RESEARCH MIDDLE EAST INSTITUTE

University of Pennsylvania

M.E.R.I. Special Studies

Becoming American

The Early Arab Immigrant Experience

ALIXA NAFF

Southern Illinois University Press

Carbondale and Edwardsville

To my parents and their pioneer companions—
A generation truly to be honored

Copyright © 1985 by the Board of Trustees,
  Southern Illinois University
All rights reserved
Printed in the United States of America
Edited by Teresa White
Designed by Frank O. Williams
Production supervised by Natalia Nadraga
Paperback edition, 1993

Library of Congress Cataloging-in-Publication Data

Naff, Alixa.
Becoming American : the early Arab immigrant experience / Alixa Naff.
p. cm.
Includes bibliographical references and index.
1. Syrian Americans—History. 2. Arab Americans—History. 3. Peddlers
and peddling—United States—History. I. Title.
E184.S98N26 1993
92-33848
973′.049275691—dc20
ISBN 0-8093-1896-2 (pbk.)
CIP

Contents

Illustrations

Acknowledgments

Credit for bringing this study to fruition is shared by many. First, it was made possible through the assistance of a research grant from the National Endowment for the Humanities. Equally provident was the home which the National Center for Urban Ethnic Affairs provided for it among its family of worthy projects. Dr. John Kromkowski, NCUEA president, and his staff infused the study with hope and provided it with sustenance. My debt to my many informants, living and dead, will be obvious on every page. They patiently and graciously welcomed me into their memories and shared their personal experiences and thoughts with me. Many of them, as well as other friends on the project, provided valuable books, photographs, personal papers, and other sources of data. A few deserve special mention. Mrs. Sandra Hasser Bennett, director of the St. Louis Project which studied the Lebanese of St. Louis, made relevant data available to me. She also read and commented on the manuscript. Mrs. Elaine Hughes gave me copies of taped interviews with first- and second-generation Syrians in her community of Vicksburg, Mississippi. Finally, Karen Rolen, a staff member of the Birmingfind Project, Birmingham, Alabama, shared some of her findings about the Lebanese in her city.

Numerous others have enriched this study with articles and information I would not otherwise have had. Notable among them is the late Michael Kafoure of Indianapolis, Indiana.

I have benefited immeasurably from the comments and advice of knowledgeable friends and colleagues. I am particularly grateful to Dr. Afif Tannous and Professor Thadeus Radzialowski. Dr. Tannous is himself a product and scholar of Lebanese village culture, a specialist on Middle East rural development, and author of numerous reports and articles on the social, economic, and agricultural conditions of the region, including several related to Syrian immigration to the United States. Dr. Radzialowski, Department of History, Southwestern State University in Marshall, Minnesota, has authored many articles on Slavic immigration and theoretical ones on ethnicity and class.

Friends of the project are too numerous to thank individually; they are scattered throughout the country. For their support, encouragement and faith, I am deeply grateful.

Mitchell Kaidy contributed his journalistic and editing expertise to the final draft, offering valuable recommendations on style.

Finally, for the capable and diligent efforts as research assistants, I am much indebted to Richard Courey, Choaura Bourouh, Belgacem Bougerra, and Evelyn Americhi.

Grateful acknowledgment is made to the following for permission to reproduce photographs from their collections: the Arab-American Media Society, Inc., Detroit, Michigan (hereafter cited as Arab-American Media Society); and the Faris and Yamna Naff Family Arab-American Collection, Archives Center, National Museum of History, Smithsonian Institution (hereafter cited as Naff Collection, Smithsonian).

Notes on Transliteration

In general, the phonetic rules of transliterating Arabic words into English are applied, except when an Arabic sound is nonexistent in the English alphabet and its absence might cause difficulty in pronunciation or meaning. Symbols for long vowels are sometimes also used for the same reason.

Becoming American

Introduction

This is a book about the assimilation of the early Arabic-speaking immigrants to the United States and the role of peddling in that process. It was known before embarking on this major project that the majority of early arrivals engaged in peddling, but the extensive role it played in facilitating the assimilation of the first generation was not known. That role is evident in the in-depth testimonies of pioneer immigrants as well as their descendants and successors—about three hundred hours of taped interviews—in over twenty-five communities, in memoirs, the Arabic and American press, and other primary documents, data heretofore neither assembled nor analyzed. Such evidence was as overwhelming and irrefutable as it was unanticipated and could not be denied: if there is an "emphasis," it proceeds from the evidence. Undoubtedly there will be some readers who will challenge this notion. Until a comparable body of data is assembled to the contrary, peddling must be held to be the major factor in explaining the relatively rapid assimilation of Arabic-speaking immigrants before World War I.

This book is not about the first Arabs to set foot on American soil. Individual Arabs had sought asylum, education, and economic opportunities in the New World even before the United States became a nation.[1] Nor is it about the most recent Arab arrivals who, since the end of World War II, constitute a second significant wave of Arab migration.

It is about those migrants who discovered an entrepreneurial Eden in America in the late 1870s and those pioneers who streamed out of the mountains and plains of Syria in the next thirty years or so to make their fortune by pack peddling. They were relatively few in number—a mere one hundred thousand by 1914—compared to the millions from Europe. Yet, the departure of so many farmers and artisans from the region alarmed their Ottoman rulers. When Congress passed the Johnson-Reed Quota Act in 1924, virtually ending immigration to the United States from southern and eastern Europe and the eastern Mediterranean, most of that pioneer generation and its successors had already made their way in a chain migration—immigrants attracting or sending for family and countrymen—into cities and hamlets of every state of the Union and into the mainstream of American society. Their reminiscences are like snapshots of turn-of-the-century America, its landscape and its people, taken through the lens of peasants originating in a world as alien to Americans as America was to them. From the threads of their memories has emerged the tapestry of this narrative.

The immigrants were overwhelmingly Christians of the Eastern-rite sects—mainly Maronite, Melkite, and Eastern Orthodox—and they were predominantly from Mount Lebanon. Five to 10 percent were Sunni or Shi'a Muslims and even fewer were of the semi-Islamic Druze faith. A small number claimed the region of Palestine as their homeland. All were subjects of the Turkish Ottoman sultan whose court was in Istanbul.

Because they migrated from the Ottoman province of Syria which, until the end of the Ottoman Empire in 1917, included Mount Lebanon, they all called themselves Syrian. In the 1920s the term "Lebanese" as a national label or identity was given political legitimacy and was adopted by most immigrants originating in Mount Lebanon. In this study, therefore, immigrants to the United States from the province of Syria before 1920 will be referred to as Syrians. The term "Arab" will be reserved primarily for the post–World War II Arabic-speaking immigrants, because it more closely accords with the nationalistic reality of the times.

Momentous social and political developments, both in the homeland and in the United States, hewed a wide chasm between the first and second waves of Arab immigration—even between those who stemmed from the same geographic region.

In contrast to the earlier arrivals, the post-1948 Arab immigrants have characteristically been more educated and politicized. They are nationals of various, often competing, Arab nations, now known collectively as the Arab world—nations which finally achieved independence only after the Second World War. Most had experienced the deep and disturbing political events in their homelands which today underpin Arab nationalism and which have profoundly affected both the character and map of the Middle East. Moreover, most are Muslim. But whether Muslim or Christian, Saudi Arabian or Syrian, they wish to be called Arabs.

Unlike the pioneers, these more recent arrivals came to a United States which had filled its continent from border to border, experienced two world wars, and had become the world's leading industrial, scientific, technological, and military power. It was the American-raised and American-born descendants of the pioneers who inherited the task of bridging the chasm and coming to terms with the differences. It was they, for example, who were provoked into an Arab identity by the nationalistic reaction of the new Arab arrivals to the humiliating defeat of the Arabs in the Six Day Arab-Israeli War of 1967 and by the denigration of the Arab image in its aftermath. The Arab identity they awoke to, however, was vastly different in its frame of reference from that which had been passed on to them by their parents and grandparents.

The consequences of this development have been a debate that continues today to reverberate throughout the Arab-American community. It evokes such questions as: What is an Arab? Who is an Arab? What is Arabness? These questions, for which no common answers have been agreed on, have inhibited the development of a common Arab identity in the United States. At the basis of this unresolved issue is a flawed and inadequate understanding by the Syrian Americans, of the social and political history of their forebears and the persistence of a certain unwillingness of some sects to shed the obsolescent religiopolitical view of history and society. Both are legacies of the immigrant generation.

Collectively, the Syrians have represented one of the smaller and less studied of America's ethnic groups, aspects of whose history deserve to be much better known and understood than they are. Although fundamentally similar to that of other groups, the Syrians' assimilation experience is set apart from the rest in the way in which most of the early Syrians became American—namely through their adoption of entrepreneurial pack peddling as their immigrant occupation.

A study of this experience in the United States, however, confronts the basic problem of a lack of primary and secondary sources. The reasons are simple. The Syrians' small numbers and seemingly indistinctive assimilation patterns did not capture the attention of students of American history and society. Another is that documentation of the culture requires of the student or scholar an expertise in a non-European language whose classical form is understood mainly by the educated and is rarely spoken in informal circumstances. Its spoken, or colloquial form, moreover, is fragmented into a host of regional dialects and idioms. Before World War II, few universities or colleges in the United States offered classical Arabic, and even in the Syrian community, classes organized by churches and clubs to teach spoken Arabic were short-lived and virtually fruitless. Because of these obstacles, no reliable study of the Syrian experience in America exists, and the Syrians are rarely mentioned in general immigration or assimilation studies. Lastly, primary data on which to base such studies, if they exist at all, are as scattered as the Syrians themselves.

The Syrians also neglected to study themselves. Here again the reasons are simple. They failed to develop a program of cultural preservation or to leave to their descendants a significant body of community-generated literature or private documents that would serve as primary source materials. Most notably lacking, in the thinly dispersed Syrian community, has been the absence of community unity or a common ethnic identity. Most understandable is that the early immigrants were not only poorly educated if at all but were intent on achieving the economic goals for which they had migrated. Moreover, before 1940, very few of those who could write and speak Arabic would have considered a study of their community—or more likely their subgroup—worth their time and effort.

Not that the first generation was uninterested in history; a glance at the remaining preserves of their books reveals that history was important to them. But it was the history of the past, of the Arabs and their glorious civilization, that mattered. The history of their American experience was, by comparison, too insignificant and too fleeting to warrant recording. Finally, acceptance of the United States as their permanent home came well into their American experience for many of the pre–World War I immigrants. Meanwhile, their American-raised and American-born children were being raised up without a meaningful grounding in the family's language or ethnic heritage. Consequently, when the parents died, few children retained appreciation for the relics and documents of a poorly understood past; except for certain sentimental items, most disposed of their parents' cultural legacy.

To locate data, it was necessary to visit Syrian communities where two types of primary data were collected: taped life histories and private documents and books. A second source was the rich materials of the prolific Arabic-language press which began publishing in the United States in 1892. The work relies most heavily on these sources although the data have been corroborated and supplemented by diligent local and national archival research.

The richest data are the life histories—in-depth tape-recorded interviews—conducted by the writer with first- and second-generation Christians, Druze, and Muslims in many urban and small-town communities, with emphasis on

middlewestern states where many of the descendants of the
pioneers still reside. Some of the communities were specifically and purposefully selected. Detroit, Michigan, for example, is an industrial metropolis with a large and stable Syrian population of all faiths. Cedar Rapids, Iowa, and Peoria,
Illinois, are much smaller cities which, during the period of
America's industrial expansion at the turn of the century,
were railroad depots that primarily served agriculturally related industries. Cedar Rapids has been home to one of the
earliest continuing Muslim groups in the United States. Peoria's Syrians are predominantly of the Maronite sect originating from one village in Mount Lebanon; and although the
community claims to include three hundred families, only in
1978 was a Maronite church consecrated for their use.
Spring Valley, Illinois, on the other hand, is distinctly different. One of several small mining towns strung together in the
heart of America's corn and coal belt, its Christian community is the remnant of a once flourishing peddling settlement
that dates from the turn of the century. Furthermore, its
Eastern Rite Syrian Orthodox Church was, until 1961, the
only one in Illinois; it served as a link between the scattered
smaller Syrian groupings in surrounding hamlets and towns.

Detractors of the oral history method criticize, with some
justification, the reliability of interview data. Doubtless,
people offer their histories incompletely and subjectively and
their responses to questions are frequently selective, filtered
through biases, laced with nostalgia, and exaggerated. Yet,
for eliciting and recording from older, uneducated, or illiterate informants primary information that would otherwise
be irrevocably lost, the interview method is unequalled. In
the case of the Syrians, taped interviews were essential. They
deserve, and have received in this study, the same critical
scrutiny as published sources. Ethnic literature, such as the
few Syrian biographies and numerous journalistic items,
were authored by writers who generally looked back from an
acquired middle-class perspective. Because they often wrote
nostalgically and in poetry, their accounts lacked the accuracy and immediacy of the actual experience. In the interviews, on the other hand, conducted frequently in a mixture

of Arabic and broken English, the speakers' observations and experiences were related spontáneously and naturally. Versions of the same experience, told by various informants in different communities, provide some corroboration and often allow the analyst an opportunity to separate fact from fiction.

Of particular importance to this study was a set of taped interviews that the writer conducted among first-generation Christian Syrians who had immigrated at the turn of the century. Recorded in 1962 in several American cities for the folklore department of the University of California in Los Angeles, these interviews not only provide firsthand accounts of the important pioneer period of Syrian immigration but also corroborated the memories of informants' interviews in 1980.

The Syrians are, of course, a non-Western people. They were shaped for life by the mores and institutions of small, self-contained communities; their individual places in their community's strata and their world view differed significantly from those of mainstream Europeans and Americans. Moreover, the Syrian-American community was and, to a large extent continues to be, fragmented. It is, reflecting the homeland, a conglomeration of village and religious subgroups which share a language and a common cultural heritage, even though perceptions of that heritage differ. The story of the Syrian immigration must, therefore, be viewed against such a background.

This study of Syrian immigrants does not propose to present compilations of statistical data. Neither adequate nor reliable quantifiable data exist. Therefore, where figures are given, they are approximations based on the best available information and are intended to guide the perceptions of both the writer and the reader.

This work is not intended to be the definitive work on the assimilation of the Arabic-speaking pioneer immigrants. Rather, the objective is much more modest. A great deal more research remains to be done. It hopes only to provide a more accurate historical data base than presently exists—a narrative that derives primarily from the memories and documents of the immigrants themselves. It further hopes to stimulate additional research not only about the Syrians but about other small non-Western ethnic groups in America. Such studies add an important new dimension to the knowledge of a vastly significant period in American history that Americans have become accustomed to view largely through the assimilation experience of already well studied European peoples.

In the process which transforms aliens into loyal Americans, *becoming* American is prerequisite to *being* American. If becoming American is that process by which an immigrant reaches the stage in which, at a minimum, he accepts the American way of life and strives to emulate it, then being American takes effect when the striving ceases to be a conscious act and the immigrant feels *he is* an American. Even when the language hurdle is overcome and foreign accents are barely discernible; when tastes and manners of the larger society have been imbibed in large drafts; when Old World customs are scorned as visible tags of foreignness or hindrances not only to acceptance in American society but to feeling—to being—American; and even when, many native values are, no matter how reluctantly, compromised or dropped, assimilation need not have been achieved. It is a continuing process in the lifetime of the first generation whose inner self-identity is ineluctably encased in the essences of ancestral values. Moreover, whether it can be achieved in the lifetime of the next generation is an open question. Ample evidence of this observation is provided by the testimony of this book's informants.

Immigrant assimilation into the mainstream of American society has been for all immigrants a continuing, many-faceted process, moving unevenly and unpredictably through their lives in America's pluralistic society. Its complexities were governed by a number of variables inherent in the migration of any given people: the period of migration; the social, political, economic conditions in the host country; the size of the group; its cultural values and customs; the group's motivation for migrating; its expectations; and the degree of nationalistic sentiments held by it. These variables hold special relevance to any understanding of the assimilation of Syrians in America.

In the decades leading to World War II, Americanization was frequently pressed on immigrants by an uneasy and, at times, chauvinistic American public. The pressure intensified until it was tempered by the levelling effects of the Great Depression of the thirties. Yet, it would be misleading to imply that it was always imposed upon unsuspecting and unwilling immigrants. More than a few immigrant groups, the Syrians among them, willingly acquiesced to Americanization and, from their own perspective, to the benefits of becoming American.

The assimilation process could be said to have begun in the homeland. When the decision to migrate was made, the prospective migrants were carried to the edge of a new consciousness. Questions would mount as they tried to sort out the challenges of the new land. Answers, accurate or inaccurate, about American society and its job opportunities, and the memorization of a few, often mispronounced and disjointed, words, stimulated their imagination and alerted the prospective emigrants to change. The anticipation of change was part of the emigrants' tools of survival. It prepared them to face problems that might become wedged between themselves and the basic needs and goals of their families.

Change has a momentum of its own. Old-timers, turn-of-the-century pioneers, scoffed, in 1962 interviews, at some deeply engrained beliefs and superstitions. The evil eye, for example, was dismissed as nonsense. Yet, the preventive oaths fell from their lips as if it was still a threat. Native dishes, typically three or four, served to guests, may have been replaced by a Sunday roast, but guests were pressed to eat large portions at the persistent urging of the hosts as if the latter's honor depended on it, as indeed it did.

Even some of the most cherished Old World values were not immune to the erosive effects of Americanization. Parents began to relax their control. Daughters were allowed some freedom in their choice of husbands, and the inter-ethnic marriages of sons might be accepted as minor calamities. The traditional preferences for the birth of sons underwent a decided decline no less than did the village custom of dropping in, unannounced, for visits. And, occasionally, social and business relations were expanded to include non-Syrians.

These and countless other indexes of progressive assimilation nevertheless fell short of being complete for most pioneer immigrants and their children. Full assimilation was not to be achieved as long as there remained a nucleus of native values that resisted assimilation. For Syrians, the granite block of values—the essence of being Syrian—was the nexus of behavioral patterns that protected and perpetuated family honor and unity. The most demonstrable and durable of the patterns is the one nearly always associated with people of Arab descent—generosity and hospitality. It continues to be treasured as the "most Syrian" of traits by the descendants of the immigrants even after assimilation has distilled away all traditional bases for it.

Irrespective of whether they were born in Syria or in the United States, the immigrants' children—those offspring who were molded by their parents' traditions and values in the early years of the immigrant experience—constitute the second generation. Because they intimately shared that pioneer experience with their parents and because of their greater adherence to Old World values, if not always Old World customs, they would be distinguished from their younger siblings. Frequently, the cultural gap between the youngest American-born, growing up at a later stage in their parents' American experience, and their older American-born, let alone foreign-born, siblings could be as broad as that between themselves and their immigrant parents.

Inevitably, the extent of adjustment required to survive in America far exceeded any immigrant group's imagination and preparation; adjustment sometimes met with resistance, sometimes caused pain, sometimes resulted in indifference, depending on the group's need to maintain its identity and way of life. Irrespective of the barriers raised against the threat of assimilation to the group's most cherished beliefs and values, its members could not easily avoid adopting the basics for getting along in America. Therefore, they learned

English, attended citizenship classes, and acquired the seemingly innocuous American manners and material possessions for attracting a measure of acceptance in the new society. Whenever these accomplishments became accepted, within the group, as symbols of status and barometers of success, they were pursued with even greater vigor. In the highly competitive and status-conscious Syrian society, this factor was an effective force in the assimilation of Syrians.

Before World War II, the American attitude toward the Americanization of foreigners required, to a large degree, immigrant social and cultural conformity. Aliens were expected to be happy to shed their native identity for the privilege of participating in American life and sharing its blessings. Nativists were particularly insistent that "foreign" colonies formed "the usual solid front against Americanizing influences and tended to perpetuate the hyphenated class."[2] The Ford Motor Company of Detroit, ardent advocate of the melting pot concept, created the Ford English School to convert aliens into Americans. Its graduation ceremony was described in the *Ford Times:*

> The feature of the graduation exercises was a unique pageant, for which the big stage of the Light Guard Armory, at Detroit, in which the event was held, had been set. Across the back of the stage was shown the hull and deck of an ocean steamship docked at Ellis Island. In the center of the stage and taking up about half of the entire area was an immense caldron across which was painted the sign "Ford English School Melting Pot." From the deck of the steamship the gangway led down in to the "Melting Pot." First came the preliminaries of docking the ship and then suddenly a picturesque figure appeared at the top of the gangway. Dressed in a foreign costume and carrying his cherished possessions wrapped in a bundle suspended from a cane, he gazed about with a look of bewilderment and then slowly descended the ladder into the "Melting Pot," holding aloft a sign indicating the country from which he had come.
>
> Another figure followed, and then another—"Syria," "Greece," "Italy," "Austria," "India," read the cards, as the representatives of each of the different countries included in the class emerged dressed in American clothes, faces eager with

the stimulus of the new opportunities and responsibilities opening out before them. Every man carried a small American flag in his hand.[3]

Characteristically, historians like to divide studies into well-defined periods—as if life were lived that way. But although the early years of Syrian experience in Ameria do not lend themselves to clear chronological breakdowns, one can speak about the Syrians in roughly two overlapping stages, the second emerging out of developments in the first. No sooner had the pioneers of the first stage arrived in the United States than they began to set precedents and establish patterns that shaped the second. There were, in fact, two intersecting stages that defy periodization. Nevertheless, in order to simplify chronological reference, this study will refer to the pioneer, or peddling, period from about 1880 to about 1910 and the settled period from about 1910 to 1930.

The pioneer stage began in the second half of the 1870s when a few unrecorded immigrants spearheaded a chain migration that has since been interrupted only during the two world wars. Distinguished by the peddling trade and by these first immigrants' sense of impermanence, it was both a period of adventure and colonization. The second, or settled, stage is marked by changes that set in well before peddling reached its peak between 1895 and 1900, although Syrian immigration did not reach its apex until 1913. Peddling then entered a protracted decline; more women immigrated, longer-range aspirations replaced temporary goals, and the itinerant peddler's suitcase—the symbol of his commitment to return to the homeland—gave way to the retail shop—the symbol of confidence in the new land. Expectations were now being fulfilled, in most cases, beyond most immigrants' hopes. What had been viewed as temporary settlements evolved gradually into permanent communities; Muslims and Druze arrived in increasing, though still limited, numbers; and industrial wage labor, already the choice of some Syrians, began to attract some newcomers. The Syrians moved gradually into the ranks of America's middle class and became willing subjects of the Americanization process.

The Syrians' acceptance of America as their permanent

home was signaled by establishment of such institutions as Eastern-rite churches, an Arabic-language press, and several educational and charitable associations, mainly in the more populous East Coast urban colonies.

The Syrian immigrants of the late nineteenth and early twentieth centuries did not fit the popular impression of economically, religiously, or politically displaced peasantry who sought the American ideals symbolized by the Statue of Liberty. Although drawn from the lower economic levels of society, they had not been driven from their homeland. Like others who migrated to the United States, they came voluntarily and enthusiastically. Almost without exception, the pioneers of the first phase and many in the second came with the intention of returning home in no more than two or three years much wealthier and prouder than they came.

Indeed, they were, in most cases, not disappointed. Their experiences in America generally paid rich, although hard-earned, rewards. The discovery back home that success, as they conceived it, was open to anyone willing to seek it precipitated an exodus from Syrian villages. It was in America, while pursuing their goals, that immigrants became aware of the ideals of freedom, individual liberty, and equality of opportunity—ideals that at first had little relevance to their motivation for emigrating. As the Syrian immigrants became conscious of those ideals, however, they embraced them fervently.

The relatively high degree of Americanization among first generation Syrians and the relatively low degree of ethnic consciousness in the second generation are two of the indications that the assimilation process penetrated sectors of the Syrian community more deeply than might have been expected. The vitality of that process became evident in the taped life-history narratives. The peddling anecdotes, in particular, reveal a sense of optimism and adventure bubbling beneath the surface of stories about the hard grind and anguish of everyday life. At the same time, one can detect, in the recollections, signals of distress from those who had sensed the erosion of the cultural heritage in the Syrian community. These signals, louder after 1924 than before, were sent out by too few and generally ignored by the many; those who generated them seemed to have lacked the will and desire to slow the erosion. Consequently, the heritage with which the first generation imbued its children was more American than Syrian, more Syrian than Arab.

From the beginning, the Syrians were an enigma to Americans. The spectacle of aspects of their family and group lives overflowing into neighborhood streets of American towns and cities, as if the Syrians were still in their villages, aroused the curiosity or, occasionally, the ridicule of journalists. In 1892, the *New York Daily Tribune* devoted almost a full page to detailing the customs and wares of the city's Syrian colony.[4] In 1897, journalists in Cedar Rapids, Iowa, and Detroit, Michigan, provided their readers with colorful descriptions of the "new colonies" of peddlers who lived and worked in their midst.[5] Such articles continued to appear in newspapers and magazines well after 1900, reflecting the spread of Syrian colonies. They also reflected a confusion about who the Syrians were, referring to them variously as Arabians, Armenians, Assyrians, and Turks, often synonymously with the term Syrian.

These immigrants no less puzzled the United States immigration officials in New York and in the several other immigration ports. In 1899, acknowledging that most of the increasing flow of Turks from "Asia" were, in fact, Arabs from Syria, the Bureau of Immigration added the classification of "Syrian" to its records. Not only did this development improve the reliability of recordkeeping, but it also provided the Arabic-speaking immigrants with an identity—a way of sorting themselves out in a society teeming with foreigners from many different lands. It had not been, however, an identity they were accustomed to in their homeland.

Rarely in the Old World would they have needed to refer to themselves as "Syrians," more rarely as "Arabs." Those few who came from the Ottoman province of Palestine called themselves, of course, Palestinians. All, however, came from the historic region of Greater Syria which, under Ottoman rule, had become, by the late nineteenth century, the provinces of Palestine and Syria. This geopolitical fact made them

Syrian. For centuries the structure of Ottoman-Muslim society shaped their identities according to religion, sect, and place of origin. But while they continued this sort of identification among themselves in the United States, they referred to themselves and were known to the outside community as Syrians until the end of World War II. This was a cultural rather than a nationalistic reference, since in that entire period there was no independent Syrian political entity which would justify the latter. The occasionally used self-reference as "people from the Holy Land" was, as often as not, a shrewd sales tactic.

Even if they were unaccustomed to identifying themselves as "Arabs" those immigrants, in fact, clung tenaciously to their Arabness. Christians, Muslims, and Druze alike proudly acknowledged common Arab cultural roots, yet each group had its own perception of its Arabness. "We are all *awlād Arab* (children or sons of Arabs)," they characteristically responded to anyone who encountered them in an Arab gathering—even as they instinctively gravitated into cliques of religion, sect, and/or place of origin. And yet, before World War I, it can be doubted that more than a handful of immigrants ever discussed the broader questions of who is an Arab and what is Arabism. Such questions were more relevant to Arab intellectual circles abroad who were concerned with the incipient Arab nationalist movement.

Of course, no one religion, ideology, national identity, or sense of history and heritage defines all Arabs. A popularly held definition states, in effect, that one is an Arab who is of Arab origin or descent, who speaks the Arabic language, whose character is formed by Arab culture, and who takes pride in the glorious Arab past. This definition, simple as it is, overlooks the complexities imposed on any generalization by Arab history, geography, and society.

According to Sir Hamilton Gibb, distinguished scholar of Arab history and culture, "All those are Arabs for whom the central fact of history is the mission of Mohammad and the memory of the Arab Empire and who, in addition, cherish the Arabic tongue and its cultural heritage as their common possessions."[6] Many Christians would reject Gibb's notion of

Arabness. While they cherish the Arabic tongue and its cultural heritage, they do not, of course, accept the mission of Mohammad as the central fact of history. Staunch Christian nationalists of Mount Lebanon initiated, between World War I and World War II, a movement that continues into the present Republic of Lebanon which denies their Arabness and claims racial and cultural links with the Phoenicians—links that stretch taut the logic of identity. And, one can find Muslim extremists who deny Christians a place in the Arab fold.

In the 1920s, political developments (see chap. 1) in Syria generated an ethnic consciousness among Lebanese immigrants and ignited a controversy within the Syrian-American community. From that time, many preferred to be—even insisted on being—known as Lebanese, an identity to which Syrians on the whole (and more than a few from Mount Lebanon) would not accede. The matter appeared to be resolved after 1946 when both Syria and Mount Lebanon achieved full independence, only to surface again during the era of the cold war and McCarthyism in the 1950s. During that time, the first independent Syrian government in many centuries turned politically left. It aimed to forge a unified nation in the aftermath of twenty-six years of a "divide and rule" policy under the French Mandate, while attempting to respond to the strong anti-West, antiimperialist sentiments of its people. At the same time, the new and unstable government reacted to the widely shared perceptions of the West's one-sided pro-Israeli policy. A number of American Syrians, out of conviction and fear, found it more expedient to adopt a Lebanese identity which simultaneously cloaked them in the robe of Christianity and separated them from the rising anti-West, antiimperialist, and Arab nationalist stridency in the Middle East.

This protracted and unresolved debate, frequently fanned in the United States by political winds from the homeland, points to the central fact of Arab society, past and present. Although Arabs, including Syrians, share a common language, tradition, cultural traits, and values, their national identity is refracted primarily through the prism of religion.

This is just as true when they share a common national origin. The result is widespread factionalism and fragmentation. Yet, religion is not the sole divisive factor; roots of disunity are imbedded in centuries of interaction between the geography and history of that region. Their intricate connection has shaped the culture and society of Syria. To understand this, one must note that although Mount Lebanon is geographically linked to Greater Syria, historical forces combined with geography to drive a wedge between the two peoples—politically, socially and economically.

Thus, an introductory overview of Syrian history and society will guide the reader through the maze of cultural customs, beliefs, and institutions that differentiate Syrian subgroups from one another and Syrian immigrants, in general, from the millions of Europeans with whom they shared the experience of becoming American.

1

Land, History, and Society

THE LAND

The concept of Greater Syria dates at least to biblical times
and is basically geographic. The dream of a political Greater
Syria, which gained currency in the first quarter of the twentieth century, harks back to a glorious period of Syrian history when, under the Umayyad Caliphate, the Islamic Empire was ruled from Damascus between 661 and 750. In the
nineteenth century, the concept defined an area that was
geographically and culturally unified: from the Taurus
Mountains now in southern Turkey, it extended southward
into the northern region of what is today Saudi Arabia. It
stretched from the Mediterranean coast in the west to northern Mesopotamia and the Syrian Desert in the east. While its
western and northern borders were more or less set by natural geographic features, the eastern and southern bounda-
ries fluctuated with the ability of the central government to
defend them against bedouin incursions and enemy forces.

Its approximately 85,000-square-mile surface is divided
among highlands, valleys, plains, steppes, and desert. Moving inland from a coast dotted with port cities from Jaffa to
Alexandretta (including Tyre, Sidon, Beirut, and Tripoli), a
fertile uneven narrow plain merges into a belt of broken
highlands, the most prominent and relevant of which is the

Mount Lebanon range. This range extends from above the city of Tripoli in the north to just above the port of Tyre in the south. Beirut, outside the jurisdiction of the autonomous government of Mount Lebanon before 1920, sits on a promontory which juts into the sea midway between the two cities. The peaks of Mount Lebanon, famous for their ancient cedars, rise like a wall to over nine thousand feet in some areas and block the rain-carrying winds, leaving the eastern slopes and valleys considerably drier. The eastern descent slopes sometimes gradually, sometimes abruptly into the Beqa Plain, the most prominent and important of three fertile depressions which separate the coastal ranges from the inland ranges dominated in the south by Mount Hermon. The mountainous regions are broken by minor plains, valleys, and plateaus.

The land east of the inland ranges is mainly steppe, merging eastward and southward with the Syrian Desert. In fact, almost half of Syria's land surface is desert, with scattered oases. Damascus, Syria's capital, is located in one of the largest and best watered of them. In the nineteenth century, the desert was virtually a wasteland, occupied by animal-grazing bedouin.

Agriculture is paramount in Syria and since man first learned to cultivate the soil in the Middle East, Syrians have been accommodating the wide variety of indigenous and imported edible plants to varied soils and climates, thus producing a wide range of agricultural crops. How they are watered depends on their elevation and proximity to sea and desert. Rainfall and temperatures vary intensely. From forty to fifty inches in the western coastal highlands, rainfall levels drop to between fifteen and twenty inches inland. The winter rain season, beginning in October, gives way almost abruptly in May to summer drought brought on by continental air moving over the desert from the south and southeast. Springs and winters frequently bring hot dry winds known as *khamsin* or *shlouq*. The climate in Syria is generally characterized by hot, humid summers and cold winters.

Climate and temperature govern what is planted as much as where and when. Wheat, the predominant staple, is a winter crop and flourishes in five-thousand-foot altitudes; barley is grown in hot arid steppes; grain sorghum and summer maize are grown on the coastal plains, and oats in the cool damp highlands. In mountain zones of intense rainfall, arable land is terraced to preserve the soil cover.

Irrigation has played an important role in agriculture. Despite snowfall in the elevations and high rainfall in the coastal ranges, water is at a premium. In Mount Lebanon, for example, much of it seeps into permeable bedrock forcing the cultivators to work out sharing schemes for the waters of mountain streams and springs. Abundant sources such as the Orontes, Euphrates, Barada, and Litani rivers and their tributaries were also utilized.

Urbanization has been one of Syria's most distinguishing features; cities date from the earliest times. Middle East economist Charles Issawi attributes this phenomenon to "the scarcity of water, which prevented scattered settlement and made for concentration in large villages or towns; the insecurity of the countryside, which led many farmers cultivating land in the immediate vicinity of a town to live within its walls; the relatively flourishing condition of the handicrafts; and the active internal and international trade."[1] Damascus and Aleppo were large inland commercial and trading centers on the great east-west trade routes long before the advent of Islam. Several other cities flourished on the Mediterranean coast and inland—Jerusalem, Beirut, Haifa, Hama, Homs, to name a few. None was on Mount Lebanon. Only toward the end of the nineteenth century did Zahle, Mount Lebanon's principal market town, grow to become a small city.

Industry, on the other hand, has been Syria's least distinctive feature; nature did not favor the land with mineral and water resources. The small deposits of iron, coal, and copper that existed were virtually depleted as far back as Roman times. Other minerals have been sparse, difficult of access, and of poor quality. Lumber, Syria's most plentiful natural resource in its mountainous regions, had also been exhausted in the distant past largely through export to neighboring areas and for charcoal production. And, the country's water supply has always been insufficient to serve industry on any large scale.

HISTORY

Geography provides the setting; people make history. Because it sits strategically astride the confluence of historic trade routes of three continents and its terrain imposes no insuperable obstacles, Syria has been, since the dawn of history, a thoroughfare for caravan traders, migrants, and conquering armies. These visitors and intruders not only contributed new ideas and cultural influences, but racial diversity, evident in the modern Syrian population. Syria's commercial and trading cities were prizes for ancient-world conquerors and modern imperialists.

They came by land—up the Red Sea coast, across the Gaza Strip, through the northern plains and the southern desert, and they came by sea. Canaanites and Amorites came via the southern steppes; Hittites and Kurds from Anatolia; Persians from the east; Egyptians from the Nile Valley; Greeks, Romans, and Crusaders from Europe; and Mongols and Turks from central Asia. Bedouin from the Arabian Peninsula have migrated uninterrupted into Syria's heartland since long before Islam gave their intrusion religious sanction. Finally, and more recently—within the last two centuries—the French and British arrived via the Mediterranean Sea. And, yet with all this, since the ancient Phoenician merchants dominated the mercantile trade of the Mediterranean four thousand years ago from their base on its eastern shores, Syria has survived alternating periods of conquest and peace, fortune and destruction, glory and obscurity, ethnic and cultural assimilation.

Syria is timeless. No known Columbus discovered it and no date celebrates its discovery. It stands genealogically at the base of the West's family tree of civilization of which the American branch is the most recent. America suffered one revolution in which it cast out a country whose language and values it inherited but which today it regards benevolently as the motherland; it was left free to work out its own destiny. Syria, on the other hand, has witnessed no revolution in history in which it overthrew its alien ruler. Since adopting Islam in the seventh century, it generally accepted foreign rule—as long as that ruler was Muslim—and it resented its non-Muslim conquerors. Ultimately, the nation was granted—it did not win—independence from Christian rulers in 1946 after World War II. Through most of its history, Syria's political destiny has been dictated by outside forces. Ironically, even its current political borders were mandated by foreign powers.

Religion has played an integral part in Syria's complex history. Like Judaism centuries earlier, Christianity was born on Syrian soil sixty-four years after Rome conquered the region. Three centuries later, the religion emerged as a dynamic social force which the Roman Empire could no longer ignore. When Rome adopted Christianity as the state religion in the fourth century, the political and economic center of the Roman Empire had already shifted to its eastern capital on the Bosphorus. In time, the eastern Roman Empire absorbed the intellectual and artistic culture of the Near East, particularly the Greek, and came to be known as the Byzantine Empire; its capital was Constantinople.

Under the strong and efficient government of Byzantium, Syria flourished. Its cities blossomed and enjoyed a busy commercial life while its agriculture expanded. The Syrians shared in the intercourse of ideas that moved freely on the great transportation and communication arteries provided by the empire. Syrian merchants, artisans, politicians, and intellectuals made significant contributions to both Roman and Byzantine civilizations and thereby to Western civilization. Among them was the idea of an alphabet, which Syria had inherited from the Phoenicians, and the concept of monotheism; the principle of codified law was developed in Beirut's Roman law colleges. Antioch, an important Syrian city, became one of early Christianity's five patriarchal seats.

Syrians, over the centuries, became disaffected with Byzantine rule. The most deep-seated grievances stemmed from the controversial theological and doctrinal positions adopted and enforced by the Byzantine court—positions, heatedly debated in early Christian councils and opposed by many Syrians. Consequent heretical movements were suppressed there and many of the sectarian minorities took refuge in the mountains of Lebanon. They would later be joined by Islamic heretical minorities. It was Byzantium's misfortune that its political, military, and economic decline and the heightened disaffection of its Syrian population coincided with the rise of Islam.

Throughout the seven hundred years of Greco-Roman rule, Syria retained its Semitic character. Although Latin or Greek were spoken in the cities, Syriac—a Semitic language—survived in the countryside. Arabic, another Semitic language, filtered into Syria with traders and bedouin long before its conquest by Islam in 637. Consequently, when Muslims invaded Syria, "the native Semites of Syria and Palestine," wrote historian Philip K. Hitti, "looked upon the Arabian newcomers as nearer of kin than their hated and oppressive alien overlords."[2]

With the conquest of Syria by Islam in 637, not only did its population cease to be predominantly Christian, but its universe—social, cultural, political and economic—became Islamic. Thus, the history of Syria and its people, into the present, can only be understood in this Arab Islamic context.

Mobilized by the fervor of a new faith and the promise of booty, Arab tribes rode out of the Arabian Peninsula in the fourth decade of the seventh century carrying to unbelievers the message of their Prophet, Muhammad. In just one hundred years, they succeeded in uniting under their rule peoples of diverse cultures and languages—from the inhabitants of parts of China to those of North Africa and Spain. In building their vast empire, the Muslims did not so much destroy the heritages of their conquered subjects as absorb and build on them.

Thirty years after the Prophet's death, the problem of who would succeed him as the temporal and spiritual ruler of Islam, for which he left no guidelines, shattered his vision of a community unified by its adherence to Islam. Of those closest to him, one faction believed that his successor must come from the Prophet's inner circle of believers and helpers. A second faction insisted that succession should pass to his son-in-law and cousin, Ali, who was also a member of the Prophet's inner circle. The schism which this early dispute produced was as deep as that which cleaved Catholics and Protestants in Christian Europe. Moreover, it was inevitable that the insistence of Islamic rulers on the concept of a community in which conquered religiously and ethnically diverse peoples would be unified on the basis of a religion that claimed superiority over others, was bound to generate additional rifts and spawn numerous sects.

The schism produced two major Muslim sects. The majority Sunni, or Orthodox, sect adheres for earthly guidance to the precedent set by the Prophet during his life. The minority, or Shiʿa sect, was mobilized around the claims to the caliphate of Ali and his descendants. It held that since the Prophet governed as the agent of God, his descendants were the matchless and rightful hereditary successors to his spiritual and temporal powers. It began as a political party but, losing its claim to succession to the opposition, it turned into a dissident sect which attempted to achieve its essentially political aims through religion. The Shiʿa fashioned their own theology, philosophy, and ethics. Eventually, when Shiʿism was adopted as the state religion of Persia in the sixteenth century, Shiʿas controlled their own government. Their experience provided the prototype in the Middle East for merging political and social discontent with religious principles. Shiʿism itself then fragmented into a number of splinter sects which scattered throughout the Islamic world. Among them was the Druze sect. Expelled in the eleventh century from its birthplace in Cairo, Egypt, it made its home in the heart of Mount Lebanon, southeast of Beirut, and in more southerly mountainous regions of Syria. The sect began as followers of Al-Hākim bi-amr Allah, a Fatimid caliph in Cairo, who, before his mysterious disappearance, had proclaimed himself the incarnation of the Divine Reason.[3] As it evolved, the sect's distinctive esoteric beliefs and practices so diverged from its Islamic origins as to be considered semi-Islamic by some Muslims and non-Islamic by others. Present-day Arab-American Druze have adopted the latter opinion.

From a simple belief system, Islam developed into one of the world's great civilizations. Between the tenth and thirteenth centuries, when it was at the peak of its power and influence, its three capital cities of Baghdad, Cairo, and Cordova in Spain were among the world's major centers of learning and culture. Architecture, music and art, literature and philosophy, astronomy and navigation, mathematics and medicine, all flourished under Islamic rule; European culture was not to reach such heights until the Renaissance—and then only after the achievements of Islam had been transmitted to Europe.

But dark days lay ahead. In the thirteenth century, Islamic lands east of the Mediterranean were devasted by Mongol hordes, the most brutally destructive of the two-centuries-old westward migration of warrior Turkish tribes from the steppes of central Asia. As a rule, Islam assimilated the Turkish as it had previously absorbed the Persian and Byzantine elements into its cultural mosaic. As converts to the religion and to the cultural life of Islamic cities, the Turks had since the tenth century defended, ruled, and advanced Muslim territory until by 1453, Ottoman Turks conquered Constantinople and put an end to the moribund Byzantine Empire. In 1517, the Ottomans conquered the Arab lands as far as Egypt and incorporated them into their vast empire which at that time extended from Mesopotamia to the outskirts of Vienna.

Ottoman administration and institutions gave Islam unity and stability while its military protected and extended its domains. Yet, after little more than a century of glory, these same institutions became rigid. For the next two and a half centuries a conservative Ottoman court withdrew behind a curtain of self-sufficiency and complacency. Meanwhile, the deterioration and stagnation of Ottoman institutions were to have the most adverse effect on the provinces. Adversity was compounded by the failure of the ruling and religious classes to see the technical, scientific, economic, and military advances of Europe and to comprehend them for the threat they posed.

To feed their industrial machines as well as to gain markets, European nations rivaled each other for raw materials, and by the nineteenth century they were competing for domination of the feeble Ottoman court. The necessity of preventing the empire's collapse while competing for its domination guided European foreign policy at least until World War I. Much of the strategy was played out in Arab lands with long-range social and political consequences for their inhabitants. Notwithstanding efforts of reforming sultans, Europe, by 1914, controlled or dominated most of the Ottoman territory. Resentment against the interfering European governments drove the Ottomans into World War I on the side of Germany and to consequent extinction.

During the four hundred years of Ottoman rule, the Syrians maintained their Arab identity. Although the Ottomans were never Arabacized, they were Muslims and, therefore, were acceptable to Syria's Muslim population. Meanwhile, the Syrian Christian minority remained relatively indifferent to the change in Muslim overlords. If most Arab aspects of Islamic civilization were eclipsed under Turkish rule, the Arabic language remained secure. In Syria, moreover, from whose capital Islam had expanded and was ruled for its first one hundred years, the people still believed themselves to be an integral part of Arab-Islamic civilization with which both Muslims and Christians identify. Yet, when these groups proudly reflect on the golden age of their heritage, Muslims tend to emphasize its Islamic content, Christians its Arab. In retrospect, both blame the degradation and impoverishment of Arab culture in recent centuries on the dismal rule of the Ottoman Empire and its weakness in the face of western Europe's imperialism which many Christians welcomed and Muslims deplored. Nevertheless, for Muslims, loyalty to an Islamic ruler, even one perceived as inept or cruel, was critical if Islam was to remain unified and if it was to withstand inimical Western Christian influences which first entered with the Crusades. Christians, on the other hand, exposed to and protected by the Christian West, attributed the decline of Arab culture to the backwardness of Islam and its Turkish rulers. Few of either faith would, however, disagree about their culture's remarkable resourcefulness and ability to regenerate despite repeated periods of conquest, exploitation, and disintegration.

The historically delicate relationship between Christians and Muslims, worked out over centuries of accommodation, was severely disrupted by the European powers. It was triggered by the ambitions of Egypt, which conquered Syria in 1832. Before the conquest, Mount Lebanon had been ruled under a unique feudal system which had evolved over centuries. Under this system, peasants and artisans were ruled in districts by hereditary aristocratic feudal lords, each with his own militia. Over them was the Lord of the Mountain, an Amir, selected by the notables from a dynastic feudal family. Theoretically, he was first among equals, responsible for amassing the annual tribute demanded by the Ottoman government; but he answered to its representatives, usually the stronger of rival Ottoman governors in two neighboring provinces who also demanded an annual tribute. He also arbitrated between rival feudal lords and kept internal order with the help of his army. From his lords, he took an annual tribute for himself and his administration and called on them for military service. In their mountain fastnesses, the notables were virtually self-governing, subject only to occasional discipline by the Amir or extortion by unruly Ottoman governors. The Egyptians, routed by the Europeans in 1840, left in their wake twenty years of political chaos and religious conflicts in Mount Lebanon. The Amirate system of government was destroyed, and European intervention became more overt and divisive.

In competition for dominance over the tottering Ottoman government, the Europeans focused mainly on the rival Christian sects of Syria. By mid-century, each major sect was supported by a European power: the Maronite and Melkite Catholics by France, and the Eastern Orthodox by Russia with Anglican England vacillating between Christians and the Druze sect. In championing the Christian cause, the Eu-

ropean powers exacerbated the division between Muslims
and Christians and sharpened Christian sectarian hatred
that had been described in 1822 by the British traveler, John
Burckhardt, as directed "not so much against the Muham-
medeans, as against their Christian brethren, whose creed at
all differs from their own."[4]

French influence among the Syrian affiliates of the Roman
Catholic church was the most penetrating and enduring.
Through economic, educational, political, diplomatic, and
military activities on their behalf, France stimulated the Maronite dream of political dominance over Mount Lebanon.
At the same time, it alienated the Muslim sects, especially the
Druze, as well as the antipapist Orthodox Christians who
tended, and still tend, to support Muslims against Maronite
political aspirations.

Muslims and Druze, who for centuries believed in their
own religiously sanctioned superiority, were further embittered by the arrogance and airs of superiority exhibited by
many Christians, an attitude that grew from the close links
between Christian Arabs and Christian Europeans and the
higher social and economic status derived from those links.
Christian aspirations were correspondingly elevated. The
culmination of European intervention in Syrian domestic affairs was the massacre of 1860. At that time, a large number
of Christians, particularly in Maronite and Melkite Catholic
centers in Mount Lebanon, were attacked by Druze with the
tacit support of many Syrian Muslims. Accounts of the pain
and wrath of the massacre, embellished with myth and superstition, have been passed on from generation to generation of Lebanese.

The massacre of Christians provoked Europe into conven-
ing an international commission of Western powers and Ottoman representatives to shape a political structure for the
Mountain. French troops assisted the Ottomans to restore a
semblance of stability and in 1861 a new form of government, guaranteed by six European nations, was agreed to by
the sultan. The commission consolidated the new arrangement into a statute promulgated in 1864.

The mutasarrifiyya, as it was known, was administered by

a non-Lebanese Catholic Christian Ottoman governor (mutasarrif), appointed by the sultan and approved by the West. He was assisted by a central administrative council in which the Muslim and Christian sects were proportionally represented. Politically, the mutasarrifiyya of Mount Lebanon remained a Western-oriented autonomous part of the Syrian province and, although directly responsible to the Ottoman sultan, that sovereign exerted little or no power over it until it was terminated by the revolutionary Young Turk government of the Ottoman Empire in 1915.

In the words of historian Albert H. Hourani, the period from 1861 to 1915 was "a period of increasing prosperity." It was, he added, a period in which "agriculture revived, roads were built, schools were opened, and Western civilization extended its sway."[5] Philip Hitti, a native of Lebanon, noted that the people of Mount Lebanon "enjoyed a period of cultural flourish and economic prosperity and achieved a state of security and stability unattained by any Ottoman province, European or Asian. . . . It came to be acknowledged as the best governed, the most prosperous, peaceful and contented country in the Near East."[6] Those Syrians not living in Mount Lebanon envied those who did and subscribed to the oft repeated Arabic saying: "Fortunate is he who owns so much as a goat's pen in the Mountain."

The impact of the West inevitably exposed all of Syria, most directly and notably Mount Lebanon, to modern influences. During fifty years of ensuing relative security and tranquility, trade with and travel to the West, particularly by Christians, mounted; transportation and communications were improved or modernized with French capital; Western missionary schools proliferated; new intellectual ideas and ideologies were introduced; economic opportunities multiplied; consumption of staple articles increased; and health conditions improved. In Mount Lebanon, direct and indirect taxes were fixed at a much lower rate than in the rest of Syria and were, therefore, predictable; conscription was prohibited for Christians and non-Christians; and public security was more or less guaranteed by the Western powers.

Yet the benefits could not obscure the defects of the mu-

tasarrifiyya. By favoring the interests of the Christians, it
failed to heal the persistent communal cleavages; simmering
suspicions surfaced in occasional small fracases, their deeper
significance ignored by blinkered leaders. The power of the
Catholic priesthood over its flock, always strong in spiritual
matters, now extended more than ever into politics. This was
especially true of the majority Maronite sect under the tute-
lage of its French mentors. No force existed to check the in-
trigues in power struggles among the clergy, ambitious Lebanese of all stripes, Turkish officials, and European
representatives. Stephen H. Longrigg observed in 1958 that
"the formation of autonomous Lebanon by armed foreign
intervention, overriding the Sultan's sovereignty and serving
the interests of a single sect, was well-intentioned to save
Christian lives; but it was retrograde as a move in modern
national government, was quite unearned and could be justified solely by the impotence or malice of the then existing
rulers."[7]

The political fortunes of the rest of Syria under the Ottoman Empire contrasted sharply with those of Mount Lebanon. Weakness in the central government throughout the
first half of the century manifested itself in public insecurity
and political and social oppression by provincial Ottoman officials. The rapacity of rival local governors, avaricious tax
farmers, self-interested feudal landlords and undisciplined
bedouin tribes tyrannized the peasantry and sapped its initiative.[8] Turmoil gripped the cities and towns as unruly military
and political factionalism wrought havoc on Muslims and
Christians alike. From the middle of the nineteenth century,
when Europe began to intervene in Syria, the Muslim majority, anti-Christian and loyal to its Muslim rulers, resented and
feared this Western intrusion. Muslims and Druze perceived
that the Europeans' objective was exploitation. Caught between age-encrusted tradition and modernization in its
struggle to survive, the Ottoman government could only respond by becoming more autocratic.

Economic and political reform by sultans in the second
half of the nineteenth century succeeded in bringing some
stability, security, and economic improvement to Syria. The

rebellious bedouin tribes and renegade military units were controlled by the better-equipped forces of more determined Ottoman governors, but taxation and military conscription continued to be dreaded by the people. Christians, under an earlier imperial attempt to redress the inequality between Muslims and non-Muslims became subject to conscription but were allowed to pay a heavy exemption fee. This arrangement pleased Muslims and Christians alike who, for reasons of their own, preferred the status quo ante.

Syrians were more hard pressed compared with the Lebanese. In the agricultural villages of the Syrian Beqa Plain adjacent to the Mountain, Syrian Christians and many Muslims began to claim permanent residence and citizenship in Mount Lebanon, depriving the Syrian government of much-needed revenue and precipitating an unwanted controversy between the two governments.[9] Others were lured to Egypt. Toward the end of the century, it appeared to French and British consuls, who measured Ottoman progress almost exclusively by their own national interests and values, that the internal situation was rapidly deteriorating and that discontent, corruption, and anarchy were spreading alarmingly.[10]

The most deliberate act of Ottoman oppression in the second half of the nineteenth century was not directed at the general population but at the empire's intellectual minority whose writings were perceived as threatening. Sultan Abd al-Hamid II, intending to stem the fermenting spread of Western-influenced ideas and ideologies such as nationalism, and to silence his critics, reinforced and extended censorship over all published material.[11] In the great cities of Syria, where a nascent Arab nationalism based on the Arabic language and cultural heritage coincided with an Arabic literary revival, censorship forced journalists and intellectuals, most of them Christians, to depart Syria for the freer atmosphere of British-ruled Egypt.

In 1908, the Young Turks, a Turkish nationalist military junta, deposed the sultan. Resentful of Western interference and fearful for the fate of the empire, the new government intensified military conscription, enforcing it on all Ottoman subjects except those in Mount Lebanon. It also made the fatal decision to enter World War I on the side of the Germans.

When the Young Turks, threatened by defeat during the war, installed its authority over the Mountain in 1915, untold numbers of its citizens were allowed to starve, partly because the staple foods, which Lebanon had had to import from nearby agricultural regions, were diverted to the military. This act symbolized not only Mount Lebanon's vulnerability but the Turks' apparent unconcern for the welfare of its Arab, especially Christian, subjects. In Syria, the Arabs were alienated by the Young Turks' deposition of the sultan—the Muslim temporal and spiritual authority—by the new stress on Turkish nationalism and by the imposition of a policy of Turkification. Discontent fueled the slow-developing Arab nationalist movement. Young Turk policies, although designed to preserve the empire, served only to hasten its demise and, in the process, widened the split between Syrians and Lebanese.

The rift between the two regions of the former Ottoman Syrian province became almost complete after the war. In 1920, the vacuum left in Syria by the demise of the Ottoman Empire was filled by France. With its military superiority, the European nation deposed the legitimate Arab ruler and seized the reins of government in Damascus. Thus, the promise to the Arabs of an independent Arab nation, made by the British during the war in return for Arab assistance to the Allied cause, was not only shattered but confirmed a revelation by Russia's Bolshevik government in 1917 of a secret agreement whereby Arab lands would be divided among the successful Allied powers. Nevertheless, France and Britain were given, by the new League of Nations, mandatory power over the region. France governed Syria, north of Palestine. The Maronites of Mount Lebanon, of course, welcomed the French; the more nationalistic, non-Catholic Syrians, on the other hand, who had dreamed of an independent Arab nation based on the historic idea of a Greater Syria, resented them.

Under the Mandate System, Greater Syria was artificially divided until only a truncated Syria remained. First, a Maronite-dominated Greater Lebanon was created by extending the eastern borders of Mount Lebanon inland across the Beqa Plain and into the middle of the anti-Lebanon range. The new Lebanon also incorporated four of Syria's port cities: Tyre, Sidon, Beirut, and Tripoli, leaving to Syria only a fraction of its former access to the Mediterranean. Lebanon was enlarged to extend its cultivable land and to minimize the possibility of starvation by an enemy; to bring the strategic ports under French-Maronite control; and to reward the Maronites for their loyalty. From an administrative standpoint, France could now better impose its rule over dissident Syrians. However, by incorporating the port cities and the Beqa, it incorporated thousands of Muslims which greatly diminished the numerical Christian majority of Lebanon.

In addition, Britain created a new country—Transjordan—out of Greater Syrian land and promised a homeland for Jews in Palestine over which it maintained direct rule. Later, France would cede to Turkey the Hatay district in northern Syria, which included the port city of Alexandretta and the important Christian city of Antioch. All of this was done over the expressed objections of the Syrians.

Under France's policy of divide and rule, old separatist religious and political feelings hardened, and new ones were created. Divisions among the sects of Mount Lebanon, and between Christians and Muslims, were accentuated, triggering another Druze rebellion in 1925 which French forces quelled. In 1926, France proclaimed Lebanon a republic and promulgated a constitution within the framework of the mandatory arrangement. Although amended and suspended more than once, the constitution remained in force until independence in 1946. Under the French, the Lebanese, observed one political analyst, "had all the accoutrements of a sovereign state but not the authority."[12] It was not until 1930 that a constitution for the state of Syria was written.

Most Syrians remember the mandatory period as one of resentment and frustration; of rebellions and riots incited by Western interference; of broken promises, fallen aspirations, and subjugation. Ultimately, after World War II, dissatisfied

Christians and Muslims would shape an Arab nationalist ideology along Western lines and use it against the West.

Not unexpectedly, the Christians of Lebanon and Syria advanced most under French rule. Again, the Muslims and Druze felt humiliated by the favoritism shown to Christians and again they were suspicious and fearful for their political and cultural survival. The psychological and social barriers raised by the warnings of their leaders delayed for some time the effects of Wetern culture, both spiritual and material. Nevertheless, Westernization penetrated their insularity. Gradually, some of them took advantage of Western schools in Syria and became involved in Western trade and commerce which slowly dissolved their apprehensions and broadened their world view.

During this period, American political influence was nonexistent in Syria. As a fledgeling, halfhearted imperialist nation at the turn of the century, America avoided intruding into European spheres of influence, although its merchant ships occasionally steamed into Syrian ports. A favorable impression of America in the minds of Syrians was made by the King-Crane Commission which surveyed Syrian opinion to determine the political disposition after the war. Their report, ignored by the peacemakers at Versailles but published in 1922, revealed a preference for an Arab nation united with the Palestine region governed by a constitutional monarchy, and including an autonomous Lebanon. Failing acceptance of that plan by the Western powers, the Syrians would accept a temporary United States mandatory government.

The most visible Americans at that time had been Protestant missionaries whose proselytizing, since about 1831, met with disappointing success. Their educational successes, on the other hand, left a legacy of far-reaching social significance for Syria, creating a bond between its people and America that remained unfrayed until after America's recognition of the state of Israel in 1948.

Before 1860, amid opposition from religious and political authorities, the American Protestant Mission had diligently opened schools and churches and distributed missionary material. In the more favorable political climate of Syria after 1864, the embryonic network of schools was expanded to include a larger number of towns and villages where several thousand boys and girls were taught rudimuentary skills in Arabic. These skills would later be developed by immigrants in the United States for writing letters home and reading newspapers. A few villagers were introduced to English; perhaps also to history, arithmetic, and Christian scriptures. Over all, however, the numbers of those who attended American missionary schools were relatively small, not only because of native resistence and disinterest, but because of the missions personnel and financial difficulties and the "circumstances of competing agencies."[13]

The proliferation of primary and secondary schools and the numerous graduates in medicine, the sciences, and humanities from the American University of Beirut were testimony enough to the extent of American influence in Syria. But there was another important agent of American influence: the American mission press. This produced and printed a new translation of the Bible in Arabic and published religious tracts and polemics. Its most durable contribution was the production of secular textbooks in such areas as Arabic, grammar, algebra, geometry, and geography.[14] Because these subjects were acceptable to all religious communities, they gradually advanced the progress of Syrian education.

Finally, with the help of the American mission press, working under the intellectual guidance of the American University faculty, a group of Syrian writers, most of them Christians, evolved "a modern Arabic idiom and style suitable for the expression of Western ideas."[15] giving rise to an articulate, Western-influenced intelligensia and a journalistic and literary movement. Later, from New York, disciples of the movement would revolutionize an Arabic literary style which had endured the rigors of tradition for centuries. In addition, by raising the political and social consciousness of more literate leaders—mainly in towns and cities outside of Mount Lebanon—American educational influence laid the intellectual basis for the Arab nationalist movement that would become articulate during the French mandate between the world wars.

Since American missionaries, unlike their European colleagues, had not aimed to serve the national interests of their country in addition to serving God, the Syrian Protestant College (later the American University in Beirut) made "no attempt at any 'Americanization' whatsoever."[16] Although in their institutions they emphasized the three R's and religion, they nevertheless inadvertently, and perhaps inevitably, sharpened the Muslim (and Druze)-Christian split. For one thing, the education offered by Americans and Europeans was primarily Christian and centered mainly on Christian Mount Lebanon; the selective quality of the schools' locales, student body, and curricula imparted a sense of superiority and higher status to those thus set apart. Consequently, the distance widened not only between Christians and non-Christians but between Lebanese and Syrians. Moreover, although it had its roots in a literary and intellectual renaissance connected with the American University, the Arab nationalist movement was basically antiimperialist. Its leaders were drawn primarily from among non-Catholic Christians, Muslims, and Druze of Syria, whereas the Catholic Uniate Christians—Maronites and some Melkites—of Mount Lebanon were pro-French.

America's most enduring success was the favorable impression left with Syrians. Education and humanitarian work—medical and nutritional relief in times of crises such as earthquakes, epidemics, famines, and rebellions—resulted in an image of the United States as a land of "good and honorable" people. The continued Syrian immigration to the United States is evidence of the sustained high regard in which it was held despite disagreement with its later Middle East foreign policy, particularly as it related to the Arab-Israeli conflict.

The expansion of educational activity by the American Protestants invited European competition. The French increased their Catholic missionary schools and, in 1875, founded a Jesuit university in Beirut. Russian Orthodox, German Lutherans, and British Anglicans joined in; even the Ottoman government began to create its own schools along Western lines.[17] By World War I, the Levant coast, according to one observer, had "over three hundred foreign schools educating more than twenty-five thousand students."[18]

Because Christians readily sent their children to them, Westerners tended to establish their schools in Christian towns and villages. By the 1890s, Christian Zahle, with a population of about fifteen thousand that boasted of its religious exclusivity, had two Jesuit boys' schools, a Roman Catholic girls' school, a Russian Orthodox school, a British Anglican school and one American Protestant school; it also had a Jesuit college and one Catholic and one American library.[19] Rashayya al-Wadi, a mountain village in Syria with a population of about five thousand divided almost equally between Christians and Druze, had a French Catholic, a Russian Orthodox, an American Protestant, a privately operated (by a converted Syrian) Baptist, and a native local school.[20] Not all Christian villages were so fortunate, however; many had no school, and where Christians were not numerous enough to be a determining factor, Muslim and Druze villages and towns, fearing proselytization by Western missionaries, continued to resist the establishment of schools. Late in the century, however, some wealthy and educated Muslim and Druze families became conscious of the economic and social value of Western education and gradually began to enroll their children—generally in the less suspect American schools. To the credit of the Americans, the medium of instruction in these schools was Arabic and the pupils were encouraged to preserve their own customs and manners.[21]

THE ECONOMY

The economies of both Syria and Mount Lebanon were based on agriculture; an important difference, however, is Syria's greater economic diversity. Rocky soil, sharp cliff faces, and heavy winter rains limited Mount Lebanon's arable land and the variety of crops it could grow. The well-watered, terraced higher elevations and coastal plains yielded mainly cereals, tobacco, and fruits, while those at more poorly watered elevations and plains were planted mainly with olive and fig trees as well as grape vines—crops traditionally well suited to the Mediterranean cycle of winter rains and summer droughts.

Despite the cultivation of virtually every available inch of suitable land and the prevalence of family gardens and private orchards, Mount Lebanon was unable to produce enough to feed its population. This perennial problem accounted for the Mountain's dependency on imports. In addition, as informants recalled and the Lebanese government was wont to note (as it did in an 1874 communication to its Ottoman sovereign who had proposed a tax on tobacco plants) because the "lands are rocky and briny, despite efforts to improve them, the farmer can hardly cover his expenses unless he seeks his fortune outside the Mountain or practices crafts or trade in addition to farming so that he can make a living."[22]

Reliance on the import of food staples mounted when, in the nineteenth century, valuable arable land was increasingly planted with mulberries for the cultivation of silkworms to meet the demand of textile mills in France and Great Britain for silk thread. Large and small landowners (many of the latter mortgaged) were enticed into sericulture until mulberry trees became Mount Lebanon's largest crop and the reeling of silk its primary home industry.

Mount Lebanon's gradual and incomplete conversion to a cash economy at that time, based on a single crop, affected landownership. The bulk of the population were small landowning farmers. However, by the middle of the nineteenth century, the demand for land on which to plant mulberry trees pushed values beyond the resistance level of the small cultivators of olives, grapes, and other crops. Land thus became concentrated in the hands of large producers. And, when a few decades later, foreign competition diminished the demand for Lebanese silk, large landowners again expanded their holdings at the expense of the mortgaged small cultivators. Emigration also contributed to higher land prices and the transfer of ownership as small landholders emigrated permanently. Those who remained in the villages hastened to take over or purchase the abandoned and salable lands with remittances from America. Moreover, conversion to a cash economy based primarily on sericulture, tied the Lebanese economy precariously to fluctuating world-market prices and foreign competition, with the economic consequences mitigated by traditional Lebanese emigration and resourcefulness as well as by income from grape products and tobacco.

The Syrian economy fared less well in the nineteenth century. Agricultural areas had been underpopulated and undercultivated because of the general aridity and, more importantly, because of economic insecurity brought on by weak and corrupt governments. The avarice of officials impoverished large segments of the population through crushing taxation and usury, leaving whole villages depopulated.[23] Nevertheless, during periods of tranquility, despite frequent droughts, locust invasions, inadequate irrigation, and primitive agricultural methods, Syria, at times, was capable of producing surplus crops for export, including grains, rice, maize, olives, fruit, cotton, tobacco, and silk.

Toward the third quarter of the century, local government, challenged in part by emigration of its inhabitants to a more favorable political and economic regions such as Mount Lebanon and Egypt, was forced to adopt reforms.[24] Although taxation remained excessive, security improved, bringing with it a resurgent population and agricultural production.[25]

The important industries of nineteenth-century Syria were primarily dependent on agricultural production; thus crises that reverberated through the agricultural sector were echoed in industry—largely in home industries. Reeling, spinning, and weaving, for instance, relied on cotton and sericulture; wine, raisins, and a grape syrup were made from grapes; olives were pressed into cooking oil and sold for the manufacture of soap; and wheat was milled into flour, *burghol* (cracked wheat), and other commonly consumed wheat by-products.

Some villages began to specialize in one product, while others combined handicraft with agriculture and sold their products in nearby town and urban markets. "The relatively extensive market for village handicraft wares," wrote a Soviet economic scholar about Syria, "is an indicator of the correspondingly high degree of development of small-scale commodity production in the . . . trading villages. The inhabitants of these villages, however, continued to farm. For example, the village of Zuq was famed for both its sericulture and viticulture. The men of Hawran and Zahle tilled the soil, etc."[26]

Both Syria's industrial and agricultural economies fluctuated with world prices and international developments. But, important handicraft trade suffered from the competition with Europe's machine-made goods in the nineteenth century. Nevertheless, as with agriculture, this trade continued to play an important part in the country's economy well into the twentieth century.[27]

On the whole, Syria, and in particular the Lebanese region, was enjoying, in the second half of the nineteenth century, a greater prosperity than its immediate neighbors. In the opinion of Dominique Chevallier, a noted French historian of nineteenth-century Syria: "During this half century [1861–1915], especially after 1870, the Syrian economy was stimulated by European investments in sericulture, by the construction of the Beirut seaport and of railways, and by commercial and banking businesses, while the Ottoman administration, despite its inherent imperfections, became more regular and efficient. Thus if Syria was dependent on Western capitalism—as the rest of the world was—its general activity profitted from the considerable development of means of communication and the growth of exchanges."[28]

Improved conditions heightened the aspirations of many Syrians who searched for means to satisfy newly emerging needs and tastes. This increased the economic pressure on families at all levels of the economy—even those which by American standards lived at or near subsistence level.

As the nineteenth century moved into its last quarter, the economies of Mount Lebanon and Syria were neither sufficiently depressed to breed despair nor brisk enough to meet rising expectations. The lower classes in villages and villagelike quarters of towns and cities subsisted in an atmosphere of subtle tension between those two conditions. Fear of destitution challenged their wits, and hope charged their energies. Even though by the criteria of most emigrants they were poor and life was difficult, they were not driven to migrate on a mass scale out of economic desperation. Until the "American fever," the average Syrian perceived few signs of impending change in his way of life. And it is doubtful whether many urban entrepreneurs saw the United States in their economic visions before the 1880s. Not only was Europe much closer to Syria than the United States, it was a more familiar entity.

PEOPLE

Religion

The essential fact about Islamic society is that religion, rather than nationality, was and remains the primary distinguishing social factor. In the nineteenth century, religious affiliation determined an individual's social status and legal rights. About a score of Christian and Muslim sects and a once sizable Jewish community contributed to the parochialism which characterized the Syrian population.

The majority in Syria were Muslim and, by far, most belonged to the orthodox Sunni sect. The Druze were a relatively small minority. Accurate figures for the period before World War I are not available, but it is estimated that Christians constituted less than 25 percent of the Syrian population at that time, and over 50 percent of the population of Mount Lebanon. In the Mountain, Maronites, Greek (later to be known in the United States as Syrian and then Antiochian) Orthodox, and Melkites were by far the largest Christian sects. Of the three, only the Maronites, the majority sect in the nineteenth century, claimed it as their exclusive home, a claim they shared with its Druze. The Orthodox outnumbered other Christian sects in Syria, but in Mount Lebanon, they were outnumbered by the Maronites. The Melkite sect was the smallest of the three in both sections of the province.

When Islam overran Byzantine Syria in the seventh cen-

tury, a number of rival sects were already there, the Maronites among them. Followers of an ascetic monk, they
adopted, in the seventh century, the then heretic Monothelite
doctrine which stated that Christ possessed one will but two
natures. The church's liturgical language was and remains
Syriac, since the sect was an offshoot of the very early Syriac
church. In the twelfth century, the church renounced its heretical belief and affiliated with the Roman Catholic church,
making the Maronites one of the oldest of the Eastern-rite
uniate churches.

Eastern, or Greek Orthodox, is, as its name implies, the
Eastern half of the universal Christian church which officially
split in 1054. At the time of the schism, the Western half,
centered in Rome, evolved into the Roman Catholic church,
while the Eastern half maintained its Byzantine reference.
The divergences between the churches remain broad and
deep on a number of doctrinal as well as ceremonial and disciplinary matters. Moreover, Latin became the official language of the Roman liturgy, while Greek remained that of
the Byzantine. After Greece gained independence from the
Ottoman Empire in the early nineteenth century and the
church hierarchy in Syria became Arab, Arabic gradually
dominated Greek in the liturgy in that region. The Eastern
church, as might be expected, rejected the Western church's
claim to universal papal supremacy.

In Syria, adherents of the official, or Orthodox, theology
of Byzantium were known by the Arabic terms "Melkites"
(royalists) and "Rum" (Byzantine or Roman). Since the mid-
eighteenth century, however, the Melkite appelation has
applied only to that faction which, influenced by Jesuit
missionaries, had broken away from the main body of Melkites affiliated with Byzantium and became, like the Maronites, a uniate church. Since affiliation with the Latin church
did not require a change in language, ritual, or symbols of a
uniate rite, the accoutrements of the Melkite church remained the same as that of the Orthodox with minor concessions to Catholicism. Despite this internal split in the Byzantine church, the separation between the two factions at the
personal level was not as great as the chasm which separated

the Eastern Orthodox and the Maronite communicants. Persecuted by the majority Greek Orthodox for about a century after their breakaway, many Greek Catholics, as they were also called, sought refuge in Mount Lebanon and made Zahle their stronghold; Damascus, however, remained the official See in Syria.

Islam, meaning the submission to one God, was the third of the great monotheistic religions to originate in the Middle East. It was revealed in Arabic to an Arab prophet in the Arabian Peninsula. The cornerstone of its faith is the belief in the unity of an all-powerful, compassionate, merciful, and transcendent God who tolerates no sharing of his divinity or power. All Muslims, irrespective of sect, adhere to this doctrine.

In Islamic belief, Muhammad is considered to be the last and greatest in a line of prophets from Adam through Moses to Jesus who were chosen by God to remind mankind of the Day of Judgment and to warn people to mend their errant ways. God's final words of warning and guidance, dictated to Muhammad by the Angel Gabriel, were compiled by his friends and followers into the Koran, the Holy Book of Islam. Inasmuch as Jews and Christians are also people with a holy book, they were to be protected by Muslims and were not to be forced to convert to Islam. This "Doctrine of the Book" allowed for a great deal of religious tolerance within the world of Islam where Jews, Christians, and people of other faiths lived and flourished, albeit in a "protected" or "second-class" status. In various times and places, however, some Muslims and their rulers ignored this tenet of tolerance and Christians and Jews were persecuted.

In Islam, as in Judaism, government, religion, and society are inseparable. Since Muhammad regarded Islam as the successor to the earlier monotheistic traditions, he drew many of the basic Islamic tenets, such as the concept of Judgment Day, from both Judaism and Christianity. In order to guide the faithful and prepare them for that day, theologians and jurists searched the Koran and drew on the Prophet's pronouncements and practices to compile and codify the *Shariʿa*, or Holy Law, which governs every activity in the life of believers. It is explicit on a wide range of civil, personal, criminal, and fiscal questions, including the prohibition of pork and intoxicating beverages and rewards for the manumission of slaves and the protection of orphans. Property rights, inheritance, marriage and divorce, and punishments for theft, adultery, usury, and bribery are also ruled upon.

The Holy Law is believed to be the will of God and it is to the law that the faithful submit. Therefore, observance of it is more highly valued than observance of religious practices. In theory, it stands above the ruler, and upon him lies the responsibility for its implementation and the consequent salvation of the Muslim community of believers, the *umma*.

All Muslims are required to perform a prescribed set of practices which are considered to be the "five pillars" of the faith. The first, and indeed the foremost, is the profession of the faith. To be a Muslim, one must profess belief in the unity of God and the prophecy of Muhammad. By saying (and believing) the words "There is no God but the One God and Muhammad is His Messenger," one is initiated. Second, he must pray at prescribed hours, after he has performed the ritual of ablution in a prescribed manner, repeating in Arabic, prescribed prayers five times a day—morning, noon, midafternoon, sunset, and night—accompanied by a prescribed number of bows toward Mecca. Since the faithful may conduct the daily prayers wherever convenient—at home, work, or outdoors—as long as the location is clean and "uncontaminated," Muslims frequently use prayer mats.

Although the mosque is the central religious edifice and a sanctuary for prayer, meditation, and religious learning, corporate prayer on the Muslim sabbath is not obligatory. Prayer is considered an individual matter even in mosques where Muslims flock to attend the weekly prayers on Fridays. There they enjoy the spiritual experience of communing with God and fellow believers in a sanctified place and listening to Koranic verses chanted as well as to a sermon on religious, political, or other topics delivered by an *imam*. The imam is not a priest. Islam ordains no clergy, although many of an imam's functions as well as his status are similar to a priest's. He is a religious teacher and leader of prayers; among other duties, he performs marriages, burial rituals, circumcisions, and religious ceremonies. He teaches the Koran, explains and oversees religious obligations, counsels believers, and resolves conflicts. At a minimum, he is trained to recite the Koran from memory and to teach it. Most imams, however, are literate, and many may also be graduates of an Islamic university. Women, if they pray in a mosque, are segregated, usually behind screens.

A third pillar of Islam is charity—both voluntary and obligatory. Almsgiving and the feeding and clothing of the poor are ordinary forms of voluntary giving. However, a pious Muslim might, if he can afford one, build a mosque, school, hospital, or orphanage. An act of charity required under this pillar could compensate for the failure to perform any of the other religious obligations, save the first. Obligatory offerings are, in practice, a tithe which in the past were used to defend and extend the domain of Islam. Non-Muslims, forbidden to join the military whose purpose was to defend and extend the faith, were also taxed as "protected" peoples. At present, in the Muslim world, funds which help to build and maintain religious institutions come from private endowments (*waqf, awqaf*) and government coffers.

The fourth pillar is total fasting, from sunset to sunrise, during the holy month of Ramadan, a period devoted to spiritual renewal. Spiritual renewal is also one of the objectives of the fifth pillar. Believers, male and female, are enjoined to make a pilgrimage to Mecca, the holiest city of Islam, at least once, where, along with hundreds of thousands of faithful, they reenact a seven-day ritual adapted from pre-Islamic times. This uplifting experience binds a believer not only to the Islamic umma but to the Arabic roots of the faith. The pilgrim is also rewarded with the honorific title of *hajj*.

In its formative centuries, Orthodox, or Sunni, Islam, like Christianity, faced heated and divisive controversies involving a variety of complex theological problems. Resolution to one of the most significant and complex of them in the tenth century rejected man's free will, virtually draining religious practice of mystical experience with God and bringing to the forefront of the issue a movement of believers, the Sufis, that drew strength from the inherent mysticism in the Islamic faith based on the love of God. Reconciliation of the two seemingly incompatible views of Islamic beliefs in the twelfth century, became the creed of Sunnism. Over the centuries, Orthodox Islam proved adaptable to change. While it stood guard over the traditional religious dogmas and values, it nevertheless allowed their evolution to conform with changing needs by an emphasis on the study and interpretation of law and has therefore been instrumental in maintaining the cultural unity of Islam through the ages.

The reconciliation of these two theological principles, however, did nothing to reconcile the schism between the Sunni and Shi'a sects. Just as Protestantism is faithful to the fundamental precepts of Christianity, so Shi'ism is faithful to those of Islam. Yet, the Shi'as continued to adopt doctrines and practices which emphasized their particularism and widened the breach.

The Shi'a belief in the hereditary principle of succession led ultimately to the doctrine of the hidden, sinless, and infallible Imam who, it is believed, divinely rules the world from his concealment until his return to unite the world with righteousness. Therefore, the fourth caliph, Ali, the Prophet's cousin, who was martyred in the struggle for succession, became the first Shi'a Imam. All other rulers of Islam, including the first three successors, are considered usurpers. Until "the return," the "Learned in the Faith" represent the Hidden Imam on earth. Influenced by pre-Islamic religions, Shi'ism diverges from Sunnism in a number of other beliefs and practices, among them the principle of atonement, the right of interpretation of the Koran, cults of saints, and the efficacy of shrines. Although Sunnism eschews saints and shrines, belief in them is widespread among Sunnis.

The early history of Druze persecution by other Muslim sects shaped the nature of Druze religion and society. First, it forced the Druze into a secrecy about their religious beliefs and practices that endures; it caused them to cease proselytyzing and accepting new converts; and, to dissemble in defense of community and faith when confronted by a foe.

Moreover, it reinforced a time-honored cultural interdiction against interfaith marriages. Only children fathered by a Druze are accepted into the faith.

Druze dogma is veiled in esoteric inner meanings of the sacred books known only to the initiated—men steeped in the wisdom and mysteries of the religion—who are pledged to secrecy. These elders, *shaykhs* or *uqqal*, distinguished by their apparel and beards, interpret the faith and lead the uninitiated masses along the righteous path but leave them ignorant of the mysteries and symbols of the faith. "Though many may well be uninitiated into the inner sanctum of the true theosophy of their faith, *Al-Tauhid*," wrote Henry Flehan, "all were taught, since birth, its basic meaning: the Oneness of God, the One and Only, the First and Last Cause to matter and form. However, as felt by the Elders of this sect, the *Mashayikh*, this theosophy must only be revealed in its true meanings to those Druze who can commit their lives to the practice of its true revelation. . . . [The uninitiated] are taught . . . some principles of Al-Tauhid, mainly that God directs our destiny and that a soul never dies, but as a plant may die and wither away, only to bloom again in another season [so is man reincarnated]."[29]

Despite this explanation by one of the uninitiated, Druze, in practice, have difficulty explaining their faith. Little understood by the outside world, Druze silence about their beliefs has spawned legends. Of the uqqal, the late Ambassador Abdullah Najjar, himself a Druze, wrote: "The Druze majority looked upon this well-informed minority among them in awe and with due respect. They didn't want to disturb it in its devotional life and reclusion. They avoided its displeasure and were wary of facing its potential reprisals."[30]

The *majlis* is the inner sanctum of the elders where, closed to the uninitiated, they secretly conduct work and prayers, and where apprentices (men and some women) are trained and take vows to maintain purity of mind and body; that is, they must, among other things, abstain from such habits as smoking and drinking; they need not, however, be celibate. The uninitiated, on the other hand, meet in a *khalwa* (meaning a retreat) which could be a community hall or a private home, wherever two or more Druze come together. There, on the Sabbath, which is observed from sundown Thursday to sundown Friday, they read from *Al-Hikma*, the nonsecret *Book of Wisdom*, or discourse on religious and community matters. Despite the distinction in the functions of the two, the word "majlis" is more frequently used by Druze in America when referring to a Druze place of worship.

Like Islam, the Druze faith subscribes to the authority of the Koran but with much less spiritual and doctrinal compulsion and rigidity. Also, no sanction attends nonattendance of congregational Sabbath prayer. The Druze faith accepts the five pillars of Islam in principle only; Druze are not obligated to practice them with the rigor and literalism of Muslims, a consequence of the religion's interpretation of the inner meanings of the precepts of Islam. Like Muslims, prayer, for Druze, is primarily an individual matter, but unlike Muslims who are obligated to bow in prayer at prescribed times, Druze are not required to bow; nor must they adhere to precise times; ablutions may be obviated by an individual's declaration of intent allowing him to pray any place, even in the midst of work. Fasting during Ramadan is also not obligatory; and Druze deviate from Islam in the celebration of religious holidays. Of the several holidays, Druze celebrate only one, *Eid al-Adha* (the Great Feast) commemorating the final day of the ten-day pilgrimage to Mecca—the day on which families traditionally sacrifice a sheep and share the meat with the poor.

In search of refuge from the dominant Islamic sects, the Druze migrated into the Syrian mountains where they adapted their tribal ways to mountain peasant life. They are said to be clannish, warriorlike and courageous fighters, suspicious, if not unfriendly, to strangers in their villages, and capable of intense loyalty and tough endurance. Mr. Flehan defined the nature of a Druze and his fidelity to his origins and identity: "He is a Druze first and last wherever you find him. He is a person who can adapt to many cultures, only to enhance his betterment, yet never lose sight of his identity. He is most covetous of his heritage and his identity among other societies in the world. He is originally a tribal warrior;

... throughout his existence, he is a person most protective of his name, honor, family, country, and friends. He is, and for a good reason, referred to in the Motherland as 'Beni Ma'ruf'—the tribe of tributes and honor—a justifiable reference to [Druze] merits and deeds in spite of their minimal number in the Middle East. The Druze were and still are, an important integral part of Lebanon and Syria, including Palestine."[31]

Najjar says of his people: "For the last thousand years they conducted a mode of secluded community life as Druze, which strictly discouraged any further mixture of blood. They kept their lineage, as history testifies, undiluted and untouched. They are ethnically, therefore, the purest of Arabs, and in that respect they make a fetish of their origins and of their loyalty."[32]

Syrian Society

Since the advent of Islam, Syria's multi-religious society had been organized on the basis of two Islamic principles: the Prophet's concept that the Muslim community would be regulated according to Koranic precepts and secondly, the concept that Christians and Jews were a "protected" class. The result was society organized according to religious beliefs. Not until the introduction of the Western concept of nationalism in the nineteenth century did race and ethnic origin become factors in the social consciousness of Islamic society.

Since the conquest, protected religious minorities have been allowed to regulate their own communities. Each community was administered by its highest religious authority who controlled civil, spiritual, educational, and personal matters (marriage, divorce, and inheritance). He had jurisdiction over legal cases, except criminal, and was responsible for the collection of taxes and maintaining order within his community. The religious communities were not compact segregated entities; their members were scattered and were relatively free to move about within the Ottoman Empire as long as they kept their place in society. Nevertheless, they tended to gravitate, in cities, towns, and villages, into rela-

tively homogeneous quarters, or *haras*. While the system of
organizing society by creed dates from the time of the
Prophet, it became institutionalized into the *millet* system
under Ottoman rule when it served the interests of the dynastic, autocratic, and militaristic state. It was a formula for
maintaining social order among the numerous religious and
national minorities and for collecting revenues with minimum conflict and cost.[33]

In some ways, the non-Muslim millets were more fortunate
than the Muslim community. Under some measure of autonomy, which each group jealously guarded, its members were
considerably freer of direct state and bureaucratic authority;
they were also exempt from military service. Although the
system ceased officially with the end of the Ottoman Empire,
its legacy lingers into the present. By centuries of condition-
ing, divisive attitudes and behavior reinforced often fanatical
sectarian and religious identities which fed endless rivalries.
The millet system permitted Western missionary, educational, and economic influences to reach the non-Muslim minorities and allowed the rival Western powers to manipulate
them and exacerbate Muslim-Christian relations.

Under the millet system, the Maronite primate resided in
Mount Lebanon, whereas the primate of the more scattered
Eastern Orthodox faithful, the Patriarch of Antioch, made
his headquarters in Damascus. The Melkite patriarch divided his time between Damascus and Zahle. The Druze
community was administered by its elders in Mount Lebanon.

In a general way, religion also explains the distribution of
the sects in Syria. One fundamental fact of distribution has
been noted, that is, the majority in nineteenth century
Mount Lebanon was Christian, while in Syria it was overwhelmingly Muslim. Another is that within that larger geographic framework, whole sections of Syria were and continue to be dominated by one sect or another. The Druze,
who have for centuries made the Shuf district their stronghold in Mount Lebanon, also had tribal and kinship ties with
Druze in southern regions of Greater Syria. The northern

half of the Mountain has historically been dominated by Maronites, with the exception of the Kura district which is predominantly Orthodox. In the late eighteenth century, Melkites migrating from the Kura and Syria after the Orthodox-Melkite schism, settled in the gorge that is Zahle and adopted it as their capital. For generations, the Shi'as have dominated the southern plains. Over the centuries, population shifts and internal political and economic changes brought peoples of different faiths together to form many religiously mixed villages.

Mixed villages were the most common feature of Syria, although geographic separation of the faiths was as prevalent there as in Lebanon. Whole villages and frequently clusters of villages would be occupied by adherents of one faith. However, in religiously mixed cities, towns, and villages, inhabitants tended to self-divide into quarters by kinship or place of origin.

Using the vantages of their mountain fastness, Lebanese Maronite and Druze sects, both consisting of warlike independent-minded peasants, achieved virtual autonomy in which religion was woven into politics and administration.

Whereas Maronites and Druze were characteristically mountaineers, Orthodox and Melkites tended to concentrate in Syria's towns and cities. "In the long run," according to historian Zeine N. Zeine, "most of the prosperous merchants all over the Empire were the Christians."[34] They were the most economically active and prosperous, trading on a grand scale and acquiring European languages, tastes, and manners. Their family names were associated not only with the largest, most historic trading houses in Syria but with a variety of crafts which they dominated. As agents and merchants, this small but growing class pushed its way to the center of a new era of entrepreneurial opportunity ushered in by European manufactured goods. They were no strangers to change; moreover, they were in a far better position to take advantage of economic innovation than were the farmers. On the other hand, the Orthodox of the Kura district of Mt. Lebanon have farmed there almost as long as their Maronite neighbors predating the Orthodox-Melkite split. The sizable Melkite community of trading and commercial farmers in Zahle dates from the late eighteenth century.[35]

Shiʿa Muslims, expelled from Mount Lebanon in the fourteenth century, made the Beqa and the district south of the Mountain their home region, subsisting off the land. Sunni Muslims, never numerous in Mount Lebanon, dominated Syrian villages. They were also prominant in Syria's coastal and interior cities where they shared with many Orthodox and Melkites the wider economic and social horizons of urban commerce.

City dwellers, rich or poor, considered peasants to be inferior and Lebanese mountaineers less civilized.[36] Outside of feudal Mount Lebanon, the upper stratum of Syrian society dwelled in the cities. At the pinnacle were the Ottoman-appointed ruling class, notables, and religious dignitaries followed by a thin layer of men of wealth and status consisting mainly of great merchants, absentee landowners of large holdings, shipowners, and a few industrialists, men of letters, and professionals. In Mount Lebanon, which lacked seaports and cities, wealth and status were vested primarily in holdings devoted to sericulture, and worked by tenant farmers and sharecroppers, as well as in animal and grain trade.

The gap between the wealthy and the vast majority of poor was wide, bridged only by a historic class of men engaged in small business and industry. The lower class of artisans, petty tradesmen, day laborers, and the broad mass of agriculturists measured their lives by the daily struggle for survival. Yet abject poverty was not widespread. Even the poorest "made a living, with God's help," said Nemer K., who emigrated in 1905, echoing similar statements made by other pioneers. Although he and his mother had nothing when his father and brother emigrated, "we got along," he added. "I worked as a cobbler's apprentice for two years and was paid nothing. Then I got [the equivalent of] five cents a week. My mother used to bake for people in an earth oven.... We always walked barefooted and when we had to wear shoes, we carried them till we got to where we were going so the shoes would not wear out. But, ooohhh, when I look back now I say 'What did we have there?' We were so poor."[37]

Landownership among the Syrian peasants was widespread, particularly in Mount Lebanon, and it was, everywhere, a status symbol. However, the tradition of landownership was weaker in Syria than in the Mountain and the system of land tenure less secure. Until World War I, many farm families owned no land; instead, they held a share of village land. Periodically, village land was divided according to quality and distributed by shares among the families according to family size.[38] However, inasmuch as the plots were often small, disconnected, and distant from the village, and because agricultural methods were archaic, the land yielded little in return for a hard day's labor. Peasants on the outposts of the cultivated areas were further hampered by insecurity, as much from government forces as from pillaging bedouin. The most secure, like the Lebanese, lived and labored in the mountains. Those who owned too little land or were landless, including sons of farmers, toiled longer for less in the fields of others. Most peasant families were forced to supplement their incomes by engaging in trade or crafts; family-owned mule or donkey caravans also carried goods from one region to another as their entrepreneurial owners bartered and sold within a network of petty trade. Consequently, the distinction between peasant, artisan, and tradesman tended, outside the cities, to be blurred.

Like the townspeople, the peasantry had become accustomed, but hardly resigned, to a low standard of living—lower in Syria than in Mount Lebanon. But in the context of nineteenth century Syria, people's aspirations corresponded to their perceptions of what was possible. To attain the possible—to break through the limits of their economic status, they employed bold personal enterprise and the utmost resourcefulness. Faris N.'s account of his youth before emigrating in 1895, is characteristic. He began his memoir with "My father died . . . and left my mother . . . with not a thing. . . . My mother started to do all kinds of work to raise me and my two sisters." After some schooling and work as a thresher,

he apprenticed with a weaver and dyer at the age of twelve.
The three small, disjointed vineyards owned by the family,
required little care and were tended by his mother and sisters
when not working the fields of others. In addition to weaving
and dying, Faris used "to go to the district of . . . Ayn al-
Sha'ra and would bring the coarse cotton from the peasants
and dye them. I would return them during harvest and collect the cost in foodstuffs." His sisters left the household as
child brides, and he tended the vineyards and bartered and
sold the products of his craft in villages as much as a day's
walking distance from home. When Faris was nineteen, in
1894, his brother-in-law, a blacksmith, invited him to go
along to Hawran as helper and to sell his woven and dyed
cloth. The brother-in-law annually spent several months
during harvest in that major grain-growing Druze region.
"You could profit more in three months than working here
for two years," he told Faris. "I said, 'God will help.' I left the
shop . . . took some cloth that would sell in Hawran and I
also took my share of cloth from the shop which I had
woven. . . . We stayed in Damascus three days until we found
someone to accompany to Hawran."

Enroute, they encountered thieves and raiding bedouin.
After several day's journey, they reached their destination
and spread out their goods. His brother-in-law sent him to
another village because "there they plant tobacco and you
could sell the goods for tobacco and then we could sell the
tobacco to the Arabs [bedouin]." They continued to trade in
cloth, tobacco and grain until September. Faris helped with
blacksmithing tools and plows for the farmers. "Now autumn
was beginning and the season of trade was at an end, and
those who were itinerant were returning to their homes. . . .
I sold the grain and returned to Rashayya."[39]

In Syria's uncertain economy, villagers and townspeople
buffeted by forces beyond their control, as well as by whims
of a weak or corrupt government, the elements, and what
happened in worlds they never heard of, could hardly afford
to overlook any exigency or opportunity and were ready for
it. Karam N.'s father, who owned land in Ayn Arab, Syria,
"which was not much, but he made a living," taught his son

the value of preparedness. Karam helped in the family vineyards until he was twelve when he accompanied his father on
the latter's second trip to the United States. This was in 1893.
They peddled together for three years and returned to the
village. There, Karam became restless and his father finally
decided that his son "would not make a good farmer." So the
boy was sent to Zahle, across the Beqa Plain, to learn shoemaking. "My father said if something happened and I
couldn't work on my feet, I could always make a living at
shoemaking because I could sit down. . . . When I learned
that, he said now you should learn another trade; so he sent
me to learn to be a carpenter. Then he made me learn how
to be a [house] painter. Then he said, now you know all these
trades and you have a good start in merchandising and farming. Now you can go to America and see what you can do for
yourself. I was seventeen years old then."[40]

The Syrian lower class constantly scrabbled for ways to improve its condition. Deeply ingrained fatalism may have
ruled most of their lives, but when it came to economic survival, they were pragmatic, grasping at opportunities that
were informed mainly by the lessons in the struggle.

Syrian Values and Traits

Arab values were born in the crucible of the desert and
forged by nomadic tribes into a system during centuries of
accommodation to a harsh environment and the scarcity of
life-sustaining resources. It was a system better suited to desert survival than to modern living. Continuity is not resistant
to time and place nor is substance changed by form. Although modes of behavior alter and bend under different
environments, modes of thought and attitudes, deeply ingrained, persist.

Centuries of trade between Syrians and the Arabs of the
Arabian Peninsula as well as the settlement of bedouin tribes
in Syria, had paved the way for the integration of Syrian and
Arab values and traits. Moreover, Syriac and Arabic are siblings of the Semitic family of languages. Thus, if some Syrians shunned the Arab's new religion, few were unaffected by
the Arab's values and language after centuries of accultura-

tion under Islamic rule. Acceptance of these forms the
strongest universal bond among those who identify as Arabs
and links them culturally with the pre-Islamic roots of Arabism—the bedouin culture of the Peninsula.

Even while affecting disdain and contempt for the bedouin's undisciplined, marauding, and nomadic way of life, Arabs everywhere revere the bedouin's social ideals—the so-
called noble virtues and cherished values. Admired for
manliness and sense of honor, individualism and group loyalty, magnanimity and munificence, as well as heroism, the
bedouin has, through the ages, been idealized in poetry,
tales, and song. On the other hand, less romantic analysts,
like the Syrian literary scholar, A. Kh. Kinany, perceived him
as one "who rode a perfect switchback from misery to eu-
phoria in the spirit of the clan yet be an individual, proud of
his achievement and aware of his importance. He had the
temperament to combine opposite qualities in the same situation—grossness, fineness, extreme hatred and magnanimity, foaming fury and self-control, tenderness and cruelty,
glowing sentimentality and apathy. He lived for the present
and had not time to contemplate anything except the practical needs of the moment. . . . Psychologically, [the bedouin]
were prone to excesses, but their sentiments were genuine."[41]

To some extent all of these complex and contrasting qualities survived in Syria, nowhere more than in mountain villages where the arts of valor and honor were, and are, perpetuated and preserved in village and family lore.[42] Syrians
have been described by both friends and scholars as generous, hospitable, individualistic, and proud—a people who
cherish strong family ties and group loyalty leading to clannishness, jealousy, factionalism, and volatile emotionalism.[43]

Syrians in America recognized these characteristics in
themselves and were frequently as outspoken in self-criticism
as they were ardent in self-praise. In an article of 18 May
1898, entitled "Some Causes for the Retardation of the Syrians in the United States," the author blamed sectarian factionalism and jealousy for the lack of unity that he believed
was essential to Syrian progress.[44] Historian Philip Hitti criticized the Syrians' individualism. "Of all the immigrant

races," he wrote in 1924, "the Syrians seem to be the most jealous of those of their number who aspire to leadership and are consequently most leaderless. Intensely individualistic with a history and geography that militate against cooperative effort, the modern Syrian has come to look upon organization with suspicion and contempt."[45]

The complexities of Arab values and their effects on Syrian society and character defy simple explication, yet essentially can be identified. A strong sense of honor, pronounced in older cultures and prevalent among peoples of the Mediterranean, explains, above all, the social conduct of Syrians. Through the single lens of that quality, a vast realm of human experience was, and is, viewed, weighed, and responded to. Yet, the sense of honor has not been, in traditional Arab society, an individual's alone. In the distant past, it derived from the tribe—that primary source of one's being and identity. In more recent times, that source became the extended family. Family honor is passed patrilineally from the ancestral fount, actual or fictitious, where it is usually enshrined. "I am an Arab" expressed in Arabic translates to "I am the son or daughter of an Arab [Anna ibn or bint Arab]." Before last names were required, tradition preserved the lineage in the father's name, extending for two or more generations. "My name is," a man would say, "Yusuf, the son of Khalil, the son of Yusuf, the son of Ibrahim." Implicitly, the honor of one's ancestry and his Arab heritage were inextricably intertwined and became indistinguishable from his own. An existence apart from kin or primary group was almost inconceivable for an individual.

From early youth, family members learned that they were expected to uphold the family honor—defending it with their lives if they must. Reciprocally, the family protected its members, invested them with honor, and assured them an identity and status in society. Not to identify with a family was to be bereft of status, virtually isolated. In return, the family demanded loyalty and conformity to its will. To assure loyalty and sensitivity to offenses against the family honor, it so instills in them a sense of pride constantly interwoven with the fear of *ayb*, an Arabic term usually translated as "shame" or "disgrace" but which goes much further than that. Under certain circumstances, as when loss of face is involved, "ayb" can be an exceedingly forceful regulatory device. Both pride and "ayb" are equivalent in value to the sense of honor, and when the three become fused they form one highly charged sensor manifested frequently in individual Syrians as a sense of inflated self-importance coupled with an obsession to save face.

While the essence of one's identity—and thus honor—is the family, other identity factors linked to it become perceived as inseparable from the family and become infused with its honor. In a religiously oriented society, divided into the tiny worlds of "we" and "they," two factors achieved primary but somewhat unequal significance—religious affiliation and place of origin, if that place was associated in a person's mind with his forebears. The place could be a region, town, village, city, or even quarter. An affront to one might be construed as an affront to all, requiring defense. Numerous illustrations of the importance of these two identity factors can be found in the colorful litany of compliments or curses one Syrian can heap on another.

The way in which Syrians formulated their identity affected relations between groups as well as between individuals. When a Syrian asked "who are you?" he asked, implicitly or explicitly, "to whom do you belong?"—that is, "whose son or daughter are you?" and he pursued his inquiries until he was satisfactorily informed: family name, religion, and place of origin (a married woman covered her husband's background as well)—whatever triggered some subconscious mode of behavior because implicit in any relationship is the individual's unbending belief in the superior or at least equal status of his family's honor. The objective in any social interplay was to gauge one's honor and status relative to that of the "other" and to assure that the perception of equality was maintained and that of superiority was gained over others. A common tactic employed in social interplays was to try to elevate one's own and to humble and discredit the other's honor and status.

The notion of "equal or better" extended to other aspects of Syrian society. In primitive society, generally, reciprocity evolved as essential to social harmony. Nowhere was it more indispensable than in the desert environment of the bedouin. There, it became intricately interwoven with the most minute and hairsplitting aspects of the honor-centered value system. It also became finely calibrated for measuring the "other's" perception of one's family honor and status. In a society that placed so much value on personal relationships, reciprocal favors, gifts, or compliments, for example, had to abide by the unwritten behavioral code that to give less than one had received was to convey a disregard, if not disrespect, for the receiver's honor. Such a transgression produced disharmony in the relationship and placed the giver under a burdensome obligation to the former. To avoid so intolerable a situation and uphold, if not emphasize, one's honor, the tendency was to transgress in the other direction—to exaggerate the giving. In more modern times, the symbols of Syrian munificence center on the serving on food. When the Arab's pride and honor are engaged, tables often groan under the weight of ostentatious quantities of food and, in a duel of etiquette, servings are pressed on the guests. "Just a little more, for my sake," the hosts urge, as the guests politely protest. Tasteless immoderation by both hosts and guests has characteristically been checked by the fear of ridicule—of "ayb," the relentless and ever-present wounder of pride.

Family honor was a given; every family displayed pretensions to it, warranted or not. The line between a family's honor and the perception of its status is, however, worked out through the family's relations with other members of the community. It is incumbent on its members, individually and collectively, to gain acceptance for that perception of status, assert it if necessary, and enhance it. Today, of course, noble ancestry and strength that once guaranteed family status have been supplanted almost exclusively by wealth. A more weighty criterion for honor and status is upholding the social values and moral conduct manifested "nobly." Wealth thus allows the family to "perform nobly," that is, to demonstrate the cherished virtues of magnanimity and munificence (*shar-raf* and *karam*). Social graciousness is, therefore, not only the most noble goal of Arab families; it is a way of life.

At the upper level of Syrian society, a family's pretensions to honor qualified it to exert influence and power. In the lower strata, the most that it can achieve is respect, and must, in the competition, assert its honor by steadfastly maintaining an inner conviction of self-worth. Here are statements about immigrants to the United States made by two villagers interviewed in Zahle in 1968:

    a. Here I would be ashamed to be a laborer or work at a job— not I, a man of family with a horse and land—not even if it brought me wealth. Over there, I would do it without shame as everyone was doing the same thing. No one would know me. No one could say "He's the son of so and so and his father rode a horse." There I would be like everyone else.

    b. The Zahlawi won't work at a job that he thinks is beneath him. He thinks himself as "ibn [son of] Zahle." He would rather not work. He is so proud that if he bought something and it had to be put in a bag, he would hire someone to carry it for him. Over there, he lost this pride in order to make money and because no one knew him. His pride came first. What mattered most was how he saw himself in the eyes of his townsmen. In America, he would shine shoes, but not here—not if he was starving. He'd be afraid someone would reproach him some day saying "That one? He shined shoes."[46]

The competition for honor and status gave rise to another trait, the concern—commonly bordering on obsession—with public image. More precisely, this image was created by the individual comensurate with his perception of his honor and status, one that is veritably etched on his mind's eye. One's inner concern centered on how he projected it and his outer concern was with the public reaction to it. What *they* think or say, or what *they* appear to think or say, mattered deeply. What was reflected from the mirror of the mind or into it triggered a particular mode of behavior.

To redress an affront, real or imagined, and to minimize the potential for open conflict, an individual might engage his opponent in a conventionally refined art of verbal dueling to test the latter's resolve and signal his own displeasure. Generally beginning with embarrassing flattery of the opponent's honor, it could, if pressed, deteriorate into a feud. This method of resolving conflicts offers the challenger a face-saving possibility. He could gracefully withdraw, pointing to the surface meanings of his "complimentary" statements, unless his opponent chooses to pursue the challenge implied in the underlying meanings. The contest is culturally specific, the rules being known fully to the participants.

Such a system of values breeds complex contradictory personality traits and behavioral patterns whose effect on the texture of life is immeasurable. Preoccupation with the assessment of others shields against self-examination, lest some flaw in one's "mirror" image be detected; it encourages the inclination to externalize blame and to sublimate reality, while limiting the ability to laugh at one's self. For the individual who must remain honor conscious, little relief is afforded from the tensions of responsibility. It requires a sense of security to admit one's falibility or to accept criticism. So much depends on the individual's performance that the inevitable undercurrent of anxiety must be veiled by haughtiness and contempt for the ability of others, even one's betters. Even Ibn Khaldun, the fourteenth-century Muslim historian who is credited as the father of sociology, noted that an Arab tends to be jealous of leadership and to disdain authority. "Every Arab," he has written, "is eager to be a leader. Scarcely one of them would cede his power to even his father, his brother or the eldest (most important) member of his family."[47] An often-cited Arab proverb states "Myself and my brother against my [parallel first] cousin; myself and my cousin against the stranger."

An inflated self-esteem, born of the need to perform well while concealing anxieties, frequently manifests itself in overstatement, equivocation, intractability, intense emotionalism, and at times, aggressiveness. Hate is as strongly felt as devotion and loyalty; compassion as deep as contempt. An individual could be as faithful to his word as he is defiant in his will, and as friendly as he could be rude and deceptive.

With identity tied intricately to the narrow primary group, the tendency toward clannishness and factionalism is inescapable and, in turn, inhibits the Syrian's ability to subordinate his interest to the interests of higher, broader social or political goals.

Another side of the Syrians' social personality—indeed that of all Arabs—is quite positive. What appear as negative traits in one time, place, or situation are generally the obverse side of positive qualities under other circumstances. The Syrians' dignity, generosity, hospitality, warmth, and compassion are traits recognizable as characteristic by friends and foes alike and are as traceable to their culture's emphasis on family honor and status as their competitive spirit and individualistic behavior. Individualism, along with loyalty, piety, and close family relations, as the Syrians in America were to discover, were compatible with the most cherished American values. Moreover, pride and the determination to elevate group status bred an ethic of hard work, thrift, perseverance, initiative, shrewdness, resourcefulness, and conservatism. Syrians were characteristically unafraid to take physical or economic risks to achieve their imperatives. Given the economic opportunities and the system of values Syrians found in America, their traits flourished just as the first generation had brought them, and served all Syrians well in their new environment. Syrians readily and enthusiastically became success-oriented free enterprisers. No two more dissimilar molds could have produced more similar products.

Precisely because the fear of shame was linked in the Syrian mind with family honor, it functioned to restrain crime and indigence and to promote mutual help within the community. Age and wisdom, highly cherished in a society that revered its ancestors, guided and controlled social morality. The tradition of giving succor and aid to poor families in one's own village and neighborhood resulted in the entrance of very few Syrians into the rolls as public charges in America—and most of those only under temporary or emergency conditions.

Over the centuries, values and traits of the ideal Arab heroes mellowed and transformed. Although Islam had preserved them and deposited them wherever it spread, it also exposed them to the civilizing effects of conquered civilizations. Bedouin influences, like bedouin numbers, however, have declined to relative insignificance; yet, the heroic values and traits have never been expunged. They continued to survive and adapt to new environments.

The Village

Most Syrians who immigrated to the United States came from, and identified with, religiously self-segregated neighborhoods and quarters in villages, towns, and cities. Since the quarters and neighborhoods were themselves, like villages, virtually closed social units, and the people in them lived by the same beliefs and customs, it would not fundamentally distort the portrayal of Syrian society in this broad overview to classify the Syrian immigrants as villagers and their places of origin as villages.

Generalizations have their exceptions; no more so than in so culturally complex a region as the Middle East. For example, although economic life in the cities, such as Aleppo, Damascus, and Beirut, contrasted sharply with life in farm villages, and although some city quarters were more religiously mixed, relations between the faiths and sexes varied mostly in degree.

Life in the villages conformed to the otherworldly orientation of religion and to the obligations required by the real world's customs and economic necessities. Between these two poles, life-styles ranged from the simple to the lavish, and although concessions were made to the ideals of status, a life of hard work, sobriety, and frugality was the rule. Strong social pressure was exerted to produce "right and proper" conduct. Certain aspects of tradition, however, varied according to class, religion, and residence. Unlike the lowest class, the upper class, the middling affluent, and even those poor with claims to family status disdained, for example, both manual labor and working women. Rules of behavior relative to age, sex, and class were closely watched for deviation, and transgressors openly criticized.

Social relations between religious groups were also established by custom. On the whole, they were characterized more by courtesy and distance—except in times of crisis—than by hostility. Hostility, nevertheless, bubbled just below the surface. The lessons of a long history of periodic outbursts of religious and sectarian violence, often influenced and fueled by a fanatic clergy, dictated moderation and prudence. Yet, a curse uttered in the heat of anger, touching one's family or religion, could provoke a conflict which an alert religious and lay leadership hastened to contain.

Syrian leadership qualities were age, noble ancestry, exemplifying the noble virtues, wealth, and perhaps even learning—one or two of them were often adequate. Occasionally, leadership, however, was expressed through councils, sometimes by individuals, usually heads of families. Most villages, including their quarters, possessed two or more competing venerable families with claims to noble ancestry or who seemed to embody the noble virtues. Rashayya al-Wadi, for example, had two; Btallun had five; and Zahle had seven. They did not govern or represent the authorities; they led. Each family had its own retinue of followers drawn from their village, most likely their quarter. Individually or collectively, the status and strength of these families could, at times, override religious and political authority. The relationship between this kind of personal leader (za'im) and his clients was based on loyalty and reciprocity. In return for their support, each za'im committed himself to protect and foster his followers' economic, social, and political interests.

The villager's identity with his leader and group was complete; it carried the same sense of honor and pride that the villagers attached to other identity factors. Frequently, the group's activities and the relationship between the men afforded opportunities to demonstrate the social ideals of the heroic and legendary desert Arabs.

Personal leaders were not, however, indefinitely secure in their position. Because every follower craved to lead and behaved as though he could and should, there was unremitting pressure on the leaders to deliver. Further, because leaders had more to lose—status and livelihood as well as their lives in extreme cases—they had to live up to the expectations of their followers. Equally important, they had to contain the fractious tendencies of their followers to avoid showdowns which might threaten their position, disrupt unity, or bring reprisals against the community from authorities or its adversaries.

Fealty to a person rather than to his solution to problems was widespread in Syria. Nowhere was it stronger than in Mount Lebanon where for centuries it had been reinforced by the Lebanese feudal system and where allegiance to a central authority was the more pragmatic, but fragile, alternative to chaos than expression of national loyalty and unity.

Physically, the streets of Syrian village and town quarters were generally a random network of narrow dirt paths and passageways leading to a church or mosque and, perhaps, to a marketplace. Except for those owned by some urban elite and mountain "lords," there was hardly a home remarkable for its size or appearance. A close cluster of dwellings housed an extended family. Some might be single dwellings; many were multiple with two or more rooms facing a walled-in courtyard. In mountain villages, tiers of adobe and stone-block houses covered the slopes. Their dull pinkish color and whitewashed doors contrasted with the green of the fields and orchards that surrounded the village. Better homes boasted windows and slab-stone floors, but dirt floors and small apertures close to the ceiling were common, so that much of family life, weather permitting, was conducted in the open.

In the house lived up to three generations of the patrilineal family. This might include the nuclear family, unmarried children, and perhaps the eldest son with his family, although the last could occupy a residence next to his father's. There might also be a widowed mother or sister. Living was crowded, and privacy almost nonexistent. The alfresco feature of Syrian life—in the yard, courtyard, or the flat roof—added space to the cramped quarters. Winter provisions were prepared and stored in these areas, clothes were washed and dried, children played, friends visited, and in suitable weather, members of the family ate and slept under the shade of trees or arbors.

No class was self-sufficient, but families provided as much of their food supplies as their plots and gardens allowed. Gardens played an integral role in Syrian life. What could not be produced or purchased locally was procured from itinerant traders or nearby marketplaces. A midwife and barber administering age-old cures were often the only medical assistance available.

Syrian women dressed simply: a loose-fitting garment or a long skirt, worn with a blouse, covered the body to the ankles. A light shawl or kerchief covered her head; some Muslim families required their women to veil themselves in public. Somber colors, usually black, were worn by older women. Men could choose between a dresslike garment, sashed at the waist (*qumbāz*), or a white collarless shirt and black trousers. The trousers were distinctive—bagging in multiple folds from the hip to the crotch and tapering tightly to the ankles. Called *shirwāl*, they were functional for men dependent on animals for transportation and combat. A black vest and waist sash completed the outfit. A large fringed square shawl was the common headdress. Its placement on the head, its color, cloth, and what was worn under it to shape it varied with creed, place, status, and sometimes occupation. In the cities, one frequently spotted men of status dressed in western suits and a fez.

The Syrian diet abounded with a variety of vegetables and fruits. Staples of rice, wheat, barley, lentils, and beans, as well as vegetables cooked in olive oil or in rendered butter—occasionally with meat or fish—and served with fresh fruits and vegetables made the diet highly nutritional. Meat, almost exclusively lamb, was reserved for special occasions. Pork was, and remains, religiously proscribed to Muslims and Druze. It was disdained by many Christians; in the United States, it took a period of time before many of them consented to eat it. Olives, preserves, *dibs* (the grape syrup), and dairy products such as cheese and *laban* (yogurt), made mainly from goat's milk, were important dietary supplements. Milk was rarely used as a beverage. The food was consumed with large quantities of flat leavened bread.

Provisioning for winter began in late summer and continued into late fall. Women dried or preserved vegetables and, along with the men, boiled cracked wheat into burghol and prepared other grains and legumes for storage. Olives were treated for the table and pressed for cooking oil, grapes were boiled into dibs, and fruits were preserved. A sheep, probably fattened by the family or purchased in the market, was slaughtered, and its chopped flesh and fat cooked into a base (*qawwarma*) for winter dishes.

Social life, for the most part, was carried on within the quarter or village in the company of relatives and neighbors. Religious institutions gave meaning to community life. With their prescribed obligations and calendar of holidays, they set the rhythm of social activities just as the seasons set the rhythm of economic activities. Ceremonies and rituals were occasions for collective socializing—most often kinship or religious, sometimes village—that could last for two or three days. Events were numerous: marriages and births, baptisms for Christians and circumcisions for Muslims, funerals, birthday of the Prophet, and saints days, blessings of the fields and harvests, and others particular to a locale. Such events set in motion cooperative preparation and participation. And, above all, the role of religion was prominent: each ceremony and celebration affirmed the unity of the group. Christian priests, Muslim imams, and Druze shaykhs were closely involved in the daily lives of their congregations. Yet, below the villagers' formal religiosity, concerns with superstition and magical practices underpinned their lives.

Between celebrations and rituals, the most important recreation was visiting among relatives. Such visits were among the few recreational activities open to women unaccompanied by a male relative. Men, however, were not so restricted. They could take strolls or visit with friends and relatives in coffeehouses where they quaffed demitasses of rich, thick Arabic coffee, exchanged well-spun heroic tales, listened to or sang folk songs, played backgammon, or discussed work; they also drank *araq*, a homemade liquor. On occasion, too, the villagers held indoor and outdoor gatherings, called *haf-las* or *mahrajans*, marked by feasting, dancing, and singing. Although men and women might arrive together, they separated to enjoy the festivities with members of their own sex.

Whereas in the United States such gatherings would become important fund-raising events for a church or mosque and for social or charitable clubs, in the intimate daily interaction of Syrian village families, social clubs, in the late nineteenth century, would have been irrelevant. Charity for proud Syrians was foremost the responsibility of the family and secondarily that of religious institutions administered through a committee of elders and funded sometimes by endowments. Most of the funds to build and maintain places of worship frequently came from endowments of the pious and wealthy. Such endowments were held in trust by the central religious authority of a faith which occasionally was called on to supplement church funds from its treasury. Parishes were not required to fund places of prayer or clergy entirely from their own resources.

Until the advent of missionary schools, education had always been the prerogative of men of the cloth who, at the village level, were, as often as not, barely literate. They taught, mainly by rote, religion as well as the rudiments of Arabic essential to reading the holy books. Sometimes a literate villager, for a few piasters a day, taught language and basic arithmetic to boys, sometimes to girls. School attendance was dependent more on the economic, rather than on the learning, needs of the family, and classes were small and sporadic. In principle, all sects recognized the merits of educating their sons. In practice, however, poverty, the simple village economy, which offered limited opportunity for education-based achievement, and the lack of newspapers or journals, except in towns and cities, provided little incentive for educating even sons beyond the most elementary levels. As for daughters, early and near-obligatory marriage made their education, in the opinion of their parents, quite irrelevant.

Notwithstanding the dearth of schools, education by the end of the nineteenth century was gaining. Both foreign missionary and indigenous religious schools contributed to and raised its value. Gradually the schools filled with Christian boys, but nothing was more striking than the attitudinal change involved in the education of girls. As classes and schools proliferated, female education slowly kept pace. It was education of the lower classes that gained the least ground.

Belatedly, upper-class Muslims and Druze began to enroll their sons and some daughters in missionary schools, particularly American ones. Tradition-bound families, however, continued to prefer the religious schools. Where schools did not exist, apathy toward education persisted until it was stimulated by family remittances from America as well as the challenges of greater opportunities projected eastward from the New World.

Family

The paramount institution of Syrian culture, invested with profound emotional significance, was the extended family. Ties of blood and affection, inculcated from early childhood, bound the family both in work and in leisure. Every member was dedicated to its welfare, honor, and status.

The Syrian family, including all of its nuclear units, living under the same roof or in separate households, was almost unexceptionally patriarchal, the patriarch being the eldest male member. Theoretically, his authority was absolute; strict obedience was not only expected but enforced. In practice, however, his authority was limited. First, by considerations of family unity and the strong bonds of loyalty and affection that flow from it; second, the role of the first son who was, in effect, his father's alter ego, lieutenant, and heir to the family responsibilities and authority; finally, the role of his wife as child bearer and rearer. Nevertheless, to maintain, before the world, his honor and status as head of the family, the father must not give an impression of weakness or deficient control over his household. Least of all might he be seen to have relinquished his authority to any of his womenfolk—with the possible exception of his mother. Mothers and wives were not without influence; they achieved their will subtly and effectively, but invisibly—even in the present, a well-developed art.

Master of the household, the patriarch was also master of the family finances and property which he held in his name and managed for the family as a unit. Even when he toiled long hours, the duties of family members remained under his direction. All were accountable to him and dependent on him, since he dispensed the fruits of labor. It was his responsibility to maintain as well as to extend the family's wealth, measured in income and property. The preference for marriages between patrilineal kin and the preference given to sons in inheritance laws are based on that concept. To keep the family property intact, it was not uncommon for a daughter who owned property to leave it to a brother if she married outside the kinship group or migrated.

The relationship between the sexes was the most complex relationship in the family and bore on a number of the community's mores. At the center of that relationship was the woman's sexuality. A woman, whether married or unmarried encompassed, in her sexuality, the honor of the family—of her father under whose authority she was raised. When she married, she had the added responsibility of her husband's honor by whose masculinity she bore sons. There were and remain three insults which a Syrian man believes he cannot abide: against his faith, his ancestors, and the one most likely to elicit a violent reaction—against the chastity of his women, that is, his wife, sister, daughter, and mother. Thus, the protection of a woman's person and reputation was the responsibility of her male kin. From puberty, her father, brothers, paternal first cousins and, after marriage, her husband and sons formed around her a protective and sensitive shield that was almost ironclad. Thus too, was formed the web of limitations on her independence and freedom of action, reinforced through the ages by social taboos and sanctioned by tradition, more strictly enforced in Muslim and Druze societies than among Christians, more in towns and villages than in cities, and more in lower than in upper classes.

The limitations ranged from the impropriety of leaving the vicinity of their homes unaccompanied by a family member to which males looked upon them, talked to them, and married them. Muslims and Druze, more than Christians, protected their women from the gaze of nonkin males, relegating them to women's quarters or veiling them. If Christian women were able to leave their quarters and remain unveiled, they nevertheless, had to avoid compromising contacts—even one-to-one conversations—with men to whom they were unrelated or unbetrothed. To accomplish these ends, some men went so far as to undertake the shopping needs of the family in the market, including buying their women's apparel.

Although at one time some urban Christian women covered their faces, veiling, the outward symbol of male dominance and female propriety, was largely confined to Muslim societies. In practice, the veil was more evident among city families and the fundamentalist poor. In village societies where women's work was essential to the family economy, the veil was impractical and was worn primarily when women left their neighborhoods. On such ocasions, some preferred to cover themselves from head to foot; others, like the Druze, simply drew their shawls across half the face or cast their eyes away from nonkin males. All three faiths required women to conceal their hair, the symbol of their sexuality and pride, from covetous eyes. While this practice had religious and social sanction, there was also the underlying concern with hygiene.

Social segregation, another form of restriction, was practiced in all communities. Almost from puberty, females were forbidden from freely intermingling with nonkin males. Christian women, however, were far more visible than Muslim and Druze in their respective societies. In social gatherings, while Christian women gathered in a separate room that need not be closed off, non-Christian women remained in concealed quarters. In churches, men and women worshipped from opposite sides of the aisle, although in a few traditional communities women might be segregated to the rear or in a secluded area. Muslim women, if they prayed in the mosque, did so in a concealed area. At a Christian dinner table, it was proper only for a matron, if she desire, to join the men—the younger women served, postponing their meal until later. However, women were not necessarily forbidden to sit with men. Muslim and Druze women ate in their quarters after the men had completed their meal. Unlike their non-Christian sisters, no special disgrace was attached to Christian women being greeted by nonkin males if proper decorum was observed.

In Christian, Muslim, and Druze societies, girls of marriageable age were guarded against mingling with the opposite sex to ensure not only their chastity and respectability but their chances of marriage. Unchaperoned premarital courtship was strictly forbidden. The marriage of children was a special concern for the family from a child's adolescent years; matchmaking was more than a village pastime; it was a village preoccupation. For the family, considerations of mates was interwoven with considerations of honor and status as well as economic ones. There were daughters' dowries, sons' bride prices, and the costs of a "respectable" wedding. On the family's reputation depended both the marriage chances and choices of the children as well as better afinal alliances. Unmarried children in the household, especially daughters, could jeopardize the family reputation, deprive it of alliances, and drain its income. Inasmuch as the family was, among other things, an economic unit and the children were financially dependent on the father, the choice of spouses was arranged by the parents. The traditional preferential treatment of boys allowed them some choice, if the father's consent was obtained. Should a son dissent from that choice, he and his fiancee, with the parents' consent, might elope. A priest would then perform a quiet ceremony. This practice served as a cultural safety valve.[48] Only rarely was freedom of choice or dissent extended to females; rarely would they violate their deep sense of loyalty and obedience.

The potential for a harmonious marriage, it was held, lay within the kinship group "because we know them and they know us." Traditional first-cousin parallel marriages, considerably more prevalent among Muslims and Druze than Christians, continued into the late nineteenth and the twentieth centuries albeit with diminishing frequency. The required dispensation by church authorities not only made such marriages more problematic for some Christians but somewhat discredited them as well. Village endogamy was also overwhelmingly favored over marrying one's daughter to "foreigners," a decision sometimes interpreted by the villagers as a misfortune or a desperate move to marry off one's daughter. It was, in any case, not an occasion for great joy.

Perhaps the ultimate precaution against a girl's vulnerability was early marriage. Although marriage at the ages of fourteen or fifteen was common, girls were sometimes betrothed before puberty, and many were married upon reaching it. Poverty sometimes compelled such child marriages, or they might be used to form a binding alliance. In such cases, the daughters might be married to considerably older men who would not only treat them compassionately and delicately but ensure the girls' moral and economic protection. Age differences of twenty-five to thirty years between females and their husbands were not viewed as undesirable.

Too frequently a girl entered marriage bewildered and frightened because her sexual role was only briefly explained to her, often only on her wedding night. Until then, ignorance, superstitions, and taboos surrounded her sexuality. Menstruation, sex, and pregnancy were never discussed in her presence. This was as true for immigrants as it was in the village. "It was considered disgraceful for a mother to tell her daughter such things," recalled Budelia M. and Amelia A. M., both American-born daughters of pioneer immigrants. "When women visited my mother and the subject was about sex or pregnancy or something like that and I came into the house, my mother would just look at me and indicate with her eyes that I should not enter the living room. Then she'd follow me to the kitchen and ask me to make coffee or lemonade to make sure I wasn't listening."[49]

"Oh no," chimed in Amelia, "When I began menstruating I knew nothing. . . . I ran to the bathroom and was terrified and cried. . . . My paternal uncle's wife was wise and . . . she put it straight to me. I begged her not to tell my mother. . . . Then she warned me: 'From now on you must never let a boy touch you.' She never told me why, but the implication was left that if he touched your finger you'd become pregnant."[50]

Since the majority of marriages were arranged by parents, duty and respect governed the relationship between husbnd and wife. A wife was required to be as obedient and respectful of her husband as she was of her father, and she remained as committed to upholding the honor of her parental family as that of her husband. For Christian women, divorce from an ill-suited marriage was unthinkable. It was not much easier for Muslim or Druze women. Divorce, permitted by Islam, is customarily initiated by the husband, except under unusual circumstances. It should be noted, that polygamy— up to four wives—permitted by Islam, had by the late nineteenth and early twentieth centuries, declined significantly.

Intersectarian marriages were rare, but interreligious ones were even rarer. Couples who infringed the religious barrier invited the harshest penalties—seldom death, more commonly ostracization from the family. Not surprisingly, the penalties fell more harshly on the daughter than on the son because the girl was expected to adopt her husband's faith and her children therefore would be lost to the faith and the community. A son, on the other hand, brought his wife into his community, and, even if she resisted conversion, their children represented additions both to the family and the community.

The birth of a first son was met with festive joy, and successive sons were considered the answer to parents' prayers. On the other hand, the birth of a girl was met, as often as not, with prayers for sons or condolences. From the family's point of view, sons affirmed the father's masculinity, largely shouldered the father's responsibilities, perpetuated the family name, and, unlike daughters who left the household, represented their parents' old-age security. Sisters were expected to yield their own interests and goals to their brothers', and dutifully did so. The status of the family's eldest son is demonstrated by the fact that parents proudly surrendered their first names to his. From his birth, villagers respectfully addressed them as *abu* (father of) and *umm* (mother of) that first son.

It would be grossly misleading to assume, from a Western perspective, that women yearned for reforms. Normally, their family relationships were warm and affectionate. Despite actual or potential conflicts, family members, and women in particular, accepted what appeared to them to be the natural God-given mores. If men wielded the authority to preserve these mores, women worked to maintain and transmit them to the next generation. In fact, women resisted as "ayb" changes in their way of life.

Even in traditional society, the family's unending economic struggle was not, as is commonly believed, regarded as outside the world of women. In villages where few opportunities to work for wages and where many men insisted that their women "did not have to work," many women and girls in the lower levels augmented family income by their labors. While only the neediest hired out as domestics, it was acceptable for women to work in the fields and tend the animals. Many made products for sale, such as baked goods, processed foodstuffs, and handiwork—sewing, weaving, spinning, knitting, embroidering, and crocheting. Some women who worked in cottage industries were paid by city merchants. However, women tended the silkworms on small family farms and reeled the silk thread from cocoons in factories frequently owned by Westerners. Such precedents in the homeland did not leave women totally unprepared for the unusual and more aggressive economic role they would assume in the United States.

Migration

No memorable political or economic event unleashed the Syrian migration to the United States. There was nothing to indicate that the departure of a few men from the ports of Beirut and Tripoli in the mid-1870s would become another, though minor, fountainhead of strangers streaming from the Old World to the New and that this trickle would change the lives of tens of thousands of Syrians. Departures from Syrian ports to Europe and Africa, particularly Egypt, had in the past been commonplace. Relatively few even reached the United States before the 1880s, but they did not constitute a movement. Evidence pinpointing the beginning of the popular movement of Syrians to America is fragmentary and conclusions are speculative, including this one. Adele Younis has chronicled, in some detail, the impulses of the migration of Arabic-speaking people to the United States. None adequately explains why the movement which has been described as the "American fever" happened to Syrians, even when the magnetic pull of expositions in America is cited. "The Arabic-speaking people," she has written, "under their respective governments whether in Turkey, Egypt, or other North African communities—responded to the call, either

for trade, pride, or just the adventurous spirit of their restless young men and women."[1]

That Arabic-speaking tradesmen were present at the nation's centennial exposition needs no further verification.
However, analysis of an entry in the log of the governor of
the administrative district of Zahle throws additional light on
those who opened the way for an exodus from Syria to the
United States, when, and why. On 20 March 1877, the governor recorded his reply to an order received from the
governor-general of Mount Lebanon through the Mountain's administrative council. He had informed the public of
the exhibition to be held in Paris in 1878 and "those who
wished again to show their wares, would be instructed, as
before, and the names of the individuals and their products
[will be] sent to the Governor General."[2] Undoubtedly, the
order was approved by, if not initiated in, the court of Sultan
Abd al-Hamid II, who, despite his autocratic reputation, was
"a willing and active modernizer," interested in reform and
Westernization.[3]

The reference to an exhibition was unquestionably the
Philadelphia Centennial Exposition of 1876, and Syrians
who responded to the call undoubtedly came as part of the
Turkish exhibit. Younis took the time to describe the exhibit,
relating that it included a coffeehouse, restaurant, and exotic
articles. Although the articles were "few in number," they attracted the attention of American journalists.[4] Louise Seymour Houghton, in her outstanding study of 1911, noted
that the few Syrians at the exposition were "chiefly traders
from Jerusalem" whose "stories of fabulous profits fired the
imagination of their people."[5] The vanguard of Arabic-
speaking immigrants to the exposition may indeed have been
from Palestine, but Syrians were among them and traded in
Palestinian merchandise. Available evidence indicates, however, that the pioneers who established the first Arabic-
speaking colony in New York were overwhelmingly from
trading centers in Syria. Curiously, a significant number of
the founders and pioneers were from Zahle, a prosperous
and active Christian market center and Mount Lebanon's
only semiurban community in the last decades of the nine-

teenth century.[6] One conclusion seems highly reasonable: that Western-oriented Syrians, mainly Christian urban tradesmen, if they were not the first Arabic speakers to discover American economic opportunities at Philadelphia, they at least had the foresight to take advantage of them.

Whether these trailblazers deliberately recruited others or simply reported their success in such glowing terms as to excite their neighbors will probably never be known. There is no doubt that these pioneers were soon overtaken by an influx of Syrians as word of newly made fortunes spread from town to village along the grapevine of extended families, and in the packs of itinerant tradesmen and artisans, until it reached the most secluded villages of Syria and Palestine. An informant, William D., recalled that his father and grandfather, in the late 1880s, regularly left their mountain village, not far from Damascus, for five or six months to weave and sell wool mats and blankets in small villages around Jabal al-Druze in southern Syria. "People would wait for them to come because they carried news also."[7] In 1896, Elias L., a farmer in Rashayya al-Wadi, a village in the anti-Lebanese mountain range, heard from Zahle traders in skins that "America had work and money."[8]

In the last quarter of the nineteenth century, America represented not so much a reality as a remote, distant, and incomprehensible mystery. Given the primitive state of communications, the speed with which the information was relayed to small entrepreneurs was remarkable. Even more remarkable was their readiness to confront both the remoteness and the mystery and to cast off for the New World. Before the decade of the 1880s was out, Syrians who gambled on that hope swelled the trickle of migrants into a chain migration that expanded exponentially until it drew migrants from many regions of Greater Syria.

By the 1880s, the chain migration was well under way. Nothing better confirms this than the reports of vigilant, though not impartial, foreign consuls who wrote to their home offices in Europe. In a navigation report from Beirut to the minister of foreign affairs in Paris entitled "The Question of Emigrants," dated 30 April 1889, the writer expressed concern over the "difficulties" created by the Lebanese migration. Since about two years ago, he wrote, Lebanese emigrants had become a very important element in passenger traffic aboard French ships and maritime regulations were being contravened because the migrants were being boarded beyond the anchorage and their numbers violated sanitation rules. "These are not, properly speaking, emigrants," he continued, "since almost all who leave do so with the intention of returning." However, the movement so disquieted the Ottoman government that several times it "requested the French Consul-General to take measures to debark its subjects from French ships anchored at Beirut," a request the writer rejected.[9]

A report of 28 March 1891, focused on the economics of emigration. Monsieur Quiot, French consul-general in Beirut, in his commercial report to Monsieur Ribot at the ministry in Paris, suggested that the decline of tobacco growing could be reversed if the migration "which for several years has drawn thousands of Lebanese to America," and "which has created a shortage of labor" is reversed.[10] Two years later, Monsieur G. Saint-René Taillandier reported to his government that the Lebanese flight from Beirut was "relatively important for Europeans" and "continues in considerable proportions." For several years, he pointed out, residents of the Mountain had been seeking their fortunes away from the homeland, "especially in America to which they are drawn." Those early ones who made money have generated "a veritable commercial exodus." Such rewards, he added, were a "delusion and dazzle." Lebanese need not seek their fortunes in America when they could find work in the Mountain. A day's labor in the fields and as artisans corresponded with the earnings in France and "in a general way, the remuneration of one's work is 50% higher at home than in America."[11]

Observing the migration from a different perspective, the Reverend Dr. Carslaw of the Foreign Mission of the Church of Scotland, described, in his report of 30 April 1894, the great improvements in the villages of Mount Lebanon:

On our way up the mountain, we noticed a great improvement in the villages we passed through. Building operations
were going on in many of them. Houses were having the old
clay roofs taken off, and new roofs of Marseilles tiles put on.
The outside shutters of windows, too, were getting a coat of
green paint, and everything spoke of comfort and prosperity. . . . Eighteen years ago there was not a tiled roof in the
whole district. . . . Workmen and labourers will no longer
work for the same wages as they did a few years ago and as
wages rise, everything else seems to rise too.

This appearance of prosperity seems to be caused by the
return of a great number of Syrians who, a few years ago,
emigrated to Brazil, the United States, and Australia. Having
in various ways obtained large sums of money, they have returned with the intention of enjoying life so long as the money
lasts.[12]

To stem the loss of labor and revenue, the Ottoman government tightened its regulations against travel by stationing
military police on roads leading to the port cities and at the
ports themselves. The government also required travelers to
post bonds. Syrian tradesmen had always traveled to Egypt
on business, but now they were using its ports to escape illegally to the New World. In the late 1880s and into the 1890s,
court records of the administrative district [Qada'] of Zahle
show not only more travelers posting obligatory bonds for
foreign travel but more bondsmen including America in
their bond coverage. Here is entry no. 762 of 26 December
1888: "Khalil Ubayd Issa guarantees for 100 Ottoman liras
[about $500] Elias Habib Ma'karun, newly shaven, and his
12-year-old brother, Salim. They applied for permission to
go to Egypt on business. The guarantor guarantees against
their leaving Egypt for any European country or to America.
He [Issa] will pay the sum required by the government in
case the guaranteed violates the law. He further promises
that he will secure their return to this country."[13] Mrs. Frank
A.'s father, a bondsman, several times traveled to the United
States at the turn of the century to collect such debts or return the defaulter to the homeland, she related in an interview.[14]

But, the Turkish restrictions were poorly enforced. To the determined emigrants they proved to be no deterrent. The minority who posted bonds and forfeited them reasoned that the bond penalty was an investment when, and if, they returned from America. Of course, most did not return. The majority found other means to circumvent the regulations. They put themselves in the hands of ticket agents who bribed the easily bribed Turkish police and then rowed the emigrants, under cover of night, to international ships anchored off the Mediterranean coast of Syria.

By the nineties, immigrants from several Syrian regions had reached well into the heartland of America, many of them having arrived much earlier. Mose N., an informant, related that three men from his Orthodox village in North Lebanon arrived to Chicago in 1877 and Mrs. Joseph C.'s grandfather left his Maronite village in that same region for Mankato, Minnesota, in 1880. Abe A.'s Orthodox grandmother was already peddling in Louisiana, having entered through New Orleans, when she gave birth to a daughter in 1885. In 1885, Mrs. Negebe S.'s father left his Sunni Muslim village in southern Lebanon to join a Christian friend in America, while Mrs. Rose L., a Maronite from northern Lebanon, and Selma B.'s grandmother, a Maronite from Zahle, arrived in Fort Wayne, Indiana, in 1890. By that time, Salem Bashara, an immigrant who had come from a village near Damascus, had already opened a store there to provision peddlers. A community of Melkites, mainly from Zahle and Damascus, was well enough established in Chicago to build a church in 1894.[15]

"Between 1882 and the year of the Chicago Exposition [1893]," wrote Louise Houghton, "though official data are wanting, there was without doubt a considerable emigration from Syria, which spread itself all over the country east of the Mississippi and north of the Ohio, and found its way to California without intermediate stay. Syrians are known to have entered New Orleans first in 1887, coming directly from the homeland."[16]

Immigration records for 1900–1901 show that Syrians reported destinations in forty-one states, the District of Columbia, and Indian Territory;[17] the destinations they reported in 1910 included all forty-eight states.[18]

By 1892, New York City's bustling Syrian community was described in the *New York Daily Tribune* as a "picturesque colony" of Christians and "a few Muslims" with shops of Syrian handcrafted articles, wholesalers and peddlers, coffeehouses and restaurants, societies and an Arabic-language newspaper. The article concluded that the community was "destined to become in the near future, under the leadership of men who are thoroughly acquainted with their capabilities and needs, a factor in the body politic which will make itself felt for good."[19]

WHY THEY CAME

The decision to become American—to surrender their nationality and native culture—is an act of will that may be explained by the immigrant's motivation for migrating. That motivation, in turn, would be expected to exert a powerful influence on how the group would assimilate. The particular needs, anxieties, and expectations of the Irish, for example, who fled from famine, or whole communities of east European Jews who sought refuge from religious persecution, contrast sharply with those of immigrants whose social uprooting was less traumatic or self-imposed. The freedom to exercise some control over one's destiny cushions the impact of the assimilation process. The question then, is what motivated the Syrians to migrate?

The pioneers who departed Syria before about 1905 and a large percentage of those who followed until World War I, answered the question unequivocally when interviewed: to make money and return within two or three years to live better in their villages. Throughout the interviews and in publications by and about Syrians before World War I, one theme recurred: that the Syrian pioneers, no more or less than Greeks, Armenians, and other national groups from the eastern Mediterranean, were lured to America by the notion of sudden wealth and the prestige it would confer on their return home.

Theirs was not an emergency or panic flight; it was a deliberate and calculated choice made by individual families. Informed in advance, usually by relatives and friends in America, they almost always knew their destination in the United States and believed they knew how they would prosper. Furthermore, the majority arrived with sufficient means—in hand or available from relatives—to reach their destination where work would immediately be available.

Syrian pioneers were not driven from their villages; the ties that bound them to their families were strong. Their avowed intention to return to the homeland, the constant stream of remittances to the villages, and the increased consumption of nonessential goods in them, compellingly testify to the economic reasons for emigration. Promoting family status translated into zealous ambition when the quick-wealth option was opened up. An eminent Lebanese scholar of the economic history of the Middle East minced no words on the subject when he wrote: "But one point needs to be made: this mass migration must be attributed to the energy and activity of the Lebanese not to poverty, which was much greater in the surrounding countries. This fact was recognized by the Egyptian poet, Hafiz Ibrahim, who, in a poem written before World War I, said that if they thought there was a livelihood to be made there, the Lebanese would surely migrate to Mars!"[20]

Once peddling triggered the chain migration to the United States, Syrians began migrating for other reasons. A handful left to escape official authority; some sought to escape parental authority; and others ran away from family problems.[21] A few thousand migrated to avoid military service, and several hundred left because they were unhappy with political developments in Syria as a whole after World War I. Many more came simply to join relatives and friends. Collectively, however, these various explanations are marginal to the economic reason and essentially consequential to it. Had the discovery of the moneymaking opportunities of America not turned Syrian eyes toward a new direction, Syrian migration very likely would have remained an individual, rather than a mass, matter. It should be observed that large-scale movements characteristically attract followers who march to different drummers.

If the pioneers largely left home in the hopes of boosting their fortunes, the draft avoiders were pushed to migrate by political circumstances. This was particularly true of Muslims, Druze, and Christians residing outside the protected Mountain who considered Turkish military service tantamount to extinction. Strange as it seems, enforcement of military conscription by the Young Turk government in 1909 was an attempt to implement an earlier edict promulgated by preceding sultans. The edict had aimed to appease the Western powers who pressed for Christian equality in Muslim society and expunge the stigma of inferiority. While the principle of equality was rejected by Christians and Muslims for different reasons, its implementation through military conscription was resisted unanimously for the same reason—fear of hardship and death.

Conscription fell harder on Muslims and Druze than on non-Lebanese Syrian Christians who generally opted to pay a burdensome exemption [bedel] fee when they were unable to escape to the New World. The onset of World War I removed the option as a legitimate evasion from military service.

Whereas migration, by 1909, was no longer an act of courage or a leap into the unknown for Christians, such was not entirely the case for Muslims and Druze. While several thousand Christians had formed a steady stream of emigration for a generation, only a few hundred Muslims and Druze had become sufficiently emboldened to defy the anxieties of living in a Christian country. Christian societies were perceived as unfriendly, if not hostile, to Muslims and Druze. Moreover, they feared Christian influence on their beliefs and traditions. Their slow migration prohibited the generation of a chain migration comparable to that of the Christians. In some cases, the early Muslims and Druze emigrants made the break to travel to America with Christians and to peddle with them.[22] To evade the military at home, some resorted to adopting Christian names[23] or smuggled themselves into Mount Lebanon from which they could migrate with less difficulty.[24] Otherwise, their emigration mirrored that of the Christians in almost every way.

For Muslim, Druze, and Christian emigrants, military desertion was an act not of treason but one of survival and opportunity. The pull of Syrian patriotism was either nonexistent or, if it existed, was impotent to restrain them. Their superseding loyalties were not nationalistic. Moreover, external and internal political circumstances in the Ottoman Empire which drove it into the war validated their decisions.

Apprehensive villagers, believing both rumor and fact, sought to send their eligible men out of the country. Experience of others had convinced Syrians eligible for service that once conscripted, soldiers would never be seen or heard from again; that Syrians were assigned hazardous and difficult duty in the Arabian deserts; and families, kept ignorant of their fighting men's whereabouts, could not retrieve their bodies, if the men fell in battle, for the "proper religious" burial.

Migration was advantageous for the families of draft evaders in another way. If the family's economy must suffer from the absence of its males, it seemed prudent to send them to America where not only would their lives be spared, but their increased earnings would benefit the family. Consequently, the then-weak Muslim and Druze chain migration strengthened, attracting more of their co-religionists. Nevertheless, during the 1909 to 1914 period, when Syrian migration had peaked, Muslim and Druze constituted perhaps less than 10 percent of the Syrian total.

Temporarily interrupted by World War I, the stream of Syrian migrants resumed when travel became feasible. Surviving relatives of the thousands who had starved at the hands of the Turks, particularly in Mount Lebanon, joined a small number who resented the French overthrow of the newly installed and highly popular Arab monarchy in Damascus and its replacement by French and British mandatory governments in Greater Syria, and by those who opposed the British pledge in the Balfour Declaration of 1917, to create a Jewish homeland on Arab Palestinian soil.

This migration coincided with the reentry of immigrants

who had returned to the homeland and who now reimmi-
grated with their families, and with others whose travel plans
had been thwarted by the war. All now rushed to enter the
United States before the enactment of contemplated restrictive legislation could bar their entry. Far fewer of these late-
comers intended to return to the homeland, heightening the
trend that had begun at the turn of the century.

That persecution in Syria drove Christians from their
homeland before World War I was a myth found mainly in
the post–World War II studies on Arabs in America—a myth
that tended to distort the immigration motivations as well as
the social and political realities of late nineteenth-century
Syria. In the words of Dominique Chevallier, the noted
French historian of Syria: "From 1861 to 1914 the various
provinces lived through a period of relative calm which contrasted with the extreme stress of the preceding period. This
fact should be brought out, for it has often been masked
from foreign observers by their remembrance of the 1860
massacres, Egyptian affairs, the Balkan turmoils, the Armenian massacres, the difficulties of the Turkish government,
the reinforcement of police supervision at the time of Abd
al-Hamid, and the revolution of 1908."[25]

In the limited literature written about the Syrians between
the turn of the century and the end of World War I, the
economic reason was, not surprisingly obscured by references to the "oppressive" or "terrible Turk." For staunch
American Christian journalists writing during the Victorian
era and after the war and influenced by the social and political biases of French and British writers as well as by some
American missionaries, the oppression of Christians by Ottoman Turkish Muslims was a common Western assumption
which Turkey's entry into the war on the side of Germany
seemed to confirm. Moreover, explaining it as an escape
from religious persecution made the migration of Christian
Syrians to America (ignoring Muslim and Druze migrants)
comprehensible to both the writers and their readers. Such
an explanation placed the Syrian migration midstream
among millions of immigrants, stereotyped in the American

mind, as poor and oppressed who sought refuge in the land of liberty and democracy.

Syrian Christians, emigrating from an area in which religion was the most meaningful basis of group identity and where religion and politics were hardly separable, would be expected to cite persecution as a motive for emigration when interviewed. Yet, none of the Syrian-born informants of any Christian sect, including those from Mount Lebanon, mentioned persecution and, when pressed, regarded the suggestion as amusing.

One would also have expected to have heard it from Syrians who originated outside European-protected Mount Lebanon. However, a village incident, related by two pioneers, illustrates how the European shield reached into Syria. In 1904, toward the end of the reign of Sultan Abd al-Hamid II, known for his despotism, a band of youthful Christian horsemen defied a government restriction by firing their muskets inside the town. The Turkish Muslim officials located the men hiding in their church where the village leaders had taken them. The confrontation between the Christian "heroes" and the Muslim officials reached its climax when the Muslims were dragged into the church and humiliated by the mock baptism of their leader. To block any punishment by the authorities in Damascus, communicated by telegraph through a Christian operator, the Christian religious leader threatened to turn the event into a religious conflict by reporting to the European consuls in Damascus that the Turks had desecrated the church. Underscoring his point, the priest shouted at the Turkish official saying, "You vile one, do you not know that if you so much as disturb this crown (pointing to his religious headdress), I will shake this whole province?" Allowing for the hyperbole of storytelling, this does not appear to be the behavior of an intolerably oppressed or persecuted people, but one which held its rulers in bold contempt.[26]

The anti-Turk and persecution cause for migration was brought into sharp focus in the United States in the 1920s by Syrians themselves. By the end of the war, they had become

politically more sophisticated. Arab nationalist sentiment
had, during the war, developed an ideology based on Syrian
unity and independence, reinforced by the collapse of the
Ottoman Empire. It was hardened by French and British
mandatory rule and complicated by conflicting political goals
of Syrian subgroups, particularly the differences between
Maronite Christians and the majority of Syria's population.
The conflict was echoed in the American and the Arab-
language press in the United States. Under these circumstances, Syrians—Christians and non-Christians alike, with
one eye on the homeland and the other on their future in
postwar antiforeign America, found the anti-Turk and the
persecution notion useful. Many had become American citizens with sons who had served and died in military service
against the Germans and their Turkish allies; others were
caught up in the postwar fervor of rising Arab nationalism
which was decidedly anti-Turk. Still others, mainly Christians, compounded their hatred of the Turks by projecting
the myths which surrounded the 1860 massacre of Christians
on to the tragedy of starved families in Syria during the War.
There was also the simple fact of the immigrants' ignorance
of their native social and political history, which made them
gullible to anti-Turk rhetoric.

The most ardent propagators of the persecution thesis
were the advocates of a larger French-ruled, Maronite-
dominated Lebanese entity. In the United States they were
led by Naoum Mokarzel, publisher of *Al-Hoda* in New York
City who used his highly respected Arabic-language newspaper to generate an exclusively Lebanese nationality linked
to "Phoenicianism," a claim that Lebanese descend culturally
and racially from Phoenicians. In August 1911, he organized
the League of Lebanese Progress, a nationalist, political, and
reformist organization to protect the interests and special
privileges of Mount Lebanon and to support its appeal for
improved port facilities and internal development.[27] By
1914, the league's emphasis was decidedly political, including
the return of Lebanon to its "natural and historic" borders
(which it failed to define) and the establishment of an independent constitutional government under French supervi-

sion with French military and civilian personnel performing advisory functions "as if they were Lebanese personnel."[28] Working with Maronite and French counterparts in Mount Lebanon, the American Maronite leadership used the persecution argument in the 1920s to justify Maronite and French political objectives in Mount Lebanon as well as the expansion of Lebanese borders into Syria to create a Maronite-dominated Greater Lebanon—this, notwithstanding Syrian and Arab nationalists' efforts to gain regional independence between the two wars.

Yet another group used the persecution claim. Americanized Syrians hoped to raise their status in the eyes of Americans whose antiforeign fervor had intensified. More out of pride than to deceive, they sought to win acceptance while veiling their humble origins and pecuniary motives for migration. These were people who, by the 1920s, had experienced some financial success as well as freedom of movement and expression in the United States and who, only then, appreciated and articulated, with great relish, the difference between poverty and restriction in the homeland and freedom and opportunity in America.

The mass emigration in the thirty years before World War I was novel. Traditionally in the homeland, population pressure, political discontent, and local religious disturbances had been endured or relieved by moderate emigration, not to Europe or to the United States, but to nearby Egypt and other North African regions. With the discovery of economic opportunity in the United States, families began to send fathers and sons; husbands came with wives, and some wives without husbands. Altogether they launched an unprecedented two-way traffic between Syria and the New World. Even before the turn of the century, going to "Amrika" came to mean the United States as well as Canada, South and Central America, and Australia where, whether through the deceit of steamship agents and brokers or by the emigrants' choice, communities of Syrians developed their own magnetic attraction.

Poverty was no deterrent to emigration. Most Syrians may have been poor, but those who made the decision to migrate were never so destitute that they could not pool even meager family resources, perhaps mortgaging land, to raise the nearly fifty dollars for steerage, train fare, and incidentals, including "a little something to safeguard against misfortune." In the Klondike atmosphere of the 1890s and beyond, hope pushed the poorest to borrow money. Finanical risk for the family was viewed as minimal, since it was expected that in a year or two, the investment in the traveler would be converted into considerable prestige and wealth by Syrian standards. Those for whom the promise of wealth across the seas had become a reality sent or took back to the homeland fares for others, in addition to sending remittances.

The Christian and non-Christian migrations differed in one significant way. Christian women became caught up in the adventure of the times, and as early as the 1880s a small number traveled abroad—sometimes with their men, sometimes alone, sometimes to make money, sometimes to care for their men. Only a decade or two later would they come to marry and settle. Except for a handful or two of Mulsims, the immigration of Muslim and Druze women was, at this time, virtually nonexistent. The conservatism of their societies effectively restricted their migration. Muslims "felt it was immoral to take their women to a Christian land," explained Mohammad S., a Druze, "so Muslims did not bring wives." Druze religious leaders, anticipating a host of deserted wives and a surplus of unmarried women in the villages, extracted oaths from emigrating males that the males would return to their wives and betrothed within two years or release them from obligation before their departure.[29] Many men did return to their women; some released them;[30] and others ignored the oath and its intent. Without wives and women of their faith to marry in America, immigration of Muslim and Druze men was further curbed by prohibitions against interreligious marriages.

If a measure of wealth was his purpose, peddling was the Syrian immigrant's means to earn it. During the pioneer period, as many as 90 to 95 percent arrived with the express purpose of peddling notions and dry goods and did so for a period in their immigrant experience—even if only for a day or so after arrival. In fact, it was their success at peddling that activated the chain migration. By the 1890s, whole groups were succumbing to its enticement. Mike H. was fourteen years old when he caught the "American fever" in 1895. When he became aware of America in 1892, not many people from his tiny village of Ayn Arab, close to Mount Hermon in Syria, were leaving. That year, he recalled, members of one of the village's poorest families had emigrated and, when they wrote back that they had saved eight hundred dollars, "all of Ayn Arab rushed to America—it was like a gold rush." He and his brother were among seventy-two who left the village in 1895. ". . . we were fourteen youth in our group and there were boys younger than I. We were excited and happy and having such fun as if we were in our village," he mused. Faris N. was nineteen when three cousins returned from America to spread the word. Within a few weeks, he was among a group of thirty-two men and two women who had set off to "get rich."

Others during this pioneer period recalled traveling with sixty, some with as many as two hundred, from a single town or village. Their reminiscenses were tales of a simple people filled with adventure, optimism, and confidence. Variations in each account added color to the dramatic events of simple travelers who were on their way half across a world about which they knew hardly anything except the persistent illusion that one could "shovel gold off the streets." For men and women who, on the whole, conceived of travel in terms of hours by foot or days by mule from the village, their recollections were remarkably lacking in trepidation or reservation.

En Route: A Network of Services

Fortitude was a characteristic shared by the majority of those who migrated to the United States in the late nineteenth and early twentieth centuries—to embark on a long sea voyage several weeks distant from their homelands; to endure the dangers of rough passage, the inhumane crowding in steerage, and, perhaps worst of all, the agonizing suspense at the end, after hours of herding and probing, before they would know whether they were to be accepted or rejected. But between home and destination, there were many more hazards and obstacles awaiting unsophisticated emigrants that intensified their anxieties. The Syrians were no exceptions. For them, however, these tribulations were mitigated by a network of services, if they chose to use it—the overwhelming majority found it necessary to do so.

By the mid-1890s, it became known to Syrians unaccustomed to travel but determined to do so, that they could be assisted by countrymen at every stage of their journey, from the village to destination, and be assured of work on arrival. When and how this network began is not altogether clear.

As a result of the steadily increasing commercial trade between Syria and Europe in the second half of the nineteenth century, Syrian-owned hotels and restaurants may have sprouted in European port cities such as Marseilles, France; and Liverpool, England.[31] As increasing numbers of Syrian immigrants moved westward across the Mediterranean, these facilities most likely became linked into an incipient network and expanded their functions to meet new demands. The owners probably hired or became themselves ticket agents, money changers, or runners and provided other services. In the flow of emigrant traffic of the late 1880s, cargo and passenger ships which served Syrian, Egyptian, and Cyprian ports deposited their human cargos at west European ports where agents of rival ocean-going steamship lines from North and South America and Europe competed in the lucrative market. Syrian entrepreneurs also moved in to compete in their own way. Their services could also be found in such lesser port cities as Athens, Naples, Genoa, Trieste, Cherbourg and Le Havre. None, however, developed a Syrian port colony comparable to that of Marseilles.

European ports were flooded with emigrants going to the New World. In America, the demand for cheap labor to man the burgeoning industries as well as settlers to occupy large areas of the West and South was publicized by industry, railroads, and state immigration bureaus. The steamship companies especially could foresee large profits in selling the promise of America and fanned out agents abroad to spread the word.[32] In Syria, as elsewhere, when these agents lacked the facility with foreign languages, they contacted localites.

Witnessing the flurry of activity, the foreign mission of the United States Presbyterian church, compiled the following critical report:

> The emigrant business has become a very profitable one; . . . A native usually one that has been to America visits a village, holds meetings, tells of the wonderful way to make money, where to go, what to do—in fact everything necessary for an emigrant to know. It is a poor day when he does not obtain a number of deposits for steamer tickets. This man is one of a long chain whose links are located all the way from Syria to North and South American seaports. From time to time, this chain of workers will send and receive warnings to avoid or to go to this or to that place. Word will come to avoid New York if diseased; then go to Mexico, and then go north, etc. No doubt this is an ingenious plan for making favorable commissions from steamship companies. At the present writing the flow is towards Argentina. We could tell of the harvest of gold that has been reaped by the officials, steamship agents, boatmen, etc. at the ports. It is a system that results in much human suffering, troubles, jealousies, and sometimes crime.[33]

In Beirut, perhaps also in Tripoli, brokers sent their agents to recruit in surrounding towns and villages.[34] It could not have taken more than a few years before the brokers' agents lost out to the more palatable enticements of swaggering Western-dressed townsmen returning from America, some of them commissioned to recruit by veteran Syrian peddlers who had opened stores for supplying merchandise to peddlers. Brokers competed, too, with a flood of letters from suppliers and immigrants to the most remote corners of Syria, often painting glowing pictures of exaggerated success. Moneylenders, eager to mortgage land or provide cash at usurious rates, became recruiters in their own rights, although far less effective. However, nothing was more persuasive or irresistible than the flow of dollar remittances from America.

Indirect recruitment played a role and could be said to come from the Arabic publishing community. *Al-Hilal* and

Al-Muqtataf, popular and informative periodicals published by Syrian émigrés in Cairo, for example, included numerous articles about American society and history as well as about the Syrian communities in the New World. Before 1908, articles appeared on estimates of Syrians in the United States; the merits of acquiring American citizenship; United States immigration restrictions and requirements; important events in the Syrian community; and the status of the Arabic language in the new lands. There were also notes from the editors answering many questions from readers concerning emigration and emigrants. America was idealized and eulogized. It seemed the New World had captured the interest of their readers.[35]

So successful was the recruitment process that auxiliary services were required not only to meet the needs but to circumvent Ottoman restrictions on emigrants who streamed into Beirut and, to a lesser extent, Tripoli. The emigration industry burgeoned to provide transport from village to port, inns to accommodate those who had to wait for a ship, guides, dinghies and rowers to smuggle emigrants at night to ships anchored at sea because of poor port facilities. Agents bribed the Turkish officials and hired guides to lead emigrants to hiding places and row them to the waiting ships offshore.

In the major European and American ports, there were Syrian-owned restaurants and hotels; food stores opened in response to those who preferred to cook Syrian food in their rooms. There were clothiers and interpreters and scribes were available to fill out necessary travel papers and to send and read letters and telegrams. Each had his price. At every port the opportunistic combined with the unscrupulous as well as with the compassionate and helpful; and all spoke Arabic.

What ultimately developed out of seeming chaos was a network of self-contained, spontaneous, interdependent, entrepreneurial services whose component parts reached from the homeland across the Atlantic and minimized the worst anxieties and adverse incidents for humble Syrian migrants. Like connecting dots on an international map, the network served as a communications line between the homeland and the New World, bringing the two closer together. It was culturally derived and functionally relevant to the goals of the immigrants. That the network was not deliberately structured or under the control of any one individual or group was irrelevant to its success.

While it began in Syria, it had originated in the peddling trade in North and South America and, in turn, by facilitating travel, it fostered further emigration. Emigrants traveling before the turn of the century came to rely on it almost totally. If they tried to circumvent it, they often found themselves helpless and confused, their problems and anxieties exacerbated. The experience of Elizabeth B. and her family is illustrative.

Her father submitted to the persuasions of a naturalized Syrian who had returned to the village. "You could shovel gold," he told his townsmen, and fifty to seventy-five people allowed him to lead them to America. Her father hid the family treasures and took his wife and daughter Elizabeth, with him on his temporary expedition.

> We were to board near Batrun. . . . We had to wait there about a week for a sail boat to take us to the ship and each night they'd say "Get ready," and each time it was a false alarm. My father finally said to him, "We are wasting our money." Then my father decided to take us to Beirut where we were to meet the rest to tell them we were leaving and found they had all gone to Minat Jbayl, fifteen miles away and had been caught. As for us, the next day we took a carriage from Minat Jbayl to Beirut. My father again complained about the price and the men warned him that the others had been caught and the authorities were on the lookout for emigrants, that he had better get in. The driver took us to a khan in Beirut. . . . We were then taken in a dinghy at night to our ship and got to Egypt. Then we found ourselves back in Beirut but we didn't get off and went on to Cyprus. We heard that the others got caught in a severe storm and were caught again [arrested by Turkish police] in Beirut.[36]

Increasingly, many emigrants were alerted to the hazards of the network by letter from America and by word of mouth by returnees. When finally the fraudulent practices of agents attracted the attention of the Arabic press in the United States, the emigrants' shrewdness and alertness were sharpened. They were told which services to use and what deceptions to guard against. Being informed was the best defense against exploitation. In fact, exploitation notwithstanding, thousands made use of the network in the early years rather than risk entrapment in the web of ignorance and bureaucratic restrictions. Mike H.'s group of seventy-two went directly from Ayn Arab, across the Beqa Plain, to Beirut, knowing what to expect. "We in Syria were ruled by Turks and they did not permit Christians to emigrate. There was more freedom in Mount Lebanon. There were agents in Beirut who smuggled us to Mount Lebanon and promised to get us passports with Christian names of people who lived there, but they did not succeed. We remained in the Mountain eight days, living outdoors. It wasn't cold. Finally, one night the agents . . . directed us through a small canyon and we walked to the ocean. They bribed three Turkish officers and put us in an open boat which took us to Cyprus where we boarded a French ship which reached Marseilles twelve days later."

The blackmarket trade in passports and money flourished so notoriously that the Turkish government in Beirut was moved to appoint a commission in 1898.[37] United States citizenship papers apparently also found their way to the Beirut blackmarkets, even if that was not the intent of the senders. Citizenship papers, illegally issued by zealous American politicans in election years to newly arrived immigrants, were sometimes sent to Syrian villages for use by relatives. After a two-year investigation of the Syrian community in Cedar Rapids, Iowa, in 1910, the Department of Justice arrested a Syrian upon discovering that there were

> certain irregularities in not only their [the Syrians'] naturalization papers, but also in the manner in which some of them came into this country. It seems that when a Syrian who has been naturalized dies, his papers are returned to the "King" of the colony who sends them back to the old country and another Syrian comes over on them. Also that it is not necessary for a Syrian to die in order to do this as the papers of

> scores of men who are now living here have sent back and
> other Syrians passed the officials at Ellis Island through hav-
> ing them.
>
> It is stated that the government agent located one instance
> where the naturalization papers of a dead man have been sent
> back to the old country three times.[38]

The defendant, who received the full support of his townsmen, was fined, and the matter, according to the United
States district attorney, was "brought to the attention of the
local Syrians in a manner that will give them to understand
that when they come to this country they must live up to the
country's laws."[39] There was no allegation that the papers
were being sold; George N. emigrated using his father's papers.[40]

The system misrouted hundreds of its patrons and in the
process inflicted perhaps its most painful effect on them—it
separated families—sometimes for decades, sometimes for-
ever. Hundreds of stories circulated about emigrants being
misrouted to strange destinations depending on the advantage, ignorance, or indifference of the agent. One observer
noted that "They might be sent to Argentina, while the
friends to whom they were going were in Massachusetts.
They might be sent to Sierra Leone or to Capetown, but it
was all to America" in the minds of the emigrants.[41] It was
said that Syrian communities planted in Australia, New Zea-
land, and the Philippines were the result of such agent avarice. Clark S. Knowlton, who studied the Syrian community
of São Paulo, Brazil, cites the trickery of steamship agents as
accounting for a large Arab migration to South America:
"envious of the profits made by companies ferrying emigrants to the United States . . .[and] in order to share in the
lucrative business, several companies informed prospective
immigrants that they also took emigrants to America. Many
emigrants sailed with them and landed in Rio or Santos believing that it was a part of the United States."[42]

Usually without the immediate option of changing course,
the misrouted settled in the countries they were sent to,
formed a nucleus of attraction, and dutifully sent remittances home. An uncountable number who remained deter-

mined to reach the United States to rejoin family or friend:
later made the journey, not as Syrians, but as Brazilians oɪ
Jamaicans or Mexicans.

It was in the European ports that emigrants were most vuɪ
nerable to exploitation. Without the knowledge of Europeaɪ
languages, currency, immigration regulations at the port o
debarkation, and ships' schedules, the emigrants were com
pletely at the mercy of the agents and hotelkeepers. Time ha
dimmed memories of hotel filth and inedible restaurant fooɔ
but had left vivid those of the uncertainty of getting the righ
passage, the boredom of long waits, and the fear of exploi
tation that would deplete meager funds and leave then
stranded. Many recalled waiting weeks and months foɪ
American relatives to wire or mail additional funds.

In a satirical account of the experiences of two Syrian em
igrants, the eminent Arab writer, Ameen Rihani, combineɔ
fiction with fact to capsulize the traps laid for the unsuspect
ing emigrants in Marseilles, the most notorious of Europeaɪ
ports. The travelers in the story, Shakib, a writer, and hi
companion, Khalid, left Beirut for "the gold-swept shores o
the Paradise of the World. . . . huddled like sheep on deck.'
In Marseilles they were

> rudely shaken by the sharpers, who differ only from the boat-
> men of Beirut in that they . . . intersperse their Arabic with a
> jargon of French. These brokers, like rapacious bats, hover
> around the emigrant and before his purse is opened for the
> fourth time, the trick is done. . . . From the steamer, the emi-
> grant is led to a dealer in frippery, where he is required to
> doff his baggy trousers, and crimson cap, and put on a suit of
> linsey-woolsey and a hat of hispid felt: end of First Act; *open
> the purse*. From the dealer of frippery, . . . he is taken to the
> hostelry, where he is detained a fortnight, sometimes a month,
> on the pretext of having to wait for the best steamer: end of
> Second Act; *open the purse*. From the hostelry to the steamship
> agent, where they secure for him a third-class passage on the
> fourth-class ship across the Atlantic: end of Third Act; *open
> the purse*. And now that the purse is almost empty, the poor
> emigrant is permitted to leave. . . . But the purse of the dis-
> tressed emigrant now being empty. . . .the rapacious bats
> hover not around him, and the door of the verminous hos-

telry is shut in his face. He is left to starve on the western shores of the Mediterranean.

. . . Shakib from his cage of fancy lets loose upon them his hyenas of satire. . . . "The voyage to America is the Via Dolorosa of the emigrant; and the Port of Beirut, the verminous hostelries of Marseilles, the Island of Ellis in New York, are the three stations thereof. And if your hopes are not crucified at the third and last station, you pass into the Paradise of your dreams. . . ."

And when the emigrant has a surplus of gold, . . . the ingenious ones proceed with the Fourth Act of *Open Thy Purse.* "Instead of starting in New York as a peddler," they say, " . . . why not do so as a merchant?" And the emigrant opens his purse for the fourth time in the office of some French Manufacturer, where he purchases a few boxes of trinketry—scapulars, prayer beads, crosses, jewelry, gewgaws, and such like,—all said to be made in the Holy Land. These he brings over with him as his stock in trade.[43]

Syrian agents, merchants, bounders, and men of all shades of good and evil were thrown together in Marseilles which, like other Western port cities, teemed with emigrants, each a prospective patron or dupe. With few exceptions, these entrepreneurs were bent on fortunes in a boom era with little concern for how—only for how much. The spirit of go-getter and the pragmatism of men who took advantage of the boom mirrored every facet of the capitalistic ethic.

In some corner of the port cities there formed self-contained Syrian colonies where the humanitarian elements of the network coexisted with the heartless. In the villagelike atmosphere, hundreds of Syrians, "from Zahle, from B'albek, from everywhere . . . all going to America,"[44] found other countrymen in hotels, restaurants, and on the street. They re-met old friends and made new ones. More importantly, they exchanged news with rejects and returnees and asked questions: What was it like in America? Can one get rich? What should one watch out for? They also inquired about friends and relatives from whom they had become separated or whom they were to meet. From the experience of others they learned, planned, and drew courage.

In these colonies, many needs were met. In the company

of their countrymen, the trauma of rejection was temporarily mitigated, fears alleviated, boredom and loneliness relieved. The ill were cared for; and the stranded aided. When honor needed protection, even if misguided, there were those who rose to the occasion. Only by the mature judgment of his older brother was young Mike H. and his friend prevented from attacking what he was told were Muslim boatmen who had "violated the honor" of a Christian woman stranded in Marseilles for six years. Since all were under the same novel stimulus and in the same bewildering circumstances, comradeship burgeoned in these colonies, so that it seemed to the emigrants that they were bound to each other's care. Seen from a larger compass, the Syrian colonies must have been miniscule compared to those which served emigrants from eastern and southern Europe.

The unfailing bond was their language. The familiar babble of Arabic was both assuring and comforting. To have perplexing circumstances explained and questions answered, accurately or not, in their own language made a deep impression. Half a century after his experience, Faris N. recounted the joy of hearing Arabic where he and his group of thirty-three least expected it. Having been booked by an agent in Marseilles on a ship leaving from Le Havre, the group traveled by train and were to change trains in Paris. En route, two of them jumped out of the window of the slow-moving train to retrieve a newly purchased fedora hat, the villagers' symbol of immigration to America. His companion and cousin jumped after him. The rest continued to Paris where, at the train station, they awaited word about their companions:

> The company at the international station in Paris sent a man to tell us about two of our group who had jumped from the train and to relieve our minds. He was good looking and cordial. I started to say that we are simple folk and that our friends are full of [practical] jokes, but the man opened his mouth and said in Arabic "Are you Arabs?" The words hardly left his mouth before we all came at him like eagles crying out "hey, hey" . . . like town criers or field guards. "An Arab!" we said, and eyes would be amazed to see how the rest of us ran

from all corners of the station and surrounded him like eagles after their prey. He said, "Calm down so that I can tell you," because we had given him no chance to speak. . . .

In the battle of wits between agents and villagers, there were winners and losers, but few fatalities. Typically, the villagers dealt with agents as they had dealt with Turkish tax and military officials—with suspicion and cunning—trying to outwit them or to turn a given situation to their advantage. Faris N. was one who was prepared in advance. In Marseilles, he took a letter of introduction, from his cousin, who had been to America, to a specific agent. As instructed in the letter, the agent helped Faris and his group purchase Western-style clothes and steamship tickets. Then "she asked me for seven liras, but I told her that I would give them to her at the hotel. My cousin had told me not to pay her until after the purchase. I told her 'I brought you all of these travelers and you want from me the price of a ticket?' Then she said, 'Never mind.'"

Port colonies frequently served as halfway stations for the rejected, the impecunious, and the lost. Men like Joe A., who did not have sufficient funds to enter the United States in 1901, had to wait in Marseilles until a friend wired him some money. Anxious and lost, single girls like Yamna A. were deported from New York to Marseilles because their families had failed to meet them.[45] None, however, felt the terror of rejection as much as those who were turned down because of trachoma. Considered by the U.S. Bureau of Immigration as a "contagious and loathesome" disease, the eye ailment overwhelmingly accounted for the rejection of Syrians. As a result, children were separated from parents and husbands from wives. The hapless turnaways either returned the thousands of disheartening miles to their villages or lingered in the port colonies awaiting funds to take them home. Others sought ways to circumvent the regulation; not many could afford the costly and time-consuming treatment of the disease. Among them was a bewildered thirteen-year-old who, in 1905, was left in Liverpool to be treated and cured. Seven months later, certificate in hand, Eli B. found his way to his parents in Worcester, Massachusetts, via Halifax, Nova Scotia.[46] Rahmy F., herself only seventeen, emigrated to join parents she had not seen in eleven years. In her care was her brother, an infant when the parents had emigrated, and her father's sister, an adolescent. In Marseilles, she was horror-stricken when the boy was rejected for having trachoma. Terrified and helpless, the trio was rescued by a countryman who arranged for the boy's treatment. Meanwhile, the girl endured several anxious weeks until her father sent money from Kentucky to repay the rescuer.[47]

Others cleverly returned to the United States in cabin class where detailed questions and physical examinations were deemed unnecessary by the U.S. Bureau of Immigration.[48] Untold numbers entered at alternate ports—New Orleans, Boston, Philadelphia, Providence, and Baltimore—where enforcement of immigration regulations was lax. Still others made their way through Caribbean, Canadian, and Mexican ports. The routes were circuitous, often taking months, and the anxiety prolonged, but entry was generally certain. Two incidents were related by Ghandura H. and Wardi N.

Ghandura shuddered at the telling fifty-two years after her ordeal. With her infant son in her arms, she embarked with eleven townsmen, mostly relatives, to join her husband who was then peddling in Nebraska. Their leader, a cousin who had been to America, spoke some English and "could even read a map." When his wife and sister were rejected in Marseilles for trachoma, he decided to reroute the group through Mexico. The ship they boarded carried cargo and, recalled Ghandura, it "circled the world" for six months. "We went to Brazil and some place where there was a mountain that flamed. We also stopped at Puerto Rico and Guatemala. In Central America we crossed a river on the backs of oxen and we walked in mountains and through forests. We were led by a Mexican. How we suffered! We were terrified all the time that some animal would jump out at us. I carried my bundle and my son on my back and tried to keep an eye on others who wanted to take my hand. We finally reached Laredo, Mexico, where my husband met us, but we couldn't pass because of the trachoma. So we took a train to Monterey and then to El Paso. He met us there and we got through."[49]

Wardi's experience was not as traumatic; indeed it was pleasant, but she too entered illegally from Mexico. Twelve years old when she was separated from her parents and brother in New York for trachoma, she was deported to Marseilles with four other youths. It was several months before they boarded a ship headed for Mexico and several more before they arrived. Meanwhile, the children had been cared for by friends abroad while, at their destination in Cedar Rapids, the parents had arranged for her voyage and prepared for her entry into the United States. They had hired two Syrians from Wichita, Kansas, who apparently had become experts in arranging such entries, to meet the youths in Mexico and bring them across the Mexican border.[50]

The discomfort of weeks at sea was endured with patience. Strangely, none of the smells, the crowding, sleepless nights, strange and inedible food, and seasickness during their journeys were accented in the recollections. Informants remembered the homesickness, however, and how the women wept silently and continually; they remembered, too, the weariness and boredom. Sometimes they sang or told stories and played practical jokes on each other; and they wrote mental letters to the family back home. Some practiced a few English words taught by returnees and relatives: yes; no; father; brother; good morning; Buy sumthin', Maam?; Holy Land; and the like—useful words. Or they rehearsed instructions in Arabic: Tell them you are a farmer, Americans admit farmers;[51] tell them you are going to live with and work for your father or a relative, you will not be admitted if they think that you have agreed in advance to work for others. Tell them your husband, fiance, or father is waiting to meet you; tell them you do not believe in marrying more than one wife; remember the address, show them the letter; don't lose your money, they will ask you to show it. Each new United States regulation was printed in the Arabic press and letters relayed them to families back home. Knowing what to do and doing it properly could spell the crucial difference between being admitted and being rejected.

The young Rahmy F. finally arrived at Ellis Island with her two younger wards. What she was not aware of was that an immigration ruling, to combat "white slavery," prevented single girls from debarking alone. Rhamy had come neither to marry nor to work. She came to be reunited with her parents, but since she had not seen them since childhood, she did not recognize the father who had come to meet them. Neither could he identify his children and sister. Rahmy cried and protested; finally parent and children were asked to identify each other from lineups. In desperation, she broke from the lineup and called out in Arabic to a man she thought might be her father. He responded. Still suspicious, the immigration officer sent the father back to Lexington, Kentucky, where he had been a respected businessman for almost a decade, for character and financial references before the children were allowed to proceed a month later.

New York was the penultimate stage in the journey, although it represented the ultimate hurdle. With the exploitation, indignities, and inconveniences of European port cities behind them, the emigrants anticipated their arrival in America with unconcealed anxiety and impatience underlaid with a sense of exhilaration. The heartbreaking prospect of deportation at the threshold of the Promised Land was exceeded by the heartbreak of family separation.

Much of the confusion and anxiety of Ellis Island was alleviated for Syrians when an Arab interpreter was hired, perhaps in the 1890s, by the Bureau of Immigration upon the realization that most arrivals from the Ottoman Empire were Arabic-speaking. The first-known interpreter was Najib Arbeely, son of Dr. Joseph Arbeely who had brought his family to the United States through New Orleans in 1878. The family moved to New York in 1881, and eleven years later, in 1892, Najib, assisted by his brother, Ibrahim, founded the first Arabic newspaper, *Kawkab Amrika* (*Star of America*) in that city. Three years later, Ibrahim published an English-Arabic primer to teach English to Syrians, providing them with examples of a wide range of American business forms and letters as well as social courtesies, tastes and manners.[52] For years, Najib guided Syrian immigrants through the labyrinth of examiners, answered questions, consoled and counseled them; when it was necessary, he put them on trains labeled with their destinations. He contacted relatives and friends, put strays into the care of the New York Syrian colony, or directed them to Syrian leaders or communities of their faith or region of origin. The only interpreter remembered reverently by name, he was described by several informants as helpful and compassionate.

Although not an entrepreneurial link in the network of services, the role of interpreter both at Ellis Island and at the Paris train station was the result of the network's success and became an integral component in facilitating the immigrants' journey.

Once out of Ellis Island, the immigrants who planned to stop in the New York colony, rather than board trains directly for their destinations, faced another hurdle. Swindlers and thieves, recruiters of industrial and farm labor, state immigration bureau agents, boardinghouse runners, and horse-drawn taxis—all swarmed around the confused immigrants.[53] This trap was also relayed to the homeland. Faris N., still following his cousin's written instructions and still cautious, turned down two men with five rented buggies who approached him and his companions as they left Ellis Island. He explained why.

> I had sent a letter from Marseilles to Salem Bashara in Ft. Wayne, Ind., in accordance with what I understood from my cousin, Mousa. I told him I had 20 travelers and that we were coming to him and asked if he would help us. After Salem received the letter, he sent word to Yousuf Bek al-Ma'oushi and Ibrahim Maksoud in New York to help us and whatever they spend on us he would be responsible for the payment according to an agreement between themselves. These people prepared to meet us and they, each of them, rented five buggies and they continued to wait for us until we left the island and we went to claim our baggage and we got them and each of us carried our own on our back as we were accustomed to do in the old country. Ibrahim Maksoud and Yousuf al-Ma'oushi came to meet us and said "Are you the men of Salem Bashara in Ft. Wayne?" "Yes," we said. "Here are the buggies; put your bags in them and welcome. Come, ride with us." We said to them, "Impossible. You cannot take our money from us. We can walk." We had been told that there was much trick-

ery at the hands of whoever approached us. They said to us, "Where are you heading?" "To Ibrahim al-Maksoud," we said. He said, "Damn you, I am he. What stupidity!" We said, "Go ahead of us," and we continued to carry our packs on our backs until we arrived at the place of Ibrahim al-Maksoud.

By 1905 or 1910—the date is difficult to pinpoint—one can no longer speak only of pioneers or the pioneering spirit. Syrian travelers had become more sophisticated. Moreover, seasoned relatives in the New World were now paying most of the fares in order to bypass the network. Instead of money, emigrants received prepaid tickets from point of departure to destination. The three major Arabic newspapers carried advertisements of Syrian travel agents who would make direct arrangements to and from the homeland.[54] Articles were published exposing the excesses of the system and discrediting it. On 5 March 1899, in an article entitled "Emigrants and Agents in Marseilles," *Al-Hoda* noted that poor emigrants were being cheated and asked the emigrants to notify the French authorities.[55] As a result, the agents and other components of the system could no longer prey on the innocence and ignorance of emigrants with impunity, and their value to the traveler diminished. Ironically, the network's decline coincided with the sharp increase in the annual rate of Syrian immigration after the turn of the century. Nevertheless, in 1911, *Al-Bayan*, the Druze and Muslim Arabic newspaper in New York, strongly criticized a Syrian agent for preying on poor women, robbing one of four hundred dollars and another of five hundred dollars, indicating that the decline of the network was both gradual and incomplete.[56] On the other hand, immigrants who arrived after 1910 could recall no memorable experience with agents.

In retrospect, the coalescing of the various component parts into a network was an inevitable, even indispensable, feature of a mass movement. Exploitation of the ignorant and naïve became rampant and wanton. Yet, in the determination of thousands to reach the Promised Land, chaos was inevitable and inevitably there were people who capitalized on it. Hardly a shrewd venture was overlooked; only the goal mattered. Right and wrong, morality and immorality became blurred; ignorance, anger and fear were countered with cunning, and cunning with resourcefulness. Such was the tempo of the times that only in retrospect was the system evaluated by those who had used it; there were few reproaches and fewer regrets.

The collective excesses of the system hardly detered emigration. As long as the harm was not irreparable or fatal, or the vexation too intolerable, even the most timorous emigrants weighed losses against gains—personal and economic—and accommodated to the demands of the system with a very strong sense of pragmatism and fatalism. For the hundreds it wronged, there were thousands for whom it opened the way to opportunities that might otherwise have been lost to them.

Quite apart from the heartless frauds it perpetrated on many, the network can be described as a set of functions which were validated by the Syrian value system. The behavior of the entrepreneurs was culturally recognizable to most clients who themselves had been conditioned to do business in traditional Middle Eastern bazaars. Arguably, too, the links in the system were psychologically reassuring for many who faced transplantation.

THE IMMIGRANTS

Who were those Syrians who followed the Pied Piper of peddling? From what segments of their society were they drawn? How did the pioneers differ from those who followed them? These are questions for which the immigrant literature offers scanty clues. Perhaps, however, the most difficult questions are those which deal with numbers. Such questions as how many Syrians came to the United States before World War II; how many were Christian, how many were Muslim and Druze; how many were skilled; how many were literate—all these have no reliable answers. Fragments of information that emerge from the interviews do no more than confound conjectures and estimates in published sources on the Syrians in the United States and cast doubt on official data.

The lack of dependable official statistics has resulted in widely disparate estimates. Louise Houghton, working with sheets furnished by the U.S. Department of Commerce and Labor, estimated that 41,404 Syrians were admitted between 1899 and 1907. "Although," she added, "100,000 is the usual estimate, 70,000 is that of the best informed Syrians."[57] In 1908, *Al-Hilal* quoted "reliable sources" who said, "There are between 100,000 and 150,000 Syrians in the United States." The author, however, believed that the figure was more like 100,000.[58] The *Literary Digest* published a figure of 400,000 in 1919.[59] Philip Hitti, writing in 1924, doubted the results of the United States Thirteenth Census of 1910 because it reduced "the figures of the foreign stock speaking 'Syrian and Arabic' to the ludicrous number of 46,727." His estimate was considerably higher: "Counting those who entered during the twenty years previous to that [1899], and those who were born here from Syrian parents, and making allowances for those who returned to Syria or died, it is safe to assume that there are at present about 200,000, foreign born and born of Syrian parents in the United States."[60] Four years after the United States Congress passed the restrictive Quota Act of 1924, Salloum Mokarzel, brother of the publisher of *Al-Hoda* and a respected author, editor, and publisher, claimed a Syrian population of approximately 250,000.[61]

The unreliability of the United States immigration and census data begins with the attempts of bureaucracies to classify millions of previously unclassified foreigners.[62] Before 1899, classification of immigrants by country of origin or nativity did not answer questions of religion or national identity. Emigrating from a multinational empire where country of origin did not correspond with national identity and where the latter was as much determined by religion as by language and culture, the Syrians were not distinguished from other Ottoman subjects. Lumped together with Turks, Greeks, and Armenians (emigrants from the Ottoman Empire), under the classification "Turkey in Asia," there is nothing to distinguish them from other Ottoman nationals.

Secondly, errors in immigration recordkeeping caused by the language barrier casts further doubt on the credibility of the statistics. Moreover, their value is further diminished by the deliberate falsification of information provided by the immigrants. Syrian craftsmen, for example, were told to say they were farmers on the assumption that America preferred immigrants with a farming background.[63] Furthermore, true ages were exaggerated or lowered and single women entered as married or divorced. Untold numbers, as has been noted, slipped undetected across Canadian and Mexican borders for decades. Sometimes they entered as immigrants from these countries; frequently they smuggled friends and relatives with them.[64] Many of those who were mistakenly left in Australia, South America, and the Caribbean later entered the United States listed on ships' manifests as immigrants from those regions. And, how many entered on relatives' passports and naturalization papers is another question mark. Moreover, Syrians tended to travel frequently to and from their homeland—three, four, or five times were not uncommon—to fulfill promises made to the family, to marry, to handle economic affairs, as well as for a variety of other reasons. Until immigration regulations were reformed in 1893, many of these were counted more than once. Some remained in the homeland for up to a decade or more before returning to America.

Records of the Bureau of the Census dealing with the Arabic-speaking people and Syrians in particular also lead one down a vague and confused path. Most of the problem stems from the impossibility of comparing categories of data (and their definitions) from census to census. Whereas the Bureau of Immigration began in 1899 to distinguish Syrians and Palestinians by "race" from other Turkish subjects, the census of 1910 continued to include them under the category "Turkey in Asia." Furthermore, until the decline of peddling, the peripatetic nature of that trade kept a large number of Syrians from being enumerated. Syrians, too, were accustomed, when confronted with questioning officials, to withhold or falsify information for fear of "trouble." In short, there exists no source or means that will provide accurate demographic data on Syrians in the United States before World War II.

Despite the figures' general unreliability, they do reveal useful trends and characteristics. By 1899, the Bureau of Immigration had concluded that classification of immigrants by country of birth did not "afford a satisfactory clue to the actual racial or ethnical status of such immigrants." It thus began to compile data by race or people as well as by country of birth or origin.[65] Between 1869 and 1898, with figures for several years not available, 20,690 aliens were admitted from "Turkey in Asia." However, by comparing the figures shown for immigrants recorded under that classification for the years 1899 to 1910 with figures given for the racial classification of "Syrian" for the same period, the Syrian count is the higher one by far. Of the 85,791 immigrants originating in "Turkey in Asia" during these eleven years, 56,909 were Syrians, or slightly more than 66 percent of the total.[66] Thus, it might reasonably be concluded that of the number of immigrants originating in "Turkey in Asia" before the "racial" classification of "Syrian" was instituted in 1899, a high percentage was Syrian.

Immigration from the eastern Mediterranean before the mid-1880s was negligible. A total of 74 was recorded between 1869 and 1885; fifteen arrived in 1886. But once the chain migration began to take effect, the figures inclined dramatically, with 208 arrivals shown for 1887 and, on average, more than doubled annually until they reached a high of 4,732 in 1897 (figures for 1892 to 1894 are missing). By any standard, Syrian migration had become an exodus by the 1890s. With few exceptions (some that might be attributed to enforced restrictions in the homeland), Syrian immigration maintained a steady climb for the next quarter of a century, averaging an increase of from 500 to 1,000 annually. In 1910, however, men escaping Turkish military service pushed the figures upward by approximately 2,500—from 3,668 to 6,317; with the onset of World War I, the figures reached their highest levels: 9,210 in 1913 and 9,023 in 1914. A total of 86,111 Syrians, recorded between 1899 and 1914, joined those who had come previously and uncountable hundreds of their unrecorded countrymen.[67]

Restricted wartime travel reduced entries of Syrians to approximately 3,700. Figures for the years following the war are, however, more interesting. In 1920, the floodgates opened and between that year and 1924, when they were virtually closed, 12,288 arrived, 45 percent of them women, reflecting the reentry of Syrians with their families and relatives as well as the arrival of newcomers. They were joined by immigrants unhappy with the imposition of mandatory governments. Despite the annual quota of 100 allowed to Syrians after 1924 by the Quota Act, 5,314 Syrians, an average of almost 500 a year, entered from 1924 through 1939. During this period, the number of female arrivals at first almost equalled, and then exceeded, those of males. The depression years of the 1930s, in the end, proved to be more restrictive than the immigration laws; only 1,182 entered during the entire decade.[68]

Palestinian immigration was, from the 1880s to 1940, relatively negligible if the figures in the records are to be accepted. Palestinians began to appear on immigration records around the turn of the century; from 1901 through 1919, only about 2,800 are shown as admitted. Their migration accelerated moderately under the British mandatory government in the early 1920s. In the four years from 1920 through 1923, 1,471 arrived, reflecting, perhaps, the effects of a chain migration. On the other hand, some of it may have been generated by political unrest after the war, provoked by the influx of European Jews to build the promised homeland in Palestine. The year 1924 marked a high point in Palestinian migration when 1,351 arrived. Thereafter, despite immigration restrictions, they continued to enter at an average of 270 annually until the end of the decade. The Great Depression cut that rate by two-thirds. In the last three years of the 1930s, corresponding with the Arab rebellion of 1936–39 against mounting Zionist migration and dominance, immigration increased somewhat, averaging, nevertheless, only about 250 a year. The total number of Palestinians shown to have been admitted to the United States from 1901 through 1939 is a mere 8,425, raising the same doubts about these statistics as about Syrian ones.[69] Many Palestinians may also have been recorded as Turks from Asia or as

Syrians, since they emigrated from the same general area of the Ottoman Empire.

Palestinian migration seems to have been less affected by political unrest in the homeland than one would be led to expect. The low volume of migration was probably due to the economically depressed conditions of the Palestinian peasant who was more subjected to the oppressions of absentee landlordism, and perhaps also to the lack of communication between the Palestinian province and Syria, the center of Middle Eastern migration to America. Perhaps, too, the Palestinian chain migration was directed more to South than to North America.[70]

Migration from other Arabic-speaking regions of the Middle East appears to be that of transitory individuals. Fragmentary figures show 12 arrivals from the Arabian Peninsula to 1940, 178 from Morocco, 939 from Egypt, and 145 from Iraq. None of these groups seems to have generated a chain migration, formed settled communities, or made social or economic contacts with Syrians or Palestinians of any faith in the United States.[71]

The largest majority of Syrian immigrants before World War II were Christians—perhaps as much as 95 percent; the rest were Muslims and Druze. The latter were so few that they hardly warranted passing mention in the literature on Syrians at the turn of the century.[72] Secondly, perhaps 90 to 95 percent originated in Mount Lebanon. In the vanguard of the Syrian migrants were young, single men who, for the most part, were between the ages of fourteen and forty. They were adventurous, tough, and ambitious mountaineers, determined to grapple with the unknown for promised rewards. Among them was the surplus population—those who would, when times were out of joint, migrate elsewhere anyway—as well as the unemployed, underemployed, and discontented. Women, few to be sure, joined the movement even in its incipient stages, along with a small (counted in the tens rather than the hundreds) but significant group of intellectuals and professionals.

Most were mobile tradesmen, artisans, and skilled laborers of various trades. Landless sons of farmers and farm laborers were among them. These were joined by farmers—owners of small plots of land. But since it is too often difficult to distinguish the Middle East artisan-farmer or tradesman-farmer from the full-time small farmer, the majority of the Syrian immigrants, it is reasonable to say, came from the land.

All too commonly, immigrants to the United States in the late nineteenth and early twentieth centuries have been portrayed as poor, landless, and oppressed peasants, deprived of a cherished way of life when severe economic depression or religious oppression forced their migration. With some exceptions, and despite the universal value of land as a status symbol, this characterization of the Syrian immigrants did not fit the mold. The average Syrian peasant was a landowner; his relationship with the land was, on the whole, more pragmatic, physical, and economic than emotional. The exceptions, more often than not, were drawn from among the wealthy landowners who had enlarged their holdings in the last third of the nineteenth century as well as from among the upper-class gentry and village nobility whose status was vested in family estates held for generations. Small farmers had little reason to treasure the land if, by other means, they could provide for their families and elevate their status. In the nineteenth century, their small parcels of land were usually scattered, sometimes as much as an hour's walk from their homes in the village; the work was backbreaking, since beasts of burden were either scarce or relatively useless in mountainous, terraced terrain; farm techniques were archaic; watering a common problem; and outside of Mount Lebanon, taxes were crippling. Moreover, the possiblity was remote of ever increasing their holdings from their income.

One other little-known point affecting the farmer's attachment to his land involves the systems of land measurement and evaluation. In nineteenth century Syria, including Mount Lebanon, land wealth was measured not in surface area but in the estimated monetary value of the yield. Thus, a family's land, irrespective of surface area, was registered in government cadestres in *dirham* and *qirat*; taxes as well as loans, even though in some cases land surfaces might be

measured in *dunum* or *feddan*, were calculated accordingly.[73]
Yield was frequently barely sufficient to do more than sustain
the family after long and arduous labor, frequently requiring
the family to supplement its income by other means. Such
conditions were not conducive to developing a deep emotional attachment to farming. What land they owned, they
clung to; it was the source of their livelihood and the symbol
of their independence; it also gave them a place in their society. Many had hoped to return with American wealth, free
themselves of debt, and perhaps even to increase their holdings. But once they foresaw the potentialities in America,
there was little hesitation to leave their farms and vineyards.
Many deserted their plots even after paying off their mortgages with American earnings; others endowed them to
churches or mosques; still others sold or gave them to relatives who remained behind. If there were hesitations about
emigrating permanently, they centered on the emotional attachment to village life with its intricate web of deep personal
relationships which the first generation had idealized in its
enduring nostalgia.

Although the Syrian immigrants were generally from the
lower stratum of their society, they were not among the poorest of America's "new" immigrants. Immigration data after
1899 confirm this. It cannot be reliably ascertained how
much money they carried with them on entering the United
States before that date because such data was not compiled
by the Immigration Bureau. However, data after 1899, even
taking into consideration money and travel fares sent from
America, places the Syrians in the middle range of all immigrants showing money at ports of entry. Comparing Syrians
with Poles and Greeks—two immigrant groups who also migrated primarily for economic reasons—for the period 1899
to 1903, one finds that the average amount per capita, based
on official statistics was: $12.26 for Poles; $21.32 for Greeks;
and $31.85 for Syrians.[74] According to testimony of several
informants, travel, entry fees, and incidental money were
provided primarily from family resources.

Bureau of Immigration accounts indicate that illiteracy
was high among Syrians, particularly among Syrian women.

Of the 47,834 Syrians over fourteen years of age who entered between 1899 and 1910, 53.3 percent are reported to have been unable to read or write.[75] A breakdown of this statistic, compiled from the *Annual Reports of the Commissioner General of Immigration* for the years 1896 to 1910, shows that 31,781 could neither read nor write, 153 could read but not write, and none could read and write.[76] Yet, so illiterate a population supported a prolific Arabic press. No fewer than twenty-one newspapers and magazines appeared from 1892 to 1914 and published not only news of Syria and America but the literary works of luminaries of Arabic literature in America, among them Gibran Kahlil Gibran. Although most of the publications' life-spans were short, at least five survived well past the 1920s when the use of Arabic fell into decline. In addition, there were numerous tabloids and journals issued in local Syrian communities.

Of the majority listed as illiterate, many may have acquired at least the rudiments of Arabic in Syrian missionary schools. In the homeland, literacy in classical Arabic would have served few practical purposes save to read the Bible or the Koran and few would have had the time or the motivation to develop their literacy skills. In the United States, they may not always have had the time, but the motivation was present. They were anxious to read and write letters and read newspapers for information about the homeland as well as about the new land. They taught themselves, or each other, to read and write Arabic in the United States, building on their elementary knowledge. Some had brought with them grammar and children's storybooks or purchased them from New York distributors who not only sold Arabic books published in that city but imported a large variety from Syria and Egypt.[77]

Women, of course, were a part of the earliest Syrian migration. Before 1899, they constituted about 27 percent of the available immigration figures, or 5,565 females to 15,125 males. Between 1899 and 1910, women, motivated by the same economic desire as men, as well as by the desire to join husbands or to enhance their marriage possibilities (since villages were being emptied of single men), raised the percentage to 32. It was pushed upward markedly to 47.5 percent from 1919 to 1930 by the arrival of wives, brides, and mothers who came to live in more settled Syrian communites.[78]

The economic impetus behind Syrian immigration is underlined in the age breakdown of the migrants. From 1899 to 1914, 69,595 men and women between the ages of fourteen and forty-five are recorded by the Bureau of Immigration, while 12,924 were under fourteen years of age and 3,556 were over forty-five.[79] The proportion of children under age fourteen from 1889 to 1910 was higher than for any other Mediterranean people: 16.4 percent as compared to 6 percent for Greeks, 14 percent for Armenians, and 12 percent for Southern Italians.

Generally, a high rate of immigrant children is characteristic of family migrations and permanent settlement in the new land. Although this may have been true for a small percentage of the pioneer Syrian migrants, the difference must be accounted for by the number of children, males in particular, who accompanied a parent to peddle. Children already accustomed to an economic role, would, it was thought, hasten achievement of the family's economic goal and the return to the village. Rarely were children unaccompanied by an adult kinsman or townsman. Many more children, of course, were left in the care of relatives, usually paternal grandparents. Some were left behind to spare them the dangers of the unknown; others because one or both parents wanted the freedom to work unencumbered by domestic responsibilities; still others were "hostages" to the tradition of family unity and responsibility. Grandparents, unable to contemplate possible permanent separation from their sons by unfathomable distances, withheld, particularly if both parents emigrated, one or more of their grandchildren to ensure the return of the sons and daughter-in-laws. If there was any anguish in this practice, it was endured by the migrating mother who had to succumb to tradition and the will of her in-laws.[80]

Immigration records disclose that about 25 percent of the 107,593 Syrians admitted between 1899 and 1940 returned to the homeland. That they were mainly single males who, more often than not, came back to America, suggests a restlessness of individuals, returning home temporarily for brides or other personal matters. Only the most timid rejected the dream of America—those who were unable to adapt to changing behavior patterns, those who feared a failure to achieve expectations and consequent loss of face, or those whose resources and responsibilities did not allow them to remain permanently. Altogether, they were too few to affect the overall dimensions of Syrian migration.[81]

By 1920, the bird-of-passage mentality which had predominated before 1910 had virtually faded; by 1940, over 200,000 Syrians called America their permanent home.

Divided almost equally between males and females, the census of 1910 recorded 59,729 Syrians born in Turkey in Asia. The 1929 census initiated separate classifications for Syrians and Palestinians under the category of "Foreign-born white population." In that census, Syrians numbered 51,909, 40 percent of them females. Of the 3,203 Palestinians, 35 percent were females. The 1930 census shows 57,227 Syrians and 6,136 Palestinians, with women constituting 43 and 40 percent respectively. The Syrian population shown in the 1940 census was 50,859 and that of Palestinians 7,047. More telling are the figures which included not only the foreign-born but the "native white stock of foreign parentage." In 1930, there were 89,349 Syrians and 4,311 Palestinians born in the United States of mixed parentage. When combined with the foreign born, the total shows 137,576 Syrians and 10,446 Palestinians. By adding these figures to the total Syrian and Palestinian population for 1940, the result is an estimated 206,128 Americans of Syrian and Palestinian origin and descent.

3

"Amrika"

Syrians called it "Amrika"; sometimes "Nay Yark." From across the seas its light appeared golden, its promise certain. Life would be "always the season of olives waiting to be harvested," Mose N. was told by his aunt on his departure.[1] In the bright glow of hope, they discerned no flaws nor anticipated any.

Syrians who came to seek their fortunes in the last two decades of the nineteenth century were ignorant of the social and economic contrasts engulfing America. Rapid growth and change, exciting and welcome to some, was troubling to many more on farms, in small towns, and in the urban middle and lower economic classes, even though they had shared in the benefits; in short, those segments of American society the Syrians would encounter most frequently in their peddling rounds.

Syrians would have scoffed cynically had they been told that many Americans felt a growing sense of insecurity and self-doubt. They would have been indifferent at least, incredulous at best, to reports that there were Americans who feared the unbridled technological innovations, industrialization, urbanization, the closing of the frontier and whatever else they thought was eroding America's cherished ideals and values. To the Syrians, these elements represented precisely the symbols of progress and promise for which America stood.

Ironically, few Americans, even those most disturbed by the changes, would have disagreed with that glowing characterization of their country. As ardently critical as they may have been at any given time, they would nevertheless have added, in typical Fourth of July rhetoric, that it was a land of opportunity for all, where freedom and equality of the individual were emphasized, where social and economic mobility seemed to transgress class cleavages, where status was based on achievement rather than heredity, and where diverse peoples were miracuously blended into one nationality. Such lofty social concepts were outside the Syrians' experience and comprehension and, in any case, irrelevant to their plans.

The burgeoning change which touched virtually every segment of society and elicited a variety of responses from Americans provided precisely the conditions that benefited the Syrians—without their being caught up in the problems of Americans as other immigrant groups had been.

With their expectations pointed in a single direction, the Syrians were oblivious to the economic and social currents that dogged so many Americans. America was an incoherence from which they tried to grasp whatever meaning they could. They understood few of its values and shared even fewer of its concerns. Would they succeed in the New World or would they fail?—this was their primary concern, however masked with confidence and optimism.

The quickening of industrialization since the Civil War had produced a network of railroad lines which facilitated freight and passenger transport, knitting disparate communities into a national market and ending the isolation of many small towns and farms. New towns, following the railroad lines and the frontier, sprang up where none had been before. Larger cities became metropolises and small towns burgeoned into cities.

Industrial expansion spurred urbanization and drew more people to the cities. Many self-made men left their farms and small towns for the cities to become wage earners; many more, attracted by industrial jobs, migrated from Europe and Asia at an average rate of about a million a year. More than 13,345,000 or 14.5 percent of the American population in 1910—a population of 91,972,266—were foreign born. From the viewpoint of small town and rural America, the city was subverting the economic and cultural dominance of the countryside.

Industrial growth precipitated revolutions in communication, transportation, and sources of energy. Exploration yielded several new oil and coal regions, while refining and mining methods improved production to meet demand. Fabulous deposits of gold, discovered in Alaska, the Yukon, and along the Klondike Creek, generated "gold fever" throughout the country. Telegraph lines, paralleling the spread of railroad lines, served practically every hamlet in the nation by the 1890s. During the 1880s telephone systems were found in virtually every American city and although relatively rare in rural areas, the telephone and, more effectively the telegraph, eroded the provincialism of small towns, which became increasingly oriented toward the cities. Electrically operated interurban and urban trolley lines stimulated mobility of far more Americans than the few subways and elevated trains in the largest cities.

But it was the automobile that effected the greatest change in the lives of Americans more so than any of the major inventions of the nineteenth and early twentieth centuries. Although the automobile remained insignificant—a toy of the rich—before the turn of the century, by World War I it was mass-produced. The Ford Motor Company alone pushed its production from 10,607 automobiles in 1908 to 250,000 in 1913 and almost 1 million in 1920.[2] Automobiles were purchased even though few roads had been paved outside the cities, a fact that remained true for decades.

America was moving rapidly into the age of mass production, mass distribution, and mass consumption so characteristic of the post–World War I period. Yet, in the late nineteenth and early twentieth centuries, a larger variety of manufactured products reached more markets in a shorter time in greater quantities and frequently at lower cost than ever before. New sales techniques were perfected to serve the markets opened up by the railroads. As early as 1872, Montgomery Ward introduced the mail-order process and was soon followed by Sears Roebuck. Assisted by rural free delivery and parcel post, a farmwife or small-town homemaker could purchase virtually anything available to urban women in department stores—if she was in no urgent need of her purchase. Advertising in a host of new publications created new appetites for new products. Consumer goods—from timesaving gadgets and ready-to-wear clothes to machinery and tools—began to overspread the market.

Farmers, responding to the needs of expanding urban markets, began to rely on modern agricultural machinery and methods. In the process, they lost their self-sufficiency and were buffeted by the unpredictability of domestic and world markets. Private initiative, conditioned to the free market, had to defer to more efficient monopolistic big business, capitalistic merchandising, and controlled competition. Small-town entrepreneurs, sharing with farmers the social ideal of free enterprise, struggled for their economic survival. Progress was purchased at the price of their economic principles and values. Moreover, the entrepreneurs' civic prestige was being tested by the captains of urban industry, and they were drawn inexorably into a bewildering and impersonal complex of business relationships. Both farmers and entrepreneurs felt threatened by forces outside their comprehension and control. Hard work, prudence, thrift, and self-reliance—ideals to which they had fervently adhered—were becoming incongruent in the late nineteenth century. The self-made man was no longer supreme, except perhaps in his own estimation.

For the old-stock Americans, the rising urban middle class, anxious about upward mobility, respectability, and changing values, the city came to symbolize much that they thought wrong with America—economic insecurity, recurrent depressions, exploitation by unregulated big business, and an indifferent government. Corruption, immorality, and a general depersonalization of life were all blamed on the city. The Americans deplored the endless lines of unemployed and they feared labor's often violent attempts to organize. Unionization, they believed, was based on "alien" ideologies imported by the millions of unassimilated immigrants crammed into wretchedly overcrowded and ill-smelling slums.

Uncertain of the present and alarmed about the future, provincial Americans joined urban entrepreneurs and wage earners in turning their resentment against the bold and sweeping power of the great corporations. In the view of the traditionalists, free enterprise was under challenge. America was changing at a bewildering pace. A wide range of Americans, bewildered by circumstances not previously encountered, demanded reforms.

Toward such matters as regulating monopolies, the Syrian immigrants were oblivious, and the Arabic press indifferent. They were attuned, however, to congressional regulation of immigration. The upsurge of nativist feelings, fanned by pseudoscientific theories propounding Nordic superiority, clamored to halt immigration as well as to eradicate the foreignness of those admitted. In response, Congress adopted a series of restrictive laws which, beginning with the Contract Labor Law of 1885 to the Quota Act of 1924, tightened and refined previous ones while expanding the list of excludables. While some were intended to protect immigrants against exploitation and white slavery, they were viewed by helpless immigrant groups as biased and unfair stratagems to restrict entry of their kin and countrymen to this country. Angered and frustrated, Western Asians, like the Syrians and Armenians, contested in court attempts by nativist naturalization examiners and judges to classify them under the Asian exclusion regulation. By 1917, Congress passed a literacy requirement over President Woodrow Wilson's veto.

Yet, compared to post–World War fervor, public pressures against immigration before the war paled. Attributed mainly to foreign causes at home and abroad, uncertainty and insecurity resurged. Peace itself became disillusioning. To some who felt threatened, Bolshevik revolutionary ideology seemed to leap the protective seas along with immigration; unemployment and crime swelled as farm prices dropped, and the nation was shaken by a series of militant labor strikes. America's fears and prejudices increasingly were vented on the immigrants. In the excesses of the Red scare of the early 1920s, some groups were denied basic American democratic rights and even subjected to physical abuse and personal humiliation. Without apparent justification, arrests and deportations became common. Anti-alien antipathy often focused on what was "American" and what was "un-American." Advocates of "100-percent Americanism" dismissed the accelerated programs of private and public institutions to Americanize aliens and, along with extremist groups, pressured government to close the immigration gates. Among the extremists was a revitalized and expanded Ku Klux Klan.

The result of the pressure on government was the Quota Act of 1921. Earlier immigration legislation had been concerned with the quality and character of aliens; after the war, fear of the past mingled with apprehensions of the present and future to impose numerical limitations. Intended initially as a temporary measure, the Quota Act was made permanent by Congress as the Johnson-Reed Immigration Act of 1924. The law limited total immigration to approximately 150,000 annually, based on the population of groups resident in the United States as of 1920. The result was discrimination based on nationality, favoring western Europeans, and virtually severing immigration at its sources. The quota of only 100 persons annually from each of the eastern European and Mediterranean nations was intended to keep America "American."

It would be easy to exaggerate the visible effects of change outside the populous urban-industrial centers before World War I. When Arizona achieved statehood in 1910, vast stretches of vacant territory west of Iowa and Kansas were still open for homesteading, while Indians lived on the fringes of towns, many of which were distant from railroad

lines.[3] Travel on dirt roads was tiresome, dusty, and, in incle-
ment weather, almost prohibitive. Not everywhere had technology invaded. Only a small percentage of city families possessed telephones or automobiles; hardly anyone in the
countryside had seen, much less owned them.

Most small towns and rural communities were slow in
adapting to the industrial age. Families conducted their lives
much as they always had: they worked and lived frugally, attended church, and raised their children according to their
religious tenets. Conformity to their beliefs and values—predominantly those of western Europe and the Protestant
faith—and to a rigid Puritan morality was not only expected,
but imposed by the church and school around which community life centered. Socially and ethically, homogeneous
communities easily ostracized nonconformists. Strangers
either visiting or boarding (if such accommodation was available) were not always welcome and were made to feel suspect.

Small-town homes, like many in lower middle-class urban
neighborhoods, on average, housed a man, his family, and a
relative or two. Lacking timesaving devices or the services of
maids—who were accessible and affordable mostly to city
dwellers—maintaining houses usually cluttered with furni-
ture, bric-a-brac, family pictures, doilies, linen table covers,
icons, and much more required the help of all the women in
the household. Little leisure time was left, especially since
most women sewed their own or their families' apparel, even
though ready-made clothing was available by mail order or
in small shops on Main streets. Farm households, on the
other hand, depended on general stores which were commonly ill equipped to meet all of their needs.

Whether in country or city, at home or work, it was common to labor from sunrise to sunset with little time for shopping. Moreover, when women shopped, they wore layers of
clothing and dragged long skirts along dusty walks or to the
nearest trolley line; it was a major effort. Not many rural
families owned carriages, and those which did, used them
mainly on Sundays.

Pack peddlers in the urban streets and dusty country roads
of turn-of-the-century America should have been an anach-

ronism but were instead a common sight. Housewives came to rely on the bazaars brought to their doors by peddlers. "A pleasing incongruity in modern life," wrote Lillian Hart Tryon in 1915,

> showing that as yet we are neither correct nor efficient to any alarming degree, is the presence of the peddler. By all socio-logical theory and economic law, he should be discouraged from interrupting the peace of household routine, and gently persuaded to adopt some productive occupation. Yet, here he is, in proof that buying at the door has survived a certain amount of reasonableness. Progress has not availed against him. He has changed his dress and wares, but he remains eternally the same. . . .
> . . . The glory has vanished from the trade. The peddler now travels humbly and unattended, but his nature is as op-timistic and his conversation as grandiloquent as ever. With a little tact and patience you may still buy a story along with your bargain.

Among her back door visitors was a "man from 'Dah-mahs-koos.'"[4]

Working in the open spaces of the still-incomplete eco-nomic structure forged by corporate and financial institu-tions, peddlers performed a special yet hardly noticed func-tion in the onrush of industrialization and urbanization. Tenacious, roaming the most remote and forbidding sections of the country, flexible in accepting payment in kind rather than cash, they promoted commerce where money was scarce. To markets not accessible by other means, they took the products of small American industries, thus expanding the markets and stimulating production of such items as but-tons, suspenders, and laces. They spared many a small in-dustry an untimely death. By creating new appetites for goods, they supported the proliferation of small industries. These petty roving entrepreneurs, thriving in the age of great capitalistic merchandising, seemed like something sus-pended in a time warp.

While technology was supposed to have sounded the death knoll of peddling in America as early as 1860, immigrants so inflated its ranks by the turn of the century that it enjoyed a revival. World War I thinned its ranks considerably, but the Great Depression of the thirties swelled them again as several thousands turned to peddling as a way for proud and desperate people to avoid joblessness and demoralization.

In the strange way that movements converge, Syrian immigration and rapid modernization were fortuitously compatible. Petty capitalists themselves, Syrians accepted the visual consequences of progress with awe and admiration. Their first impressions of America and their attitude to it were shaped not by what they understood but by what they saw. They were, on the one hand, awed by the bustling streets and tall buildings of the cities. "I used to count the stories of every one I saw," mused Frank A.[5] Lighted streets, electrically-lit rooms, telephones, and the abundance of consumer goods filled them with wonder. Tafeeda B. saw her first elevator in the New York Syrian colony: "What! Had I ever seen an elevator in my time?" Then she was taken to Hartford City, Indiana; she was six years old. "Well . . . it was just near Christmas time, the lights were all lit, you know. . . . They took me downtown. . . . It was snowing—the snow was knee-deep and I had not seen much of that. . . . They took me down to buy me . . . an overcoat and . . . a warm hat; of course, I didn't come equipped with anything. And then's where I got my first glimpse of stores. . . . Then the next day, the second day, and the third day and the fourth day, I found my own way back downtown and then I roamed the streets . . . and I looked in these store windows till I was flabbergasted. . . . I was in another world; I couldn't speak." Mechanical gadgets delighted them; toilets and bathtubs confused them: "We didn't know what to do with it, the toilet, I mean. We argued whether to wash in it or drink from it. We finally decided it was to wash our feet in, so we did."[6]

On the other hand, they were perplexed by a variety of unsorted fragments of American life which they witnessed in their roaming: Fourth of July and Thanksgiving Day celebrations, a raucous political parade, a senator who listened to the problems of citizens on the street, a roundup of voters who were paid to vote, the president of the United States who shook hands with everyone and was called "Mr." like ordinary people; workers' strikes, hooded men burning crosses, and many more curious things—police who were unfeared: "I was never afraid of the police here; in the old country, the police are quick to hit you. . . . [A customer's] son took me to the police station and told them to 'keep that poor boy all night because he can't find a place to sleep.' So I slept on some paper there all night."

When the Syrians sought explanations for what perplexed them, they turned to veteran immigrants as well as to the Arabic press. These natural leaders tended to interpret American life as they understood it, through myths of an older America rather than through the comprehension of the issues that loomed large for the native population. While the old American order had debated its plight and sought answers from the past, Syrians were concerned only with the present. Lacking the hindsight of "the good old days," they merely adapted situations they encountered to their own ends. Intensely preoccupied with the present, they had little time to ponder the larger implications of what swirled around them and had little interest in doing so. They were, after all, on a temporary sojourn—so they thought.

Deeply impressed by the financial possibilities and relishing the release from social, political, and economic restrictions of the homeland, their emerging conception of America would seem to have overlooked its flaws. Meanwhile, they sallied forth, following the lure of wealth as well as the logic of their individual ambitions.

4

Pack Peddling

PEDDLING AND THE DISTRIBUTION OF SYRIANS

The most fundamental factor in the assimilation of Syrians in America was pack peddling. It was the primary source of the tangible bounty on which their hopes and survival depended. Not only did they leave their villages to follow its promise of quick wealth with a herd instinct, but they pursued that promise to every quarter of the American continent; no region was to prove too remote or forbidding.

The basic virtues of peddling were many. Immigrants could earn immediately; it required no real advanced training, capital or language skills; and it suited their individualistic nature and sense of impermanence. In short, it allowed them to operate on their own terms. Moreover, it spared them the uncertainties of finding work, of long job lines, and of layoffs. Furthermore, the sense of impermanence set their minds to accepting change as expedient necessities to achieving their goal, while ambition set their minds to absorbing whatever might enhance that goal.

Many Syrians had traded at home; yet pack peddling entailed a radical change in the way they earned their livelihood. But its scope and nature, the demands on the peddlers' physical and psychological resources, and the way it would irrevocably reorient their lives—these they had not

128

anticipated. Even after they had tested its realities in America—tasted its loneliness and suffered its hazards—most still, on the whole, preferred it to the drudgery of the factory as well as the isolation of American farm life. Providing a firsthand, closeup introduction to American life, it served as a window to new ideas and values, tested the Syrians' inclination to return to the homeland, raised their expectations, and improved their skills.

Not by any means did all Syrians accept the inevitability of peddling. Some found it too demeaning—"too much like begging"—and some feared it was too aggressive a trade for which they had neither the fortitude nor the inclination. Those who felt this way joined the labor force or gambled, without language or capital, on a small business, perhaps a fruitstand. Others, with some means, regarding it as a tedious path to wealth, gambled on a larger enterprise and endured cycles of failures before succeeding. And yet those who eschewed peddling entirely constituted a small minority. Many others found themselves returning to it time and again—the disgruntled worker who could not bear bosses or confinement, and unsuccessful shopkeepers who used it like a revolving door. There were still others who bent under its strenuous demands and left it for good. The majority, however, were diehard opportunists who turned the trade to their purposes.

Habib Ibrahim Katibah, journalist and author, has described the pioneer period as "the most romantic and colorful period, the period of discovery, adventure, and colonization."[1] This characterization is echoed in the reminiscences of the peddlers themselves and in anecdotes they have left behind in which humor only partially veils the trials of adventure. The anecdotes re-create a period but they also celebrate a breed who had a tenacity, resourcefulness, vision, and self-sufficiency which eluded many of their progeny. The pioneer years were a time in which the Syrians' basic sturdiness of character asserted itself in what seems to have been a titanic exertion of will.

Peddling was not, of course, unique to the Syrian immigrants. Greeks, Italians, Armenians, and east European Jews had also used it as an expedient initial occupation. Generally, however, they preferred the pushcart to the pack and the city to the country. Yet, Karam N. encountered Irish, Swedish, as well as Jewish peddlers in the northern prairie states where he peddled in 1908. What is unique about the Syrians in the late nineteenth and early twentieth centuries was their deep and broad identification with pack peddling, an identification comparable to that of the Yankee peddler and the itinerant German-Jewish merchants with whom the Syrians felt an affinity. "We learned about peddling in this country from the Jews," some pioneer Syrians are wont to say, and like the Jews, they used the trade as a stepping stone on the upward path to success and middle-class status.

Having adopted pack peddling as their own, the Syrians' entreaty to "buy sumthin', Maam," had penetrated, before the turn of the century, deep into the country. "Syrian peddlers," Louise Houghton has noted, "were roaming over North Dakota in 1888."[2] If uncertainty ever haunted them, they left the outcome to Allah [God] and to those who would receive them at the end of their journey. Distance and geography had only the haziest relevance to why they had come or where they were going.

As soon as they were processed at Ellis Island, groups of young men and women, who had been drawn closer together en route by the adventure they shared, separated in New York. "All joy left us," said Mike H., describing a common experience of leaving village companions. "One day we were children, playing and enjoying ourselves, but now we cried." Some of his friends went to Fort Wayne, some to Grand Rapids, some elsewhere—he didn't know where.[3] He and his brother went to Bloomington, Illinois, in search of a brother-in-law who had opened a store in the country.

How did these simple villagers know of the existence of small American towns and cities whose names they could hardly pronounce? "Do you think I looked at a map and said I want to go there?" retorted Elias L. who arrived in 1896. "No! I couldn't speak a work of English, let alone read it. I came straight to Salem Bashara in Fort Wayne. . . . There were many who came there from Rashayya at the same time.

Salem had been here a good while before I came. . . . He had
a store for supplying peddlers. I had Salem's name and address and showed it to Mr. Arbeely, the interpreter, and he
put us on the train. Salem met us." To say, as they usually did,
that there was a relative or friend "there," begs the question.
Who first went "there" and why? How did men like Salem
gravitate to remote towns and cities scattered between New
York and Los Angeles, Minneapolis, and New Orleans? What
factors impelled the dispersion of Syrians throughout the
United States within one generation? It is late to question the
impulses on which men acted one hundred years ago. Like
many basic historical questions, there is here no certain answer, only the challenge of weaving fragments of acts with
legend into plausible answers.

The evidence is fairly clear that a sprawling network of
peddling settlements spread in which immigrants lived and
worked under the guidance of men with foresight and enterprise who established themselves as merchandise suppliers.
Radiating in all directions with their small notions cases (kashshi), the "primer" of peddling, and their packs, they mostly
followed their instincts, or the advice of veterans, deeper and
deeper into the outlands. The story of how Nick R. reached
Arizona, as told by his nephew, is typical: "In 1887, Nick was
in New York and he heard about New Mexico. He was a peddler and liked to travel. He just peddled until he got to New
Mexico and then he heard about Arizona and he peddled
there and then to Mexico. He peddled back and forth across
the line. Then he sent for his sister and my uncles [Nick's
brothers]. This was how the Syrian community began in Arizona. Most of them were from Ablah near Zahle."[4]

There must have come a moment when some veterans, like
Nick, with a bit of surplus capital in hand, and a little more
courage and shrewdness than their companions, decided to
lay down their packs, choose a suitable site, and enter business as suppliers of peddlers. Whatever the impetus, for the
next decade the nation was crisscrossed by a network of suppliers.

The supplier became pivotal in the distribution of Syrians
in the United States, and his settlement the crucial factor in

facilitating adjustment of immigrant peddlers in the pioneer period, the quality of which affected the adjustment of those who followed them, as kin drew kin, and villager drew villager. The network opened up opportunities for thousands of new arrivals.

The inspiration and model for a prospective supplier and his settlement was unquestionably the successful Syrian colony in New York. It was the mother settlement and the one which stimulated further immigration. Nothing was so infectious as success; and in the 1890s the New York colony seemed, by all accounts, brimming with it; its businessmen were casting about for more business. The *New York Tribune* reporter who described it in 1892 penetrated beyond its picturesqueness and painted a picture of a buzzing trading center and Middle Eastern bazaar transplanted to the First Ward of Manhattan Island where the "North and East Rivers meet." Bounded by Rector, Greenwich, Morris, and Washington streets, it was the wellspring of Syrian peddling in America. "The houses, especially on the Washington st. side of the block," the reporter observed,

> are old, weatherbeaten, dingy and sometimes dirty, the cellars are devoted to trade and packed full of everything which a pedler can carry in his pack or find a market for in his wanderings, and the first or ground floor is generally used as a display-room and office where goods are sorted out and bargains made—and these sojourners from the far East are sharp traders. . . .
>
> Go inside one of these stores where pins by the hundred gross rest against shoe-blacking by the case, and scapularies and rosaries, beads and prayer-books are almost hidden from view by boxes of cheap cologne and ornamental shell-work. . . .your eyes are dazzled by a great square of yellow satin covered with delicate tracery of silver wire. . . . Out from a drawer . . . is tossed a great fleecy cloud . . . of soft white silk with blue stripes. . . . Silks and satin lacework, embroideries, follow each other in rapid succession until the eyes are revelling in a bewildering maze of gorgeous, fantastic and beautiful colors. . . .
>
> Pick up a filmy gossamer web of silken lace with a line from the Koran running around its border and in your ear is whis-

pered the magic word, "Baghdad." Shade of Haroun-al Raschid! . . . he has some rugs there which are a delight to the eye. . . . And the quaint specimens of Oriental carving, the marquetry work, the little tables in which the wood is lost in the wealth of inlaid pearl with which it is adorned, the long, curved sword of Damascus steel, whose edge is as keen as a razor. . . . And in the midst of all this riot of the beautiful and odd stands the dealer, the natural gravity of his features relaxed into a smile of satisfaction at the wonder and delight expressed by his American visitor. . . .

These wholesale dealers, who will do a retail trade if opportunity offers, are of great help to their poorer countrymen, often advancing to them not only goods but money with which to trade, and though there are large sums outstanding at times, and often goods of much value on hand, the Syrian Colony has yet to furnish a case of bankruptcy, and the credit of the tradesmen is first-class.[5]

Other accounts of the colony recall a multitude of transient and resident peddlers crowding the morning streets, stuffing their suitcases from suppliers, ambling along selecting items from the many basement and living-room shops, and finally moving out in groups in all directions—veterans with newcomers in tow.

Spring naturally was the season of briskest activity. Long-distance peddlers returned to revitalize their spirits and refill their packs; groups of new arrivals swarmed in to cram the neighborhood and heighten the cacophony in the streets. The district has been aptly characterized by Lucius Miller as the "dumping ground of new arrivals."[6] Some, heading for their initiation into peddling beyond the city, took the opportunity to meet friends in it and, like Mike H. and his brother, to acquire supplies at what they were told were bargain rates before moving on to their destination. Mike was taken, he said, by hotel agents from Ellis Island to Washington Street "where all the Syrians were. They were living, some in basements, some above. They were everywhere. . . . They took us there. They had someone there and he took money from each of us. So we went and stayed in his hotel. . . . There was a man on the boat who befriended my brother and asked him if he had any extra money. My brother said yes. He said to my brother 'Go to a man in New York who has a store for Arabs and buy goods from him. You're going to buy anyway and you'll save 30 percent. He took us there and we bought $40 worth of goods.'"

Others stopped at the colony, as at a way station, before heading for their destinations, usually by arrangement among hotel owners and relatives and suppliers. Faris N. and his group, for example, remained two days at the hotel of Ibrahim Maksoud before being labeled "Fort Wayne, Indiana" on their lapels and placed on the train. Meanwhile, they were well treated. One day they asked Mr. Maksoud: "'When are we going to leave for Fort Wayne to Salem Bashara?' He said, 'Whenever you wish. If you like, stay here until you are rested. . . .' We asked, 'And the food?' He said, 'As you wish. Would you like to buy from the market or would you like to eat in the hotel?' We said, 'We would prefer to buy our own food.' He said, 'No matter.'"[7]

Still others went to the New York colony because they had no other destination in mind. Admitted at Ellis Island, they entered it and were absorbed into the only industry offered at the time. Ameen Rihani's two fictional sojourners, upon arriving at Washington Street, rented a cellar, stocked it with a variety of goods purchased from the wholesalers, and pack-peddled for three years. Rihani induces one of them to reflect: "A peddler is superior to a merchant; we travel and earn money; our compatriots the merchants rust in their cellars and lose it. To be sure, peddling in the good old days was most attractive. For the exercise, the gain, the experience— these are rich requirements."[8]

Abraham Mitry Rihbani did not, however, share his literary colleague's views. He found the colony's single-minded infatuation with the trade repulsive.

> The Syrian colony of New York consisted in those days of a few stores and restaurant keepers, a multitude of peddlers of "jewelry and notions," and a few silk merchants. . . . My inquiries for something to do precipitated usually the following questions from older colonists, who seemed to me to be steeped in wisdom:—
> Do you have money so that you can at least buy an interest

in a store, or deal in silk?" "No, I have no money at all." "Do you have letters of recommendation from missionaries in Syria to persons in this country?" "No." "Can you speak the English language?" "Not so that I can be understood." "How old are you?" "22." "22! Too old to master the English language. The only thing you can do, and which thousands of Syrians are doing, would be to peddle 'jewelry and notions.'"

Call it pride, vanity, or whatever you please, whenever I thought of peddling "jewelry and notions," death lost its terror for me.[9]

They turned the paved streets and crowded brownstone row houses of their little section of the city into Little Syria, giving it color with their alien tongue and colorful appearance as observed by W. Benough on a Sunday in 1895: "There is a queer mingling of American and Syrian costumes. Some of the prosperous young women are arrayed in all the glory of the latest picture-hats and most startling costumes of color, putting off the old and taking on with the new with such vigor that there is no doubt at all about their American aspirations; others less ambitious and less prosperous, still wear their picturesque lace or colored head-dress."[10] One might even have seen a fez on the head of a man who continued to see in it the symbol of status it had carried in the village. Women cooked the traditional dishes from ingredients imported from the homeland and visited, in airless rooms or on the stoops, while men gathered in restaurants on Washington Street where they were observed by the *Tribune* reporter playing backgammon, drinking Turkish coffee, smoking narghilehs (Middle Eastern water pipes) and discussing trade. The restaurants, he noted, were, in reality, the "common rooms of boarding houses, for as at least sixty per cent of the men either have no families or have left them behind in Syria, the boarding house is necessary. . . . Of home life . . . there was little in the colony. The population is constantly shifting and the families who are here find their homes utilized as headquarters by those who are not yet settled.[11]

From the hectic atmosphere, a fair number of leaders emerged to lend the colony some sense of order. They gained a grip on the economic potential that was fermenting around them and turned what had been a colony into a community. No immigrant group poured more high hopes and energy into the minds of their people than these great merchants of the New York colony and their spokesmen, the editors and publishers of the Christian Arabic newspapers. Before the end of the century, an industry of manufacturers, importers, and wholesalers had mushroomed. Between 1890 and 1895, three sectarian churches were established; *Kawkab Amrika* was quickly followed by several other Arabic newspapers; and in 1892, the Syrian Society was organized by Dr. Ameen F. Haddad, "a graduate of Beirut College and mission schools and of the New York University" for the purpose of "providing an educational and industrial institution for natives of that [the Syrian] race, founded on Christian principles, by which they shall be taught the English language and such branches of learning and industry as may assist them to support themselves, and to become intelligent American citizens."[12]

By priority, complexity, and prosperity, the New York community was the model some early pioneers tried to re-create in other parts of the vast American market. They envisioned not only rewards from the ensuing profits but also the enhanced prestige that identification with a successful enterprise, however modest, would bring. When bolder veteran peddlers settled down to convert the vision into reality, initially they no doubt did so with the encouragement and perhaps the assistance of the New York manufacturers and wholesalers who were the major sources of peddlers' supplies. Not uncommonly, the New Yorkers dispatched representatives to peddling settlements to offer merchandise on consignment or credit.

Suitable places to establish peddling settlements were bountiful. Railroads had opened up vast unexploited areas—farmlands, ranges, forests, and mineral deposits—spurring the growth of new towns and transporting immigrants to new industrialized communities. Fort Wayne, for example, a community of 4,282 before railroads reached it in 1860, steadily expanded into a city of 26,880 by 1880 and 45,115 by 1900.[13] During that period, the population of Cedar Rapids, Iowa, expanded from 10,104 to 25,656,[14] while that of Peoria, Illinois, from approximately 20,000 to 56,000.[15] Spring Valley, Illinois, a coal town founded in 1884 with a population of 1,500, expanded to 6,214 by 1900.[16]

The peddlers characteristically sought their markets where vigorous industrial development exhibited economic vitality. Occasionally, they chose the place to plant their settlements judiciously, sometimes intuitively; but they considered not only the town's market potential but its surrounding area. "They would hear there was something there and there would be money to be made—a brass foundry or an oil company opening up or something like that," related Tafeeda B.[17] They also heard—and heeded—reports about the coalfields of Appalachia, central Illinois, and Missouri; they followed the Alaskan gold rush and the reconstruction of San Francisco after the 1906 earthquake and fire. Mannington, West Virginia, was an oil boomtown when Syrian peddlers reached it in the early 1890s.[18] Of her sister-in-law, Eva F. said: "She peddled with her husband in Wisconsin and got all the way to Green Bay. She peddled in town and made customers. She was a very shrewd woman. Then she heard about the territory of Oklahoma becoming a state and decided to move there.... About 1910, they took a train there. . . .and opened a dry goods store."

Nor was there ever a shortage of peddling recruits or recruiters—neither in New York nor in Syria. A supplier opened his shop and set the process in motion by sending for his relatives and townsmen. If their expectations were met by the supplier, peddlers became prospective recruiters. Glowing letters from the settlement describing undreamed-of wealth, containing tangible evidence in the form of remittances, acted like magnets. If there was a quid pro quo in this or any kind of recruitment, it was insignificant, atypical, or unknown.

Exaggerated letters home were surpassed only by the swagger and boasting of immigrants visiting their old villages. Letters to the villages usually preceded the travelers, and curious villagers gathered eagerly to gape and listen.

Western suits, fedoras, leather shoes, gold watch fobs, and a smattering of English were as dazzling as the embellished tales of quick wealth. Sometimes, a supplier induced such a visitor to the homeland to recruit. Faris N. recorded his moment of acquiescence that day in 1895 when his cousins returned to Rashayya from America:

> I went to visit them and asked them about work there. They said that work was in trading and one could make $15.00 which is about three English pounds. I said "Three English pounds!" Then I said to one of them, "Musa, what do you sell?" He said [speaking in Arabic-English] "Aw rayt, tell it." I said, "What do you mean?" He said, "Sumthin' gud." I said to myself [sarcastically] "Look how his Arabic has thickened already." Then I returned home and said "Mamma, what do you think? I want to go to America and I will be away from you for two years. . . . She said, "What is this talk? I want to get you married before anything else. . . . Take her with you so she can work for her family . . . they are in need." "Never mind," I said, "God will help [them]."

For the men and women from Rashayya who decided to make their fortunes in America, Musa wrote detailed traveling instructions and provided letters of introduction; he also provided the supplier's name and credentials—a positive destination and assurance of work.

Suppliers proliferated and eager would-be peddlers began arriving in droves. At Ellis Island, Najib Arbeely, the Syrian interpreter, himself became a willing recruiter. He could recommend a settlement or supplier to undecided immigrants, perhaps one of their faith or village. Suppliers who traveled to New York on business often befriended him. Around the turn of the century, Louis L.'s brother "used to come to New York from Chicago to buy linens and he would go to the coffeehouses and the immigration officer was pointed out to him and they became friends."[19] Salem Bashara went there on occasion to purchase supplies and perhaps to arrange with hotelkeepers to meet his recruits, if not to enlist them to recruit.[20] Mr. Arbeely knew him; he once chided an immigrant who had been instructed to say he was going to his "Uncle Salem" in Fort Wayne. "How is it that a Druze is related to a Christian?"[21] Abe K.'s father, a supplier in Cedar Rapids, "would take a train to New York. Sometimes he'd meet one or two dozen people and bring them back to Cedar Rapids, and start them peddling; he would sell them [merchandise] on credit."[22]

A relatively small number of the immigrants who arrived on the get-rich-quick peddling caravan decided to eschew that trade or abandon it at the first opportunity to join the unskilled or skilled labor force. In turn, they generated nuclei of wage earners, particularly in the eastern states. The textile towns of Fall River, Lowell, and Lawrence, Massachusetts, are prime examples.

NETWORKS OF PEDDLING SETTLEMENTS

By the turn of the century, emboldened Syrians had covered the nation in a network of peddling settlements. Not surprisingly, most were located in the populous eastern and middle western states but were also well sprinkled around the South and along the West Coast. Amid the open spaces of the Rocky Mountain region, they were highly scattered. Many were located in metropolitan areas; the majority, however, seem to have been clustered around small cities and towns on the fringes of agricultural areas, especially along railroad lines.

The national network was connected by a series of subnetworks, the result of a process of splintering and resplintering. Each settlement in the subnetwork was linked, as might be expected, by the peddlers' places of origin, sect, and/or kin, which stretched group cohesion along a nexus of small dispersed colonies. Yet, village and kin relationships were not weakened; rather, they were tightened as each subnetwork drew in and scattered, among its settlements, more relatives and friends. From the settlements within each subnetwork, men drew the courage and strength to roam further afield with one eye remaining on the home settlement and the other fixed on the road ahead. Not only were the subnetwork settlements invaluable launching bases for peddlers, they provided indispensable sources of psychological and material support in times of need. Moreover, men seeking bloodline or village brides competed within the small pool of marriageable women that gradually collected there. Intermarriage between settlements reinforced ties between new and remote settlements and the more established communities. Few settlements are known to have become totally isolated from other settlements. If such was the case, they must have been tiny and have since vanished through assimilation or been abandoned.

The proliferation of settlements not only opened up greater opportunities for new arrivals but constituted undeniable evidence of the Syrians' belief in the promise of America. It also contained imperceptible seeds of the complicated, piecemeal transition of transients into citizens. It was in the peddling settlements that most immigrants experienced many of the elements of the assimilation process: they learned the rudiments of peddling, shared experiences with companions, warded off potential demoralization inherent in this immigrant occupation, and discovered that the gold they sought in America was, in fact, the opportunities it offered.

Subnetworks often intersected. As a result, many settlements were dominated by two or more groups of differing faiths or village origin. Only by sifting through snatches and echoes in the interviews was it possible to trace the shadowy outlines of some of them. If their geographic directions were dissimilar, the process was nonetheless similar. It is not known, for example, where or when the string of Syrian Orthodox settlements in Mississippi began. However, first- and second-generation residents of the Arabic-speaking community in Vicksburg have kinship and village ties with those in Jackson, Hermansville, Greenville, Port Gibson, Meridian, Natchez, and other railroad and river towns, as well as in the states of Louisiana and Texas. Most Syrians in these communities are descendants of early peddlers who originated from seven contiguous villages in the Kura district of Mount Lebanon. They first came to Mississippi, said eighty-four-year-old Wadi N., who arrived in the well-developed settlement of Vicksburg in 1911, because "they peddled their way south from New York. The climate was more moderate and they liked it and stayed. . . . They peddled in Louisiana, Mississippi, east Texas, Tennessee, Kentucky, and Virginia which was thickly populated by Negroes and there were farmers to whom they peddled."[23]

At least one subnetwork sprouted from Chicago. The Syrian colony in that city sprang up almost full grown during the World's Columbia Exposition of 1893. It had a substantial complement of Melkites from Zahle and Damascus. Some Zahle peddlers then trekked northward and established a settlement in Milwaukee. From there, smaller settlements began to dot eastern Wisconsin—in Oconomowac, Watertown, Fond du Lac, Oshkosh, and Green Bay. State borders were no barrier and the Zahle Melkites crossed into Escanabo, Iron Mountain, Sault Ste. Marie, among other Michigan towns.[24]

Maronites from Biskinta, in Mount Lebanon, are found in a network of settlements that began in Utica, New York and spread to Amsterdam and Little Falls, among other towns in that state. "Utica became one of the most prominent way-stations in a Biskinta network of peddling settlements emanating from suppliers in New York City," wrote Eugene Paul Nassar of Utica. "Bachara Ganim in 1895, Joseph Tady in 1897, and Daher Hobaica in 1901, were engaged in dry goods to supply the local peddlers from Biskinta. . . . A large percentage of Utica area Lebanese are Biskinta descendants. The second largest percentage is from the area of Akkar, northern Lebanon, especially the town of B'arzla. Moses Acee, who is listed in 1895 as a dry goods merchant in Utica, was supplier to the Akkar contingent of peddlers."[25]

The process of colonizing and subnetworking becomes more clear as the trails of two other examples are traced. Syrian Orthodox from the neighboring villages of Ayn Arab and Rashayya al-Wadi moved out in different directions from a settlement on East Main Street in Fort Wayne, Indiana, one of the earliest Syrian enclaves in the Middle West.

It may be extravagant, but only barely so, to describe Fort Wayne as a prototype of peddling settlements and Salem

Bashara, its founder, the prototype of pioneer suppliers. The temptation seems unavoidable because more is known about him than other suppliers and because his name recurred frequently in the reminiscences of several former pioneer peddlers and suppliers. "He was a king among Syrians; everybody came to him. He was the head man," reflected his sister-in-law, Elizabeth. Some of his contemporaries might have found this characterization somewhat exalted, but those who lived to recount their stories, remembered him as a shrewd, energetic, and an honest man who helped his people. He was born in Dahr al-Ahmar, one of many villages, which, like Rashayya and Ayn Arab, dotted the valleys and slopes of the anti-Lebanon range, not far from Damascus.

Salem and his two brothers were brought to Fort Wayne on their father's second trip to America in 1887; his first had been in 1882. They settled there probably because the father had previously peddled in the town and had chosen it as a supplier's site. Elizabeth speculated that they came to Fort Wayne because, like Columbus, Ohio, where she had peddled with her parents until she became a child bride to Salem's brother Khalil, in 1896, it was a large town and they believed they could make money. The town was then an indistinct American industrial and commercial city located at a division point on the Pennsylvania Railroad's main line.

Salem proved to be the boldest and most enterprising. Khalil and a third brother, Bashara, opened fruit stands on street corners while Salem and his father peddled. Initially, they all prospered. Then, about 1890, Salem bought a building housing three stores. When Elizabeth joined the family, Salem was already a major supplier. "There were quite a number of peddlers in Fort Wayne. . . . and men took rooms upstairs," she added. Before his marriage, Khalil had opened a supply store in Columbus. Peddlers who stopped in Columbus patronized Khalil; when they went to Fort Wayne, they patronized Salem—the brothers referred peddlers to each other.

Ultimately, however, Khalil's store in Columbus failed. With Salem's help, he opened another in Hartford City, Indiana, where he had previously peddled. At that time, Hartford City was a town booming from gas and oil refineries. Elizabeth operated the store while Khalil continued to peddle. Every Sunday, the family commuted by train to Fort Wayne, their "real home." Eleven years later, a depressed economy, perhaps the result of the Panic of 1907, forced Khalil to close the store. That was when they moved permanently to Fort Wayne where Khalil's days ended in poor health and near-failure.[26] By that time, however, peddling, as a Syrian immigrant occupation, was diminishing and only a small group of families remained to constitute the permanent community.

It has been forgotten by the informants how many peddlers worked out of Fort Wayne, but during the nineties, it was a vigorous settlement. Peddlers were described as having descended from trains in groups labeled on their lapels to Salem who usually met them. They came from several villages, most in the general region of his own: Rashayya, Aytha, Irna, Ayn Arab, Bloudan—even from Zahle and Beirut.[27] Fort Wayne, like other settlements, was then a revolving door; peddlers came and left as it suited them. Stable core groups formed, however. The most dominant in Fort Wayne were from Rashayya and Aytha. The Ayn Arab Syrians were among those who did not form a core group. Religiously, the Syrian Orthodox far outnumbered the other sects. Elizabeth remembered the arrival of fifty or sixty people from Aytha "carrying their bundles on their shoulders and [the women] were dressed in long colored dresses with open necklines and with many skirts under their dresses. Salem met them at the train station and gave them everything they needed." Faris N. arrived with his group from Rashayya, which had dwindled to about twenty-five, in 1895.[28]

There could be no doubt that Fort Wayne was then among the largest and most flourishing peddling settlements in the United States. The Right Reverend Raphael Hawaweeny, the first Syrian Orthodox bishop in America, counted his congregation in 1898. The populous multi-sectarian New York

colony headed the list with 575 Orthodox; Fort Wayne
ranked second with 424 and Worcester, Massachusetts, third
with 152.[29]

Census taking of peddlers was as difficult for the bishop as
it had been for the U.S. Bureau of the Census, and the bishop's methods, although he visited his communicants in their
dispersed settlements from time to time, were less adequate
to the task. On the one hand, there was the peddlers' itiner-
ancy; on the other, many immigrants were birds of passage,
returning to the home village every few years. Absences of
six months to a year selling on the road and several years
back in the homeland were not uncommon. Further, a supplier conducted his business more by credit than by cash, and
names of peddlers remained on the books for years. Therefore, it seems prudent to accept the estimate of eyewitnesses
that in its heyday, during the 1890s, as many as 150 peddlers
and residents lived in the Fort Wayne settlement at any given
time.[30]

Salem proved to be an astute entrepreneur. His instincts
told him that satisfied peddlers were not only good recruiters
but good customers. The more they sold, the greater his profits and, therefore, he sought lucrative markets to which he
could direct them. He was literate and probably learned English well enough to read about industrial and commercial
developments in the Middle West. He also doubtless learned
much from the peddlers who returned intermittently for
recreation and supplies. Moreover, friendly local politicians
who solicited the votes of peddlers and illegally naturalized
them, and the banker with whom Salem banked the peddlers' savings might have shared economic information with
him. In any case, he used the information resourcefully,
sending his peddlers to coal-mining regions in Illinois and
the industrial towns of Ohio, Indiana, and Michigan.

Salem's success inevitably invited competition. Tafeeda B.'s
comment that "all the peddlers dreamed of imitating him,"
contained more truth than the boasting of a daughter-in-law,
for in the second half of the nineties, Salem had no less than
three competitors. Not surprisingly, competition developed

along village lines. Faris N., who had come from the lower district of his mountain village, wrote about his townsmen: "Damus Ayub had emigrated from Rashayya to New York and then to Ft. Wayne and had opened a dry goods store which was, in general, like that of Salem Bashara's and the people of the upper district of Rashayya, all of them, would buy goods from Damus. . . . I was staying with Salem from whom I bought goods."[31] A man from Irna supplied his fellow villagers;[32] and fifty to seventy-five peddlers from Aytha followed Khalil Shaheen who turned a rented house into a supply store and boardinghouse.[33] Faris saw spite in the breakway of the Aytha group: "There was rivalry in trade between Salem and the people of Aytha and Yusuf Dahruj, George Razuk, and Milhem Haykal al-Khuri and several others from Aytha were behind in their debts for merchandise purchased from Salem Bashara and they were incited by Yusuf and his group not to pay."[34] Attitudes, like the times, had changed. The spirit of adventure and apprehension that had united the men in comradeship subtly gave way to self-interest and the traditional village competition.

Fort Wayne, paralleling the decline in peddling generally, had passed its prime as a peddling settlement around the turn of the century. Peddlers, with numerous other settlements to go to—perhaps along their own village or sectarian subnetworks—ceased to pour in, and its Syrian population began to dwindle and then to stabilize. Salem sold his business about 1906, and his remaining competitors followed suit or remained to serve only the non-Syrian public. Having lost much of his wealth and health, Salem died before 1910 in his late middle age.[35]

By about that time, pioneer peddlers everywhere had been gradually turning to "other things and new ones did some peddling but were better equipped with money and English. They no longer needed a supplier. They were ordering directly from New York and many were beginning to buy cars. Only a few ordered from a supplier."[36] Many of the peddlers graduated into selling Oriental rugs and imported linens and laces; in that line, they were no longer the humble pack peddler. They saw themselves and acted as "classier salesmen dealing with classier people."[37] The period of adventure and impermanence had been gradually phasing into a period of permanence and community building.

Salem was typical of the trailblazing supplier—the archetypical supplier. His settlement was generically similar to numerous others formed throughout the national network from which peddlers fanned out to open their own supply stores and settlements. Salem's own peddlers, testing their prospects with more nerve than knowledge, populated the Middle West with their tiny colonies.

The Ayn Arab and Rashayya Subnetworks

It was from Fort Wayne that the faint trail of the Ayn Arab and Rashayya subnetworks emerged and meandered across several state lines. In retracing their imprecise development, points on the subnetworks may be overlooked, yet the general outlines are discernible from the interviews. Peddlers from Aytha reportedly spread into Ohio, western Pennsylvania, and Michigan, forming a possible third subnetwork.

Before 1895, the few Ayn Arab immigrants that had joined the influx of peddlers to Fort Wayne were, like many other of Salem's peddlers, directed toward the coal and agricultural fields of central Illinois. Faris N. was there and recorded how "in the old days" peddlers set out from the settlement and how they usually trudged from farmhouse to farmhouse in small village and family groups. One group that left Fort Wayne "was composed of members of the Ayub family—six or more of them, including three young [single] women. . . . [They] roamed in the open areas of the state of Ohio and by accident they met a group from Aythat al-Fakhar in a hotel in the city of Lima, Ohio, and they spent Sunday in the hotel together." Faris left at the same time with companions from his village but they peddled in another direction until they reached Bloomington, Illinois.

In that year, 1895, Mike H. and his brother reached Bloomington from Ayn Arab only to find that the brother-in-law they had sought had moved on to open a store in the country. They found, however, that "there had been sent there a man from Fort Wayne called Jiryus Thiyab and another man, Habib Skaff. . . . They had opened a store for Arabs." By the time Karam N. arrived at Bloomington in 1898, it was an Ayn Arab settlement: "All our people from Ayn Arab were there. The people of Rashayya went to Fort Wayne and they bought their goods from Salem Bashara. We had our own man and peddlers bought from him."

Bloomington became the fountainhead of the Ayn Arab network. Its path can be picked up in the wanderings of Mike H. He and his brother equipped themselves with a kashshi (notions case) and suitcases filled with the goods they had purchased in New York and a larger supply purchased in Bloomington. Mike continues "Our first cousin there took us out and now we were peddling. . . . Our trainers left us and we kept walking until we got to Iowa. The first year we walked; the second one we got a horse and buggy. . . . We carried maps and we would head in a direction and in each town, we'd ask how far to the next town. . . . We continued in this way until 1898 when we arrived in Lenox, Iowa."

Mike peddled for six years before returning to Ayn Arab. He married, and when he returned in 1907, he trekked over Iowa and Minnesota. One of his stops that first year was Sioux City, Iowa, where many Ayn Arab peddlers had formed a settlement. Other relatives lived in Cedar Rapids. Finally in 1910, his wife joined him in Hot Springs, Nebraska. "We didn't have relatives there," he said, "but I had been there and decided to stop peddling and opened a dry goods store."

Karam N.'s father and future father-in-law had arrived in Bloomington in 1893. On the father's second trip to the United States in 1898, he brought nine-year-old Karam to peddle with him. They bought a rig and peddled their way to Burlington, Iowa, then went on to Ottumwa. "When we were through in Ottumwa, we went on from town to town to Sioux City. There were lots of our relatives there," he said. Three years later, both father and son returned to Ayn Arab.

The boy, who returned to Syria in 1901, came back to the
United States a man in 1906: "I got a horse and buggy and
started peddling from Cedar Rapids. I went to Sioux City,
then to Nebraska and to South and North Dakota. I didn't
like North Dakota. . . . There were not too many Syrian families there, but what there were, were all from Ayn Arab and
related to us . . . with the exception of maybe two or three
families."

Karam was tempted to homestead with his uncle in Den-
hoff, North Dakota, but after a particularly severe and hazardous winter in 1908, he decided "No more of this for me"
and went to Cedar Rapids in search of a bride. Soon after
their betrothal, the fiancée, a distant cousin, moved with her
parents to Albert Lea, Minnesota, where she, Karam, and
Mike H. had relatives. After the wedding, officiated by the
priest of Saint George's Orthodox Church in Kearney, Nebraska, they settled in Albert Lea and opened a dry goods
store. There were only a few Syrians there, but combined
with those that lived in nearby small towns, including relatives in Thompson, Iowa, and Minneapolis, "that made quite
a few of us," said Mrs. N.

Before the end of the nineties, the Ayn Arab people, gravitating northward, seem to have abandoned Bloomington.
One of the attractions was Cedar Rapids, an Ayn Arab settlement that probably predated the Sioux City colony by a year
or two. When Karam found his bride in Cedar Rapids in
1908, the colony was in its second decade, populated mainly
by his relatives and townsmen. "It is a fact not generally
known," began an article in the *Cedar Rapids Evening Gazette*
of 9 March 1897,

> that Cedar Rapids now has a fair-sized colony of genuine Ara-
> bians which is being augmented rapidly and bids fair to be-
> come a feature of our cosmopolitan population.
>
> In a little store room at No. 920 South Third Street, Tom
> Bashara, the recognized head of the colony, lives amid a het-
> erogeneous mixture of American and foreign made goods,
> including all the articles that peddlers ever carry in their
> "packs." . . . Several of the party had only been in this country
> a few months and all were Tom's friends. . . . Now they are

really working for him carrying their great burdens about the country and peddling the various articles with which Tom supplies them.[39]

The settlement had been well located in the heart of the rich agricultural area along the swift-surging rapids of the Cedar River. As the principal industrial city of east central Iowa, Cedar Rapids attracted both skilled labor and immigrants. When Syrian peddlers arrived, its population was booming and Czechoslovakians were the dominant ethnic group. Some Syrians, without realizing the difference, learned to speak "Bohemian" before they learned English.[40]

The *Gazette* went on to state that Tom had emigrated from a village near Damascus—Ayn Arab, according to George N.—six years earlier (about 1892) and first located in Fort Wayne. After Tom had accumulated enough money, he returned to his Syrian village. Then back in the United States, he lived for a time in Chicago and Bloomington. He turned up in Cedar Rapids late in 1896, the year he founded the settlement. On one of several trips between Cedar Rapids and Syria, he was reported by informants, to have stopped in Brazil for a short time, perhaps to peddle, perhaps to recruit because South America—Brazil in particular—was attracting many Syrians. While there, he befriended Abdullah A., a Shiʿa Muslim, and together they traveled to Cedar Rapids in 1905.[41] But, within months, Abdullah chose to settle in Fort Dodge, Iowa, where three Shiʿa Muslim brothers had opened a supply store several years earlier.[42]

Tom Bashara was no less a recruiter than Salem, to whom he may have been related. He drew in friends and relatives from Bloomington as well as others like Lillian K. H.'s father, a distant relative, who had peddled "in the Ohio hills for nine years before coming to Cedar Rapids because Tom was here."[43] He reached out to his own and nearby villages for peddlers, sometimes financing their travel and supplying them with merchandise.[44] Others simply wandered in. His peddlers too, in turn, wrote to their friends and relatives and "would say 'come here and peddle; we're making money,' and they would come."[45] Those who came were predominantly Syrian Orthodox from Ayn Arab. There is no evidence that

Muslims other than Abdullah A. were among these pioneering recruits.

Established relatively late in the pioneer period, Cedar Rapids' peddling settlement status was short-lived, although peddling continued to be a vital occupation into the World War I years. While the Syrian population comprised no more than twenty-five or thirty families by informants' count, three suppliers served peddlers in any given year from 1909 to 1915 according to Cedar Rapids city directories.[46] Tom enlarged his operation before 1909; in that year he entered into a partnership with two cousins.[47] By 1912, the partnership had become two individual supply stores. One of them had a barn for the peddlers' rigs in his back yard where "there were always ten to fifteen wagons parked."[48] Toward the end of 1911, Tom took Aleck S., a newly arrived Shi'a Muslim, as partner, and in a few months sold out to him to leave, it was thought, for California.[49]

Cedar Rapids was neither the first nor the last link in the Ayn Arab subnetwork. Tom's "boys" scattered "out like spokes in a wagon wheel" and the networking process continued until its relevance declined with the peddling trade.[50]

The Rashayya subnetwork began much as that of Ayn Arab but was diverted mid-course. The Rashayya people peddled from Fort Wayne and roamed freely over Illinois, Indiana, Ohio, and Michigan. Some crossed the Mississippi River westward, and individuals are known to have reached Denver and El Paso, but the bulk, it would appear, made the Middle West their home. They settled in such communities as Spring Valley, Illinois; Terre Haute, Indiana; Grand Rapids, Michigan; Rochester, Pennsylvania; Manchester, New Hampshire; and Canton, Akron, and Toledo, Ohio.[51] Only in Fort Wayne, Spring Valley, and Grand Rapids, however, did they colonize in sufficient numbers to form the majority in what might be called "Rashayya settlements."

The Rashayya people were well on their way to developing a network comparable to that of the Ayn Arab when they became drawn to a mushrooming settlement, not in the United States, but in Canada. Since about 1882, a misrouted group of Riyyashni (as they were called) purportedly settled in Montreal, Quebec, and began to attract townsmen from abroad and the United States by 1900, outstripping other Rashayya settlements in size. Initially, its growth was due to the more lenient Canadian immigration laws, but it also proved to be a lucrative peddling area. Like New York, Montreal was an important port city and, similarly, it would become a major receiving colony with numerous immigrant shops, residences, restaurants, and a Syrian commercial center of manufacturers, importers, and wholesalers. Riyyashni flocked there, fanning out into nearby provinces as well as into the American stream with relative ease. Immigrants crossed the international border in both directions, often illegally, all the while maintaining communications between the center and its satellites.

For most of the early period, Fort Wayne was the primary Rashayya settlement in the United States. It ceded that place to Grand Rapids to which it had sent, if not the first Syrian, as Alexander M. believed, then the first Rashayya immigrant.[52] By the turn of the century, this industrial town began to appear, from the perspective of the Spring Valley settlers, like the "hub of Riyyashni."[53] Although the colony had at least two suppliers, some Syrians had already left peddling for more permanent enterprises and factory jobs. Meanwhile, Syrians from several villages migrated into the town, drawn by its peddling and job market, but Riyyashni were also gravitating there from Fort Wayne and Montreal. By World War I, the Riyyashni had assumed not only the majority but the leadership. There, as in Fort Wayne, the other numerous group was from Aytha.

Spring Valley was neither a commercial nor an industrial center in the late nineteenth century. Until the mines closed in 1927, it was a soft coal mining town with four mines in the immediate vicinity and seventeen others within a radius of eight or nine miles. Although situated in the heart of the rich farming country of the Illinois River Valley, midway between Chicago and Rock Island, it had been established in 1884 by the Spring Valley Coal Company, in conjunction with the Chicago and Northwestern Railroad, to exploit the coalfields. The coal company's advertisements for miners drew prospects from numerous European countries and turned the area into an immigrant's haven. Spring Valley almost immediately became "a cosmopolitan city," according to its historian, Bernice Sweeney: "it was a boom town, the population swelled to 5,000 in 1886." Its population never exceeded 7,914 when mines were in full production between 1910 and 1913.[54]

Almost from the beginning, the town was so plagued by labor strife that by the turn of the century, a Chicago newspaper designated it, with some exaggeration, as the "banner anarchist city of the United States."[55] Today, as a reminder of its coal-mining origins, a huge slag dump dominates the town and several other dumps are prominent in the surrounding landscape.

Into this unsettled but prosperous region wandered the Syrian peddlers. Hasiby A. remembered Salīm B. saying: "There was a man from Fort Wayne who used to organize them [the peddlers]. He'd send one peddling to Spring Valley and another to another place. . . . He [Salīm] would tell stories about how he used to go to Fort Wayne and there the peddlers would be directed to go here or there and would be sent where they could peddle and make money."

Hasiby's father, his brother, and his brother-in-law were in the vanguard of Riyyashni from Fort Wayne about 1898, and although men from Tripoli (Syria), Mhaytha, and other villages also came, the Riyyashni constituted, according to its old-timers, almost a two to one majority, including several women. Sometimes, they came from Fort Wayne and Montreal; sometimes they came directly from Rashayya. With the exception of Hasiby's parents and uncles who were Melkite, all were Syrian Orthodox.

Before the century was out, Spring Valley had become a bustling peddling settlement, the leading one in the extensive bituminous coal region of north central Illinois, a distinction it held into the 1920s. Peddlers came and went. No one remembers the exact totals, but it seemed there were always fifty or sixty around.[56] Each morning they left town in groups of men and women to ply their trade in nearby immigrant-populated mining towns and the countryside.

Hardly a peddler could not recite the names and locations of Illinois towns and hamlets as if he were reading a road map; he could also describe their prominent landmarks.

The Spring Valley colony almost resembled a "Little Syria." When Hasiby A. arrived from Rashayya as a young bride in 1911, there were twenty five or thirty families and many single men and women. "There was plenty of business for all because the coal mines were working," she explained. William D. was certain that "the coal company's payroll was $200,000 every Saturday" and compared the town expansively with Madison Avenue. By 1913, the Main Street businesses included a Syrian-owned fruit wholesaler, grocer, poolroom, barber, and confectioner. Three dry goods stores still served peddlers as well as the general public.[57] The first and largest had been opened by Hasiby's father about 1899.

Peddling survived in Spring Valley long after it waned as an important Syrian trade in most of America. In a practical sense, it was lucrative. At least, to quote Nemer K., who peddled until 1939, "they made enough money to satisfy them." At the same time, the narrow range of the town's economic options left little incentive to change. There was little industry in the immediate area and the thought of working underground at the low wages then paid to miners exacerbated the Syrians' innate disdain for wage labor. Besides, Main Street bulged with sales and service shops, including those of the Syrians; the town's small and stable population could hardly support the abundance of competing entrepreneurs. Syrians who wished to move up the economic ladder before World War I, opened shops on the "Main" streets of neighboring towns; many more sought opportunities elsewhere—in Toledo, Grand Rapids, or Canton, Ohio, for example. Meanwhile, the colony continued to receive immigrants who welcomed the opportunity to adapt to America in this continuing "school" of peddling.

On a more abstract level, the colonists became captivated by their environment. Surrounded by an idyllic countryside and bountiful farms, they had re-created much of the ethos of the home village—the close personal relationships, mutual dependence, and simple village pleasures—while enjoying a higher standard of living and greater freedom than they had experienced in Syria. In addition, having conquered the initial hazards and hardships of peddling and having developed familiar routes and clienteles, there was no urgent impulse to give up their suitcases.

Spring Valley itself spawned no new settlements; it was created too late in the pioneer period. While it maintained a relatively stable population, Syrians moved into it primarily from other Illinois towns like Kewanee and Streator, and others moved out. There was hardly a town or hamlet in north central Illinois, as far as the Iowa border, that did not count one or more Syrian families with village or kinship ties in Spring Valley. Insofar as its place in the subnetwork is concerned, the colony remained an important contact point for the scattered pockets of Riyyashni in the Middle West, linking them with other enclaves.

The current state of research into the distribution and settlement of the relatively small number of Muslims and Druze allows only the most shadowy speculation and imprecise comparison with Christian communities. During this study, no pre-1908 immigrant was found for interview and the testimony of their survivors and successors throws little light on the pioneers' activities. Nor are the few available studies helpful since they are, on the whole, social science dissertations and theses on Muslims prepared after World War II. Regrettably, they all lack detailed empirical historical data. No major study of a Druze community is known to exist.

Only vague traces of any non-Christian subnetwork exists. The Muslim and Druze suppliers, with one possible exception, did not seem to have played the pivotal role in recruitment and leadership as those of the Christian, probably because of the tenuous chain migration. On the other hand, no discernible lack of entrepreneurial skills and ambitions differentiated them from the Christians; and the absence of suppliers proved no insuperable obstacle to their goals. Mohammad S., who peddled from Tennessee to Virginia in 1913, the year he arrived, purchased his merchandise locally or mail-ordered it from the New York colony. Aliya H.'s father and his fellow peddlers, living in Sioux Falls, South Dakota, at the turn of the century, ordered their goods collectively from Chicago, Minneapolis, and New York "and they would divide it between them." Sometimes her father drove his horse and buggy to Omaha, Nebraska, for supplies. "There was really no supplier as such," she said. Independent and determined men, they fended for themselves.

The few thousand Muslims and Druze were well scattered throughout the United States. Louise Houghton found, in 1911, that they were "still few in number, the majority of those considered Moslem being Druses. There are a few of the unorthodox Moslem sect, the Metualey [Syrian Shi'a]. . . . The largest Moslem community is perhaps in Providence [Rhode Island], where they number 150, many of these, however, being Turks from Asia Minor. The most important Druse communities are in Pittsfield and North Adams, Mass.; the largest if not the only Metualey community in America is in Sioux City [Iowa]."[58] By the time Tom Bashara ceased to be the moving spirit behind the Christian settlement in Cedar Rapids, a few Muslim families had collected there, but none was related to Abdullah A., Tom's traveling companion from Brazil. From 1908, a total of four brothers and two cousins joined Abdullah from the village of Insar in Fort Dodge and Urbana, Iowa, helped by Abdullah. In the late 1920s one of the A. brothers finally moved to Cedar Rapids.[59]

Why Shi'a Muslims from Jib Jenine in the western Beqa Valley trickled into the predominantly Christian colony is still largely an unanswered question. Perhaps they came from Sioux City; another uncertain explanation holds that a chain migration was triggered by Negebe S.'s father, despite his Sunni Muslim beliefs. He was an influential man who, before the turn of the century, had visited a Christian friend in the United States. Failing to find the friend, he went on to Cedar Rapids and worked with Tom. He may have peddled to Cedar Rapids from Iowa City where he reportedly had a Muslim friend and creditor.

At first, there were no more than a handful of single Muslim men living in rooms near the Christian settlement. Some peddled for a short while but soon joined the trend toward wage labor and opening stores. In their work and leisure, they freely mingled with the Christians; however, as families formed, the two religious groups gradually drifted apart. Despite a number of religiocultural differences which inhibited formal social relations, the two groups maintained quite cordial, albeit detached, relationships. As for the relations in the colony between Muslims of different villages, Hasebe A. observed that "all the Syrians were divided by village. People from Jib Jenine may not always have liked each other, but they were closer to each other than with those from Insar." Before World War I, Christian families in the colony outnumbered the Muslims five or six to one; in the state, the disparity was more pronounced.

Another early concentration, gradually formed in three areas of North Dakota about 1902. Muslims from Damascus, they settled near Crookston, Minnesota, where they became peddlers of dry goods, reported the *Fargo Forum* on 8 December 1967:

> At first these pioneer Moslems peddled their wares on foot throughout North Dakota, but used horse and buggy when they could afford it. Some of the more successful bargainers were even able to purchase automobiles.
>
> Finding North Dakota a good place to live, they soon moved from Crookston and clustered in three localities—the Stanley-Ross area, Rolla-Dunseith, and Glenfield-Binford.
>
> . . . And when they had saved and borrowed enough money and had learned the rudiments of the language, they became homesteaders or operated small stores. In turn, they taught the newer immigrants the skills of peddling—and so on the cycle—until they were all settled in their new homeland.
>
> By 1925, the Moslem population near Stanley had grown to 30 or 40 families.[60]

Aliya H.'s father and his small group collected in Sioux Falls, South Dakota, about 1900, and like their compatriots to the north, they found their way along peddling routes, through Minnesota, from other parts of the United States. A tiny settlement in Alpine, Michigan, may have been an offshoot of a small group of Muslims and Druze living in Detroit. Elkholy, in his study of Muslims, states that Detroit, "perhaps the oldest Arab Moslem community in the United States," was founded about the beginning of the twentieth century, some twenty years after the Christian community.[61] In all likelihood, they too peddled before settling down to work in the budding automotive industry or opening their own businesses.

If Detroit was the earliest, Chicago might have been the largest. The Muslim Palestinians who began arriving there around the turn of the century ultimately formed a sizable Muslim center that resembled the larger, older neighboring Christian community. Their experiences were similar:

> I came to Chicago in 1912 with my brother. At that time, we already had an uncle and a cousin here. They got us a furnished room on 18th Street and the very next day after our arrival, we started to work. In those days the Arabs had a couple of wholesale dry goods stores on 18th Street where us peddlers used to get our stock. We carried a suitcase in which there was linen tablecloths, napkins, small rugs, handerkerchiefs and stuff like that. On the first day when my uncle handed me a suitcase and told me what I had to do, I got scared out of my wits. I couldn't speak a word of English so how could I go from door to door selling the stuff?[62]

There were, no doubt, many other peddling enclaves where Muslims settled, but their locations and histories have not been recorded.

Druze, probably fewer than Muslims, peddled their way, before 1900, to such widely separated regions as West Virginia and Seattle. The first Druze to arrive in West Virginia may have meandered southward along the East Coast in 1885, passing through the Pennsylvania coal districts. Before he returned to his village three years later, according to one of that pioneer's descendants, he started a chain migration of males within his extended family to that area which, in time, became an important nucleus of Druze. From there, small clusters of Druze men settled neighboring Virginia, North Carolina, Kentucky, and Tennessee, forming what appears to have become, after 1908, a hub of settlements from

which Druze spread southward and westward as far as Texas
and Oklahoma. Some also formed enclaves in Cleveland, Akron, and Dayton, Ohio.[63]

Farther west, a group of Druze settlements centered on
Seattle, their origins now forgotten. However, the Seattle
group appears to have taken the lead in organizing the first
Druze association in the United States in February 1908.
Called "Bakurat al-Dirziyya," its Articles of Incorporation
were signed, in Arabic, by over seventy members on 25 July
1911. The association pledged to unite the Druze in America
and to assist its members in particular and Syrians in general,
spiritually and materially.[64] In addition, it disseminated information on the Druze, their religion, and culture both in
the United States and in the homeland.[65]

In the Middle West, about 1890, a Druze supplier opened
a store in Hannibal, Missouri, and attracted coreligionists to
his peddling settlement, sold them goods on credit, trained
and launched them into their American experience.[66] From
time to time, he sent merchandise to Druze peddlers in Oelwein, Iowa. The oldest of three R. brothers had arrived in
that tiny agricultural town, located on a railroad stop, about
1912 while peddling and decided to settle there. The first of
them arrived in the United States about 1910 and was joined
by two brothers. Although a few relatives caught up with
them in Oelwein, they did not start a supply store for peddlers, but ordered goods from nearby suppliers, probably
Cedar Rapids and certainly Hannibal, until the oldest
brother opened a restaurant in 1914.[67]

Flint, Michigan, became the home of another extended
Druze family. The first of its migrants arrived in the United
States about 1898. Perhaps he peddled, no one seems certain; but, about 1908, he reportedly weeded sugar beet fields
around Carol, Michigan. In the two years he remained there,
other members joined him. Then in 1910, he and some relatives moved to Flint, attracted by the incipient automotive
industry, and worked in General Motors' Buick plant. Within
a year or two, he opened a small grocery store and used some
of its profits to finance the immigration of additional relatives from Syria. The family business grew with the expan-

sion of Flint's industry, and by 1925, the family was operating a chain of grocery stores, thought to be the forerunner of that trend.[68]

Pioneer Druze settled in other states—in Massachusetts, as Louise Houghton observed, in Connecticut, and in the District of Columbia, among others.[69]

The migratory momentum of Muslims and Druze, generated after 1908, was, even then, too limited to form sufficiently large settlements from which splintering on the scale practiced by the Christians could take place. Perhaps more importantly, because most arrived when the peddling trade was already in decline, the newcomers relied less on that trade than on privately owned business and factory work, and even less on farming. Moreover, by that time, they tended to be less mobile, settling in or near the points of attraction. Later, they would make contact with other enclaves of their respective faiths.

Muslims tended to gravitate to highly industrial urban centers, while Druze were more generally distributed. Post–1908 Muslim centers—Toledo, Ohio; Michigan City, Indiana; and Highland Park, Michigan, for example, where Christians and Muslims shared the same neighborhoods—owed their existence essentially to industrial labor rather than to peddling. Dearborn, Michigan, currently the largest Muslim community in the United States, grew out of the relocation of Ford Motor Company's Highland Park plant in 1916.[70] Druze, a highly individualistic people, seemed to have shunned industrial work in general, preferring the independence of entrepreneurship.

Collectively, the subnetworks facilitated the tendency of a peddling people to become widely distributed. On the other hand, the pattern of recruitment set the character of the permanent communities that were to succeed the settlements and left legacies that continue to echo in Arabic-speaking communities. First, an immigration of single individuals who believed themselves to be on a temporary sojourn, left behind the traditional guardians of community values and mores. Absent from most settlements (for as much as a generation in many cases) was guidance from religious institutions and the traditional secular leadership. Moreover, social sanctions of family, neighborhood, and village were loosened. Consequently, attempts to preserve Old World values and customs were weakened. Enforcing them and guarding them against change became difficult at best. New leaders, trying to re-create Syrians institutions in permanent communities, found the force of the new far stronger than the authority of the old.

Second, the family-village emphasis in the recruitment process perpetuated the deeply ingrained religious and sectarian divisions endemic in Syrian society. People of one faith and/or place of origin, coalescing early in the settlements and in urban neighborhoods, inhibited, if they did not preclude, a unified national ethnic community by perpetuating as many Syrian—frequently rival—identities on American soil as they were on the identity grid in the homeland.

Rashayya al-Wadi, Mount Lebanon, in the 1920s.

Nineteenth-century Syrian family.

Family portrait, Damascus, nineteenth century.

Star Theater cast for *Romeo and Juliet*, Utica, New York, 1914.

Professor Joseph Arbeely, his six sons, and niece, who were
pioneer Syrian immigrants in 1896.

Syrian restaurant, Lawrence, Massachusetts, ca. 1911.

Saint George Syrian Orthodox Church, built in 1926, Spring
Valley, Illinois.

Looking west on Saint Paul Street, Spring Valley, Illinois.

Syrian peddler, before World War I.

A Syrian peddler selling to a homesteading North Dakota farm family.

Peddling in or near Williston, North Dakota.

Peddler boy carrying notions case (*kashshi*).

Aossey's switch from rig to truck, date and place unknown (probably 1920s).

Exhibit of Butros & Butros, importers of laces, New York City.

Syrian dry goods store ca. 1930 (opened 1908 or 1910).

Opening of Syrian-owned grocery store in 1916 at Clifford and
Henry streets, Detroit, Michigan; brothers Albert (*left*) and Louis
(*middle*) Ajamy.

Interior of early Syrian-owned grocery store in the late 1920s, owned by Albert Ajamy.

First board of directors, Saint George Orthodox Church, Detroit, Michigan, 1916.

Dedication of Saint George Orthodox Church, Detroit, Michigan, World War I era.

Lebanese Maronite girl, Detroit, Michigan; Palm Sunday, early 1920s.

Sunday afternoon in Spring Valley, Illinois, in the 1920s.

5

On the Road

To the second generation, the American-raised and American-born generation, the peddling experience of their parents has proved murky, humbling, and frequently embarrassing. The children of the pioneers were too focused on hewing out their own course in American society; few could appreciate the challenges and strengths of peddling. Today, most of them conceive of that period in Horatio Alger terms in which poor illiterate immigrants, with little or no English, succeeded by ingenuity and hard work. References to Horatio Alger are, of course, apt. The second generation also prefers to talk of salesmen, or merchandisers, not pack peddlers. Few appreciate the way in which the peddling trade actually facilitated the adjustment of those immigrants to American life. Something in the second generation's mental struggle with its own past deflected it from penetrating beyond the shabby dress, the foreignness, and fatigue, to the romance and adventure of life on the road that captivated the memories of their parents and has been preserved in Arabic satirical short stories and poems.[1] Nowhere, however, is the lore of the road better preserved than in the corpus of peddling anecdotes in which hardships are overshadowed by the Syrians' appreciation of cunning and wit.

Old-timers—those conscious of themselves as pioneers—
will nod approvingly at the Horatio Alger analogy but unravel their past in anecdote after anecdote. They will grin,
chuckle, deprecate the miseries—"Oh, how we suffered! Oh,
what we endured!"—with hardly a hint of bitter brooding.
They will sigh long and nostalgically; a gleam will appear in
the pensive eyes, and they will inevitably begin: "There was
that time when I . . ." From their now comfortable middle-
class living rooms, they will beckon the listener back to the
days when the pioneers trudged along unpaved country
roads, knocked on strangers' doors, and communicated in
sign language, trying to make a sale or desperately pleading
for a cold night's lodging:

It was cold in Nebraska that night; I was tired and hungry.
Farmhouses weren't close together in those days, sometimes a
couple of miles apart—maybe more. It was getting late and
I'd been trying to get a place to sleep since the sun went down,
but no one let me in. So I knocked at the door. I was determined. The woman opened the door and I made a gesture
like this [putting his two hands to one side of his head] that I
wanted to sleep. While she was telling me that her husband
wasn't home from the fields yet, and she had no room, I said
"thank you," and pushed past her into the house. There was
a warm fire glowing and I went straight to it as she continued
to try to make me understand that she had no room, I said,
"thank you," and continued to warm myself. I smelled the dinner cooking and saw the table was set and I prayed she would
let me stay at least long enough to eat. Then her husband
came in. She began to explain to him about this poor peddler
who keeps saying thank you and who must be cold and wants
a place to sleep and she told him that she tried to make me
understand. While they were doing this kind of talking and
before they could turn me away, I said "thank you," and sat at
the table. Well, the husband said "all right" and we all sat
down to eat. I thanked God, but could not relax yet. Was he
going to throw me out into the cold again? He said something
to his wife which I could not hear and went to my pack. I
watched him; if he carried it toward the outer door, I would
plead, but if . . .; well, he took them toward the bedrooms and
gestured for me to follow. I said, "thank you," and went.

I had a good night's sleep; the bed was warm and clean, not like some I've slept in. I awoke early the next morning and joined the wife and her two daughters in the kitchen. I opened my pack and took out three expensive linen handkerchiefs and presented one to each of them, saying how grateful I was—peddlers always paid something for their lodgings—and how nice the bed was and she said, quite surprised, "But you speak English." I had learned a lot in the three years I'd been peddling. "Yes, Maam," I answered, "but if I'd spoken it last night, I'd be out in the cold and frozen to death by now." We all laughed and I returned to their house several times after that and was welcomed.[2]

By the end of the tale, they are bubbling with laughter and blotting the corners of their eyes with neatly folded handkerchiefs.

Syrian pack peddlers were, it seems, indefatigable men and women of steely determination who trekked along, ladened like beasts of burden. A heavy suitcase strapped to the back, a kashshi to the chest, and one satchel in each hand was the typical portrait of a peddler. Wadi N. described how peddlers "would start out. . . . with their packs worth from $100 to $300—as much as a man could carry. You strap your heavy pack on your back and cover it with oil-cloth and the strap had a hook to which you hooked a small notions case. In it were scissors, razors, pins, buttons, and it weighs thirty pounds in addition to the heavy one on your back. The notions case would hang on your chest and you could rest your hand on it, but that makes it heavier, and you walked from one place to another."

Cunning and perseverance were an indispensible and almost unanimously applied prescription for success. In that sense they were optimistic, for they were well grounded in both qualities. In retrospect, their optimism was justified and when they look back, it may not always be with nostalgia, but almost never is it with regret. Their story possessed its own drama and humor beginning with the day they presented themselves, alien and olive-skinned, bent under the weight of their packs, at the door of a customer.

Scores of anecdotes convey the conflict between the old

and the new, of transition and of the capability to overcome adversity by native wit and ingenuity. Yet, the old-timers make no effort to conceal the anguish, pain, bewilderment, disappointment, and insecurity of a people roaming in a strange world for which they had been ill prepared. Nevertheless, theirs is no litany of despair. Even the most biting and embarrassing stories, told and retold at the peddlers' expense, have been embellished and transformed by fertile imaginations. In the process, anxieties of the road became dissolved in wit and irony. At once bitter and humorous, when shared with comrades and kinsmen, rebuffs and insults were objectified and trivialized; dignity lost among strangers was restored among those who cared; and solutions were found to problems, not previously encountered in the homeland or soluble by an institution or agency brought with them. Moreover, group-oriented and group-sustained, the anecdotes became a form of common identification with each other and with the trade itself—largely irrelevant and incomprehensive to outsiders.

Perhaps only a Syrian would find humor in the desperate act of a newly arrived Muslim peddler who, after a hard day near Sioux Falls, South Dakota, and repeated rejections for a place to sleep, seized the beard of the next farmer at whose door he knocked and kissed it. The confused and outraged Norwegian began to throttle the cowering immigrant whose companion and trainer, waiting by the roadside, rushed to his aid. "May your mind be troubled [*Yishghal balak*]," the veteran admonished the novice, "why are you fighting with this man?" "I'm not," cried the bewildered peddler, "I'm kissing his beard so he will take us in." Had the Norwegian known that an Arab's beard is a symbol of honor and integrity by which an Arab swears and that in Arab tradition, honor compels a man whose beard is kissed to fulfill the request of a supplicant, the farmer may have understood the young man's feelings of desperation.[3] One of the most circulated anecdotes concerns two peddlers, again in search of a place to sleep. When one knocked on the door and requested it, he was told "Sorry, no room." Befuddled, he returned to his friend. "How," he asked, "did she know I was Rūm; she

doesn't accept Rūm." His friend offered to try. His knock
evoked the same response. "Hones', Laydee," he pleaded,
"Ana [I] no Rūm, ana Cathōlīc." The humor is buried in the
knowledge of Syrian intersectarian relations and in the Syrian meaning of Rūm, a reference to Byzantine or Syrian Orthodox.

Training for the road was minimal. Besides, most newcomers were impatient; they had come to make money quickly
and were eager to get on with it. Within a day or two, someone put a kashshi in their hands and took them out for their
first day's earning. Veteran peddlers, usually kinsmen, were
generous with advice. Welcoming gatherings in the supplier's
quarters or in peddlers' rooms became orientation sessions
as the newcomers listened to anecdotes and learned the fun-
damentals of the trade. The realities they would experience
for themselves on the road. Few beginners ventured out un-
apprenticed or untutored, at least in the preliminaries.
"Those who had been here a month or two," recalled Mary
A., "would teach them a few words they [the veterans] had
already learned—to knock on a door and say 'Buy sumthin',
Maam,' or how to say they were hungry or needed a place to
sleep."[4] They learned about American currency, how to pack
suitcases to bursting point, how to sue for a housewife's attention ("hold up the rosaries and crosses, first; say they are
from the Holy Land because Americans are very religious
and don't like Jews"); how to deal with towns that require
licenses and much more. And, there was the first principle of
peddling—how to make the most profit. Watfa M. was told
"if you buy a dress for $10, sell it for $20 and take $10 from
the customer first before giving her the dress. Then, if she
wants credit, give it to her; but always get your cost first."[5]
There was little, however, with which the Syrian's innate
pragmatism could not deal, and a novice turned into a veteran within days.

In that era of freewheeling enterprise, some veterans converted the influx of novices into a profitable venture. "They
took men with them," said Mike H., himself trained by his
cousin, "and they [the newcomers] would pay five percent. . . . They [the veterans] would find hotels, teach them

routes, and guide them in other ways. And, the owners of the stores would give these men [the veterans] five percent of whatever they [the newcomers] bought from the storeowners." Faris N. claimed that he trained six countrymen, including a Druze, and received 6 percent commission on the cost of merchandise purchased from Salem Bashara.[6]

An observer, seeing men and women milling about near a supplier's store in the early hours of the morning—backs and hands ladened with suitcases—some heading for a train station, others for a trolley stop, and still others for the countryside on foot or by buggy, might think he was seeing, as Slayman N. said, "a bunch of gypsies. Women would wear the black scarves on their heads. Up to 15 of us would leave together daily. You'd see them at the street car stop. A saloon owner used to make fun of them, all packed and dressed funny and going out like gypsies. So, I told him one day, 'These people are going to make an honest living . . . ' but they really were like gypsies."[7]

Although by the end of the century, all modes of transportation were used to get the peddlers to their routes and back to the settlement, selling all the while. They departed the settlement in small groups or pairs. Some followed the recommendations of the supplier; the more confident and independent selected their own routes. Depending on the distance of the route from the settlement, a number of strategies were used: "Six or seven of us would start out peddling. We'd plan our routes for the week. We'd leave on Monday mornings and go in different directions and plan to meet on Saturday afternoon at the train depot of some town. We'd all walk. None of us got lost."[8] Some took a train to a distant point and peddled back toward the settlement, canvassing towns and farms for a week or more along the way; others followed their intuition and roamed for months.

Amity on the road was essential if members of a settlement were to earn and return as comrades. Although competition was as natural to Syrians as the sense of entrepreneurship, generally they refrained from invading each other's territory; the market was ample. Streets, towns, or regions were divided by informal agreement: "They'd tell each other [where they were going] and one would get off at the beginning of a town, then ten or twelve blocks later, another would get off and so on; and one would maybe go to another town."[9] But entrepreneurial self-interest bred many exceptions to the rule. As one close observer noted, "they used to plot their routes together so that they would not cross paths in the same town. One would say, 'Well, today I'm going to Oglesby;' the other would say, "Well, I'll go to Peru." But they would run into each other's territory and they'd get angry at each other for that. Oh, yes, they did, indeed."[10] When a supplier directed peddlers to routes, he usually took pains to avoid overlapping to prevent conflict. "He would alternate routes and peddlers from week to week. When a peddler angered a supplier, he ran the risk of being deliberately assigned to someone else's territory."[11]

If Syrian peddlers could be classified, they might fall generally into three categories according to length of time away from the settlement and distance covered on the road; there was, however, no unvarying pattern. Long-distance peddlers roamed the towns and countryside of several states far from the settlement for as long as six or twelve months, and medium-distance peddlers usually returned to the settlement after two or three weeks, maybe four. The day-peddlers remained closer to the settlement, returning each evening. Some might be away two or three days. A peddler could limit or extend his or her range according to inclination, health, or restricting responsibilities. Gradually, pragmatism overcame the sense of frugality and many peddlers succumbed to the purchase of a horse and buggy. Not only was the rig more comfortable, it increased the variety and quantity of their merchandise, and they covered more ground. Yet, walking appeared to be no inhibitor to covering distance. In general, the medium- and short-range peddlers tended to develop regular routes and a clientele from whom they took orders and sold on credit; the roving peddlers, on the other hand, might never retrace their paths. Most women, children, and older people tended to canvass nearby town and city streets, stopping at farmhouses, if there were any, along the way.

Children who peddled accompanied a member of the family. They were not, on the whole, victims of parental exploitation. As in the home village, children by the age of twelve considered themselves, and were regarded as, ready to shoulder their responsibilities in the family. Thus, they were as eager, in the United States, to prove themselves as their parents were to have them do so.

Peddling women were Christians; Muslim and Druze women, because of the conservatism of their tradition and, in part, because they migrated in the declining years of the peddling period, are not known to have peddled. On their daily rounds, women normally moved out and returned in groups and pairs. On longer trips, however, they accompanied men, at least one of whom was a close relative or family friend; in this way, their honor and self-respect were safeguarded. Traveling and peddling was not only a breach of tradition but the opening wedge to further significant changes in the status of Syrian women in the United States.

It is with the long-distance—the most stalwart—peddlers that most of the romance and adventure of the pioneer period is associated. Peripatetic merchants, they seemed to show up wherever there was a chance to sell. Following railroad lines and networks of rutted roads, they trekked from state to state. "I've heard that some walked as far as Baton Rouge, Louisiana, from New York," said Wadi N., "and peddled all the way." Nazha H.'s father was on the road for months at a time. He walked, he once told her, "from Fort Wayne, through Ohio and Pennsylvania to Manchester, New Hampshire, then went on to Montreal." Another time he walked from Montreal to Fort Wayne and, with another group of companions, ventured west until he reached El Paso, Texas.

Peddling was initially a trade in holy items: rosaries, crosses, and icons. "For this reason, there were no limits to the prices they charged," wrote Salloum Mokarzel. "Yet the Americans and other immigrants who preceded the Syrians to this country bought these items because, in general they believed them to be blessed and viewed everything the peddler had as related to the Holy Land. Eye witnesses of these first immigrants and those who spoke about them say that they used to carry the rosaries suspended on a stick or arranged on their arms and they would in this way present them to a woman or the people of the house. And, their behavior was limited to cities for they neither had the experience nor the need to penetrate to the interior."[12]

From those earliest days which seem to have faded from memory by the turn of the century, evolutionary stages in the expansion of the peddling trade followed in rapid succession. Almost certainly, carrying holy items on a stick was quickly followed by the notion's box filled with anything which a peddler could fit into its several drawers. So prevalent was this peddler's companion, that its Arabic name of kashshi (said to be "a corruption of the Spanish word for box or 'caixa'")[13] came to encompass all the peddlers' cases and even the peddlers themselves. Whereas the Arabic for merchant or trader is *tājir*, (*tajjār*, in the colloquial), in America he became known by the Syrians as "*kashshash*."

Perhaps notions led to selling cut dry goods and ribbons; perhaps customers themselves made other requests. Whatever the course of change, it pointed the way to greater varieties of merchandise for the pack peddler. Much of it was what the practical, frugal, hardworking Americans needed most—underwear, shirts, socks, garters, suspenders, and working gloves and caps. "My father's customers were farmers who lived in isolated areas, and if they needed a pair of overalls, they'd rather buy it from a peddler than go into town," said William A. of Spring Valley.[14] The only limitation became the peddlers' ability and capacity to carry what they thought they could sell. Abraham Modi of Mannington, West Virginia, gave the following account of his father's pack:

My father, Francis Abraham Modi, migrated to this country from Lebanon in 1899, coming to the little town of Mannington in the early oil excitement days. He began back peddling. . . . His pack consisted of dry goods, mostly cut yardage, and clothing, shirts, work clothing, socks, pants, and underwear. These he carried in one large pack weighing 200 or more pounds. The pack was supported by a strap which went over his shoulder, and although the strap was rather wide, it rubbed his shoulder enough to make a calloused place. The callous remained on his shoulder until his death, many years after he quit peddling on foot. In addition to the large back-pack, he carried a hand grip, which held combs, thread, needles, and all such notions that women and men would need, like shaving soap, straight razors, and just about all the non-toiletries the farm folks would need. The women would ask him for powder, combs, needles, thread, and such.[15]

Some peddlers added finer goods—linens, laces, and Madeira embroideries—from importers and manufacturers in the New York Syrian colony. As buggies, and later automobiles, came into common use by Syrians, peddlers began to add heavy Oriental rugs to their stock. In fact, the combination of rugs and fancy goods became a lucrative specialization for a considerable number of Syrians well before World War I.

Essentially, however, it was the women of a household that peddlers catered to. Aside from the practical sewing needs they carried in the notions case, there were cotton prints, gingham, voile, and muslin in varying lengths and widths, as well as decorative ribbons, threads and trimmings. In another corner of a suitcase were lures to ignite buyer's curiosity or vanity. There might be jewelry, perfumes, fancy scarves, picture frames, mirrors, and other bric-a-brac, many of them wrapped in the mystery of the Holy Land, as Elias L. explained: "She'd ask, 'Where are you from?' I'd say, 'Jerusalem.' We'd say that to get their sympathy. I'd say, 'We make Jerusalem fine comb to take the lice out.' We'd call it that so she would buy." For black Americans in rural Mississippi, they carried hair cream, some of it homemade.[16] Christian and Muslim Palestinians in Chicago peddled cloth pictures which they slung over their shoulders.[17] To people in the bars of Chicago and to immigrant Italian laborers living in the back rooms of a padrone's bar, according to Louis L., Syrians sold "holy pictures of saints."

Always, the best customers were the farmers' wives who visited town only infrequently and came to depend on the peddlers. They were welcomed, too, by housebound mothers and English-shy immigrant wives who lived in industrial and mining towns or in urban lower-class neighborhoods and who appreciated the convenience of having necessities brought to the door.

Peddlers carried hand-embroidered and crocheted linen tablecloths and covers, delicately tatted doilies and dress collars, lace-trimmed pillowcases and sheets, and ribboned dusting caps which some asserted were made in the old country. In fact, they were probably in most cases made in the peddlers' homes. It did not take long for Syrians to realize that the traditional craft at which their women were so adept could turn a handsome profit.

> All the women used to work at home making things for their men to sell. As a child, I used to help make pillowcases and embroidery, and make dusting caps with wide ribbon fringes and rickrack. If a woman came up with a crocheting or tatting pattern, she'd hide it so that other women wouldn't copy it. Mrs. Slayman N. had a particularly lovely one. My mother wanted it to make for a good customer. She asked the other ladies around the town; no one knew it. One day she saw it at one of her customer's house so she borrowed it and showed it around town so all the ladies got the pattern. They crocheted wide yokes for nightgowns and slips and borders for slips and skirts. The wider the better.[18]

Some suppliers as well as importers in New York and Chicago bypassed European exporters and manufacturers and contracted with their relatives in Syrian villages for laces and embroideries. Zbayda M. worked in her mother's cottage industry before coming to the United States in 1905: "My uncle used to peddle linens in Chicago. His sister, my mother, in Zahle would send him, every two weeks, a box of crocheted and tatted linens. Many girls worked for her; they'd be paid fifteen or twenty cents making doilies and tablecloths, imitating Italian cloths which sold for five hundred and a thousand dollars. Many families did this for their relatives in the United States. It was a real trade. Mr. B. had most of Zahle working and supplying his huge store, sending money to pay for workers, like my uncle did. My father used to go to Beirut and Damascus to buy spools of thread."[19]

Few customers could distinguish between handmade and machine-made or between domestic and imported products; often the inexperienced peddlers themselves didn't know. Before the turn of the century, Syrian shops in New York were producing rosaries and beads that were sold as "imports." As the market for the prestigious goods grew and the technology advanced to imitate handmade European imports, Syrian establishments in New York and other eastern cities came to dominate the industry.[20] Nevertheless, the demand for imported merchandise never slackened as Syrian importers met the demand. Peddlers who specialized in this merchandise would appear at their customers' doors dressed in serge suits and shined shoes befitting a "salesman with a better-class clientele."

Nazha H., who made the transition from dry goods to Oriental rugs and imported linens with her husband, talked about this trade. After her husband's death in 1937, she continued in the business for almost forty years when age and arthritis forced her to retire:

> Many peddlers started selling linens and rugs or maybe they just carried linens several years before World War I. They were supplied by importers in New York who specialized in importing goods to supply peddlers. These houses would send salesmen from New York to Syrian communities. They would bring their trunks full of goods and the peddlers who were by then calling themselves "traveling salesmen" would buy their stock on consignment. The importing house would give credit up to $2,500.
>
> They would go in cars or at first in a horse and buggy, to where the rich people were—in summer resorts and rich neighborhoods—and build up a clientele. One would ask a customer and that customer would call her relatives and friends and send the peddler over. She would act as his reference and he would then be trusted. Then he might call back on his customers once a week or so. Those who sold rugs would sometimes do the cleaning and repairing. Either they would do them themselves or would take them to a cleaning place. I repaired rugs for my husband for years. How do you

think my fingers got so bent [with arthritis]. It was hard work.
We didn't have children, so I went along to help. I met his
customers and would call on them. . . .

The importers [in New York] had agents they would buy
from in Italy, China, France, etc. They got laces from France,
Madeiras from there and from Brussels. . . . They got the cut-
work from Italy. Listen, the Syrians had people make goods
for them in China and the Philippines. No, they didn't have
factories, they would pay people to make laces and embroi-
dery in their houses—a cottage industry—and were paid by
the Syrians.

Of course, selling linens and laces and rugs took a lot more
capital, but the wholesalers sold on consignment. That
helped. They began changing from dry goods to linens and
laces and rugs before World War I and there were several, but
most went into it after the war; some during the war; we
started in 1916.

Joe D. had found peddling dry goods in Brazil beneath his
dignity so, on arriving in Fort Wayne in 1911, he went directly into the linen and rug trade, buying from his brother-
in-law who was purchasing from New York importers. He
sold them to "the well-to-do," not

> like the items sold by the "kashshashi" to farmers. These items
> were very expensive, imported from Italy and China and
> Puerto Rico. I sold to professional people in the twin cities
> [Minnesota]. My customers would refer me to their friends
> and relatives. I'd sell in the north country in the summers and
> in Arizona and Texas, New Mexico, Kansas, Missouri, and
> Oklahoma in the winters. I reached as far as British Colum-
> bia, Edmonton, Alberta, and five hundred miles beyond. In
> the summer, I'd go back to Minneapolis and to North and
> South Dakota and to Colorado, and I made good money. I
> traveled by myself at first in a horse and buggy and then after
> 1919 I traveled in my Buick. I got back to Fort Wayne every
> six or seven months.

When Syrian peddlers were still green in the ways of
America, resupplying forced them to return periodically to
the settlement and their suppliers. There, a peddler might
pay his debt and resupply on credit; he might leave surplus

cash with the supplier for safekeeping and, after resting, set out again. Once he learned about parcel post and rail transport, a long distance peddler could rely on his own supplier and on purchasing on credit. "On Saturday night," explained Essa L., "we'd go to where we had arranged to have goods sent to us. On Saturdays, we'd take stock to see what we were short of or needed and we'd write to Salem and tell him where we would be next Saturday and he would have them there at the depot. It would be a big box and each of us would take what we ordered right there in the depot." A few, at times, wired wholesalers in New York. On a number of occasions, peddlers found it expedient to supplement their stock from local town merchants.

Peddlers and town merchants were natural adversaries. The peddler carried goods directly to the doors of his customers, infringing on what the petty capitalists on America's Main streets viewed as their domain. An old animus toward peddlers was reawakened by the influx of the Syrian peddlers and in retaliation, merchants in many towns demanded that license fees, instituted against the Yankee and the German Jewish peddlers of an earlier day, be raised and enforced against their new economic "menaces,"[21] while towns without peddling licenses fees began to enact them. Consequently, a few Syrians spent a night in jail and not a few were fined and escorted out of town. Most, however, had learned to avoid such indignities and the fines, as well as the fees. "I was stopped in a couple of places because I didn't have a license. In Peking, Illinois, I was fined $14.18 and put in jail for a night. I didn't buy licenses. Who could buy a license in every town—six or seven dollars a day? Police told me many times that I needed a license, but I would peddle on the outskirts of town—out of the town. The license was more than we earned some days and businessmen kept it high. . . . One of the [town] councilmen's wives called the police on me once."[22]

Everything about the Syrian peddlers, from their appearance to their accent, should have precluded relations with small-town and backcountry Americans—even with urban dwellers who at the turn of the century maintained a semirural mentality. Yet, with unshakable faith in themselves, the Syrians continued to knock on the doors of these stalwart Americans and were accepted far more frequently than they were turned away. Their introduction was "Buy sumthin', Maam," or some variation of it. Here is a wily introduction reportedly used by some women in the middle western states:

Buy sumthin', ya [Oh] Laydee wil [and the] husban' dead
Six chil'ren, ya Laydee, oo mafish [and there is no] bread
Buy sumthin', ya Laydee, bleeze [please].[23]

Syrians were proud of their trading skills. "We are natural tradesmen," they insist, and by a logic peculiarly their own, they will further claim to have descended from the ancient Phoenicians and are the natural heirs to that venerable trading tradition. From their open suitcases at a customer's doorstep, they would suspend item after item before a housewife's eyes to invite at least a cursory examination, and would persist until a sale was made. Yet, in the times and milieu in which they operated, they did not have to sell very hard. More often than not, housewives were, if not always eager to buy, willing to make some small purchase.

Syrians capitalized on the natural advantage of their women and children who lacked neither courage, tenacity, nor resourcefulness and who were willing participants in the family venture. "Lots of people would feel sorry for me because I was so young," said Essa S., "and the women would usually find some little thing to buy." He sold rosaries to French-Canadian customers in New Hampshire, and, on Saturdays when laborers were paid, he would "be there when they got out of work;" he would peddle from six to ten in the evening. Saida Rashid liked to relate her favorite childhood peddling experience to her grandchildren and as late as 1962 she told it to Chester Morrison of *Look Magazine*: "We were peddling, my mother and I. She was working one side of the street, and I was working the other, and the policeman came and wanted to see my peddler's license, which I did not have because I was too young. I could not tell him my mother was on the other side of the street. . . . and when the policeman said I would have to go to jail, I picked up a handful of sand and threw it in his eyes, and while he was blinded, I ran to the freight yard, and my mother came pretty soon, and we went away from there."[24] Elizabeth B. was almost ten in 1892 when she encountered the following experience:

My father hadn't intended to stay. . . . They didn't send me to school but I picked up English very quickly because I was young. He would take me out peddling with him. He was not young and would be turned away at night when he was looking for a place to sleep; but when the farmers would see me, a little girl, they would feel sorry for me and let us in. . . .

They [her parents] gave me a small kashshi with icons, crosses, and pictures. Once, I went not too far from home. I knocked at the door of two ladies. They looked at me. I was a small girl, and one of them said to the other, "Look at that pretty girl. I'll bet if she had a nice dress on she'd look nice." So they gave me lunch and I was getting anxious. I didn't want to be held up. I wanted to sell. Then they brought a pretty dress and a little sailor hat and dressed me in them. I only half understood what they were saying. I had to wait while they altered it to fit me—about two or three hours. I looked like a million dollars, but I was seething inside but couldn't say anything. They said, "You must always wear these" . . . and let me go. I went directly home and changed back into my own clothes because we were told that if we looked well-dressed, they wouldn't let you in to sell. I went back to finish selling on my street and they saw me. . . . They called me. I was mortified. I said "A man stopped me and hit me like this and took my clothes. They were shocked. . . . They took me to him [a Syrian who spoke English] so they could know where the clothes were. I explained to him in Arabic and he reprimanded me for my stupidity. He told them that I was saving them for church on Sunday and didn't understand what they were saying to me. But that did not satisfy them. They took me home and made me put the good dress on.

When my parents got home I told them what happened. We used to exchange stories in the evenings about what happened to us during the day. We used to have such fun.

Women were, by far, the most valuable economic asset to the trade. They were, if not superior, at least the equal of men in salesmanship: "These women, well they'd go to the small cities and go from one house to another—just got off the bus and start out, one street after another . . . and they'd put their grips down at the door and the only thing they could say was 'Buy sumthin', ya Laydee' . . . so these ladies would naturally . . . buy a pair of stockings for a dime and maybe two spools of thread for a nickle and hairpins—well, you could get a carload for a dime."[25] "A woman elicits more sympathy than a man and makes more money," admitted Charles R. "This brought many women to the United States. Some left their children back home . . . and would return to Lebanon with $1,000 or $1,500."[26] In addition, they could more easily gain access into homes than men, as Houghton rightly observed,[27] and were more trusted by their customers, thus developing lasting clienteles which, in many cases, grew into friendships. On these strengths, at least one supplier focused on women, supplying thirty or forty with the finer white goods.[28] Of their contribution to Syrian trade, Salloum Mokarzel, looking back at the history of peddling in America, wrote in 1929:

> They played a large role in increasing Syrian trade and drew attention of wholesalers to many new items. It was the woman who was the cause of their adding new items. They brought items to their attention they never dreamed of in the interior and in New York. They brought in much revenue and in the interior the woman was the greatest help to the men in their advancement and diversification also. Trade in women's apparel and bed linens became big items with the Syrian traders due to women peddlers, for when they knocked on a door, housewives would request items of clothing and bed linens and when peddlers settled down to open stores, these items were their mainstays.[29]

More than a quarter of a century earlier, an article in *Al-Hoda*, reflecting the reality of women's participation in the Syrian family's economic goals in America, concluded that peddling was compatible with women's personal honor as well as their family honor.[30]

There is no way to calculate how many women peddled nor the value of their contribution to the trade, either monetarily or in the general economic advancement of the Syrians in the United States. Nevertheless, two observations are reasonably safe. First, that perhaps 75 or 80 percent of the women peddled during the pioneer period. While most gladly gave up peddling to marry and raise a family, a surprising number continued well into the thirties and forties, long after most men had turned to other pursuits. Necessity held many to it; but so did habit, ambition, and the sense of independence it provided. Mayme F.'s mother, peddling from Vicksburg, Mississippi, was not unusual:

> My mother peddled when my father had the [supplier's] store. It was a controversy between them; he didn't want her to; he didn't like her independence. She wanted more for them. She worked hard; two or three days after my sisters were born, she would be up washing and not long after that she'd take her stuff and peddle. Once my father got mad and destroyed her satchel—in front of the other peddlers and the women who lived around there too. No, she wasn't disgraced. . . . She stopped it for a while and when she felt they needed more money, she would go. . . . But independence was a big thing in their lives. He didn't seem to want to make it for some reason and she felt like she had to.

Some who gave it up returned to it intermittently in times of economic crises, between pregnancies and even after the childbearing age. When, after the 1929 crash, Saida Rashid's husband, Jake, lost his wealth, rated by R. G. Dun and Company at over one million dollars, she went back to peddling with her husband, as did many others.[31]

Secondly, the economic participation of women, irrespective of religion or sect, contributed significantly to the general economic satisfaction of Syrian immigrants and thus the impetus to settle permanently. Relatively few families succeeded without the help of one or more women. The earnings of wives, mothers, daughters, and sisters, their sacrifices and labor, staved off poverty and failure in many cases and in many more cases enabled the family to improve and accelerate economic and social positions. Not only did they peddle, sew, and crochet, they also worked in textile mills and factories, took in paying boarders, and clerked in relatives' stores. Their collective earnings helped convey the impression of success enjoyed by Syrians during the peddling era and later. Because of them, more capital was accumulated, more small businesses started, more independence gained, more money sent to the homeland, and more fares remitted to bring relatives to the United States. Neither illiteracy nor the native attitude toward the protection of women seriously hindered them. Americans who deplored peddling by women as a form of begging, demeaning, or as "drudges of an idle husband who lived upon her hard earnings"[32] did not understand how deeply ingrained was the Syrian women's traditional dedication to the family and, in the majority of the cases, the willingness, if not the eagerness, with which they indefatigably shared the family's economic responsibilities. And, all the while, they did not shirk the homemaking roles assigned by society and expected by their men.

Many men, and sons in particular, accord their women the respect and praise they have earned. Too many, however, fearing that family honor would be sullied and their patriarchal position diminished, denied or devalued the contribution of women.

The business probity of the Syrian peddler was by no means ideal, but neither does it seem exceptional. Occasionally, it is true, he deluded inexperienced customers about the origins of certain merchandise and overrated their quality and price. Items purchased for ten or fifteen cents were frequently sold in the countryside for a dollar; lace bought for five cents a yard sold for fifteen; and holy pictures which cost ten cents went for seventy-five.[33] The margin of profit was all that the market would bear. But this was definitely in the capitalist tradition and morality of America. Not unlike the thousands of businessmen through whose towns he threaded his way, the peddler operated on the profit motive and the principle of supply and demand. Moreover, at the turn of the century, both Syrian and American petty capitalists were operating in a business milieu dominated by large powerful corporations who set their own standards of business morality.

In the Syrian immigrants' inner struggle between petty

cheating and the drive for quick gain, the latter usually prevailed. Syrians were shrewd; they were not generally corrupt. In her inquiries into the business activities of the Syrians in the United States, Mrs. Houghton concluded that "nothing, indeed, in the course of this inquiry has been more unexpected or more surprising than the almost universal testimony—including all except the few to the contrary. . . .—to the integrity and fair dealing of Syrian business men. Two or three notorious exceptions there have indeed been, the more notorious because so few. Several men and women have been convicted of smuggling, and the failure of one large Syrian business house has already been noted."[34]

Although in the earliest pioneer years, large and quick profits were the rule for all Syrian peddlers, in time, only long-distance peddlers held to it. Not as peripatetic, middle- and short-range peddlers developed regular clients. As they returned to their customers, filled special orders, sold on credit, and accepted payment in kind, they dared not seriously overcharge. They found more economic security in steady sales.

If the Syrian peddler seemed to operate by his own mores and standards, his faults could at times be redeemed by the color and novelty he brought into the routine lives of his customers. His curious appearance and mannerisms in themselves evoked questions whose answers both intrigued and amused the customers. Not the least amusing was the peddler's corrupted English. By no means did all Americans appreciate his intrusion into their daily routines, and many were openly hostile; yet on balance, Syrians were received with civility, kindness, and sympathy. Americans nursed them when they were ill, gave them money when they were robbed, and counseled them when they needed it.

In 1911, the Syrian peddler, by then a familiar figure on the American scene, captured the imagination of Lucille Baldwin Van Slyke, who portrayed him somewhat romantically and shrouded him in Eastern mystery. In her short story, a brief visit by a peddler shatters the boredom of a young New Hampshire farm maid. His quaint appearance, gentle courtesy, colorful accent, and "seductive" wares are contrasted sharply with weary Emily's routine tasks, her aunt's scoldings, and the farm's isolation. Emily has crossed her state line only once and is "getting awfully tired of it lately, seems as if I'm sick and tired of everything lately." She is tantalized by tidbits of life in the peddler's homeland where "the Bible eet ees jus' 'appened," by his gift of glass beads— "gaudy Oriental bits of color"—and by the cadences of his song about Antar, a romantic hero of ancient Arabia. "Emily found herself thinking not so much of the peddler as of the things he had said to her. She lived in a perpetual daydream; foreign lands for the first time in her life were not mere spots upon a map or something one read about in history books, but places wherein people moved and lived." The peddler departs as mysteriously as he had come, leaving her with a bit of his Eastern wisdom: "An' you, you haf a theeng to learn from me—thees do I know because of the sadness een your beeg, gray eyes. Thees ees the theeng you mus' learn, thad weesches ees not idle theengs, they ees send by Allah to save the heart."[35]

From her childhood on a farm in Minnesota, Alice E. Christgau remembered a "jolly, loveable peddler" who came often to the door and immortalized him in her children's book, *The Laugh Peddler*. In the following scene, an air of anticipation attends the approach of Yusuf Hanna to the small Miller farm in the sparsely populated Minnesota countryside:

> A figure had appeared over the rise where the big road joined their own little road. It plodded past the mailbox and came on toward the house. In another moment Sidney cried out, "I know who it is! It's the Laugh Peddler!"
>
> The faces in the kitchen suddenly brightened. . . . and Mama glancing hastily in the mirror, smoothed her hair.
>
> "I was just wondering if he wouldn't be around one of these days," she said. She shook up the stove and put in another stick of wood, . . . and filled the tea kettle.
>
> The figure was easily recognizable now. Only a foot peddler had that particular kind of hump on his back. It was made by a heavy pack strapped across his shoulders.
>
> . . . It was a suitcase, . . . filled with all sorts of things. . . .

This was his way of making a living, not an unusual one in the early 1900's when towns were small and the western half of the country sparsely settled. . . . The Farmers' Company Store in town, with its limited lines of merchandise, was the only shopping place most farm families had. Automobiles were not yet in common use, and trips to the city were not often made.

Yusuf Hanna is portrayed as a visitor who, initially distrusted by the farmer but beloved by the rest of the family, not only shatters the monotony of isolation with his wit and charm but is wise, friendly, and compassionate. He heroically saves the lives of two of the Miller children lost in a blizzard.[36] Such portrayals of the Syrian peddler confirm his ubiquitous presence in America and pay tribute to his services.

On foot, by buggy, long or short distances, peddling was a strenuous and often lonely and dangerous trade. Syrians harbored no illusions about the trade's long hours and physical strains; they came from a culture where hard work and patience were endemic, and the fear they would experience on the road had been a familiar road companion in Syria; thieves had still been terrorizing travelers at the turn of the century.[37] But, loneliness was something new for gregarious and group-oriented Syrians. Communication by means of a handful of strange words and constant travel left the distant peddlers feeling isolated. Their sole reference point in a land bereft of familiar cultural landmarks was the supplier's settlement.

Nothing really could have prepared them for the rigorous and strange life on the road. The problems and conditions they confronted could not have been anticipated by anything in their previous experience. For survival, they were thrown back on their own resourcefulness; survival exacted the utmost ingenuity.

Climate in its extreme forms—high and low temperatures and heavy rain and snowstorms—particularly when shelter was unavailable, was their most implacable foe. It is no accident that many recollections of informants about their experiences on the road were about weather and shelter. Even hardy mountaineers, accustomed to severe climes in the homeland, complained of the length and severity of midwestern and New England winters as well as their hot and humid summers. Winters left the deepest scars. "We didn't believe them until we saw them," some said. Elias L. cried, as undoubtedly many others did, because "there was so much mud and slush and cold." Buggy owners fared little better than foot peddlers.

Simple physical comforts were constantly pressing: hunger and cold, fatigue, a place to sleep; throats parched from the heat and dust of the road; blistered feet; wet clothes that clung, cold and clammy, to the skin (peddlers did not encumber their backs with many personal effects). They talked of icicles forming on mustaches;[38] of women's frozen long skirts slashing cold ankles;[39] of men, forced to sleep in their buggies, who froze to death;[40] of buggies and feet mired in mud. "Snow in those days was heavy and we'd walked fifteen to twenty miles a day in rubber boots," recalled Matt I. "One day the temperature was 41 below zero," began Frank A., "it was so cold no one would let me in. It was too cold for people to open their doors, so I didn't get into any house. . . . I couldn't feel the cold any more. I finally got a room and when I washed, my nose came off in my hands. For three years my nose was like a plum in my face." Perseverance and determination, though not always borne stoically, took its physical and emotional toll.

Sleep and the weather were companion problems. If the weather was tolerable, many slept in the open; when they did, it was often necessary to conceal themselves from stray animals and thieves, not always successfully, in bushes or under items from their packs.[41] If they were in or near a town where such facilities were available, they slept in a hotel or boardinghouse. But on the country roads, they sought lodging in farmhouses or slept outdoors. From farmhouse to farmhouse, often miles apart, they knocked on doors, made the sleep gesture, and prayed openly to be let in. Farmers were frequently sympathetic, but as frequently the peddlers were turned away by a suspicious few who carried guns and by the insensitive barking of dogs. Sometimes they were repelled for their unkempt appearance, having had to go unwashed and unshaven for a week or more; sometimes for the odors and parasites they carried from their last barn bedding. One late night in Minnesota, Elias L. knocked on a door and asked desperately for lodging. The housewife asked him to wait and brought out "a bottle with lice in it," he recounted more than a half century later in his much-improved English: "They were ugly. 'These are lice from Jerusalem,' she said. 'Are there many more of these in Jerusalem?' 'Look here, Maam,' I said, 'I'm played out. You keep me, I gif you fife dollah. You find lice tomorrow, fife dollah clean you bed. If no, you do me good deed and you haf fife dollah.' Next mornin', no lice."

Sundown each day became the signal for anxiety. Would he eat, if at all? Where would he sleep? A peddler's eyes searched the countryside, as he trudged along, for haystacks, barns, empty schoolhouses, or any enclosure that could serve as shelter. When discovered in haystacks and barns, it was usually by an angry farmer. On the road during one of his peddling trips, Faris N. took charge of a fellow villager's wife. She was forty-five years old and he was twenty. "One night," he wrote,

> when I asked for sleep and I said she was my wife, they would not believe me, and if I said my sister, they wouldn't believe me. We continued thus, asking for sleep. When they would see her, they would not give us accommodations. We continued walking until we reached a small town. There was in it not a hall nor a boardinghouse. We had left the town about one mile when I saw, on the side of the road, a small building. I jumped the fence. . . . it had windows and a round door which was closed. I opened my kashshi and I used a scissors, No. 9, and I put it under the frame of the window and it opened and we entered. We saw two cases in which they put the coffins. I told her that this room had two beds, one for her and one for me. From our fatigue and the darkness, we did not see the graves. . . . Then the moon came out. The woman looked outside and cried out. . . . "We are sleeping in a mausoleum and the dead are beneath us in the boxes." And she leaped out of the shed and I after her. We left and began walking for about two miles until we found a schoolhouse and we slept there until morning.[42]

There were also indignities to be suffered. When George A.'s father was nearly frozen and unable to find shelter in a farmhouse, he cuddled next to a pig in the barn for warmth. Tom C. cursed the fate that made him sleep next to a dog on a farmer's cold hearth. To Arabs, a dog is equivalent to a swine in the estimation of Germans.[43]

At nightfall, they dreamed of a hot meal or, in many cases, any meal. During the day, they purchased whatever was available at farmhouses or snacked on whatever they carried in their pack. Yearning for fresh fruits and vegetables, which in their country were available almost year round, they did not shrink from picking them—uninvited—from orchards and gardens. They yearned, too, for Syrian dishes. They were critical of what they called "American" food but rarely refused it when offered at an evening meal by kind farmers. If it was not offered, peddlers often slept hungry.

Fear—the farther they ventured, the more there was to fear. Prudence, therefore, dictated that they travel with companions. Generally, a small group left the settlement together, peddled in different directions, and met at a designated place and time, perhaps at the end of the day, more often at the end of a week or more. A railroad depot was a likely meeting place, especially if they were expecting supplies. Elias L. explained: "Farhat Zghayb—he was our 'boss'—would look for a boardinghouse for us at the end of a week and collect us together and take us there. . . . We'd start out with Farhat. We'd walk together to the train station and each would go to a different place to sell and, at times, we'd arrange to meet each other—one or two or three of us—and we'd spend the night together; sometimes one of us would spend the night alone." At the end of the tour some of them occasionally returned to the settlement together.

Although companions separated, there was some comfort, if not always security, in knowing that a friend was aware of one's general location and direction in case of accident, illness, or worse. Lives were saved in this way, but the arrangement was not foolproof; lives were lost—it is not known how many.

Peddlers were most vulnerable on empty roads at night, where animals would attack and nervous farmers would shoot first and ask questions later. With the exception of one who had been robbed several times, no peddlers reported carrying guns. Robbers regularly ambushed them, however, stripped them of their money and goods, and left them injured on the side of the road. People thought "peddlers carried much money, which often wasn't the case," wrote Arthur C. Pritchard, "and being foreigners it was thought they would be easy victims. This wasn't always true. . . . Once when peddling, he [Gabriel Nassif] was attacked by two men; Gabriel backed up against a nearby building, flexed his muscles, and dared the hoodlums to come get him. . . . The two backed off and left him alone. But many peddlers were not that fortunate; a number were robbed and several murdered. Mrs. Joe Francis says four or five of her fellow Lebanese peddlers from Mannington were killed."[44] Some men vanished without a trace.[45] Elias L. was among the more fortunate. Having outwitted his attackers in Minnesota, he "climbed a tree, strapped myself so I wouldn't fall and slept till morning. . . . We missed many from Rashayya." Four were his friends.

Once, Elias separated from his companions for a week to nurse his brother whom he finally sent back to Rashayya via Fort Wayne with Salem Bashara's assistance. "We get so tired that we couldn't walk any more," he explained, "or there'd be mud and puddles and rain, and suffering. Leave [the explanation for] it to God! How we suffered! Then," he continued,

> I got sick and I was alone. . . . I didn't know what my sickness was—fatigue, depression, neglecting our health—who knows? Many of us experienced illness and depression.
>
> Finally I left the room and started out and could go no further. I just dropped on the grass, put my suitcase under my head, clasped my kashshi and fell asleep. God sent me an old German couple who found me. He shook me with his boot and I didn't respond. Finally, I did but I couldn't say anything. So he carried me to his home and I stayed there for fifteen

days. The old lady washed my feet. I told them I was from Jerusalem and they were very compassionate towards me.

When I was cured, the old man gave me a horse and buggy and said it was a shame for a young man like me to kill myself peddling. 'When you make some money, you can send me what they're worth.' In those days it was twenty-five dollars. He was a wealthy farmer. I paid him back. I like Germans very much.

His companions had written him from South Dakota and he caught up with them there. Together they returned to Fort Wayne.

Broken English may not have deterred sales, but it complicated the peddlers' lives. "How do you stop a dog who is chasing you if you can't talk to it in English?" snapped Qisma M.[46] How does one order a chicken or liver or eggs if one didn't know the English words? Communication by charade was not always effective. How does the peddler explain to a generous farmer that he is forbidden, by his religion, to eat pork and make clear that he is not Jewish but Muslim; or that chicken not slaughtered properly is abhorrent? What does it matter if one conveys the question but cannot understand the answer? "Boo, boo, boo, time?" asked Wedad F.'s aunt at a railroad depot. "Ten till two," answered the stationmaster. She missed the train that passed through town once a day and later explained her delay to her family. "Two? Two? Two, I understand, but what is this 'tentil?'"[47]

Because Faris N. could not understand the conditions under which he was offered a ride in a cattle wagon, he was taken miles out of his way. Only when he was commanded to tend the animals and threatened did he realize what had happened to him. Angrily, he parted from the rancher and trudged the many miles back to his destination.[48] The absence of the p sound in Arabic was the cause of a day's frustration to a young novice who wandered, a small box of merchandise in hand, into a smallpox epidemic. At each door, he was warned to "go away, smallpox." Angry at not having made a single sale, he returned to complain to his brother: "Why did you give me such a small box? No one would buy from me. Everyone said to me "go away, small box, small box."[49]

English expressions were perceived in Arabic. "I'm sorry" was understood as *masari* (money); on hearing "I'm busy" from her customer, a peddler squatted until rescued minutes later from that position by her partner. *Qanbzi* or *ambzi* is the feminine imperative of the colloquial word meaning "to squat."

Words borrowed from English, because no equivalent existed in Arabic, were Arabacized. An Arabic-English patois became as common and natural as Arabic until the difference ceased to be discerned. "I parked the car" became "barrakkt al-car"; similarly, "we signed the paper" became "sayyanna al-baber"; and "I cleaned the house" was "callannt al-bayt." A deceased man's wife "tammarrat" when she died of a tumor (she "tumored"). An informant, speaking Arabic, told of the difficulties of proving the land they had homesteaded in South Dakota. "Barraffna al-ard [We proved the land]," she remarked, and when asked to explain, she said, "you know, fakkassnāha [we fixed it]," thinking she had chosen a clearer Arabic word. No words or idioms that had not already been put there by centuries of interaction between East and West passed the other way.[50]

For almost a decade, beginning before World War I, an itinerant priest recorded and annotated the linguistic twistings and distortions of his immigrant parishioners in several American states and eastern Canadian provinces. After he settled to become the pastor of a church, he continued to travel and record.

On the road, Syrians possessed natural and decisive advantages to satisfy their eagerness to learn English. The lessons they learned were primarily empirical—by trial and error and by constant interaction with Americans and American society. "I taught myself English by association," said Matt I. Others wrote down words from memorization: "I knew not a word of English," confessed Slayman N. "We'd go from house to house to peddle and . . . if someone said an English word, I wrote it in Arabic. In about a week, I began to catch on a little."[51] Customers, at their doors or in their homes,

corrected the peddlers' English and taught them new words.
Faris N. recounts an early lesson:

> On the fourth day [of his peddling], in the early evening, I
> asked for a place to sleep from a farmer—the first, and the
> second, and the third finally accepted me. After we had sup-
> per, we sat in the sitting room and the man began to ask me
> the first question. "How long have you been in this country?"
> I did not understand. I answered "Yes sir." He said "How long
> have you been in this country" again. I understood and an-
> swered "two weeks." He asked "Do you have parents?" I an-
> swered in English "fife," that is, five. He and his wife laughed.
> He had two children, a boy and a girl. He brought his son
> before me and said "this is my boy and I am his father and
> this is his mother," repeating the words for mother, father,
> father, mother. "Do you understand?" he asked. I understood
> and answered. When I had answered "five" I had thought he
> asked me how many sisters and brothers I had. When he
> asked "How old are you?" I thought he wanted to know about
> my religion and I answered Rūm Orthodox. He and his wife
> laughed. He brought the boy again and said "Look, he is
> seven years old; the girl is nine years old." He repeated "boy."
> I understood and answered him correctly. We continued to
> move from farmer to farmer for a period of three months.
> We returned to Ft. Wayne to change clothes and wash our
> bodies and then went out again . . . and after three months
> had passed I learned to speak a little English. I thought my-
> self to be a professor in English.[52]

As they increased their vocabularies in the "school of the
road," their knowledge of their environments was broadened. Indeed, few immigrant groups from remote cultures
had had the opportunity to learn so much about America—
the diversity of its regional customs and tastes—and on few
immigrant groups did the American culture have the opportunity to superimpose itself so directly and immediately.

While on the road, peddlers rarely spent their weekends
with farmers. Rather, they anxiously joined companions and
rented rooms in town boardinghouses or hotels on Saturday
evenings—usually for about $1.25 or $1.50 for two nights.
Some places gave "a special rate for peddlers. We'd wash our
clothes and bathe, and we'd sneak into the bathroom when

they charged extra. Sometimes we didn't bathe when the hotel didn't have a bathroom. We'd sleep two in a bed. . . . We'd talk about how much we made or how far we walked or the difficulties of finding sleep."[53] They preferred towns that had fifteen to twenty-five thousand people, according to Mike H., because "in a large city, we'd be afraid to get lost in it and wouldn't know how to cope, and in smaller towns also we wouldn't often find the kind of boardinghouse. . . . small boardinghouses that slept seven or eight and had livery barns for horses. We'd seek these out."

One weekend, Mike's group met up with another in Winona, Minnesota: "Well, they stayed in one hotel and we stayed in another and we wanted to invite them over. So we had some corn for the horses which we got on Friday from a farm and we were going to stay until Monday. So what did we do? We got a wash pan from the landlady and boiled the corn and ate it and not one of us could go to work on Monday [from indigestion]. . . . We spent some [crazy] days in those days."

On Saturday night or Sunday afternoon, they might walk downtown, window-shop, compare prices of goods with their own, perhaps even purchase secondhand clothes, as well as food to eat in their rooms. One or two might at times try their hands at pool or attend a "moving picture." Since Eastern rite churches were rare anywhere in the country, they might attend the local "American" churches—Maronites and Melkites at Roman Catholic and Orthodox at Episcopalian or Protestant. One of them might even consider eventually settling down in the town.

They observed and were observed by the townfolk. In Urbana, Illinois, a religious group invited Faris N. and his companions to participate in a local event. The peddlers had become

> acquainted with the farmers whose every relationship was based on the belief in Jesus Christ as related in the Bible. "Believe in Jesus Christ!" [they preached]. One would even see them refusing a doctor. . . .
>
> In 1903, they celebrated the seventy-fifth anniversary of the

town of Urbana. . . . Our whole group joined them and there came to us the elders of the community and asked us if we would join them, their object being to know if we knew anything of the ancient past and to perform it for them. So, we asked them for a wagon drawn by four horses.

The peddlers emulated their native dress from items in their cases and, being artisans by trade, each demonstrated his craft on the back of the wagon as it moved in the parade. "And your eyes would be amazed to see us in the parade. . . . We spent a night to remember."[54]

On the road, their weekend pleasures, dictated as much by their ignorance of American ways as by traditional values, were simple, innocent, and above all cheap. Every expenditure, carefully measured and weighed against the peddlers' objective, was restricted to the barest necessities. Continence and temperance appeared to be the rule; both undoubtedly further restrained by the Puritan morality of small-town America, as well as by the immigrants' fear of "getting into trouble." Muslims and Druze were Koranically restricted from drinking liquor. For Syrian Christians, on the other hand, liquor was traditionally served and consumed with food and shared with friends, and on occasion that tradition was reenacted in hotel rooms.

The Syrian immigrants' frugality was legendary. Forged in the villages, it was accentuated in the early years by the immigrants' fixation on accumulating quick wealth and furthered by the realization that savings promised a better future in America. Even deciding on permanent settlement in the new land was no reason to relax their frugality; rather, rising aspirations hardened their resolve to earn and save. That painfully accumulated money was not to be dissipated aimlessly became the creed—the way of life—of the first generation.

Hitti noted that trait: "It is the consensus of opinion among those who know them," he wrote, "that the Syrians are a thrifty people. This characteristic was in some form or another noted by every social worker or Americanization secretary who was asked about his knowledge of the race."[55]

Houghton arrived at a similar conclusion during her inquiries into the economic characteristics of Syrians. "The frugality and the temperance of Syrian wage earners," she learned, "enabled them to accumulate money."[56]

The pioneers remembered their sparing ways. Mike H. recalled that when he came back in 1907, he "passed by Sioux City, Iowa, and all the Arabs lived in poor houses; if you stepped on a floorboard, it would come up and hit you on the head. It wasn't that they didn't have money; they had it, but didn't like to spend it."

On the road, transportation costs for the foot peddlers were kept negligible; trains and trolleys were resorted to sparingly. To save the five-cent trolley fare they would walk five or six miles to their destinations.[57] They ate fifteen-cent meals and paid for farmhouse lodging in merchandise. Three yards of toweling, for example, cost Essa S. ten cents. Once he had purchased a secondhand pair of rubbers for ten cents and, he continued, "I lost one, but I had a union suit and one rubber and I was happy."

The hardships and sacrifices may have depressed a few peddlers some of the time, but it did not discourage most of them. "We endured a lot," reflected Matt I., "mostly from the cold and finding places to sleep, but with all that, I enjoyed this country because I was making money." Many complained; the impatient and disillusioned complained bitterly, but the percentage of those who ultimately traded the hardships of America for the prospects of a future in the Syrian village was small. As Mary M. said, "A man could live, save money, and send some home on nine or ten dollars a week in the United States. They could even raise a family." The consensus was that whatever they earned in America was better than the ten cents a day for the same long hours and hard work in Mount Lebanon or Syria.[58]

Syrians certainly felt no virtue in poverty, but they were generally a driven people. Quintessentially, it was a matter of honor to succeed in America. That was their strength. Their rigorous habits—hard work, thrift, self-denial—alleviated despair and spared them entrapment at the bottom of the American economy.

The rewards they reaped by those habits were tangible. Matt I. said: "I made $5 a day the first week and it improved week by week. Some weeks I could make $40 to $50 from which I could save. I had borrowed $100 to come here and in three months I sent my mother $110 to pay off my debt. I also paid off the debt for the merchandise I had bought to sell and still had $30 to $40 in cash." Afif Tannous, in a study published in 1943, quoted an old woman in Vicksburg, Mississippi, who told him: "For 35 years I have been living in this town; and the first thing I did after arriving here was to peddle. Yes, I carried a heavy pack on my back and roamed the countryside. . . . It was hard and tiring work indeed, but I had much money. . . . people used to pay much for our goods, and there were no stores as we have today. Believe me, during the first Christmas season I made $500."[59]

They took enormous pride in their ability to earn and save. Dr. Michael A. Shadid, founder of America's first cooperative hospital, arrived in 1898 at the age of eighteen to continue his medical education. But, he wrote in his autobiography, "first came money-making." He peddled: "I covered all the towns around New York and went farther away, stopping at cheap boarding houses, selling my trinkets in one village after another. . . . The profits were very large on these cheap imported pieces and my earnings grew rapidly. . . . At the end of two years in America I was able to repay the loan Uncle Gabriel had made for our passage, to send a thousand dollars to my mother and brother for their trip to this country, and in addition, I had savings of two thousand dollars in the keeping of my New York cousins. It was not only successful selling but also the most frugal living that built up my funds so quickly."[60]

Tom Bashara's small settlement in Cedar Rapids aroused the incredulity of that town's bankers and press when in 1901, about five years after it was established, its people

purchased exchange for $12,000 which they sent to their native land. . . . This crowd of about fifty foreigners, huddled together in a few buildings . . . , has certainly accomplished the feat of heaping up this large amount of wealth with no

capital on which to begin unless it be a few pennies with which
to purchase a small "pack" stock. Of the $12,000 accumulated
$5,000 apparently belonged to one man, as exchange for that
amount was given to him.

To the many young Americans who are struggling along to
make a respectable living such an announcement raises in
their minds the queries, How do they earn their money; how
do they live, and why do they send it over the briny deep to
that Asiatic country from which they emigrated?[61]

Weekly profits, according to testimonies, averaged from
$30 to $50. Houghton calculated a lower annual range of
$200 to $1,500. "As for the higher class of peddlers . . . their
profits must be, and they are admitted to be, large."[62]

Some measure of the peddlers' earnings could be gained
from the remittances sent to the homeland. Hitti noted that
"according to certain claims, the Syrians send, per capita,
more money home than almost any other immigrant
group."[63] The Board of Foreign Missions of the Presbyterian
Church reported in 1891 that "an unlettered man goes to
America and in the course of six months sends back a check
for $300 to $400 more than the salary of a teacher or a
preacher for more than two years. For months past the
money coming to Zahleh from America has averaged from
$400 to $500 daily. Nearly all this goes to pay old debts, to
lift mortgages, and to carry other emigrants across the
seas."[64]

A closer approximation of peddlers' earnings would also
have to take into account fares paid to visit the home village
and to import family members to the United States as well as
the returns from the pervasive practice of barter. Few kept
records, except perhaps for monies owed to or held in safekeeping by the supplier; and these usually on fugitive slips
of paper and disposable pocket notebooks.

Peddlers tended to trade and bargain as their daily business required, with an emphasis on the immediate. Calculations were fairly straightforward and simple and required no
pen or paper: sales, minus cost, equaled profit.

Bartering transactions were almost always profitable: ten
cents worth of toweling or fifteen cents worth of calico pur-

chased a night's lodging and a meal; a dusting cap or a crocheted lace collar bought a chicken and several dozens of
eggs. Through barter, peddlers' families were well provi-
sioned. From late summer until late fall, wives and daughters
preserved the pecks and bushels of bartered fruits and vegetables brought home in addition to their own garden yield.
Not all bartered food was preserved or consumed. Men with
rigs and later automobiles filled them with crates of eggs and
other farm products and sold them in nearby towns, significantly compounding their profits. They counted the cash at
the end of the week and praised Allah. Never mind that they
did not or could not keep records.

It was difficult enough for many to keep economic records
in Arabic, a script which most either did not know or had not
mastered. It was near impossible if one could neither understand nor pronounce what one had heard in unfamiliar English accents. Budelia M.'s mother took orders from her customers, but, said Budelia, who likes to tell this story, "Mother
didn't know the difference between pearl and ivory buttons.
One day she asked me to buy her . . . two cards of 'billow
buttnes.' I'd say, 'Mother, what's that?' She'd say, 'how do I
know. This is what was ordered. Just ask for it at Nick's store.
They'll know.'" They didn't, and the next day her mother
went herself and found what her customer wanted: they
were pearl buttons.

Even more puzzling were customers' names, particularly
when customers were, like themselves, immigrants. One day,
according to Victoria A., her mother "contemplated life and
death" because she "didn't even know the names of her customers to whom she gave credit. She peddled to German
people and tried to translate their names into Arabic."[65] Others solved the problem by identifying customers by some
prominent characteristics. They, therefore, referred to "the
lady with the green door," or "the lady of the flies," or "she
of the checkered table cloth."[66] Orders were taken and delivered and credit extended on the basis of such identifications.

The larger surpluses of cash and additional opportunities
to amass them differentiated the experience of the Syrian
peddler from that of the Syrian wage earner. Although the

latter were no less frugal and self-denying, the wage earner,
under the same felt obligation to accumulate money, labored
under greater disadvantages. Like peddlers, they lived in
crowded and cold rooms, walked miles to their jobs to save
trolley fares, and zealously watched every cent. However,
before 1914 and the Ford Motor Company's inauguration
of the five-dollar-a-day, eight-hours-a-day wage, industrial
wages fluctuated from year to year, even from month to
month, and varied from skill to skill, industry to industry and
city to city. The weekly industrial wage around the turn of
the century averaged between seven and fifteen dollars a
week. Immigrants earned at the lower end of the scale and
were subject to layoffs and extended periods of unemployment. Nevertheless, many Syrian wage earners in America,
with similar ambitions as peddlers, managed to set aside
some capital. Charles T. said he earned four or five dollars a
week in a jewelry factory and lived within his income on fifty
cents a day until he became a self-employed carpenter. Essa
S. was able to save two dollars from a weekly salary of $3.55,
but like many other wage earners, he left his factory job to
peddle.

On average, however, the upward mobility of Syrian wage
earners was slow, more measured, and less experimental
than that of peddlers, who with more opportunity to accumulate capital and understand America, were motivated to
move upward. Those who reached out and up before they
were ready, sometimes fell back into peddling. It was their
cushion—their security—against abject failure and humiliation. Qisma M.'s experience was not uncommon. He arrived
in 1902 and at first he "carried a heavy load and walked in
bitter cold and snow." Then he bought a rig and accumulated
some capital which he invested in a movie house in 1910. He
hired employees to operate it, brought in singers and danc-
ers, charged five cents, and gave away ice-cream cones. His
business failed; so he sold it, returned to peddling, and accumulated more capital. He then opened a small factory
which manufactured overalls. When that failed, he peddled
again and then opened a dry goods store. He too risked and
experimented but, he said, "I never borrowed money. I al-

ways saved money from peddling to start again and I continued like this until 1935. Trade is success or failure. . . . I had
nothing to lose in it—no wages to be stolen. I was my own
boss."

If figures were available, they would undoubtedly show
that the Syrian peddling trade mushroomed into a multimillion-dollar business between 1880 and 1914. Document-
ing that opinion is impossible, but a few calculations, using
minimal figures and focusing on the pack-peddling trade
(excluding suppliers, wholesalers, manufacturers, and other
related enterprises) and on the first decade of the twentieth
century, make the point and indicate the contribution of the
Syrian peddling trade to the American economy.

Leaving aside the thousands who had arrived between
1880 and 1899, one might assume, for example, that if only
30,000 of the almost 57,000 Syrians who are reported to
have immigrated between 1899 and 1910, peddled, and they
netted a daily average of $5, the total daily earnings would
be $150,000. Further, allowing for illnesses, Sundays, holi-
days and other rest days, as well as visits to the homeland,
and assuming that a peddler averaged only 200 work days
annually, the collective annual earnings would at least total
$30 million at a minimum. And, if the profit margin was only
100 percent, total gross sales would amount to $60 million.
This is not an inconsiderable contribution to the United
States' gross national product for so small an immigrant
group. Doubling the totals is probably closer to the reality.

During the period 1899 to 1910, the United States' gross
national product, in current dollars, rose from 17.4 to 35.4
billion dollars, averaging an increase of 1.6 billion dollars annually. The American population swelled from 76,212,108 in
1900 to 92,228,496 in 1910. At the same time, the per capita
annual income rose from $233 to $382 in 1910.[67]

Finally, if a peddler worked 200 days and earned an average of $5 a day, average individual annual earnings would be
$1,000. By comparison, the average annual earnings (in cur-
rent dollars) in 1910, for full-time employees working in agriculture was $233; in manufacturing, $651; in mining bituminous coal, $657; and in wholesale and retail sales, $630.[68]

Louise Houghton noted that "The small storekeepers, usually allied with peddlers, clear from $1,500 to $2,000 a year.[69]

But the contribution of the Syrians' humble trade to the American economy should not be judged solely in dollar terms. By their exceptional energy rather than by their capital investment, the Syrian immigrants revitalized, for about a quarter of a century, an anachronistic enterprise and made it function successfully within a technologically oriented economy increasingly dependent on the efficiency of multimillion-dollar corporations. They were hard opportunists who unwittingly served as agents of products and promoted commerce. They distributed American consumer products in scattered areas where transportation inhibited, if it did not altogether prohibit, their marketing. At the same time, they stimulated a change in buying habits of consumers whose tastes had been uninfluenced by foreign contacts and whose predelictions had been mainly toward the practical and the ordinary. Further, the peddlers played out their economic role in America without displacing or threatening any of the indigenous segments of the labor force. And, much of the capital they generated was invested in America: Syrian shopkeepers and owners of Syrian manufacturing, wholesale, and banking establishments employed hundreds of compatriots as well as non-Syrians.[70] Syrian capital, which left the country in the form of remittances, flowed back in considerable measure in the form of new arrivals who swelled the ranks of peddlers and invested both energy and their American-earned capital in this and other enterprises.

Of course, the pioneer immigrants were not conscious of, nor were they concerned about, improving the American economy or building a better future in a country in which the majority believed they were, by choice, only temporary guests. The Promised Land for the pioneers was, at first, not intended to be the United States; the future they planned to build was back in the village with family and townsmen. They came to America equating success with wealth and found, through peddling, something that for all their labors in the homeland seemed unattainable; they found a feeling of equality and status. They discovered that while their work in the United States enhanced their self-esteem, the tangible symbols of status, which their remittances purchased for the family in the village, fulfilled the original hope of enhanced family honor and status. The immigrants remained in the United States and became staunch advocates of personal liberty, an open society, and democracy.

It was inevitable that peddling would become virtually obsolete before World War I. Because it hastened the acculturation process, it contributed to its own obsolescence. The peddlers learned English relatively quickly, accumulated capital, and acquired new values and directions. Economically, the unexpected financial returns allowed them to transform their circumstances. They used peddling as a bridge which they crossed from one kind of enterprise to another. The level of their aspirations was determined by their motives for migration and, while none knew for certain the parameters of achievement, they were overwhelmed by what was practically possible and got caught up in a passionate desire to achieve. Moreover, given their intense sense of pride and individualism, it was the perfect alternative to working in factories at a time when American corporate giants were pressing upon the immigrant labor force a sense of inferiority. In addition, it spared the great majority of them the compression of living in urban ghettos.

Socially, the deep satisfaction with America which accompanied their peddling success redirected their goals from those of temporary migrants to permanent citizens. In their trade, the unavoidable contacts with American society broke down resistance to learning by interacting with and imitating many aspects of American life. Any barrier that Syrian leaders would later erect against the tide of Americanization would be built on the quicksands of the peddling experience.

The in-between state of mind—the sense of being neither American nor Syrian—could not long be endured. Born to a tradition which conditioned its people from birth to the virtues of home and family, they yearned to fulfill the social roles expected of them and which they had postponed in order to build a better future. They began to yearn for a family life and a home with a garden and fruit trees they could tend and enjoy. Of those who returned to live in the Syrian villages, the largest majority found it too narrow to contain their new world view and decided to become American. As more women immigrated to peddle, to marry, and to join their menfolk, it was inevitable that the roving peddlers would exchange their nomadic life for stability and continuity in their adopted land—once they had the capital to make it possible.

Meanwhile, American capitalist ingenuity continued its rapid pace. Mass production for mass consumption spurred by mass advertising would eventually make the peddler virtually obsolete. Not only did the combination of mail order and parcel post cut into his business, but in and around cities, department stores and a network of five-and-ten-cent stores, advertising in mass-distributed nickle magazines, were convincing increasing numbers of housewives that better bargains were obtainable if they did not buy at the door. At the same time the Syrian was outgrowing his trade, American society was outgrowing his services.

6

Off the Road

Pioneer peddling settlements didn't so much retard assimilation as they served as corridors to it. Off the road, as on it, there was little to seriously dim the immigrants' hopes or blunt their vision. Out of the cloth of impermanence and frugality, the pioneers fashioned small societies of rich and poor, educated and unschooled—societies that were incomplete extensions of the home villages, flung across the broad expanse of the United States.

Some of the settlements were little more than small clusters of peddlers and peddlers' families, more or less homogeneous in religious beliefs and village origins. In larger industrial centers, however, Syrians of different faiths and origins mingled in poorer immigrant neighborhoods in relative proximity to one another where peddlers and wage earners lived side by side. Irrespective of creed or origin, no Syrian seemed to have been deliberately excluded from a collectivity; when it existed, exclusion was self-imposed. Each cluster was initially and fundamentally established to further the economic goals of its members and was held together almost instinctively by a common system of values and traditions.

Pioneer peddling settlements were essentially informal

201

groupings. Not intended as bases for permanent communities, the Syrians called them *mahattat* (singular: *mahatta*)
meaning "stopping places" or "stations," reflecting their expedient and transitory characters, which served common,
immediate needs and aspirations. The appellation was apt.
Whether in the heartland of small-town America or inter-
mingled in their urban neighborhoods, these settlements
were, in fact way stations—havens of continuity with the past
which helped to ease the adjustment shock of the present. Of
formal ethnic authority and institutional life, there was little,
and all were characterized by shifting memberships. As in
the homeland, face-to-face relationships prevailed.

As experience washed away the mystery and uncertainty
of working and living in the new land, some settlements, beginning in the nineties, began maturing into communities
with generally stable populations; some organized ethnic
clubs and churches. Often, a settlement evolved into a small
group of families, too small to support the building of a
church or mosque but large enough to reinforce its members' religious, village, and Syrian identities, especially as absorbed and understood by the adult American-born and
American-raised children of the early pioneers.

Almost from the beginning, the tendency was toward increasing stability and permanence. By 1910, despite continued vows of immigrants to return home, the tide had turned
decidedly in favor of remaining. As men sent for their families and more women arrived, the settlements began to acquire characteristics of permanent communities. Although
peddling had by no means disappeared, scattered family residences slowly replaced communal living. Men began to
shorten their peddling absences or to abandon the nomadic
life for more sedentary work, and parents became concerned
over the future of their school-age children. As these developments were taking place, suppliers no longer had to depend primarily on peddlers for business but concentrated
more on attracting public patronage and serving American
customers. New arrivals increasingly began to depend on
their relatives and friends for initiation into American life.

Even as new settlements were sprouting around the nation

during the 1890s, older ones were maturing. By the turn of the century, colonies in New York, Boston, and Chicago could no longer be regarded as settlements; communal life was organizing around ethnic institutions.

Among the first signs of permanence were home purchases and the formation of voluntary associations. Some associations were social, formed mainly to preserve ethnic identity; some combined the social with the educational, such as teaching English and preparing immigrants for naturalization; more often they were organized to build places of worship, their leadership drawn from among the most veteran and prosperous men and women. Of five churches built in the 1890s, four were located in the older colonies: New York, which had two, Boston, and Chicago; the fifth was in Beaumont, Texas. Of twenty-seven churches established between 1900 and 1910, the majority were concentrated in New York, Massachusetts, and Pennsylvania; Connecticut, the District of Columbia, West Virginia, Mississippi, and Michigan each had one; Minnesota and Nebraska two. From 1910 to 1920, the total almost doubled, and eleven additional states possessed at least one Eastern-rite church.[1]

Although little is known of Muslim and Druze pioneer settlement life, their process of assimilation appears not to have differed in principle from that of the Christians. Smaller and more scattered, but limited to male kinsmen, their settlements were also built on the expectation of quick wealth; and, like the Christians, their experiences on the road heightened expectations and triggered the same process of social and economic mobility. Similarly, they clung to traditional values and customs, perhaps more strongly than most Christians, but were more ambivalent toward American culture. The pioneers who remained in the United States ultimately succeeded by their example and urging, in turning the attention of co-religionists to America as a refuge from conscription and as a Promised Land.

Syrian communities flourished, and neighborhoods radiated from remnants of the peddlers' broad network of settlements. In time, these communities became rooted in their respective locales; their members adopted the social attitudes, manners, and regional accents of their environment, becoming New Englanders or southerners, or midwesterners. Experiencing little, if any, serious prejudice or discrimination, they began to sense a closer affinity for their immediate American communities than for the remote Syrian communities. In the process of becoming American, the permanent communities built on the social and economic foundations of the innovative and trailblazing suppliers and peddlers.

SETTLEMENT LIFE

Generally, the settlements were "Little Syrias" only insofar as the members identified with and shared the security, values, and customs of their countrymen in a familiar language. Each settlement was, in fact, a stage on which the memories of village life were reenacted. Rarely were settlements, however, self-sufficient. Outside of the larger urban concentrations, none is known to have had its own ethnic bakeries, restaurants, and food stores. Even the venerated coffeehouse and church were seldom in evidence; mosques not at all. Outsiders, observing these aliens conducting portions of their lives outdoors—shuttling between homes on visits, engaging in animated street conversations, celebrating religious or family festivals, and quarreling—can be forgiven for considering these settlements to be "Little Syrias."

For one thing, a Syrian settlement was typically not exclusively Syrian. Syrian residences usually were scattered among a variety of immigrants in low-class neighborhoods. Separation of groups was, in some cases, as marked between Syrian and Syrian as between Syrian and non-Syrian. Characteristically, they clustered in a neighborhood by sect. For example, the Melkites of Worcester, Massachusetts, lived on Wall Street, while its Maronites were found on Shrewsbury.[2] In Peoria, Illinois, the handful of Orthodox and Melkites lived apart from the Maronite majority, all from the Maronite village of Itoo in Mount Lebanon. "Some Itoos lived on Washington Street; some on Jefferson Street, a block apart. First and Second Streets were not an Itoo neighborhood. People there were [Orthodox and Melkites] from Zahle and Beirut."[3]

Detroit's Congress Street, paralleling the Detroit River and near it, was dubbed "Syrian town" by its Maronite inhabitants, yet their neighbors were not Syrian Orthodox or Melkites; they were "Italians, Irish, and blacks, and children of different nationalities were friends."[4] In Spring Valley, their neighbors were Italian, Irish, and Polish miners; and in Cedar Rapids, they were German, Czechoslovakian, Russian, and Jewish laborers and shopkeepers. It would have been difficult to find more than a block or two in any settlement, outside the big cities, entirely populated by Syrians.

Settlements were not ghettos nor were they cultural islands. The Christians certainly erected no religious, cultural, or ideological barriers against American culture. Muslims and Druze, on the other hand, for all their wariness and defensiveness, rarely shut themselves off from contact with America. In fact, their vulnerability was compounded by the relative isolation of their smaller, dispersed groups from other Syrians. Not until after World War I, when Muslim and Druze women and children began to arrive in anything resembling significant numbers, were some barriers erected. While meaningful socialization between Syrians and their non-Syrian neighbors was practically nonexistent, contact between Syrians and their new world was inevitable. They undoubtedly greeted neighbors, observed them, and met them in the "American" churches. Indeed, a few Muslims and many Druze attended churches now and again. It was not always necessary for Syrians to venture far from settlement homes to observe and be observed.

Occasionally, the Syrians' conduct aroused curiosity and sometimes antipathy. Once, four Syrians in Grand Rapids were arrested, on the complaint of neighbors, for relaxing on their own porch in "nightgowns" while smoking their narghili (water pipe) and sipping araq at day's end, as was their custom in the village. The men were released after the supplier explained to police that the Syrians' garb was, in fact, a native costume (*qumbaz*) usually worn outdoors in the village.[5]

In another incident, reported in the *Cedar Rapids Evening Gazette* in 1901, Syrians occupied two buildings, "one had a store downstairs and two apartments."[6] The neighborhood residents had petitioned the "city fathers" to "take charge of their foreign element" because of the "dislike for foreigners' methods." The neighbors complained about

> the deportment of the fifty Arabians who represent the colony living in a building . . . at 1220 South Third Street.
> . . . In this document it is alleged that the members of the colony throw filth and refuse upon the ground where it becomes a nuisance because of the disagreeable odors which arise. . . . It is further claimed by women who have young girls . . . that the Arabs have no curtains or blinds on their windows and that the antics of the Asiatic people are not such as are the best for the moral training of young Americans . . . and though their strange actions may be in accordance with the manners and customs of Arabia, they are not the most pleasing to the eyes of the nearby residents.[7]

Crowding, a common feature of settlement life, was not a new experience for the immigrants. In the village, however, one crowded in one's home with one's kin; in the settlement, one might share a tight space not only with relatives or fellow villagers but with strangers. Consequently, the settlement provided opportunities for new relationships not usually available in the village.

Despite the crowding, it was frequently said that "if someone came from the old country and didn't have a place to stay, Syrians would give him a place to stay and feed him."[8] Yet not all remained where they had been welcomed. Christian informants could not remember a Muslim or Druze who had remained very long among them. Without fellow sectarians or villagers, stragglers felt isolated and uncomfortable. Some moved on; others, like Slayman N., who immigrated to the U.S. from the village of Mhaytha, stayed. "It was difficult at first because there was no one from my village. I came here [Spring Valley] because I heard of this supplier and I didn't know how they would receive me. Then one of them took me peddling with him and I've been among them since." As an Orthodox, he integrated into the majority Rashayya group which, except for two Melkite families, was Orthodox.

Crowding suited the immigrants' purposes; it was frugal. Suppliers who arranged to house immigrants understood this and left the living arrangements to the peddlers. Sometimes five, ten, or more crammed into a room in ramshackle buildings, above stores, or behind the supplier's quarters. Frequently, they rented houses which were known as peddlers' houses. On the whole, the rooms were bare, cold, and devoid of electricity and other decent amenities; many were airless. Nevertheless, peddlers sought no better accommodations for themselves.

Slayman, on his arrival in Spring Valley, was directed to the peddlers' house on Minnesota Street, which was south of the "Silk Stocking" district, across Main Street, toward the Illinois River and the railroad station. It was a few minutes' walk from the store of George A., the supplier who had arranged for the house. "It was right where the Orthodox church is now," recalled George's daughters. "It was used by all the peddlers when they were in town. It had one kitchen and often about two dozen at a time—both men and women, husbands and wives, single men and single women—slept there on the floor, two or three families in one room. A man and his wife maybe partitioned off with a drape or something, and they used orange and apple crates for cupboards, and the dishes would fall all over."[9] With several others, Slayman shared the room rent, which they paid directly to the owner. He slept on the floor. "There were no beds, not that they didn't have the money to buy beds, they didn't want to. They didn't buy much food either, not that they went hungry, but they were frugal. They watched what they spent carefully." "We didn't spend money for beds," said his friend Tom A., "we were here only temporarily."[10] About twenty other men and women shared a large open room above a nearby side-street store, which had no kitchen or bathroom and no water. Even when the settlement spread into neighboring streets in a four or five-square block area, and married peddlers started filling up the small mining cottages, they "still used to sleep five or six in a room."[11]

They were just as crowded in Fort Wayne. In Salem's building, the store was located downstairs and "upstairs was a lot of rooms; it must have been an old hotel once upon a time . . . and he'd charge them maybe five or ten dollars a month rent . . . and they had one big room they all cooked in."[12]

Warmth in winter climes was a luxury; stoves were not always provided in living and sleeping areas, not even when snow blew in from broken windows while they slept. So, many slept in their clothes to keep warm. Stoves, usually found in the kitchen and heated by coal and wood scavenged from rail yards and nearby woods, were used mainly for cooking and heating water. Gas water heaters were used about once a week.[13] The house in which Essa S. and his neighbor, Peter F., rented rooms in Manchester, New Hampshire, had no bathroom or sinks; water was carried from the basement.[14] Essa paid $1.50 a week for room and board. "I ate at home with fifteen or sixteen others; we were all single and shared expenses. . . . A stove was not for warmth; only for cooking. We wouldn't pay five cents for a cup of coffee in a coffeehouse, so we stayed at home."

The common kitchen replaced, in many ways, the social and functional hearth of the Syrian village home as the center of folk life and stands out in the immigrants' memories as the locus of treasured moments. There, cold winter evenings were made tolerable; there too, they shared meals and stories to bibulous laughter, and they drank, played cards, sang, and danced. On occasion, marriages were matched and babies were birthed. A common Saturday ritual in the kitchen was the bath. Tafeeda B. described it in Fort Wayne:

> They had a community washtub. They'd heat water on the stove. . . . and [they'd] put the washtub on the stove so they wouldn't freeze to death and they'd scrub themselves with a loofa real good and they'd take this water [she demonstrated how they would trickle the water over themselves with a scooping pan]—water was so scarce, you know. They had to carry it—rainwater, you know. Just like a spit bath. Every Sat-

urday when they would come from peddling. . . . They really paid very much attention to their cleanliness. . . . But they would be very sparing with that [rain] water for just their clothes and bath.

In addition, because their rooms could not serve the purpose, many Syrians saw the common kitchen as their surrogate home, the place where they could be quintessentially Arab, demonstrating those most quintessential Arab values—generosity and hospitality—of which food was the quintessential symbol. Because these two values were the most gratifyingly expressive of Arab values and because they seemed to characterize the essence of Arabness, they have survived assimilation almost intact.

The Syrians made frequent forays outside their neighborhoods—to shop, to attend church, and to "take the air." These little excursions, seemingly trivial and frequently comical, were, nevertheless, open channels to Americanization. If the lack of English-language skills reduced contact in church to a nod and a silent handshake, this lack could not so easily be circumvented in a shop. While Syrians, for the most part, concentrated on the basic necessities of food and clothing, there was much else like kitchen utensils and gadgets to attract their attention and to trigger their seemingly innate propensity to ask questions.

Their preference was naturally for their own food, and although some of the special ingredients, such as cracked wheat (burghol) and Middle Eastern herbs, were ordered in bulk (sometimes by the supplier) from New York importers, most of their needs were purchased locally. What they could not identify visually, they requested by sign language. "Cluck, cluck, lady" and the butcher brought out a hen; rocking an imaginary baby in one's arms, making sheeplike sounds and pointing to the thigh, and a leg of lamb was produced. Invariably, the embarrassment of shopping by charades was turned into an English lesson.

They also needed clothing—warm and cool clothes, clothes for school children, and that special dress for church or "company." Except for the most intractable old women who kept to their homes, most Syrians quickly discarded the village dress for Western clothes when they arrived in the United States. Actually, stressed Salema S., "since we boarded the ship we didn't continue to dress as in the Old Country."[15] By the turn of the century, women immigrants "cared how they looked." Wives and prospective wives, women like Haseby A., liked to dress well. "They wore blouses and long skirts with cinched belts, stood up straight, dyed their hair, plucked their eyebrows, and wore makeup." From all of these small but important springs, America seeped into their consciousness.

Visitors to the settlement afforded the Syrians the opportunity to act from the fullness of tradition. "And these people there [Fort Wayne] with their hospitality, if you didn't have a cent, you had food to serve your guests," recalled Tafeeda B. One's guests were often feted by others in the community as well—a gesture of honor and respect for their neighbor. It was unthinkable to allow visitors with no close relatives in the community to stay at a hotel. "Even at church meetings, when people came from different cities, people took them in—as many as they could and for as long as they wanted to stay."[16]

Neither were wayfarers turned away. It was on such occasions that hospitality and generosity shaded into mutual aid and, more delicately, into charity. The latter—mutual aid and charity, and sometimes hospitality—are considered by Arabs to be acts of *hasani*, that is, benefactions pleasing to God. They are also considered noble acts of honor. Usually undifferentiated, the two impulses were compelling forces for good. As they are acts of honor (face), they are subject to the honor-related code of behavior. Failure to extend them, therefore, was *'ayb*, or disgrace. Acts of aid or charity had to take into account the presumption of equality and reciprocity between giver and recipient. Any implication to the contrary, especially in an act of direct charity, put the recipient in the abhorrent subordinate position of debtor, damaging to his honor. Because it was as embarrassing to extend charity as it was galling to accept it, pains were taken to conceal or disguise the purpose of both the giving and the taking. No institution they brought with them or which they established in America would replace the traditional attitudes of guarding against failure, indigence, and the need for charity. Abe A.'s mother was one of those who considered extended-family concern a hasani. "It was felt," explained Abe, "that it was their responsibility to take another person of their blood—like a nephew or cousin—to provide a home and give them a chance to get on their feet, and usually the house was already crowded with children."[17]

Hasani turned one family or individual's troubles into a colony affair. Relatives and neighbors rallied to assist, commiserate, and condole in times of such crises as illness, birth, and death. Women brought food, looked after children, and busied themselves in the kitchen to serve Arabic coffee or food (as custom prescribed) to those who streamed in and out of a home to show their concern. Above all, said Mike H. "we took their minds off of their troubles and we shared their suffering; if someone got sick, or God forbid, someone died, they [the people of the colony] would stay with the family three days, no matter how inconvenient." In such times, sectarian differences frequently evaporated and religious barriers sometimes came down.

In the settlement, pregnant women, when they could no longer peddle, gave birth and were looked after by their female companions, according to Tafeeda B., "for a couple of days and they'd kill a chicken for them and give them soup. . . . It didn't take longer than that . . . and she'd lay on a couch or bed and the ladies would wait on her."

Hasani also spared many a weak and insecure immigrant from demoralization and becoming a public charge. The treatment of Salem M. and Joseph M. by their community was a case in point. Unmarried, unrelated to each other, and with no close relatives in the colony, they arrived from different villages at different times. Both, however, were Syrian Orthodox. They seemed unable to adapt to immigrant life. Unskilled, illiterate, and proud, they shunned the rigors of peddling and the discipline of industrial labor. They found their security among the people of the colony and never left it.

Salem was simple and good-natured—"he liked to make people laugh"—but lacked the drive to improve himself. The relatives he had come to join had moved on. Joseph was older, well into middle age; slightly bent and slow-witted, he ambled around town, sometimes muttering to himself. He was one of those personalities that children mocked and women teased. Existence was precarious for both of these men, but the community protected them from destitution. It gave them odd jobs, invited them to meals, nursed their illnesses, and at times included them in festive occasions. Countrymen, sensitive to their pride, scrupulously avoided insinuations of charity. When the men died, about the late twenties or early thirties, they were buried in the Syrian cemetery on the outskirts of the town.[18]

Since it was ʿayb not to aid the needy in one's family or community and a hasani to do so, virtually no one was left unaided. The emphasis on family and group cohesion and honor—of "taking care of one's own"—kept the Syrians, with remarkably few exceptions, off of the relief rolls and police blotters. Their crimes were generally for minor offenses, most arising from a foreigner's naïveté and America's ignorance of, and antipathy toward, foreigners and their cultures.

As havens of revitalization, settlements were indispensable for those who absented themselves on the road for long periods of time. It was in the settlements that peddlers revived their spirit and reveled in a sense of belonging. Here they rediscovered continuity with the past; values, which often seemed out of place elsewhere, were validated. It was here that life's vitality, numbed by the frustrations of the road, was restored; here people of their own kind spoke the same language, laughed at the same humor, called their names, and bantered in familiar accents. Here, they bathed, perhaps for the first time in weeks, and savored tastes they had craved. Emotions, pent up on the road, poured forth in the settlements. Here, too, the curtain of information was lifted. Arabic newspapers disclosed events in the homeland, in other settlements, and about America itself. Talk and gossip conveyed news of homeland villages, of friends still on the road, of those who returned, who arrived, who married and who died.

It was, however, the mail which brought them back to a reality which the limbo of the road tended to dim or distort. It reminded them, if they needed it, of their obligations. "We miss you and need you," the letters usually read. "When are you coming home? Why haven't you written? The crops were . . .; the mortgage is . . .; please send money . . .; can you send for . . .; it is time you married . . .; your mother cries . . .; your father says . . ." As the strings and knots of family ties were pulled, some men felt strengthened; others strained. Reality was changing for them and the dilemma of what to do about it was worked out in letters exchanged with those they left behind. Increasingly, these letters began to include not only the dutiful remittances, but prepaid fares.

Frequently the return of long-distance peddlers, especially on weekends and religious holidays, were occasions for food, fun, and fellowship. In Cedar Rapids, peddlers came to Abe K.'s home and his mother cooked for them. "Sometimes, she made two hundred loaves of [flat, leavened Arabic] bread. She also washed their clothes." Peddlers in Spring Valley would "cook a huge meal," recalled Amelia A. M., "and everyone was welcome." In Salem Bashara's house, Tafeeda B. was told, they "would have 'soirees.' They wouldn't go anywhere—they would be right there in their rooms and poor Mrs. Bashara, they'd tell me, she'd work the whole week, she and [Salem's] mother, to make the bread and the sweets. They'd know that these peddlers were coming and it was the holiday [Easter] and they were going to bring in their money and they were going to buy from her husband and she had to rise to the obligation due them."

Almost on arrival male and female peddlers gathered around the table in the common kitchen or at a veteran's house and talked about home and how much each had earned, what they had seen, and "they exchanged peddling stories . . . and had such fun laughing about them."[19] Sometimes, they "liked to jump rope, wrestle, and barbeque lamb, and they had a wonderful time."[20] There were times when Faris N. entertained his Fort Wayne friends by imitating minstrel men he had seen at a sideshow somewhere on the road.[21] Instrumentalists, found in almost any group, accompanied rhythmic handclaps with their reeds, while men danced the *dabka*, a line dance, with great vigor. Or, the peddlers settled down with araq and *mazza* (hors d'oeuvres) to revel in sonorous laments and ballads while the women watched and listened. When the settlements expanded into individual residences, "this kind of merriment would make the rounds; each night at a different house," recounted Amelia A. M. "And how they loved to play jokes on each other," she added: "I'd hear my mother say that she'd cook stuffed grape leaves and a few of the men would find out about it because how can you keep a secret?—and a couple of men would come and steal it off the fire and no one would get angry. Once they stole a cooked chicken and returned the bones. . . . It was a big joke. They were all single men . . . and full of life. They'd have water fights and such fun. . . . None of them had much money, but they enjoyed themselves more than now."

Salem Bashara equipped his peddlers' common kitchen with several marble mortars and wooden pestles to pulverize lean lamb and burghol into kibbie, the favorite dish. Roommates often cooked together, and the women baked bread.[32] Frequently, the women cooked for the single men. "There were several young men from Rashayya staying with Salem Bashara," wrote Faris N., "and we had agreed to share the price of . . . supper. Each put in 25 cents and we collected $3.50 and we bought meat, potatoes, bread, and so on. Those who drank whiskey bought a bottle for 25 cents each and we gave the groceries to the ladies who were present and they took over the cooking and we, the young men, busied ourselves with drinking and a good time."[23] Meanwhile, the men took note and the matchmakers matched. "That's why so many of the girls got married so quickly when they'd come to this country. . . . Just as soon as one came along that knew how to cook *mjaddarra* [a common lentil dish], they'd marry her off."[24] Never, not even in the home village, were the bonds stronger nor camaraderie more genuine than in those pioneer days.

LEADERSHIP AND THE ROLE OF THE SUPPLIER

In the literature about Syrian immigrants, the pivotal role of the early suppliers in the economic and social life of the settlement has been largely overlooked and misunderstood. Data are limited and unanswered questions remain. No pioneer supplier is alive to speak of his personal experiences and reminiscences. Pioneer peddlers, recounting their own experiences, took the supplier's role so much for granted that it seemed to require little distinction and no elaboration. He was one of them and yet, he loomed larger than any—a sometimes shadowy father figure, countryman, friend, counselor, protector, and sometimes, because occasional resistance was inevitable, adversary. In the earliest years, a supplier and his peddlers formed an interdependent relationship suspended between the counterweights of mutual economic goals and the canons of tradition.

Suppliers seemed to have emerged as a class by affirmation of their followers. Joe D., who had known suppliers in several settlements, drew a sketchy portrait of a successor to Salem Bashara. "They had a sort of leadership," he began, speaking of settlements in general, "but divisions among them prevented . . ." he paused abruptly and continued thoughtfully,

> Qizma [his brother-in-law, a successful merchant of imported rugs and linens] was a leader among them. He wasn't appointed or elected. They just turned to him. The [itinerant] priests would come to his home; guests [from out of town] would come to his home; bishops and other prominent people, they would come to his house and the people would visit them there. He would guide and advise the Syrians of Fort Wayne and intervene on their behalf with the authorities. There was no one person who sort of presided over all of them. There was none of that.
>
> It was like the tradition in the old country. The person

whose home was open would receive the guests because there was much poverty there. Not all had the means. . . . Yes, wealth was important and so was position, but what was more important was the fact of his house being open to his people. If it wasn't, people would not turn to him. This was as true in the United States as in the old country. This is an Arab tradition.

Whether the portrait of this or any supplier, pieced together from fragmentary data about a few, resembled the many in the United States is an open question.[25] The evolution of peddling, diverse locales of settlements, and varying personalities of suppliers shaped their personal styles. Certainly, the suppliers of 1900 were not the trailblazers of a decade earlier; nor did the settlements in northeastern states reflect the same pioneer characteristics of those which spread westward into the Mississippi valley and beyond.

From a distance, the settlement society appeared to be classless. All who belonged shared the same goals and rose in the morning to the same hard day's labor. Newcomers, undistinguished by clothes, language, or skills, blended in with the group or moved on. On closer examination, however, one could detect subtle, informal social gradations. Seniority had value, and senior shopkeepers had more value than senior peddlers; peddlers of imported linens and rugs valued themselves above dry goods peddlers. Leaders were drawn from the most experienced and enterprising, rather than from the highborn. Gradations in status, however, were not necessarily class distinctions; they meant relatively little in the relationship between members of the settlement.

The most important relationship was between suppliers and peddlers. Among his men, the supplier was first among equals. Since suppliers and peddlers usually originated from virtually the same social and economic class in Syria, class distinction in the settlements of America was hollow. The so-called family name and noble ancestry, no matter how often asserted, counted for little as long as almost anyone with ambition could become a supplier. Airs of superiority were simply out of place, even subject to ridicule. Thus, although the supplier's leadership was validated by the peddlers' dependence on him, no special title was attached to him, nor was abject obedience demanded. He had to earn the continued loyalty of his people.

On the other hand, the supplier's higher status was provisional on his fulfilling his followers' expectations. They expected social and economic services which most suppliers delivered, especially in the early years. Not only did the supplier advance them credit, train them, and arrange for housing, he held their savings, often for years, mediated between them and local authorities, adjudicated quarrels, wrote and received letters, advised on naturalization, and assisted in personal crises, among other services. On the other hand, and equally significant, his leadership was also evaluated by his exemplifying the traditional nobility of character, particularly the qualities of munificence and magnanimity. Friends and family of Salem Bashara both agreed that his hospitality and generosity was consistently exemplary.

In return, suppliers were accorded the respect due to prominent guests and friends. His followers might, as in the case of Salem and Daher Hobaica, a supplier in Utica, New York, be given such an honor as godfathering their children. Mr. Hobaica, it was said, was godfather to more than 140 children.[26] Tafeeda B. said of Salem that "the minute they'd bear a child, he'd have to be the godfather. Because on the Catholic book in the Cathedral in Fort Wayne—I went in there one day to look up a birth certificate. . . . He [the priest] opened up that year and there it was—Salem Bashara. I said, "can I go back a couple of years?" He said, "Yeah, help yourself, there's the books." And so help me, if he was a godfather to one, it must have been twenty-five that I saw."

Occupying a vague middle level between the supplier and the peddlers were a few veteran immigrants who, having reached the fringes of success—symbolized by their facility in English and an apparent adjustment to American society—had also acquired some prestige, if not a secondary right to leadership. They might compete for leadership with the supplier or share it, but to achieve and maintain a semblance of status, they, too, had to demonstrate the valued qualities.

Homeland group relations preordained group relations in the settlement. If its residents were sufficiently numerous and diversified by sect and village, they gravitated together to form village or sectarian groups, each with its own leader. Frequently during the pioneer years, that person was a supplier. Relations at the leadership level governed the overall relations in the settlement.

The authority of the supplier, as leader, should not be overestimated. He guided rather than commanded. He harmonized, for his followers, the unknown in the new land with the familiar cultural sentiments of the old, and by providing a road map by which they could meet their goals and personal needs, he regulated the present. In so doing, he led the way toward adjustment. For this, he was accorded, and accepted, the status of leader by a loose consensus of his followers. On them, however, depended his livelihood as well as his status. The peddlers, for their part, exhibited enough self-possession to perceive that weakness in his position, leaving him more vulnerable to concessions than they. Uninstitutionalized, and with too much of the provisional in it, the supplier's authority ultimately lacked effective means of enforcement.

The very canons of tradition that validated his leadership also militated against the supplier's excesses. For his part, he relied on the traditional means to affect the peddlers' conduct—means which generally proved much less effective in the open and fluid settlement society than in the tightly knit ethos of the village. Appeals to family honor and the peddler's noble character (*sharraf*)—touching as they do the most sensitive chords in the Arab's nerve center—were frequently less persuasive than the economic leverage of the supplier. He could send them on unprofitable routes, but more importantly, he could refuse them credit or threaten to withhold their savings.

In his role as economic leader, a supplier, whether on Washington Street in New York, South Sixth Street in Cedar

Rapids, or Main Street in Spring Valley, was foremost a businessman who pursued his own economic interests. His followers expected him to profit reasonably from their business relationship, a relationship that was as personal over the counter as in their living quarters. He was not, however, as some observers thought, exploitative as were, say, the Italian and Greek padrones. The United States Commission, in its reports on immigration and on education erroneously confused the supplier with the padrone. The following is an excerpt from a testimony of 24 July 1899, entitled "The Padrone System:"

Q. [Referring to "eastern Asiatic immigration," that is, primarily Armenians, Greeks, Syrians, and Turks] What are their callings and professions?

A. Usually merchants and laborers. . . . The Syrians—on the other hand, if these have gone into producing pursuits, I have not known of it—are mostly peddlers. They have certain distributing agencies all over the country. They are peddlers and go around the country under the control, as I understand it, of certain people interested in notions. . . .

Q. [After speaking of Italians and the padrone system] We have all through the south colonists of—we call them "dago" down there, or peddlers—who live together and seem to be under the leadership of one man, and they travel all over the country for 50 miles around. Are they Italians?

A. I think they are Orientals [meaning Syrians].

Q. A different race, but it seems to be the same system.

A. It is the same system, only a different basis. We have been unable to get very definite information as to the methods of bringing the Orientals to this country on account of our inability to know their language, to converse with them. As I said, it is very suspicious that large numbers of this class arrive here with a stated amount of American gold, and I think it is established beyond doubt that these people are controlled by a centralized body of notion peddlers, with general headquarters in New York and with branches all over the United States and that these people are representatives of some branch of this padrone traffic.[27]

In another section, the report attacked the "merchant (so called)" class for its "cupidity and indolence, reenforced by an exaggerated patriarchal authority," and for its abuse of the "peasant people." It continued: "Particularly does this class of Syrians realize the worst attributes of the parasite—the man is brutally arrogant to the poorer members of his own race and fawningly servile to Americans and all those from whom he considers there is something to be gained."[28]

The concern and confusion of the commission report reflected the dominant opinion of a time when immigration was flooding America in unprecedented numbers, most from unfamiliar cultures. With regard to the Syrians, the misimpression seems to have sprung from inaccurate observations by commission representatives in East Coast cities.

Exploitation of the Syrian peddlers by suppliers was difficult, and judging by the testimonies of the peddlers themselves, virtually nonexistent. Among the services a supplier performed for his peddlers, there were similarities with those of the Italian or Greek padrone. The Syrian supplier was not, however, the employer nor the employment agent of his men—the central role of the padrone. A peddler was, as he insisted on being, "his own boss"—a self-employed entrepreneur and, therefore, free to exercise a large measure of his individualism and free will. If supplier and peddler disagreed, it was frequently the supplier who made concessions, since his status and honor, as well as his income, were at risk. The peddler could act more unscrupulously than the supplier; he was free to transfer his business elsewhere and, if inclined, without even settling his debts with the supplier. Of this there is ample evidence in the interviews.

Those close to Salem Bashara claimed, in fact, that the peddlers "ruined" him because "a lot of them never paid him . . . and some of them he would stake and [they would] go to Illinois, and so on, and they would never come back. . . . People just ate him up. He trusted everybody to such an extent."[29] Alexander M. of Grand Rapids, Michigan, reflecting on the relations between Salem and his peddlers, recalled that "on Saturday nights in Fort Wayne, the peddlers would assemble at his home, which was a hotel for them; they would give him their money, he would take what was owed him and what was left, he would save for them. He was at the same time their supplier, banker, protector, and provider."[30]

In Mankato, Minnesota, Mr. Tubi, remembered Amelia U., "was the leader of the community. He resolved problems and was a father to them all. . . . Peddlers didn't have anyone to rely on in case of trouble except Mr. Tubi . . . and he never cheated any peddlers." Lillian H. said that many of her father's peddlers did not repay the credit extended to them. "They took advantage of him. He would never ask them— they'd give him a hard-luck story. He was too proud to ask them and they felt he was well off and didn't need the money." Had it ever been attempted, it seems doubtful that the padrone system would have been effective against the individualism and competitiveness of Syrians in America.

Maintaining order and mediating conflicts were undoubtedly the most important and trying aspects of the supplier's leadership. A value system which emphasized personal rivalry, individualism, and valor tied to family honor, impinged as compellingly on the conduct of leaders as on that of the followers. Not only did this system heighten the potential for conflict on both levels, but it also restricted the parameters of authority.

The Syrian personality seemed to require an informal leadership, personalized in flesh and blood. The usual criteria of same sect, vicinity of origin, and the ability to demonstrate nobility of character were not enough. Syrians also wanted someone with whom they could deal personally— someone whose personality and mettle they could not only measure but test against their own, and whom they could approach with their needs. In the personal relationship, supplier and peddler made a reciprocal claim on each other— one in which neither party appeared to subordinate the other. The ability to deflect the inevitable challenges to his leadership afforded the leader the opportunity to demonstrate a kind of strength and charisma appreciated by his followers. Authority to lead and a semblance of deferrence were granted to the supplier as long as he could artfully balance elements of the criteria demanded of him. An equilibrium had to be maintained between tacit authority and the traditional means of mediation and compromise—an equilibrium that was difficult to attain and to maintain in a society of individualists.

In practice, the most effective tool in a leader's kit was personal persuasion. Neither too forcefully nor intrusively, he nevertheless had to assert his authority sufficiently to avoid the perception of weakness or inaction: weak leadership invited conflict as readily as would a show of unwarranted force.

Nothing was more characteristic of Syrian communal life than petty personal conflicts. They were quick to flare up, yet frequently just as quick to quell, usually through the mediation of friends or neighbors. When an incident became violent or threatened to spread, the supplier intervened, relying on his prestige to mediate or arbitrate; sometimes he came as a friend. In either case, it was to contain any excesses of his followers. He might be joined by veteran peddlers who added their weight to the persuasion. Many times, however, such traditional means failed and conflicts had to be resolved by outsiders. One case in point: as early as 1897, a charge of assault in Cedar Rapids was resolved in court, ironically, not by a judge but by the supplier.

Joe George, praised by an informant as "a real man among the Arabs," and apparently a factional leader, was arrested for reportedly wounding Less Corey with a chair. "Both are Armenian [sic] peddlers," reported the *Cedar Rapids Evening Gazette,*

> who make their headquarters with about thirty others with Tom Bashara.... He refers to all of them as "his boys" and takes great interest in them....
>
> The evidence before Justice Rall this morning was all given by Armenians.... But as to who was the offender, Justice Rall was unable to determine. He was under the necessity of discharging the prisoner which would have again given Corey the worst of it leaving him to pay the attorney for prosecution.
>
> Then Tom Bashara tried his hand at dispensing justice.... He held that Corey and George had both been fighting; that they were alike at fault, and equally to blame for the quarrel.

It was a secondary matter as to who got the worst of a business which Tom considered thoroughly disreputable. . . . [He] has his idea of behavior from which he does not and will not suffer "his boys" to depart.

Consequently he held that. . . . they were equally responsible in the financial as well as in the moral phase of the action, and should pay half and half, including the fee of the prosecuting attorney. That there is no warrant in law for such proceedings does not interfere with its strict justice in this case, and if another action comes up from the Armenian colony, Justice Rall will not be averse to allowing Bashara to occupy the bench, arbitrate the case in his own rugged way and allow the matter to go without record.[31]

Tom's arbitration and resolution epitomized Syrian informal, personalized leadership. More by reflex than concern for justice, he knew too well that conflict resolution between individuals, particularly those from different groups, lay not in punishing the guilty but in a compromise that left neither, with prides wounded, feeling subordinate to the other. Factional bitterness is not easily eradicated; it merely subsides only to surface again at the slightest provocation. To have judged otherwise would have subjected the group to mounting discord and division and jeopardized Tom's ability to lead and control.

The best testimony to the limitation of the supplier's leadership and authority was the natural and inevitable tendency of Syrians to factionalize. As the settlements diversified and acquired a more permanent character, the particularistic barriers, which the trials of pioneering had temporarily submerged, gradually reemerged, in many cases before the decade of the 1890s was out. Competing suppliers also weakened the bonds of brotherhood, resulting in the fragmentation of leadership. Thereafter, in few settlements could one person claim to be the leader for the whole. Each supplier spoke only for his group, increasing the potential for conflict from the top.

Open conflict in a fragmented leadership often trickled down to a leader's personal followers; discipline, then, was difficult to impose and consequently required outside inter-

vention, usually civil authority. One case was the New York
factional battle in October 1905, the most extreme known
case of Syrian conflict in the United States.

The New York Syrian colony was untypically large and
heterogeneous. By 1905, religious, social, financial, industrial, and publishing institutions had nourished a body of
highly accomplished leaders and intelligentsia, several na-
tionally recognized and respected by their countrymen; no
one, however, was the sole authority or spokesman for the
community.

The *New York Times*'s lead article on 24 October 1905, was
headed: "Syrians Riot in the Streets and Many Are Hurt:
Reserves of Three Precincts End Knife-Pistol Battle."[32] The
headline of the *New York Herald*'s full-page feature on October 29 was "Brother against Brother, Villages against Villages
and Old-Time Friends Are Parted."[33] The battle lasted about
a quarter of an hour, by the *Times*'s estimate, and casualties
were numerous, although none was fatal. "Only five men
were locked up for stabbing—the others who might have
been arrested disappeared."

No one could be certain of the cause. The *Times* thought
that "the dispute and quarrels which led up to the climax last
night might make a long story. A difference in religious views
is at the beginning of it. The three principal figures in the
story are Syrian [Orthodox] Bishop Hawaweeny, Editor Najeeb Diab of the Mirror of the West [*Meraat al-Gharb*], and
Najeeb Maloof, a merchant of 17 Broadway. The Bishop and
the editor are on the same side, Maloof is their opponent."[34]
The *Herald*, admitting its inability to unravel the convoluted
charges and countercharges, nevertheless portrayed the fra-
cas as one of merchants versus the Arabic press, sect versus
sect, individuals against individuals, and reformers defending their reforms against traditionalists.

Initially, the battle was fought on the pages of the Maronite
Al-Hoda and the Orthodox *Meraat Al-Gharb*. Later, it moved
from the newspaper columns into the coffeehouses and then
before Magistrate Wahle who knew "all about their quarrels
and the hopelessness of trying to settle them in court."[35] Finally, it spilled into the streets of Manhattan where, everyone

having taken sides, it spread throughout the Christian community (the few Muslim and Druze residents remained uninvolved) ultimately engaging Manhattan Syrian against Brooklyn Syrian. A coffeehouse waiter offered his informed opinion of the violence to the *Herald's* observer. Small confrontations were unsatisfying to the combatants, he said. "I do not know what is the trouble; I only know there is much of it and the men sit late in the cafes and are liberal with their tips. I know of the fighting of last Monday night. It was because, I believe the respected Magistrate Wahle said he would make peace. Then they said to one another, 'Let us go out and have one more good night before the respected Magistrate accomplishes what he desires.' And . . . did they not?"[36]

Conflict had gripped the leaders of various factions and ignited old unsettled scores. The leaders, unable to agree among themselves or to discipline their followers, were also unable to mediate an end to the conflict. As in the homeland, extrinsic measures became necessary to stop the violence.

Syrians were not unaware of their penchant for factionalism and its potential for conflict. Indeed, this trait had been condemned publicly and privately for its harmful consequences to the budding Syrian community internally, as well as for the public embarrassment that it caused. Hitti had observed in 1924 that "Leaderless in many ways, yet deluged with petty and self-made leaders, Syrians in this country present a lamentable sight."[37] The Reverend Basil M. Kherbawi, historian and dean of Saint Nicholas Syrian-Greek Orthodox Cathedral of Brooklyn, laid the blame firmly on the newspaper owners and the "masters of the pen" who, he said, stimulated factionalism and fueled fanaticism and hate by printing invectives rather than providing much-needed leadership in the new land.[38]

Opportunities for leadership proliferated with the spread of Syrian groups throughout the nation, often attracting ambitious status-seeking men—Hitti's "petty and self-made leaders"—whose self-interest took precedence over quality leadership. For many, the easiest path to leadership was participation in a church-building or church-supporting body where their generous donations conferred status upon them.

The typical overzealous and poorly educated clergy who immigrated to officiate in the churches were not only dependent on and answerable to these bodies but helped to perpetuate sectarian fanaticism.

Several years before the New York incident, sectarian conflicts in the United States drew the condemnation of the editor of the Cairo-published *Al-Hilal*. In the April 1897 issue,
he chastised the Syrians everywhere for their continuing rivalry.[39] A contributor to *Al-Hoda* in May 1898 termed the
Syrian penchant for sectarian factionalism backward and divisive. Had they forgotten, he asked, the Arabic proverb
which says: "A stranger to a stranger in a strange land is a
kinsman?"[40] When five people were injured in a violent conflict between Maronites and Orthodox in Butler, Pennsylvania, in 1914, the editor of *Al-Hoda* again urged unity and
turning a new chapter in religous relationships.[41] Exhorta-
tions and self-criticism seemed, however, to be ineffective
against attitudes hardened by two thousand years of history.

Factions endured and the conflicts, though numerous,
were short. Tempers cooled, wounded prides healed,
breaches closed, and people went about their daily lives. The
sporadic disruptions in settlement life were sufficiently negligible as to merit the following assessment from Louise
Houghton in 1911: "The most universal testimony is that our
Syrian citizens are quiet, peaceable, and law-abiding, and,
considering their antecedents [that is, conditions under
Turkish rule], remarkably able morally to stand alone. They
do quarrel, chiefly on religious grounds. . . . generally the
Moslems appear to be as law-abiding as the Christians."[42]
Writing a decade later, William I. Cole posed the question:
"What sort of residents and citizens do the Syrians in this
country make or are in the way of making?" and answered
it: "This question can be answered in the spirit of prophecy.
But taking into account their inheritance, their native mental
and moral traits, and the way in which, on the whole, they
are conducting themselves here, it would not seem too much
to say that when, through the opportunities and influences
of America, they shall have come fully to their own, we shall

number among our 'foreign-born neighbors' no better residents and citizens than this people from Syria."[43]

Inexperienced in leadership and far removed from the home village, most suppliers, by and large, carried the mantle of leadership with remarkable skill for the short span they were on the scene. Considerable though this role was, the suppliers passed unremarked from the memories of the pioneers, their successors, and descendants.

WIVES AND BRIDES

Syrians traditionally placed a high value on marriage and the family. If the majority of the pioneer immigrants enjoyed or endured, as the case may be, a respite from family responsibilities, they knew it was only temporary. The decision to settle in America was made almost simultaneously with the decision to end bachelorhood, usually with a great sense of relief.

As soon as they were able, married men were reunited with families. Many sent for wives and children they had left behind. It was common for immigrant husbands to visit their families back home every few years—sometimes ten or more. Some remained in the village for several years to relish the rewards of their American experience. Mortgages were paid, land was purchased, new homes were built or upgraded, old trades resumed, and/or more children fathered before returning to America to replenish savings or pave the way for the family's emigration. Ultimately, the decision to become American ended the costly cycle of visits and absences. Single men, numerous in most settlements, thought of marriage, preferrably to girls chosen or approved by their parents. Finding the right choice—or any Syrian girl—in America, was, however, a problem, for marriageable Syrian girls were few.

Although Christian women had been arriving in a small but steady stream since the beginning of Syrian immigration, the ratio of men to women averaged at least four or five to one until after World War I. Among them were the unmarried sisters and daughters of men who, at the first scent of success, had sent for them as housekeepers and helpers.

"Very few women immigrated," said Elizabeth B., herself a bride at thirteen. "There weren't many at all in Fort Wayne. . . . The men were all young. . . . seventeen, eighteen, twenty, twenty-two years old. There weren't enough women for the men here. An old man from Fort Wayne brought his sixteen-year-old son over here and there was a single girl in Columbus [Ohio] who was about to marry a Syrian. . . . But this old man wanted her for his son, so he went to Columbus and took her away. . . . He brought her to Fort Wayne and married her to his son. She was thirty or thirty-five years old and the two went peddling together." Few men resorted to such drastic measures, but the competition was keen.

Some journeyed back to the village to marry girls already selected by their families. Men, returning to their villages for brides, had ample kinship and sectarian choices and were favored. Moreover, they married with all the joys of familiar customs and rituals—from parental blessings to rejoicing with kith and kin—not always as gratifying or possible in the settlement.

Others, finding return to the homeland impractical or expensive, searched other channels for brides. Some men sent to the village for brides, entrusting the often delicate selection and arrangements to family and friends. Most of the prospective mates came willingly; some had to be persuaded to trust their destinies to the unimaginable; and some, in the words of Alice A., were "tricked nicely."

Her marriage to her cousin in 1909 was arranged by her uncle. When she agreed to leave her family in Mount Lebanon at the age of fifteen, it was, she believed, to work and send money to her mother. Instead, she was married almost on arrival to "a good man." Among the more fortunate, she had no regrets.[44]

Mary S., a Maronite, was also fifteen when she arrived alone in 1908. A cousin had arranged for her marriage to an immigrant, neither of her faith, family, nor village. The arrangement had included, in addition to Mary's fare and a Maronite ceremony, five hundred dollars to purchase a return ticket to Syria should she reject the man. The option proved empty. The real purpose for her journey hidden from her, she arrived knowing no one, not even the prospective Orthodox husband who received her. Yet within two days she was married by a Maronite priest summoned from West Virginia over the objections of Maronites in the settlement who tried to prevent her marriage to an Orthodox. She cried constantly.[45]

Many eligible men discovered not only that marriageable Syrian girls were scarce, but that choices were further limited by sectarian prohibitions and the preference for village endogamy. Even if the men were willing to bypass tradition, the girl and her kin might not. So men enlisted the help of friends and relatives and scouted other settlements in their search. Tom Bashara tried in Chicago. "Long time ago," he confided to a Cedar Rapids reporter, "I go down to Chicago to get me a girl. A man he tell me that I get a girl of my own race and I spend thirty-five dollars to go down to Chicago. I hunt two or three days and I no find any girl, so I come home. A man who runs a big store there tell me that he watch for nice girl and sometimes I come down and get her. I tell him I go in couple of months when my cousin comes to tend store for me. Then I go and get nice girl, and I have nice home . . . and I have something good to eat all the time."[46]

Girls of all ages were fair game. Nazira N. was barely fifteen when she married, but she had been courted for about three years, albeit indirectly through the grandmother with whom she lived. One of her suitors was old enough to be her father, she mused. "What did I know? There were four or five men wanting to get married and they were waiting for me to get to a marriageable age. They had all come to Rugby, North Dakota, to homestead, too. They would homestead land for a while, then sell it. Syrians would come to St. Paul, peddle a while, then go to Rugby to homestead, and they wanted to get married."[47]

One of Tom's men married a fourteen-year-old girl and waited for her to grow up because, as Tom told the Cedar Rapids Evening Gazette reporter, "He 'fraid nudder mans take her away." In the reporter's words, "the groom considered

that the tender age of his bride-to-be made it impossible for
her to assume household cares, but that he didn't propose to
take any chances and therefore cinched the thing on the
spot. . . . The payment of $200 for this girl for her brother
was amply large enough. The girl is to remain away from her
husband for two years. If during the probationary time, the
girl carries on a flirtation or in any way offends her liege lord,
the brother is to forfeit $100."[48]

Since to Syrians, the state of being single was both unnatural and deplorable, the unmarried lived in unrelenting
scrutiny from self-appointed matchmakers who, besides filling an important traditional role, acted as surrogate parents
and invoked as many of the traditional mores as they could
under the new circumstances. To hear Tafeeda B., who de-
fiantly married a man she loved, these matchmakers married
the man to "just any old woman." On the other hand, they
would all say

> "Poor girl, . . . protect this poor girl, marry her [off] so that
> she won't have to go around and sell." Well, maybe there
> would be fifteen men to two women, see, and they knew they
> had to make a home and had to make a fortune and they
> knew they couldn't go back to the old country and marry right
> away, so these girls would come from the old country and they
> [the people of the settlement] would know them. Either they
> would come from their own village or they'd know their back-
> ground, and girls that today would never pass would be mar-
> ried off and they [the girls] knew the value of the dollar—that
> was the beauty about them. They put up with all that poverty.
> They put up with frugality and the hardships and the doing
> without because they had gone through that.

Tafeeda's is the cynicism of a woman who as a girl had
worked long and arduous hours in her father's fruit store.
She hadn't peddled or experienced the hardships of the
road. No one will ever know how many girls who peddled
yearned for some man, any man, to free them from the
drudgery. Elizabeth B. knew a half-frozen peddler who
tossed her kashshi away and prayed tearfully to be rid of it,

vowing to "marry any man to be finished with that miserable trade."

The economic advantage in taking a wife, so prevalent in the homeland, lost none of its validity in the new land. "I get lonesome here and I make more money when I have girl to stay in store for me," was Tom Bashara's rationale for marrying.[49] Johnny N., a grocer in 1925, married for the same reasons. "I decided to marry after I was in the store by myself for one year. It's hard not to have someone to give you a hand—to cook and wash and relieve you at work for banking or resting; and also I was twenty-six years old and I needed a companion.... I can't run a store by myself." He found her in Meridian, Mississippi. Few women were deceived that marriage in America was better than in the homeland. They usually stepped into the role of wife, homemaker, and earning partner knowing what to expect, perhaps hoping for a change, but anticipating none.

In the attention they paid to matrimonial affairs, elders showed little inclination to countenance deviations from the social norms. They were as vigilant in the settlement as they would have been in the village and as quick to judge and act. Usually, their censoriousness carried with it effective sanctions, even when they were misplaced as they were when Faris N. was falsely accused of rejecting a girl he had promised to marry. In a section of his memoir entitled "Forced Marriage," he recounted the experience.

He had been in the habit of writing letters for friends in the settlement and hardly knew young Marina who had emigrated from the higher elevations of Rashayya when she asked him one weekend to write a letter for her. She had been promised, unconsulted, by her brother to a peddler from Aytha. In her room, Marina tearfully dictated the letter to her mother and he tried to console her. "Since you do not like him, what is your hurry?" he asked; "there are many young men from Rashayya here." When he finished the letter, they both rejoined their friends. A week later, he was back in the settlement. Meanwhile, the stage had been set for the events that awaited him. A friend found him in the com-

mon kitchen with his companions. "I have come to warn
you," he told Faris, "that you are about to lose your bride.
The people from Aytha have come to claim her." Faris was
stunned. "I answered," he wrote,

> "Which bride?" He [the friend] said, "Marina. . . ." I said to
> him, "I did not open this subject to her nor do I want to
> marry." He said, "didn't you say to her "Why should you go
> to Aytha . . . ? I told him that I had said to her ". . . Wait and
> God will grant you another. Go tell her that I promised my
> mother that I would not marry except in Rashayya. . . ." Sud-
> denly, Salem and his wife [who had come into the kitchen]
> said to me, "We are going to bring you your bride [who had
> taken refuge from her brother in Salem's house]." I went crazy
> and said firmly, "Don't do that! I do not want to marry. What-
> ever you do about her, do as you please, but I am not going to
> marry her."

Salem and some of the Rashayya faction nevertheless persisted, insisting that his "promise" was now a matter of
honor. They escorted him to City Hall for a license while
others took Marina by another route "because there had developed a fight between the people of Rashayya and those of
Aytha and they [the people of Aytha] began to spread out
into the streets to see if the girl would pass." It was Saturday;
the licensing agency was closed and Faris gained a brief re-
prieve. He remained in his room while "more than 200
people" celebrated downstairs. On Monday, Salem went to
Faris's room with three senior peddlers, "and they said to me
'Now, the Chief of Police is coming and with him are three
policemen who are going to ask you questions. . . . The Aytha people have brought a complaint against you and it will
bring you five years in jail.'" Faris continued to resist and
Salem then countered with the clinching argument: "If you
do not tell them what we are going to teach you . . . , you
have with me $500 which you will not see again—not a dollar
nor a cent of them."

Faris succumbed. In his words, "I was coerced and was
married and remained in America until I completed the two
years [that he had promised to be away from his mother]."
Until he was widowed nine years later, his life remained in

turmoil. For the members of the two factions, Faris's acquiescence—whether he would (Aytha) or whether he should (Rashayya)—was a matter of honor and, his innocence notwithstanding, a case of abandoning the social values. For Salem, it was a matter of maintaining not only order and harmony in the settlement but proper relations with the American authorities.

In the opinion of many young people, the quality of social sanctions was a little too intrusive, a little too austere. Bachelors who relished release from the traditional constraints, who preferred to delay marriage for economic or personal reasons, or who wanted to shape their own destinies craved some benevolent disregard. But, that was precisely what the defenders of tradition seriously feared. Although the majority of single peddlers remained well within cultural bounds, too many, in the view of elders, were unable to resist temptation and escaped into nontraditional marital solutions. They married non-Syrians, took common-law wives, or, as the Orthodox leadership discovered, entered into "temporary" marriages with "American" girls. Traditionalists, mainly from the religious leadership, felt they could not relax their vigilance if Syrian mores—or any segment of them—were to survive and, therefore, subjected the freedom of the individual in the United States to frequent criticism.

The Reverend Iskandar Atallah believed that Syrians, who had never known freedom in their homeland, did not understand it in America. They had been blinded by the brilliant rays of the freedom to earn, he wrote. Therefore, an ignorant few stretched the meaning of freedom beyond reason and disgraced the whole Syrian community. Excessive freedom, in his view, had seriously impaired the behavior of Syrians. "I declare," he continued,

> that many of those who return to the homeland to marry, should first be asked if they were married in America. Their answer should not be accepted without proof. The reason for this is that some of them who marry Syrian girls in Syria were already married. . . . This has caused a great deal of harm and our people must be cautioned. This publication has more

than once . . . advised our countrymen, who wish to go to the homeland to marry, to take along papers from the episcopate or from the clergy of their Orthodox church, or from the clergy of any church to which they belong in order to dispell suspicion. Emigrants [to America] should likewise bring with them the same proof.[50]

The intelligentsia, with a pragmatic vision of the future, were aware that that vision involved complex social and economic changes, and raised equally complex questions: How to channel the social and economic energies of the young and adventurous away from the "subversive and immoral" and onto an upward economic path; how to reconcile the widening economic role of women with the traditional restraints; how to protect the sanctity of the family; and how to uphold the honor and integrity of Syrians were questions which subsumed, to a large extent, the issue of marriage.

The significance of marriage to the future of Syrians in America was underscored in the Arabic press. *Al-Hoda* seemed determined to educate its readers to new realities. A common theme threaded through its articles: success through trade is open to all Syrians, more open to married than to single, and more to the enlightened than to the backward; inflexible tradition is an obstacle to progress; change is essential. The following are summaries of articles illustrating how *Al-Hoda* attempted to effect change:

March 5, 1899: "Marriage and the Immigrants in America." Immigrants who postponed marriage on the pretext of "lack of money" and the desire to save before marrying are exhorted to consider the benefits of taking a wife. Bachelors value money lightly; they (presumably the urban immigrants) squander it in clubs, theaters, and houses of ill repute. All of these places are traps for immigrants in a foreign land. A man who marries and has a family is respected, responsible, and motivated to save. Therefore, men should marry—not at an early age but between the ages of twenty-two and thirty—and their mates should be chosen not for their wealth but for their education. Such wives will create enduring happiness.[51]

Immediately following was an article entitled "The Syrian

Woman in the United States" which asked "Why should a man labor hard without a wife who would share his work as she shares his life?" The thrust of the answer justifies the increased role of Syrian women in the family economy. It argued for the participation of women in the workplace in general and the manufacturing of finer merchandise in particular. There is no dishonor for women who work; women in France, England, and American have proven that. Although peddling is an honorable trade, working in the silk trade, for example, is more lucrative for Syrian women. A woman's honor, if it is pure and safeguarded, is, like pure gold, untarnishable in or out of her home. Marriage is essential to success in America, and men need not fear dishonor from marriage to a working woman.[52]

November 3, 1900: An untitled article. Referring to a previous article on marriage, the author invoked Milton and Shakespeare to support his criticism of outdated attitudes and customs surrounding the selection of spouses. A happy and successful marriage, he wrote, depends on individual preference rather than on arranged and forced choices. Fatalism has no place in bringing two people together. In the choice of mates, character and personality are more worthy than wealth. With fewer women than men in the United States, women need not marry gamblers and wastrels. Early and arranged marriages, based purely on the needs and interests of the family, are discouraged.[53]

July 3, 1908: "Immigration and the Woman." Yusuf Affendi Elia Wakim argues that women should accompany their immigrating husbands to the United States if the integrity and values of the family are to be preserved.[54]

The most difficult task for the purists was to hold their young people to the custom of religious, sectarian, and village endogamy, or indeed any aspect of that custom. The ideal marriage choice was thwarted, not only by the unbalanced sex ratios, but by the attraction of American society and a weakening in group discipline. A number of Syrians— even those who nurtured an Old World desire to marry within their primary group—broke with custom. Nevertheless, if deep-rooted village endogamy was relaxed, it was not completely ignored, and only rarely was the interdiction against intersectarian marriage among the Eastern-rite Christian sects violated.

Occasional exceptions existed for the Melkite sect which has elements in common with the Orthodox and the Maronites. Orthodox were occasionally in some cases permitted to marry Melkites on the grounds that, except for a few Roman Catholic influences, they were liturgically identical. In other cases, Melkites and Maronites married because both were Uniate sects affiliated with the Church of Rome. The influence of the Latin church in America had not yet widened the existing gap between Orthodox and Melkites or narrowed it between Melkites and Maronites.

Nothing threatened family cohesion nor met with greater resistence than defection from one's faith, and marriage offered that possibility. In the homeland, sons might well be disowned, but the consequences fell most severely on daughters. In America, as in the homeland, convention and religion allowed men much latitude in the choice of spouses, since custom demanded that wives adopt their husband's faith. Unmarried women usually remained under strict surveillance, their choices carefully controlled and arranged by the family to serve its honor and interests. They were expected to bow to parental authority—to place the family (to which they were, in any case, very loyal) above themselves. So rigid was family convention on this point, that the very passion which gave it such moral authority exposed its rigidity. The women who married outside their faith paid a price for their daring. They were painfully distanced from their families and their children were lost to the group. In spite of the latitude extended to men, and because of restrictions placed on women, the interfaith marriages of Syrian immigrants in America were minimal.

Crossing the ethnic line was far more pardonable in Syrian society than breaching the denominational barrier. Hardly an issue in the village, it was a new problem to be faced in America. Group disapproval did not necessarily translate into rejection of non-Syrian spouses. Tafeeda B. remembered that when Isber S. married an "American" woman, "unbeknownst to anybody . . . and he brought her home [to Fort Wayne]," she was accepted because, said Tafeeda, she learned Arabic, how to cook Arabic dishes well, and she was very clean; "my, how she taught these woman [new things]."

Interethnic marriages, thought to be uncommon among Syrians because they were believed both unworkable and undesirable, occurred more frequently before World War I than has been known or acknowledged. This is not to say that there was a mass defection by single men to "American" brides. One or two in a settlement, here and there, became the focus of considerable interest and gossip at the time. Louise Houghton found a "number of cases of Syrians marrying Americans and a few cases of Syrians and Greeks intermarrying, but, in general, where Syrians marry outside of their own race, it is with Americans or thoroughly Americanized foreigners."[55]

For several reasons, Syrians could not know how many of their compatriots were breaking with custom. First among them was that the impetus to mingle with and marry non-Syrians was strongest in isolated and remote settlements. Secondly, Syrians usually communicated between the settlements along the narrow network of friends and relatives. Finally, wedding rites were doubtlessly performed by a local justice of the peace or in a non-Syrian church, perhaps the church of the "American" spouse. Consequently, if figures—official or unofficial—on interethnic unions exist, they are also widely dispersed and difficult to gather.[56] Rarely did an interethnic marriage rupture family relations to such an extent that the couple left the community permanently.

That the pioneers set a precedent by marrying outside of their nationality is unmistakable from the census figures for 1910. Of 13,627 natives of white stock or foreign or mixed parentage who spoke Syrian [sic] and Arabic, 708, or 5.2 percent, had foreign fathers and 124, or .9 percent, had foreign mothers. Not unexpectedly, the numbers as well as the percentages rose in the next decade and continued upward. In 1920, 46,582 spoke Arabic and of these 3,270, or 7 percent, had a foreign father and 588, or 1.3 percent, had a foreign mother.[57] The accuracy of such figures may be questionable, since immigrants other than the Syrians and Palestinians might have been included. In the late nineteenth century, Assyrian, Armenian, Greek, and Turkish immigrants who had lived in the Ottoman province of Syria, some for generations, spoke Arabic, yet retained their own ethnic identities. The higher 1920 figures for Arabic speakers of mixed parentage, boosted upward by the liberating effects of military service, were undoubtedly the culmination of a prewar trend which had gained momentum since the turn of the century.

What was happening in a larger sense to other immigrant groups was also happening to Syrians, but at an unexpectedly higher rate for so tradition-bound and village-centered a people. Loneliness and the lack of marriageable Syrian women, of course, accounted for many interethnic marriages. Equally, however, was the desire for speedier acceptance in the American community as well as attendance at non-Syrian churches by those thousands who lacked Syrian-rite churches to attend. Finally, to these causes may be added another of some significance—the ambivalence of Syrians toward American culture.

Nothing more clearly underscores this vacillation than a debate on the question of "Syrian-American Marriages" conducted at a meeting of the Maronite Young Men's Society of New York in 1903. The "Speeches and Debates" of the meeting were printed by Al-Hoda Publishing House whose influential owner, Naoum Mokarzel, was as ardent a Maronite as he was a Lebanese nationalist, deeply rooted in his native culture. Yet, he was also an admirer of America, its business opportunities, and an advocate of Americanization. The influence of his newspaper, *Al-Hoda*, cannot be discounted in the matter of cultural ambivalence—an ambivalence that was mirrored in the society's deliberations. Several incongruent speeches variously exhorted members to preserve their quality of brotherhood and maintain material and intellectual ties with the homeland (in this case, Mount Lebanon). One called for more democratic practices within the society, and another candidly criticized the retarding effects of tenacious immigrant traditions and customs. The major item before the body, however, was the question of "Syrian-American Marriages," a reflection of that generation's inner struggles with Americanization.

As the proponent of mixed ethnic marriages, As'ad Af-fendi Ankiri, argued that, notwithstanding the differences in the two cultures, there were several advantages in marrying an "American" wife, not the least of which was her "greater" wealth, learning, and beauty. "If learning is more preferable and beneficial than ignorance and closer to that which links the heart to the mind," he reasoned, "then the marriage of a Syrian to an educated and cultured American is more beneficial to him than marriage to one of his own kind."

The traditionalist argument was presented by Shaykh Philip Nasir, who reminded the group of the harmful effects such a marriage would have on ancestral and family lineage and honor. The incompatibility of the vastly different cultural values, he continued, not only would result in an unhappy marriage but would deprive the offspring of their "rightful" cultural heritage and weaken that heritage. If a man, he warned, married a woman who was more intelligent, rich, and cultured than himself, his life would be a maze of problems. Besides, he asked, what kind of a relationship could develop between a Syrian immigrant who barely spoke English and a native American? The consequence would be divorce which is widespread in America. He concluded with an Arab proverb: "He who marries outside his own people dies from no cause save his [self-inflicted] defect."[58]

The problem of outmarriage and its solution was undoubtedly also discussed with some apprehension in coffeehouses, living rooms, and churches. Although interethnic marriages were seen by most Syrians as a threat to family unity, continuity, and honor, as well as to the cultural values, and although they deprived Syrian girls of Syrian husbands, there seemed to have been no great outcry against them, no inter-Syrian community campaign to arrest them. Any solutions that may have been devised were local, within a group or settlement. The clergy, most of it itinerant, warned and scolded, but their main concern, generally, was with interfaith marriage. But the numbers of the clergy were small and their admonitions reached only their own and intermittent parishioners. Perhaps the greatest inconsistency was that while the traditionalists-modernists debates continued in the Arabic press, no antiassimilationist forum of opinion crystallized. On balance, the press's proclivities leaned decidedly toward assimilation.

Furthermore, while Syrians feared the effects of outmarriage, they had not learned to think of it as an issue for the broader Syrian community. Impermanence was as yet a pervasive attitude by the onset of World War I. Immigrants worked hard, saved their money, and kept a keen eye on family affairs both here and abroad; but all of this was personal and immediate, quite disconnected, in their minds, from the whole. Their life consisted of small moments directed at transforming a vision into a palpable reality, not of any larger ideas or motives. Few Syrian groups saw themselves as part of an interdependent and expanding Syrian community in the United States. It is not even clear that the older, more populous urban colonies had advanced much further along that road. Given Syrian predelictions for American tastes and manners, the growing awareness that their future lay in America, and the uneven, vacillating efforts to preserve their own culture, the rate of interethnic marriages continued to rise.

What had been a trend before World War I became a gathering storm on the horizon between the wars. In the decade of the 1920s, according to census figures, 12,270 mixed marriages were recorded for Syrians and Palestinians. Of the 84,660 Syrians and Palestinians born in the United States of mixed parentage to 1930, 10,652, or 12.6 percent, had immigrant fathers and 1,618, or 1.9 percent, had immigrant mothers.[59] In response, some communities began to take institutional action to maintain their native culture and keep their children within the fold. Leaders sensed a range of new attitudes among the young—attitudes influenced by the changes and complexities in the society around them. Yearning for aspects of American middle-class life to which they had been exposed through school, movies, radio, and military service, the American-born and American-raised generation was shaking off the restraints of tradition. They were becoming Syrian Americans rather than Syrians in America as their parents had been. In an attempt to reverse the headlong trend, the community built churches—fifty between 1910 and 1920, and thirty more in the following decade—and formed social clubs as well as family and village associations.

"The Sage of Washington Street," A. Hakim, in his meditations, believed that the "dilemma of interracial marriage" of the 1920s was "becoming all the more acute in proportion to the progress of the evolutionary process which we are undergoing in our soil of transportation," and concluded that the first generation had not lived in America sufficiently long "to bring about a complete acclimatization, nor has the young generation become numerous and influential enough to cause the engulfing of the old in the invading tide of the new."[60]

The differences in the marriage problems between immigrant Christians and those of Muslims and Druze were few but significant, springing primarily from the disparity in relative numbers and the near exclusion of non-Christian women from emigration. Whereas, Muslim women were detained by custom, Druze women were strictly forbidden by the religious elders from migrating. A few Muslim and Druze women may have migrated to join husbands or to marry before World War I, but their real migration did not begin until after the war. None is known to have traveled alone either to work or to marry. With no marriageable females of their faith, Muslim and Druze males faced more acute matrimonial problems than the Christians did. The delay in the arrival of women, moreover, delayed the assimilation of many Muslim groups.

Like Christians, many of the males had left wives and children behind for extended periods and, also like the Christians, visited them from time to time. A reproachful Palestinian Muslim of Chicago told a budding sociologist who studied that community in the mid-1940s that "it's a shame the way we come over here to America when we are 19 or 20 leaving our wives with a couple of kids in Palestine waiting for us to come back. Sometimes the wives wait one year, five years, ten years, twenty years, even thirty years until their husbands come back. Sometimes they never come back but marry some mulatto here and forget about the old lady in the old country."[61] Brother John W. Shuman, on a return mission to Syria, encountered a Syrian Druze who, as an American property owner for twenty-five years, "owned practically the entire Virginia town in which he lived." The man was making his seventh trip, in the 1920s, to his family because "his wife and five children had never been to America."[62]

Because so many men could not or would not visit their families, Druze elders, before World War I, were moved to extract sworn oaths from emigrating men to return to their wives or divorce them.[63] Nafe K. thought it best to divorce his wife with whom he had had one child. Ultimately, however, the majority of Muslims and Druze were united with their wives in America.

Bachelors could either return to their villages for brides, which most did, or marry in the United States outside their religious or ethnic group, which more than a few did. Purportedly, more Druze married outside their faith than Muslims.

It might be easy to assume that as non-Christians in a Christian country, Muslims and Druze would wrap themselves tightly in their cultural armor against the effects of assimilation in general and outmarriages in particular, since for both peoples that meant interfaith marriages. The non-Christians were, on the one hand, more strictly bound to the custom of parallel cousin (father's brother's daughter) marriage than Christians were. On the other, the Muslim Holy Law and the Druze's rigid tribal loyalty served as strong deterrents against departures from custom. The Koran contained no prohibition against Muslim men marrying non-Muslims, that is, Christians and Jews, but the non-Muslim wife would be expected to convert to Islam. Yet, parents and religious leaders imposed severe penalties, especially upon women, to discourage fraternization and marriage with nonbelievers. Mohammad K., born in Highland Park, Michigan, and trained in his calling as a Sunni Muslim imam by his father, himself a Sunni imam, said that he had "witnessed cases where parents broke relations with their girls for marrying out of their ethnic [sic] group. Mostly the father and mother, but not the siblings. This was before World War II. The fathers and mothers did this out of a sense of duty so their other children would not copy. Their hearts were broken, but they did it."[64]

Druze elders, on the other hand, indoctrinated their faithful with the "fear that if a man becomes a part of an alien culture or marries a non-Druze, he would lose the privileges of belonging to a unique faith and the blessings that his faith accrued to him."[65]

Traditional and religious restraints were not effective enough. Muslim and Druze informants reported several pre–World War I mixed marriages. Moreover, at least three of the roughly thirty Muslim families in the relatively isolated North Dakota community were mixed households; the wives were Irish Catholics.[66] How many of the mixed marriages recorded in the census figures were Muslim and Druze cannot be determined. Salloum Mokarzel, in an article on "Christian-Moslem Marriages," published in the *Syrian World* in 1928, wrote that although statistics are not available, such unions occurred because of the absence of women of Druze faith. He quoted a Druze source who claimed that 125 Druze had married American women, many ending in divorce.[67] Fidelity to custom weakened under the pressures to Americanize and, like Christians, Druze and Muslims crossed the religious and ethnic barriers. A few married Syrian Christians; more took American brides. This alarmed leaders on both sides of the ocean and provoked discussions on the pages of *Al-Bayan*, the Arabic-language spokesman for Druze and Muslims in America.

A lengthy article, published on 17 February 1914, attacked the conservative view. It pinned the disturbing rise in Druze outmarriages squarely on the denial of emigration to Druze women. Opposition to male emigration in the belief that they would not return, the article stated, had been proved unfounded by those courageous few who had left and returned much wealthier. Even Christians who had migrated with their families were reported to have returned. Denying the right of women to emigrate, it continued, deprived them of husbands. Marriageable sisters and daughters who had been left behind could have been married and have borne children. Moreover, the denial virtually drove the men to marry outside of their faith. The laws of nature on which the universe was created, like the law of gravity, applies to the union of men and women. Their compulsory separation is therefore unnatural. Inevitably, the author feared, it would result in a population decline and psychological and economic crises. In this dubious bachelorhood, he warned, if a man's kin were unavailable, he would take refuge in a foreign marriage; he would adopt the nationality of his wife and be lost to his people. The author found evidence of this among Druze immigrants, some of whom had married foreigners and severed relationships with their people, even to exchanging letters. They had forgotten their obligations to their parents, kin, and people. But most serious and harmful was the fact that wives had been abandoned without support or hope of it. He argued not only for the emigration of women but for enough freedom in the new land for them to adapt the best of the American culture to their own—in America from American women who, by their freedom and education, have progressed further than the Druze. They could learn to organize their homes, bring up children, and attend to their husbands' comforts.[68]

More than a year later, articles were still appearing in *Al-Bayan* about the real or imagined behavior of Muslims and Druze in the United States. "He Who Is Married in the Homeland," an article published on 29 April 1915, might have been printed as a warning. "One of the most despicable acts of a man who is married in his own land," it began, "is to marry a second woman during his emigration—one of the women of the street, or, stated more clearly, daughters of chance." Such men would be virtual outcasts in their villages, and the wives "who preserved their chastity and honor throughout the waiting years" would not take them back nor help them when they returned, enfeebled from their experience in America.[69]

The lure of a freer mode of life in America posed the same

difficult dilemmas for all Syrian immigrants. Drawn by its visions, yet gripped by their traditional moral authority of family and religion, the males were torn between two poles. In an account of the North Dakota Muslim community, which appeared in the *Minot Daily News*, the dilemma was apparent. "Those who married within their Moslem faith," it reported, "found it difficult to maintain because they lacked close contact with their native culture."[70]

Kalil B., a shaykh ministering to a small Shiʿa Muslim colony in Highland Park, Michigan, insisted, however, that between the wars very few young Muslim men married outside their religion despite the lack of religious training. "I ought to know," he said, "I married them."[71] Imam Mohammad K. had a different opinion: "Yes, young Muslims married outside of Islam before World War II. They always have, because of the environment. Also, the Muslim boy was forbidden by a girl's parents to date a Muslim girl. . . . No dates unless you want to marry; and the boy wasn't prepared to commit himself to marriage. He just wanted a date. So, he would turn to an American girl who would date him. . . . and her parents would say 'have a good time.' The American girl was fun and was available."

Abe A., a Shiʿa Muslim, married a Polish woman in 1933 because, he said, there were too few Syrian girls available. He reflected a moment and added: "I'll tell you the truth. There were girls and they liked me, but to marry them they would ask for a car and a home and to give her father money and this did not appeal to me. This is America. If we love each other we should marry, but they asked and asked. Because of that, I didn't marry a Syrian girl."[72]

Because Islamic restrictions against fraternization with non-Muslims were unenforceable, Muslim leaders were forced, in the words of Imam K., to "close our eyes to it. . . . knowing that we could hardly handle the situation. So we took a laissez-faire attitude." Even Shaykh B. admitted that he not only officiated at mixed marriages but relaxed his attitude toward them. "When Muslim youth married American or Polish girls . . . I did not oblige the girl to convert to Islam. There is freedom in this country. She kept her faith.

On the other hand, if a Muslim girl married a non-Muslim, I would not permit it because a girl has to adhere to her husband's religion. I married them [the boys] when they married non-Muslims. It didn't matter."

This trend, incipient in the first-generation Muslims of North Dakota, could hardly be stemmed or reversed even by the establishment of a mosque in the community. "As the children in the congregation grew to adulthood," wrote the *Minot Daily News*, "many of them forsook the faith and adopted the Christian religion when they married a non-Moslem."[73]

If more Muslims remained true to their conscience than slipped away, it is traceable to the pliant nuances of their Islamic teachings as well as to the wisdom of men like Shaykh B. and Imam K., and his father before him who, according to Imam K., foresaw the dangers in excessive rigidity. "An imam had to have elasticity, that is, flexibility in the American environment," he said. "My father was never rigid. Sometimes he was criticized for his liberalism. I believe, as my father did, that rigidity causes Muslims to shun Islam and [that] defeats the purpose of keeping Islam [alive in America], but within prescribed limits imposed by God. God has given latitudes. He is liberal and a God of mercy and love as well as a God of retribution."

Despite the lack of well-knit Muslim and Druze subnetworks, isolation from kindred groups, rarely complete even during the pioneer period, declined markedly after the war. Through letters from the homeland and items in *Al-Bayan*, Muslims and Druze learned the locations of others of their faith or village and were able to mitigate the effects of numerical minority status and any isolation they may have felt. Contacts were especially important for bride searches, celebration of religious festivals, and other socially significant traditions and customs. Muslims of Cedar Rapids, for example, made contacts with Muslims in such cities as Michigan City, Indiana; Highland Park (later in Dearborn), Michigan; and Toledo, Ohio. The Druze, on the other hand, tried to formalize their contacts through the creation of area chapters of the society founded in Seattle in 1908. Although lines of communication between Druze communities, were, by their own admission, tenuous, households connected through marriage and a sense of communal interrelatedness formed not so much ethnoreligious communities as social networks.

CITIZENSHIP AND THE "ASIAN" CONTROVERSY

The link between hostility to an immigrant group and the group's ultimate assimilation is incontrovertible. To the extent that a people is rejected for whatever reason—religion, race, national origin, or cultural characteristics—its attitude toward its adopted country is colored and its social and economic integration is impeded. Toward the end of the nineteenth century, coinciding with the flood of immigrants from eastern and southern Europe and the eastern Mediterranean, hostility to, and rejection of, select groups, hardly novel in America, began to mount and was reflected in restrictive legislation.[74] The hostility would ebb, however, in the 1930s.

When immigration reached its peak between 1905 and 1914, it included Syrians, their numbers almost doubling annually. Their olive skin, dark eyes, large mustaches, and shabby clothes betrayed their non-Nordic origins. They fitted the stereotypic image which contemporary biological and pseudoscientific theories had classified as inferior—types that were likely to dilute the racial purity and weaken the moral fiber of the nation. While the American nativist antipathy encompassed all non-Anglo-Saxon immigrants, it focused more on some groups—Jews, Italians, and Chinese, for example—than others; and it was sharper in some sections of the country—the South, some metropolitan centers, some rural towns—than in others.

The Syrians were among the more fortunate; in the end they emerged relatively unscathed. Pioneers who were interviewed insisted that their relations with Americans were consistently smooth and that they were well liked. Additionally, the peddlers' anecdotes, candid insights into so many aspects of the Syrian experience, disclose far less about scorn than

about sympathy and kindness, while the Arabic press over-
flowed with praise for America and Americans. If some were
called names, Syrians were not generally singled out as an
undesirable people, nor was the rate of their assimilation,
remarkable by the standards of the time, impeded.

The reasons are not difficult to discern. At no time did the
Syrian population represent a cumulative religious, political,
or social force that attracted national attention. In addition,
their small population was dispersed, making them incon-
spicuous. The religion of the Christian majority was conge-
nial to Americans; as for Muslims and Druze, their religions
were virtually unknown to Americans, who generally assumed them to be Protestants, Catholics, or Jews. They were
seldom asked about their religion and, if asked, found it easier to conceal than to explain. The epithets used against
them were those used against other nationalities and had
nothing to do with their being Syrian or Arab. In any case,
Syrian national identity was more village and sectarian than
nationalistic.

The impact of one people's hostility toward another is
predicated not only on how it is expressed but on how it is
perceived by its targets. If the pioneers sensed any deep feelings of rejection or bias, there is no evidence in the interview
data that their self-image suffered any lasting damage. On
the one hand, they realized that they were foreigners—different from the Americans whom they began rather early to
imitate and whose approval they sought. Therefore, social
pressures to Americanize were accorded little notice, particularly by the Christians. Moreover, they lived in predominantly ethnic neighborhoods, and although decidedly clannish in their in-group associations, they erected no high walls
around themselves. Finally, with their minds fastened on a
goal greater than momentary insults, they could afford to
ignore them as they had ignored the need for beds to sleep
on and blankets to warm them. "The Polish people—one
family—was against us," said Slayman N. of Spring Valley,
"but we had to live. . . . You see, people like . . . myself came
here to make $100 or $200 and go back to build a house.
This is what we wanted." Not driven to nurture a ghetto psy-

chology, their entry into the mainstream of American life was not seriously hampered by prejudice.

In the aggregate, prejudice against Syrians was neither specific nor sustained, since Americans tended to view all foreigners as one people rather than as peoples from separate and disparate cultures and backgrounds. Syrians, indistinguishable from most east European and Mediterranean immigrants, were lumped into the same American stereotyped thinking. "Before the First World War," reflected Nazha H.

> the American people looked down on foreigners. They had specific names for other ethnic groups but not for the Syrians. My mother, who was fair-skinned and dressed like other Americans, and I, would take walks on Saturday nights to the front of the courthouse in Fort Wayne where there would be band concerts—my mother liked to listen to them. Somehow, we were always spotted and called "dago." . . . Apparently, they didn't know we were "awlad 'Arab [of the Arab people]." . . . The Americans called the Syrians dago or sheeny. . . . They didn't know the difference between Syrians and Jews and called all those who sold "sheeny." . . . Name-calling was usually from kids.

Many, maybe most, Syrian immigrants could relate some incidents of prejudice. However, shielded from distinction, the Syrians, on the road and in the settlements, distinguished between what they heard and their own deep sense of identity. They were, therefore, free to slough off ridicule and revilement or to attribute either to motives unrelated to anything Syrian. Americans, some informants said, were jealous and resentful of Syrians' rapid economic advancement.[75] Friction with a few Irish miners in Spring Valley who, with Italians and other immigrants, had fought several wage battles with mine owners and scabs, was blamed on Irish drunkeness.[76]

In some areas of the South, however, discrimination was overt. Dr. H. A. El-Kouri, a prominent Syrian physician in Birmingham, defended his people against derogatory public statements made in 1907 by his congressman, who also served as an immigration commissioner. According to Dr. El-

Kouri, Congressman John L. Burnett had seen some "dirty and diseased" Syrians in Marseilles, France, and on his return, he proclaimed them to be the "most undesirable of the undesirable peoples of Asia Minor" and supported the exclusion of Asians and the restrictive literacy test for immigrants.[77] Some informants indicated that Syrians, whose attitudes toward blacks at that time differed little from those of their American neighbors, were disliked because they were friendly with the blacks with whom they traded.[78] Yet, testimony from such southern communities as Vicksburg, Mississippi, and Birmingham (too few to be conclusive), where one would expect prejudice, are remarkable for the absence of it, and where it existed, no case was based on skin color of the Syrians.

Prejudice was more evident in St. Louis and economically motivated, according to Sandra Hasser Bennett, director of "The St. Louis Project," a study of the Maronites who constituted the majority of the Syrian community in that city. It was found that discrimination was present against Syrians who lived and worked in a community composed largely of Germans and Irish. By the 1920s, the epithet "niggers" was particularly used by parochial-school children because the Syrians were "poor and some were dark-skinned." The project concluded, however, that discrimination did not affect the Maronite's social or economic mobility, nor did it prohibit their entering municipal politics before 1910 and subsequently dominating it. By that year, one or two Syrians who had worked for the street department were reported to have hired 107 of their own, which undoubtedly accounted, in some measure, for the interethnic rivalry.[79]

Confessional controversies were not new to the Syrians. Religion, rather than ethnicity, was at issue in Slayman's conflict between the Polish and the Syrians in Spring Valley. The Polish had allowed the churchless Orthodox to use their church for funeral services and, on occasion, the cemetery. Resentment among members of the parish would, however, ultimately deprive the non-Catholic Syrians of this privilege and force them, in anger, to purchase their own cemetery and build a church.[80] In Pollack, South Dakota, Amelia U.'s family became "uncomfortable" in the 1920s because "Pollack was very anti-Catholic." The residents, with the exception of the banker and two other families, were "Protestant Yankees and had their Ku Klux Klan."

Muslims were sometimes confused with Turks for whom Americans harbored a special antipathy. Hussein I. ran into prejudice when he became known as a Muslim because, he explained, "Armenians came first to the United States . . . and start to say Muslims kill my father, brother, and so on, and [this accusation] went all over the country." A blend of patriotism and mistaken identity placed Yahya A., who was peddling near Urbana, Iowa, during World War I, in a precarious situation. A Catholic farmer who had provided lodging for the night invited him to supper. Yahya's son, William, related the story. "A prayer was said and they all crossed themselves, but my father did not. They asked him, 'Aren't you Christian?' He replied that no, he was a Muslim. They did not understand what a Muslim was and he proceeded to explain . . . and he mentioned the Turkish government. . . . At this point, the farmer rose up in anger and, reaching for his gun, said, 'So, you are a Turk. I'll kill that Turk; get out of my house.' So my father left." William concluded that "the farmer considered Turks the enemies of America, since the Turkish government fought along side the Germans. He wasn't discriminating against Arabs or Muslims; he only hated America's enemy."

Not that the Syrians were impervious to insults; on the contrary, they were conditioned to react to the slightest offense relating to that hallowed repository of their identity— family honor. There was no basis for overreaction on being called "dago" or "sheeny" or "Turk," none of which reflected on their Syrian origins or their Arabness. Convinced that they were frequently mistaken for Jews, they smothered such references with proclamations of their Christian faith and Holy Land origins. Wadi al-S.'s attitude was characteristic: "We never paid any attention to it; it just went off our backs."[81]

Corresponding with the deepening of nativist feelings, prejudice became more ethnically specific and for Syrian children more frequent in the twenties. The epithets now included "camel jockey," "black" or "dirty Syrian," and more often "Turk."[82] By this time, however, Syrian children were imitating other immigrant children and settling scores with their fists in school yards and on the streets. "We fought our way into acceptance," said Abe A., of Vicksburg, Mississippi, "there was none of that in high school, though." In Worcester, Massachusetts, the youngsters were made to "feel different," wrote Dolores Courtemanche. "We couldn't afford to get into trouble," George Abodeely told her, "We were too small a force. . . . Others didn't know whether to call us white, brown, or yellow. . . . Kids always challenge; its normal. But that didn't last past the 7th or 8th grades."[83]

Muslim children may have had a more difficult time, if the experience of the Ross, North Dakota, community was typical. "Though the adults were generally accepted into the society of the community," wrote the *Fargo Forum*, "the children received some scorn from their fellow classmates because of their non-Christian religion and differing practices. Amid Hach . . . recalled how often his children had asked, 'Daddy, how come we don't go to church.' The reasons were difficult to understand for the young minds. As these children grew to manhood and womanhood, many of them forsook their father's faith and adopted the Christian religion when they married a non-Moslem."[84]

When in 1899 the Bureau of Immigration initiated the "racial" classifications of "Syrian" and "Palestinian" for immigrants from the eastern Mediterranean provinces of the Ottoman Empire, they were regarded as Caucasian. Race did not become an issue until after 1906 when immigrants from western Asia became entangled in new naturalization laws designed to determine suitability for citizenship. A Bureau of Immigration and Naturalization was established to administer a complex set of procedures designed to "eliminate the frauds, corruption and low standards for admission so characteristic of 19th-century proceedings."[85] Then, when Congress and the courts, in order to control illegal naturalization of immigrants for voting purposes, added ethnic orgins to requirements for suitability, based on a law that declared

Chinese ineligible for citizenship, the problem of race for many non-European immigrant groups surfaced. The issue was further confused when an ammended naturalization law of 1870 was used as a further basis for defining suitability for citizenship. While the law stated that free whites and aliens of "African descent or African nativity" could apply for naturalization, it failed to define "white," leaving the interpretation of that term to the subjective opinion of individuals in the courts.[86] In 1910, peoples from the eastern Mediterranean—Syrians, Palestinians, Turks, Armenians, and others—became directly drawn into the controversial relationship between national origin and naturalization when the U.S. Census Bureau classified them as "Asiatics." To further exacerbate the issue, a directive emanated from the Bureau of Immigration and Naturalization in 1911 ordering court clerks to reject applications for first papers from "aliens who were neither white persons nor persons of African birth and descent," and the directive was acted on nationwide by a bureaucracy which included bureau chiefs, naturalization examiners, and district directors.[87]

When Syrians began to be disqualified for citizenship on the basis of race and national origin, the Syrian community was unprepared. It was no coincidence that the "Asian" issue emerged for Syrians in the color-conscious South where it was more pervasive than acute. The cases, some of which reached the courts, became the most cited evidence of discrimination by Syrians against them.

Until 1909 when the first ineligibility case came to the Syrians' attention, those who had applied had been routinely naturalized—often illegally, by local political bosses. Frequently, Syrians delayed applying until after the decision to remain permanently in America. Many had become naturalized in order to facilitate reentry into the United States and the immigration of members of the family and brides.[88] Karam N. used his father's naturalization papers to reenter the United States in 1909 and did not file for his own until 1950. Moreover, pioneers who returned home to live, before World War I, found American citizenship endowed them with a certain measure of status and such privileges accorded all Westerners in the Ottoman Empire under agreements worked out centuries earlier between Sultans and west European governments. The privileges included freedom from conscription, mistreatment, and taxation. A significant number of enlistees in the United States military during World War I also became eligible for citizenship.[89]

The most irresistible, quickest, and simplest path to American citizenship was indifferent to race, religion, place of origin of the immigrant, and even the laws of the United States. Local politicians, competing for votes, made instant citizens of many of the pioneers. Salem Bashara, according to Elizabeth B., worked with Democratic politicians in Fort Wayne and "filled out the papers for his people and they would get their citizenship quickly, no questions asked, for voting purposes." A politically ambitious lawyer did the same for Dan S. of Grand Rapids. In Peoria, the "City" called Christine L.'s father one day in 1903 and "offered him citizenship papers just like that. He didn't have to take an examination or anything. They gave him a barrel of beer and one dollar. . . . He voted for Democrats ever since." There were also the veteran peddlers who recruited newcomers for ward bosses. Matt I., who had been in the country for five years but had not yet applied for naturalization, became a citizen in 1906. He had meanwhile learned to read the English-language newspapers and had become interested in politics, especially the local mayoral election in Muskogee, Oklahoma. He was, he related,

> walking on the street one day and heard a couple of men talking politics. I walked up to them and said "We have lots of Syrians here in town; if you give me my citizenship papers, I'll get them to vote for you. . . . They wanted to elect a mayor. . . . [One] was a lawyer and chairman of the Republican Committee in Muskogee. He asked me and I told him [that] we had forty or fifty Syrians or more but that they can't vote because they don't have their citizenship papers. . . . [I had] heard that if you tell them you can get them to vote, they'd give you some money. . . .
> So, I went and got about thirty-two Syrians and went to the

courthouse and [we] got our papers on Friday. The judge and everything was Republican and the judge said . . ."Do you know all of these fellahs?" I was the spokesman for all of them and their witness. I said "Yes, your Honor, I was raised with them." So, everyone signed and each one got his paper, including me. Anyway, these were our first papers and you can't vote on your first paper. . . . I told the committee chairman that we couldn't vote and he went to the judge and we tore up our first papers. We [then] said that we all came to the United States before we were sixteen. That meant we didn't need first papers. And, so we were given our second papers and on Tuesday we voted. I got about $75 out of that.

That was the first time in Muskogee history that a Republican was elected mayor. When we went to vote, the Democratic and Republican cowboys lined the streets opposite each other wearing their guns and they'd ask you who you were going to vote for and we were frightened. . . . The Syrians—lots of them—couldn't read, but they had told us how to vote.

By all these means and motives, an impressive number of Syrians became naturalized Americans by 1920. Of the recorded 55,102 foreign-born Syrians and Palestinians, about 41 percent, or 22,583, were naturalized or had received their first papers. In the next decade, the figure rose to 61.8 percent of 63,362, or 39,129.[90]

The Syrian ineligibility issue surfaced in January 1909 when Costa George Najour, a Christian from Mount Lebanon was denied citizenship on grounds that as an Asian-born subject of the Ottoman sultan, he was not a "white person."[91]

The New York community, led by the editors of the Arabic press, took up the challenge and were supported in their protest by the foreign attaché of the Ottoman embassy in Washington, D.C. It organized the Association for Syrian Unity, rallied the Syrians in the country, and raised $1,000 to appeal the decision. At a rehearing in December, Syrians were proclaimed white persons within the meaning of the 1870 naturalization law amendments, and it was stated that place of origin had no bearing on race.[92] While Najour's petition was granted, the racial question was not resolved and the Arabic press published reports of a number of rejections in southern and midwestern states. Between 1909 and 1914, three more Syrian cases were appealed and quietly won in Massachusetts, Oregon, and South Carolina.[93] It was apparent that some courts were being influenced by what was perceived as the nation's sentiment for selective and restrictive immigration legislation as reflected in exclusionary laws and the controversy over suitability for citizenship.

When pioneers reflect on discrimination, it is this period and the case of George Dow of Charleston, South Carolina, which stand out. Dow's application for naturalization came before Judge Henry Smith in February 1914. Judge Smith had once before questioned Syrian eligibility for citizenship on the basis of skin color but did not act on it, since the applicant had failed to meet eligibility requirements. Dow, however, had met all of them, even in the opinion of the judge. Noting that his skin was "darker than the usual person of white European descent," Judge Smith disallowed Dow's application.[94]

The Charleston community was humiliated, having interpreted the decision to mean that Syrians were classified as members of the "yellow race" and therefore inferior in the eyes of America. Moreover, the prospect of remaining aliens in their adopted land, of losing what they had gained, or of being deported was frightening. The Society of Syrian National Defense was then organized and it solicited the assistance of the Arabic press and the Syrian communities. The press responded enthusiastically, explaining the case to its readers, reporting its progress, and urging them and their associations to support the Charleston Society by telegraphing their congressmen. In articles throughout the next year, funds were solicited to carry the appeal through the judicial system and to the Supreme Court. The case, it warned, cast a dark cloud over the future of all Syrians who have immigrated and who wanted to immigrate. Moreover, it was necessary to resolve the issue definitively at the federal level to avoid costly and repetitive appeals on the state levels.

The society vowed that, with the help of all Syrians, it would "fight to the death to defend the rights and honor of all who speak Arabic and are born under Asian skies."[95] Appeals from the society and other groups appeared regularly, some including pleas to the Syrians to put aside their personal animosities and jealousies and to unite behind the Charleston Society. Slayman N., Mike H., Matt I., and Louis L., and many others had sent in their dollars and half dollars. By July, the Charleston Society had accumulated $937.50.[96] Meanwhile, reports of rejections from Louisiana, Texas, Mississippi, North Carolina, and Illinois were published in the press. A special committee representing the Syrians of Florida blamed "this first major Syrian crisis in America" on Judge Smith's ruling in the Dow case which, it said, was prejudicing federal examiners who in turn were influencing judges as in the case of a well-qualified Jacksonville applicant who was rejected only after the judge learned he was Syrian.[97]

As if to remind its readers of the realities of the "crisis," *Meraat al-Gharb* published, at the height of the "crisis" in April 1914, Elias Simʿan Theeb's report stating that his citizenship application had been processed quickly and easily in an Arkansas court "without the slightest opposition." He had even been assisted, he said, in the legal questions by the court recorder.[98]

At a rehearing of the Dow case before Judge Smith, the argument turned on the definition of the terms "white persons" and "Caucasian" as well as the part nativity played in those definitions. The judge held to the interpretation of the 1870 law that aliens who are not of European nativity or descent were not white persons within its meaning and recommended that Syrians appeal to a higher court for resolution of the racial issue. The Syrians did. On 15 September 1915, the case of *Dow v. The United States* was heard in the Circuit Court of Appeals, Fourth Circuit. After deliberating, the court accepted the definition of the Dillingham Report of the Immigration Commission, namely that "Physically the modern Syrians are of mixed Syrian, Arabian, and even Jewish blood. They belong to the Semitic branch of the Caucasian race, thus widely differing from their rulers, the Turks, who are in origin Mongolian."[99]

Dow was granted citizenship, and the racial issue for Syrians appeared settled, leaving, however, the question of Asian nativity unresolved and Asian-born immigrants vulnerable to nativist interpretations.

Ultimately, the question of which "non-yellow" immigrants of Asian birth were "free white persons" or "Caucasians" was addressed in the the Act of 1917 which excluded natives from a geographical area—specifically from countries east of Persia and the Caspian Sea. Yet, the determined Judge Smith once again denied the petition of a Syrian in 1923 until, in a rehearing, it was pointed out to him that Syria was not within the restricted region.[100] The Syrian question was finally resolved conclusively.

Meanwhile, many of the pioneers who had not applied for naturalization before 1915 found themselves among those entangled in the ambiguities of the eligibility question. Mike H. was one. He had received his first papers and was to appear before an examiner on 15 April 1908 for his second papers. But, on that date, he was in his Syrian village, having rushed home on news of his father's death. Meanwhile, he continued, "they sent a judge from North Platt, Nebraska, to look over papers of those applying for citizenship. He asked the county clerk, Mr. Renault, if he knew all those boys and he [the clerk] said yes. Then he [the judge] said 'Tell them they're now citizens.' I didn't know I was a citizen."

As he had turned over his store in Nebraska to his brother, he returned to settle in Minnesota and about 1912, applied for his second papers. "Well, the time I applied for my second papers was the time the U.S. was going to classify all people from Asia Minor as from the yellow race. Someone from Washington came up with that idea. . . . The son-of-a-gun inspector . . . reminded the judge of this. The inspector was from Missouri. The judge knew me, that I was peddling around there for a long time but he had to go along. . . . This was the time when Turkey was having the war and too many Syrians were coming. I was mad as the dickens." In 1915, however, Mike returned to the small Nebraska town temporarily to help his ailing brother in the store and discovered that he had been granted his citizenship papers in 1908. "I couldn't believe it!" he said.

Slayman N. was also "one of those that got hurt. . . . I was refused. When President Wilson [*sic*] said that Syrians are of the Chinese race and can't get citizenship papers, the people in New York united, collected money, and sent a lawyer to Washington. He argued that if the Syrians were Chinese, then Jesus, who was born in Syria, was Chinese. They won the case and so I went here [Spring Valley] and got my citizen[ship]."

The "yellow race" crisis vanished as suddenly as it had appeared. It had hardly dented the spirit or self-esteem of the Syrians despite the fact that nothing had so threatened their admission and acceptance into American society. Many Syrians had become frightened, angry, even hurt, but the events of those few critical years constituted an aberration that marred only the Syrians' memory of that period.

The crisis contained few, if any, of the disabilities usually associated with discrimination as practiced against other immigrant groups in the United States. The focus on racial classification rather than on Syrian origin, as Judge Smith had made clear in his comments (regardless of his intent) and as reported in the Arabic press, mitigated any exclusivity of the disparagement. Moreover, Syrians had traditionally been particularistic and parochial in defining their identity, and since, therefore, they were not sufficiently disturbed by the experience to create an isolationist attitude, feelings of inferiority, or a vengeful memory, they were largely released from the pressure to forge a strong national or group consciousness that required defending. Finally, the Act of 1917 swept away any remaining causes for racial exclusion as well as any patent obstacle to becoming American.

THE END OF AN ERA

By World War I, peddling and the settlements had accomplished their primary task. Syrian immigrants had become amply prepared to push forward along the paths of economic and social progress.

Few pioneers mourned the end of peddling. The aches and the myriad of human hardships had seemed part of the natural order at that time—both acceptable and comprehensible; more hopeful days lay ahead and they were happy to be done with the old. Yet, retrospectively, the peddling era was viewed by old-timers, who had themselves avidly pursued Americanization, as more palatable than it actually was. Most looked back with nostalgia and a sense of loss over their adventure, discovery, and comradeship. "Everybody was close together; they just lived for each other. They knew they had to stick together," recalled Tafeeda B. pensively.

However, lamentably for many, the carefree atmosphere, the cooperative spirit, and camaraderie seemed to disappear with the decline in peddling and the improvement in the peddlers' economic and social status. Some pioneers lived to see the bonds of brotherhood deteriorate and became, like Elizabeth B., embittered. "They used to get along so well together. There was none of the jealousy you see today, nor the gossip and arguments. Today, you can't call on any of them. . . . Money sowed jealousy."

Edward E., more sad than angry, said: "We lost one thing among ourselves, I am sorry to say. . . . In the early days when . . . someone needed help, we used to help them. . . . We never required them to sign a paper. We just tell them 'yes' and that meant 'yes.' That was trust. We trusted each other. . . . Now they trust everything to the dollar instead of to honor. We lost very, very much."

Disillusionment was obvious in Joe D.'s eyes and voice: "People in those days loved each other so much. Now they are separated and live away from each other and if you want to visit someone, you have to call them and ask [his voice became sarcastic] 'Are you home tonight?' In the past, whole families would drop in on someone. We used to all meet at someone's house—every night at a different home. . . . Now they're [those days] all gone—all dead."

In such statements, the hurt of old memories are mingled with the pains of rapid change. In retrospect, the Syrians may have acceded too much, too fast, to the American way of life. They were vulnerable to its magnetism and absorbed more than they could quickly integrate. Beguiled by material progress, they could not grasp its full import and cultural cost.

While the settlements, opened the way to Americanization, modifications to the immigrant culture had at first been neither harsh nor profound. From the beginning, however, there was an inexorable battle of wills between deep-seated tradition and the new culture and, almost from the beginning, the outcome was predictable.

It had not been a governing passion of the early immigrants to become American. At first they wanted only to be Syrians in America, living in familiar and treasured ways. Continuity of folk life and values seemed scarcely disturbed by the long voyage; but the doors to change were always open in the settlements, and the forces to shut that door against America's irrepressible pull were weak. First, ambition and impermanence had convinced many that there was nothing harmful in being "like" Americans for the short time they expected to be in the country. In the process, they became fascinated by America and receptive to learning and adopting that which was, from their skewed perspective, American. But, the temporary advantages soon proved seductive—acquiring an American veneer benefited them economically and socially, and it enhanced one's prestige both in the settlement and back home in the village.

Secondly, nationalistic feelings and ideologies, normally common deterrents to changing identities, were weak or absent in most Syrians and ambivalent in others. In any case, they were hardly effective against the tide of Americanization. And, not to be underestimated, was the general satisfaction with what Syrians found in America. True, they quickly came to realize that this country was not Paradise; "They did not know what work was until they came here," it was said by several informants. They worked much harder and suffered greater discomfort than in Syria, but they also earned more money here than in the villages of Syria. The consensus was "We had here what we never had there. May God continue to build this country [*Allah yu'ammir hal bilād*]." Wedad F.'s father, like so many others, "never left for work in the morn-

ing without crossing himself and concluding his brief mut-
tered prayer with 'May God bless this country.'"

There was another reason why Syrians were attracted to
America. They like to draw comparisons between themselves
and Americans. Syrians, they would reflect among themselves, were heirs to an old and wise culture, while America
was young and unsophisticated (some thought shallow), but
America was energetic and new. Hadn't Americans, by their
own ingenuity and labor, fashioned the most advanced nation on earth? Wasn't it free of the burden of tradition and
the inertia of history? Didn't it represent the wave of the future? The wisdom of the ages, they concluded, combined
with the vigor of progress was a guaranteed formula for success—and success was the prospect they dreamed of. Nothing in the conclusion turned them away from America or
Americans. Although its matchless material progress contrasted sharply with the material backwardness of their
homeland, pride in their own culture was not seriously diminished in their rationalizations.

Unable to differentiate between American behavior and
American values, the Syrians carried the comparison further.
They thought they perceived in the behavior of Americans
they encountered on the road and in the settlements, a number of similarities with themselves. Most Americans, they observed, dressed simply, labored hard, attended church and
lived by Christian values, visited neighbors, and lived frugally and morally. Since that is how they viewed themselves,
the comparison generated little cause for inferiority. They
could then say, with some conviction, that they got along well
with Americans and experienced few problems in adjusting
to American ways. If some elements of American behavior
made them feel embarrassingly backward and foreign, they
would emulate Americans. By a combination of innocence
and arrogance, they consciously tried to modify their old-
country behavior. Attempts to moderate their voices and restrain hand gestures in public, especially when they were
being observed, were among the superficial nods to American gentility. Many of the pioneers anglicized their first and/
or last names or accepted, without complaint, their anglici-

zation by American bureaucrats (immigration officers and clerks who handled applications for naturalization papers, visas, passports, licenses, and other documents). They did not so much wish to disguise their ethnic identity as to overcome the difficulties of spelling and pronouncing Arabic sounds that are alien to Americans. Members of the same family went through life not only with different spellings of the same name but with different names.

The other world also entered their world from another important direction: the Arabic press. It exhorted them to change some old-fashioned ways and encouraged them to become "good American citizens." It also published books for learning English, American customs, and naturalization procedures.

Advocates of enlightment and change, as well as the defenders of old values and tradition, used the pages of the newspapers to express their views. The readers were taught to look at their world in a new way, to expand their horizons, to be, in the words of one anonymous writer, "civilized." The duel between the old and the new was satirized by him in an imaginary conversation between an Americanized Syrian and a Syrian nationalist. Under the heading of "Wit and Humor," it appeared in *Al-Hoda* on 22 March 1898:

(Two Syrians: *A Syrian Nationalist and an Americanized Syrian*)

(The Americanized Syrian is Pro-Americanization)

AMERICANIZED SYRIAN: Are you still a villager? Haven't you become civilized?

SYRIAN NATIONALIST: Do good manners allow you to insult me this way when you are pretending to be civilized?

AMERICANIZED SYRIAN: We alone know what it is to be civilized and we regret that you are not one of us.

SYRIAN NATIONALIST: And what are the benefits of joining your kind?

AMERICANIZED SYRIAN: Don't you understand that we are all intelligent? For when we become Americanized, we are able to earn more without working hard and we help each other by gaining greater prestige.

SYRIAN NATIONALIST: But, I ȧm from the East and I prefer to preserve the honor of my forefathers.

AMERICANIZED SYRIAN: After what I have just told you, are you provoked because I called you a villager? Haven't you heard of Darwin who denies that man evolved from man? We are what we are as a result of the evolutionary process. And, your preserving the honor of your ancestors is pure ignorance and lack of education.

SYRIAN NATIONALIST: I have not read Darwin and I gladly leave that honor to you. But you can be what you want to be; I am going to remain an Easterner. My original ancestor was Adam and it is likely that his language was Arabic. Long live the East! Down with its enemies.[101]

Duels between advocates of the new and defenders of the old were not always in the realm of wit. At times they were confrontational, as illustrated in the New York riot of 1905. Najeeb Malouf, a wealthy importer, member of the short-lived Reform Society which he and his colleagues founded, was a prime antagonist in the conflict. He defended his involvement saying: "The progressive members of the Syrian colony are determined to blot out certain harmful influences at work. We want the Syrians to become Americans, to adopt American customs and American ways. The fight against us is being made by the remnants of the old influences which cannot see the people rise, preferring to exercise their old power, no matter what may become of others."[102]

In the long run, the new clearly predominated. The Syrians were being drawn along a path they did not quite understand and, fueled by self-interest, pursued a pattern of conduct they could not quite resist. With so few checks against it, assimilation crept into the settlement innocently. But its consequences, illusive and seemingly innocuous at the time, would become irreversible by 1920. The trend had, in the opinion of some leaders, moved alarmingly away from the native culture, but it was a trend to which they had contributed more than they had intended. To retrieve the old ways from oblivion, a formula was proposed by some, notably the intelligentsia in New York: becoming American and being Syrian were not mutually exclusive. It was perhaps best articulated by Kahlil Gibran, himself a champion of Americanization. In an article purportedly written for the Boston Arabic publication, *Fatat-Boston*, in 1919, he exhorted "the children of the first generation Arabs to proudly preserve their heritage in their quest for citizenship."[103] Later, he expanded on this exhortation in a message entitled "To Young Americans of Syrian Origin," published in the newly established English-language the *Syrian World*. It read in part: "It is to stand before the towers of New York, Washington, Chicago and San Francisco saying in your heart, 'I am the descendant of a people that builded Damascus, and Biblus, and Tyre and Sidon, and Antioch, and now I am here to build with you, and with a will.' It is to be proud of being an American, but it is also to be proud that your fathers and mothers came from a land upon which God laid his gracious hand and raised His messengers. Young Americans of Syrian origin, I believe in you."[104] The full text of the statement was reprinted by the journal for framing and was, at that time, circulated widely among the Syrians.

The passing of peddling signaled the end of an era. With little appreciation for its impact on the lives of their grandparents and parents in America and thus on their own, Americans of Syrian descent have tended to minimize its importance. It had produced no heroes, save perhaps the pioneers who had endured its hardships, and it left no legacy to be revered, save that of the entrepreneurial drive. It was an epoch easily forgotten except for advocates of Syrian entrepreneurship, such as Salloum Mokarzel who, in 1927, was said by A. Hakim, "the Sage of Washington Street," to have suggested in an article on the history of Syrians in New York that a statue be erected to "the enterprising spirit as symbolized by the pioneer peddler." Reflecting on that suggestion, on the peddling period, and on the excessive pride demonstrated by his people, Mr. Hakim added:

> I should think that this suggestion if carried out in some modified form would result in not only perpetuating the memory of the pioneering spirit of the race but in holding it down to some reasonable degree of modesty. Little book-ends of a peddler's figure should grace every cultured Syrian's home;

or a little statuette in bronze could be a graceful and appro-
priate ornament for every Syrian executive's desk; or still a
handsomely engraved picture of the pioneering peddler
could be framed and hung in a conspicuous position in offices
and homes. This should tend to develop some sense of false
pride. It would also have the effect of boldly attesting to our
moral courage by glorifying achievement regardless of its
humble beginnings and means. It would be a wholesome lesson to posterity and produce a sobering effect on those who
carry their sense of elation over their success to the point of
ridiculous vanity. To such a proposition all those who have the
real interest of the race at heart should readily subscribe.[105]

Neither suggestion was ever acted upon.

From Syrian to Syrian-American: Between the Wars

In Business

The decade of the twenties was a time of tremendous change in American national life as in the life of the Syrian pioneers who had been, in any case, moving with the currents of the time. The settlement mentality had faded, and on its foundation was recast a new outlook, at once freer from tradition and more open to the pull of America, yet conscious of the past. In effect, the interruption of Syrian immigration by the war and the quota restrictions imposed after 1924, fixed the relative size and character of most Syrian communities for the next twenty five years. The settlement was Syrian; the new setting was increasingly Syrian-American, its contours shaped in a more orderly environment.

Old ways of seeing themselves, notably as transients with limited goals, were being supplanted by the dynamics of new opportunities. The central concern continued to be upward mobility. With a more certain American focus, a Syrian middle class was taking shape slowly and steadily. Prosperity and advancement, as the immigrants gauged them, became more general. Building on their prewar progress, they became mainly owners of small businesses, acquired homes in better neighborhoods, and concerned themselves with their children's future.

Postwar communities less resembled the Syrian villages; the pioneer's feelings of foreignness were gradually being replaced by a sense of being American; and the Syrians began addressing the increasing complexities of American society and accommodating themselves to them on an unprecedented scale. Consequently, Syrian society appeared to be finding an equilibrium between the predominant American values and the steadily eroding native values. Yet, the distinction between the prewar and the postwar Syrian society was in some respects a broad chasm and in others a narrow path.

In the twenties, when pressures to Americanize were intensifying and cultural reinforcement from new immigrants was negligible, the Syrians began to yield more of the elements of their culture—most notably the use of the Arabic language. At the same time, attempts were made to strengthen and secure group loyalty and identity. Many leaders had, before the war, feared the consequences of mounting cultural apathy and disinterest. But, the leaders seemed merely to hint at them. They were unable to formulate convincing solutions, nor could they hold their people tightly to the cause. After the war, witnessing their worst fears being realized, they launched a crusade—too little, too late—to revive interest in the Syrian heritage. In its ambivalent way, the Arabic press rode at the head of the crusade, just behind the church. Both, however, pulled against the engine of assimilation fueled by Syrian economic progress.

Not ones to gamble, the Syrians, holding firmly to their habits of hard work and parsimony, reoriented their goals toward a sound and successful future in America. For some Syrians, success was achievable in large leaps and bounds; for the majority, who lived on the blurred edge between poor and lower middle class, it was achievable in an integrated series of small forward advances. A few reached into wholesaling, manufacturing, and real estate; the many thought themselves successful if they could open a small business that allowed them to make payments on a modest home. Entrepreneurship, of course, remained the preferred means to success, and material acquisitions, as with other Americans, its gauge.

The publication of several Syrian business directories reflect the pride Syrians took in "being in business." Although peddling was also entrepreneurial, no directory of that trade acknowledged its humble existence. The first was published for the years 1908 and 1909, after peddling as a trade had entered its decline and almost two decades into the overlapping second, or settled, stage of the Syrian experience in America. In the directory, the authors boasted that the Syrians were "the most ingenious, enterprising and crafty businessmen of the immigrant races." More on the mark, however, was the observation that, considering the Syrians' lack of experience and knowledge of the trades into which they ventured, and "even though they find themselves deprived of any capital with which to start a business even on a moderate scale, still we find them bent on being independent merchants and altogether given up to trade."[1]

The Directory has preserved the names, addresses, villages of origin of the owners, as well as the types of businesses in towns and cities of every state. Incomplete (Spring Valley, Cedar Rapids, and Vicksburg, for example, are omitted) and imprecise in its classifications, it nevertheless offers valuable insights into the range of Syrian enterprises a few years before World War I. The range was remarkable. The 3,162 businesses listed run the gamut from banking and manufacturing to small family retail and service stores. Leaving aside those endeavors which thrived mainly in the metropolises of the East and Midwest, such as banking, importing, manufacturing, publishing, and travel agents, the Syrians owned restaurants, hotels, candy kitchens, ice-cream parlors, poolrooms, and nickelodeons. They were butchers, bakers, barbers, shoemakers, cleaners, tobacconists, jewelers, and tailors. A few contractors and developers, realtors, wholesalers, farmers, dentists, doctors, pharmacists, and lawyers were also sprinkled throughout the country. Some Syrians bottled bleach and blended and packaged coffee for distribution to retail grocers.[2] Dry goods stores far outran all others.

If any pattern emerges from *The Directory*, it is that dry goods stores, the overwhelming favorite of settling pioneer peddlers, were fast losing their popularity to two new enterprises: grocery and fruit stores. A less certain pattern was their losing popularity in some of the older colonies in port states such as New York, Massachusetts, Louisiana, and Texas, than in the heartland regions and more in urban than in small and rural towns. The decline corresponded with the decline in peddling and the changing character of settlements.

Fort Wayne, for example, was listed as having five "dry goods and notions" stores, three grocers, three "confectioners, fruit, and tobacco" stores, two Oriental goods and rug dealers, and two poolrooms. Grand Rapids boasted three wholesale fruit establishments, seven stores that sold "groceries, fruits and meats," an owner of a clubhouse, a barber, baker, poolroom, general merchandise store, two dry goods stores, and a realtor. In contrast, Utica, New York, still had nine dry goods stores along with a grocer, barber, restauranteur, a horse dealer and a few other small businesses. Most dry goods stores, by 1909, had lost the imprint of the supplier and his motley crew of peddlers, nor were they any longer the most common focal point of Syrian life.

With more courage than capital and more determination than experience, many Syrians had launched into their businesses. The considerable achievement of those who had taken the gamble earlier and succeeded posed a challenge for others who, in fact, imitated. Imitation seemed to minimize the risk. A successful grocer or dry goods retailer inspired others who frequently became his competitors, on the same block or in the same neighborhood. Four Syrian dry goods stores competed on one block of Bleeker Street in Utica, and six Oriental goods dealers within four blocks of Ruxton Avenue in Manitou, Colorado.[3] The competitor a block away might have been a brother or cousin, set up by the family—a small fruit stand, perhaps, "to get him started"—and close enough to be guided and assisted. Another rival, a door or two away, might be the unwelcome but ultimately tolerated relative of another family or village.

Imitation and competition account in large part for the association of an ethnic group with one trade in some communities. For Syrians, it increasingly became the grocery business. In Detroit, Syrians began opening them before World War I. At the turn of the century, the Syrian colony, subdivided by sect and scattered in neighborhoods not far from the city center, was initially and primarily a peddling settlement. *The Directory* shows that in 1908–9, there were four Syrian dry goods stores, one of which sold groceries, one fruit, one fruit and confectionery shop, four grocers, a "repairing tailor," and two Oriental goods and rug dealers.

In 1910, the colony (including Highland Park) numbered 417 Syrians. By the end of the twenties, corresponding with its industrial growth and higher industrial wages, that population increased to 5,520. Tafeeda B. was among them. Her husband left Fort Wayne to work at the Ford Motor Company in 1915. By that year, she observed that

> . . . Most of the Syrians in Detroit were working in the Ford factory. . . . At first they peddled and got into other things, but they were getting into industry because Detroit was becoming the thing. . . . Automobiles were becoming more progressive. There were more factories built in Detroit in those days. . . . This was during the War . . .
>
> When Ford started that five dollars a day, they all rushed in there. Ford could use anybody that came in 'cause the boys were drafted. So all these Syrians got into Fords—I could truthfully say 100 of them. Then from other places they would flock in. . . . That's why the Detroit population of Syrians grew so much. . . . And those ones that worked at Fords and made that much money, they commenced to buy the little things, but not too extravagant. Just a little more convenient because they were saving for a store.

But only a fraction of those who entered the industrial labor force remained in it—most of them Muslims. For Syrians, Detroit was not so much an industrial magnet; they migrated to it from other parts of the country to share in its booming economy as entrepreneurs. Father and sons saved their factory wages until one could open the family store.

Tafeeda's husband was not employed by Ford; instead, he became a clerk in one of the three or four grocery stores

owned by Louis S., one of the earliest and leading grocers in
the city. Many Syrians, before the war, had already switched
from peddling and dry goods to the fruit and vegetable business. It was said that they had imitated some of their ethnic
neighbors. Louis began with a fruit stand shortly after his
arrival in America in 1906. By the end of the twenties, he
owned seventeen stores.[4] Tafeeda remembered that some
Syrians owned pushcarts, and she believed that they were the
"tie-in between Detroit and all its grocery stores"; others disagree.

Pushcarts were the exception, according to George S.,
Louis's son. People started in small stores because they required very little capital. Rent for the store and its attached
living quarters was usually cheap. Bread and milk companies
would provide shelves as part of their sales promotion, and
distributors sold groceries to the beginners on credit. When
Louis S. became a grocery and produce wholesaler in the
twenties, he encouraged other Syrians to enter the retail grocery business by helping them to find locations and extending them credit.[5]

When Nazha H. and her husband moved their Oriental
goods and rug business to Detroit in 1926, "there was a small
family Syrian grocery on practically every corner and Syrians
were delivering or distributing much of the merchandise
they sold." Three years later, she convinced her father to move
his family from Fort Wayne to join the numerous imitators
and competitors who started and prospered as grocers.

Writing for an issue of the *Spectator*, a Terre Haute, Indiana, magazine which on 11 October 1975 featured "Terre
Haute's Arab-Americans," Raymond S. Azar described his
Syrian community as a peddling settlement in its early period. Families in the colony, with wives "baking and selling,"
prospered enough to settle down and start small businesses.
Gradually, into the twenties, the ethnically mixed area in
which the colony was located contained many Syrian-owned
businesses founded by the early immigrants who handed
them down to sons. "Although of common ancestry," he
added,

the many Arab-American-owned businesses, especially grocery stores, were often in fierce competition with one another. On the corners of 4th and Eagle were three grocery stores at one time. The Azar Grocery was located on the Southwest corner, the Nasser grocery was on the Northwest corner and the Joe Nasser grocery was on the Southeast corner. At times price wars were fought between these various grocers, while at the same time mutual respect and affection between these Syrian-American families existed and still exists. These groceries were a part of a total of 66 groceries throughout the city that were [in 1975] Syrian-owned. Most of the groceries had residences attached, partly to hold down the cost of housing and partly to give the store owners a family life while working long hours of up to 16 hours per day, 7 days a week. The attached residences also served to give the businessmen immediate stock, cashier, or meat counter help at the sound of a shout.[6]

The propensity of Syrians to live and work in or near urban centers was borne out in *The Directory* as well as by census records. According to the latter, by the end of the twenties, almost 90 percent (including Palestinians) lived in cities with populations over 25,000, almost half between the states of Maine and Pennsylvania. Of the remainder, about two percent farmed, the rest were businessmen in small towns or rural areas.

In its emphasis on achievement, *The Directory* concealed what for the large majority of Syrians had been a slow and difficult but steady and unspectacular progression. The average Syrian business, before and after 1920, began as a small family concern, often with only enough capital to "try it out"—one or two hundred dollars for a lease and the most meager stock, much of it purchased on credit. Newcomers borrowed from relatives. During its sixteen to eighteen hours of daily operation, the store provided personal service, delivery at any hour, and almost unlimited credit. The customer was not only always right; he was master. Pressure and anxiety were constant companions of the owner, as well as of his family, whose motto typically was, like Johnny N.'s, "to work so I won't have to live on people's money." Working over one hundred hours a week required the assistance of every member of the family. Store and home were commonly a staircase or door apart and there was much shuttling back and forth.

The contribution of women to the family's economic mobility—initiated before World War I—continued after it. And, women's existence continued to be characterized by daily toil. In addition to housework and child care, they helped in stores and sometimes operated them alone while the men went to market or earned elsewhere. Sacrifice and fatigue echoed in Wagha S.'s words as in the words of most of the women interviewed.

Twenty years younger than her husband, Wagha worked with him in their newly opened grocery store when the children were infants. He needed her help, she said. With the store next door to their home, she left the young ones sleeping and took the older children with her. She ran between home and store from early morning until late night, cooking, washing, cleaning, waiting on customers, and arranging stock. When her husband rested or was away buying produce, she remained in the store alone. "I never had any time for pleasure until my children grew up," she recalled. When her son, who himself served customers at the age of five, took over the store on his father's death, she continued working. Of her tireless efforts, her son remarked, "She was not forced to work; it was more a case of 'that's my life, my lot in life, preordained by God and I will make the best of it because I love my husband and my family.'" [7]

Wagha is Christian; but for some Muslim and Druze women, the pace was the same. They had not peddled, but they faced no prohibition against working in the family store. In resourcefulness, energy, and dedication, in daily survival and adversity, they fully equaled their Christian sisters.

Maryam A. is a devout Shiʿa Muslim who helped her husband in his coffeehouse. Having explained at length the impropriety of physical contact, even to touching hands, between a Shiʿa woman and males who are not close kin, she continued: "I preserved food to fill a pantry the size of this [living room] wall and baked sweets and my husband sold them in his coffeehouse. I had a son and was nursing him at the time and he would toddle around me. . . . and I used to work at night embroidering and crocheting laces." Her husband then opened a grocery store. When he was alive and her children were young, she did not work outside the house. But "when he got sick, I worked with him in his grocery store. . . . It is honorable work. It was difficult work and long hours, but it was honorable. I worked after my husband's death for twelve years; not alone; my sons were there, but I can [now] read [English] numbers and I know the alphabet but I cannot connect them. I never learned Arabic. I worked eight to twelve hours a day and cleaned around the boxes. . . . In business there is no social contact; it is "yes sir" and "yes maam." It won't do; it is not right to socialize. . . . I learned to butcher."[8] Of his mother, George A. said, she "peddled, then she worked in a hospital cleaning . . . because father was sick and the family needed money. . . . Mother had a lot of pride but when the family needed help she went to work because the family came first."[9]

Whereas a minority of sons and daughters peddled at an early age, many—no doubt the majority of store owners' children—were prepared for life behind a counter. Infants began that life on their mother's hip or in a crib as she shuttled between domestic burdens and relieving her husband. School-age children, when not in school, were at their parents' elbows, waiting on customers, making change, stocking shelves, delivering orders, and imbibing the shrewdness of running an independent business on meager resources. They were inculcated with the parents' work and thrift ethics and the lesson that no self-denial could or should be too great for the family and its goals. On that premise, family businesses thrived, customers became regulars and shelves, once barely stocked, filled with merchandise. The family was fed and clothed, even if at times poorly, and its honor and pride preserved.

The children also experienced what family unity could accomplish. Survival was only the immediate challenge; unity empowered the family gradually to buy a home and furnish it modestly; to purchase such modern conveniences as a washing machine and automobile; perhaps to send a son to college, start a business for another son, and afford suitable weddings for their daughters. Finally, family unity ensured the family's financial security in the·event of the father's death and for the parents' old age. Each modest gain in this typical Syrian perspective, achieved over the lifetime of the average immigrant businessman, was one success in a series of successes.

For untold numbers of daughters and sisters of the first generation, the economic socialization proved to be not only regressive in Syrian cultural terms but also oppressive in American terms. Family traditions and values relating to the obligations and behavior of unmarried girls changed hardly at all for the majority. Obedience, sacrifice, and chastity were indelibly impressed on their minds; so was the notion of male superiority. In America, the family's dependence on the economic assistance of its unmarried females was more demanding physically and emotionally than it had been in Syria. Frequently, they were pillars of support in the home and business. And, since the family continued to look to its sons for its future well-being (its economic security and honor), daughters were expected to, even told they must, set aside their dreams and goals in their brothers' interests. "Our men sure knew how to use their women," remarked Nazha H. who had made many sacrifices for her father, husband, and sons during a difficult lifetime.

Raised to fasten their expectation on marriage and motherhood, girls were caught between that traditional female imperative and the new family demands. Compelled by a sense of obligation, obedience, and guilt, more than a few unmarried females in each community postponed those important steps in their lives, often past the conventionally acceptable marriage age, jeopardizing their chances for marriage as well as their status and self-esteem in both the Syrian and American societies. Thus, some settled for a less-than-desirable mate; some never married.

"My family discouraged me from getting married," said Nellie B., "because they wanted me to work" in her father's tailoring and dry-cleaning shop which opened in 1911. She started at the age of fourteen, working before and after school and on weekends. On her father's death, the oldest brother inherited the business and she "never stopped working in the family store" not for fifty years, despite a brief marriage when she was thirty-three. Before completing grade school in Vicksburg, Mrs. Queenie N. quit to help in her father's grocery store and later his sandwich shop. When her father died and she took over the business, she was twenty-eight years old. She married at thirty-two. "I couldn't get married younger," she explained, "because I had all those brothers to take care of. I worked to support my brothers."[10]

Najla S.'s dream in life had been to continue the education in Arabic, French, and English which she had begun in a girls' school in Damascus. Instead, since arriving in the United States at the age of fourteen, she became the sole provider for a mother in ill health, a father too proud to work at anything but his blacksmithing craft, and several younger siblings, among them infants. For ten hours a day, six days a week, she earned an hourly wage at a loom in Worcester and came home to housework. When at the age of nineteen, a prospective groom asked for her hand, her parents disapproved "because they needed me at home." When she was finally allowed to marry, it was, she said, to a tyrannical wastrel, and her cycle of sacrifices began again, this time for her own children.

If marriage had been the only realistic aspiration of daughters in the homeland, in America there were other personal visions and hopes. These too, however, were often set aside, left unarticulated until, more often than not, it was too late. Many yearned to finish high school and dreamed of college, but for the vast majority, the hopes were futile. "My mother was very educated and wanted me to be educated too," said Wedad F., "but my father couldn't afford to hire help in the store." So she attended only a half year of high school and has always regretted her loss. To spare her younger sister from that fate, she reported her parents to the "school authorities."[11]

Education, in folk cultures, was thought to be wasted on girls and if it did not "give them wrong ideas," it would "hinder their chances for marriage because men would not marry girls who were more intelligent or educated than themselves." Therefore, if it could afford it, the family chose to educate its sons.[12] The subdued females remained restless and frustrated; the courageous broke the mold and exercised their own will; but they were the exception and a tiny minority.

For the females who had sacrificed their personal goals, the bitterness, by their late years, had usually lost its edge. Sacrifices and lost opportunities were counted, in retrospect, as obligations that they could not abandon. To have defied tradition might subject them to alienation which, to Syrian females, was nearly intolerable.

Shopkeeping, like peddling, furthered assimilation. It bound the small entrepreneur to a complex of businesses and community relationships—with the banker, wholesaler, police and fire departments, and licensing agencies, to name a few. In turn, these relationships led the immigrant shopowners into new business opportunities and gaining respect and acknowledgement. A sure symbol of respectability was property ownership, and being innately status conscious, the Syrians invested in real estate, when they could afford it, after home and business.

If during the peddling period, the pioneers were insulated from the potentialities of property ownership, they did not hesitate, as settled American citizens, to take advantage of them. Some bought farms to lease, property to rent, and land to sell. Acreage purchased in Oklahoma Territory, for example, yielded oil.[13] At least by 1903, Syrian realtors, advertising in the Arabic press, were encouraging their people to invest in "lucrative" Niagara Falls land sales.[14] In 1925, they were offering lots for sale in the Florida land boom.[15] Twenty-four Syrian realtors were scattered throughout the country in 1909, over half of them in New York and Massachusetts.[16] By the late 1920s, there were twenty in Manhattan and Brooklyn alone.[17]

Industrial laborers, always far fewer than entrepreneurs, were slower to advance than shopowners in spite of somewhat improved incomes in the twenties. The goal of many—perhaps most—Christian and Muslim laborers was to open a store. Many left factory work as soon as they could afford to invest in a business of their own. Others did not have the courage to give up the security of a weekly salary. After thirty years as a laborer, Osman C. continued to regret not opening a store. "I could have helped my sons; I didn't help them. I could have started them in business and kept them from factory work, but I didn't. They're still factory workers."[18]

The family enterprise, according to custom, would be assumed by one of the sons, preferably the eldest—rarely by the wife or daughters—after a father's retirement or death. Many sons, but by no means all, obligingly, sometimes gratefully, accepted the responsibility, graduating from father's assistant to manager. Then, chafing at the straitened income, the limited vision, and old-fashioned ways of their parents, they modernized and expanded. The immigrant stamp was replaced by a distinctly American one.

Younger American-born and American-raised sons, however, began to reject the unpalatable legacy of long hours, of incessant work that yielded a minimum living standard, and obsequious acquiescence to the American customers. Determined to widen and elevate their horizons, they reached out to opportunities in the American economy and to achievement through a wide variety of enterprises, many that entailed greater economic risks than their fathers would have dared to take. The younger sons also began to acquire university degrees; medicine and law were, not surprisingly, favored.

To achieve became the central focus of that generation's life and absorbed a large measure of its interests and energy; for that, no explanation is necessary: it was quintessentially American. "You gotta make your own business and prove you are a success, then you are a good American," said Alice G., who influenced seven highly successful sons.[19] While the immigrants' relation to the middle class was marginal, their children were usually conveyed on the shoulders of the immigrant generation and its stringent native values which were, in many ways, strikingly similar to those cherished by the American middle class.

FAMILY

In Syria, the emphasis on family cut across all groups. In the new land, the family remained, as in the homeland, the keystone of Syrian identity and social organization. Ties of affection bound members of the immediate family to each other and to the extended family. Profound emotion was invested in family life and in the devotion of parents to their children who, in the closeness of that relationship, usually became convinced that they best understood the virtues to live by, hardly aware that those virtues derived from a different time and place.

The conservatism of the Syrian family was not impenetrable. Although many of its traditions sturdily resisted change, hardly a family, even the most traditional, remained unaffected by it. Already under way in the pioneer phase of the Syrian migration, the assimilation process gathered force when the Syrians decided to remain and raise their families in America. Its impact, however, was determined ultimately by the family's economic status, the number of Syrians in its community, and the strength of its attachment to the cultural heritage.

Among its most profound impacts on Syrian life was the disintegration of the traditional patriarchal extended family into nuclear units. This change was inevitable, not only because the extended family had lost its economic validity in America, but because American influence and education compelled sons to establish their own households as they married. Immigration had already dealt the patriarchal family a severe blow. Its members frequently settled in scattered regions of North and South America and elsewhere, dispersing along subnetworks, often leaving the patriarch behind in the homeland or in some distant settlement. Although, in a number of cases, migration cut ties with some family members permanently, the ties that had traditionally bound the family under one roof or in one community, nevertheless, were sufficiently durable and elastic to bind it from separate and remote households. Obedience to the patriarch, as well as ties of affection and concern for family welfare, persisted psychologically, if not always socially, even over great distances. In important matters—economics and marriage, for example—that might affect the family welfare, the patriarch was frequently consulted and his approval obtained, by letter, if necessary.

The immigrant experience significantly altered traditional parental roles as well. Not unexpectedly, long hours (even days) away from home, peddling or nursing a small business, eroded both the authority and disciplinary role of the pioneer fathers. This, however, can be overstated. Tradition still defined and regulated relations between husband and wife and between them and their children. Moreover, given the cultural emphasis on family honor and unity, fathers rarely relinquished their authority or the appearance of it. The discipline they might have meted out was not so much abandoned as shifted to their wives. Women had traditionally shared in this responsibility. They had been charged with the maintenance of the social and moral values, on the one hand; on the other, the children's upbringing was seen by the women's peers as the direct measure of the worth of both parents. Moreover, since it was perceived that problems could usually be attributed to their shortcomings, Syrian mothers in America were hardly passive. In their own right, they became strong disciplinarians and mainstays of the family when fathers relinquished that role either because of work absences, temperament, or lack of self-confidence; mothers were also the ever-present repositories of affection and comfort. In such cases, the burdens of the child-rearing gap fell on the mother, since the father's discipline was deemed essential to the proper upbringing of the children. But if fathers had lost ground as disciplinarians, they retained the respect, if not always the love, due as head of the family and prime authorities.

For all their attraction to what was American, Syrian parents did not want their children to grow up "like American children," not knowing what was "right," not knowing what

would be embarrassing ['ayb] to the family.[20] Filial autonomy
and independence, they feared, would lead to a breakdown
in moral behavior and family unity; at stake was the appearance of paternal weakness and consequent loss of face.
Therefore, they insisted on adherence to family values and
exercised intense parental supervision. In short, fathers continued to rule, while mothers reigned.

The overwhelming majority of first-generation fathers, according to their children and wives, capably fulfilled their
traditional roles. There was more continuity than change in
their personalities. Long absences made little difference; the
effect was the feeling that he was "the boss and the law-
giver"—the primary authority in the household. His will was
enforced by his obedient deputy, the mother. "A child without [his father's authority]," insisted Maryam A., "is not obedient. He [God] is on high and the father is down here. He
is the master of the house." It was "his word" that was the
master, irrespective of his presence or absence. Wives, Wagha
S. pointed out, never dared to contradict that word. Moreover, since mothers ministered to their children's problems
and well-being, they often developed special relationships
with their children, especially their sons to whom they looked
for comfort in old age.

Wives, daughters, and sisters continued to live within the
conventional strictures considered proper to their sex. Nothing more sharply set off the immigrants from their sisters in
Syria than the immigrants' hard-earned steps toward greater
independence. These were not major strides, by any means,
but the first generation pushed open the door and conveyed
their gains to their American-born and American-raised
daughters.

Never was there a conscious liberation movement; such a
notion would have been roundly resisted by the majority of
the women themselves. Those internalized restraints which
traditional ways had bred could not be altered instantly. Mrs.
Hanna Shakir reflected the conservatism of her sex, as well
as any white Anglo-Saxon Protestant Victorian of her time,
when she wrote in *Al-Hoda* that men are the stronger and
more intelligent sex; and women, although they are to men

what silver is to gold, should be educated to help their husband and raise their children rather than succumb to the lure of greater independence.[21] Mrs. Afifa Karam, a feminist writer and journalist, counterpointed that women are as capable as men; just as European women have worked successfully in scientific and other fields, Syrian women should take advantage of similar opportunities available to them in America.[22] With few exceptions, the majority of Syrian women no doubt sided with Mrs. Shakir, their conservatism retarding the pace of their progress, as a class, toward independence.

Domestically, they honored their marital obligations. Mistresses of the house, bearers of children, defenders of family honor, guardians of its morality, and dispensers of hospitality, they were architects of the children's character, transmitters of cultural values, as well as nurses of the ill and the aged. Since a large number were, in addition, breadwinners, often on an equal footing with their menfolk, they had little free time for trivial pleasures or cultivating free spirits. It was their poignant and perennially confounded hope that some day they would discover some free time. Nothing prepared pioneer immigrant women for what they were to encounter in the New World. More trapped than men by the choices carved out for them by tradition, women were more caught between the heritage of the past and demands of the modern world.

Perhaps nothing effected a change in their lives more than their economic role, both as peddlers and shopkeepers. From it, they gained greater confidence and self-esteem than they had known. They found new strengths to meet new circumstances and developed skills of strategy and execution that sometimes exceeded those of their men.

Nowhere were these strengths and skills more evident than when their men faltered or failed from overamibition or the lack of ambition. When men bent under the strains and lost their nerve, the strength of the women stood out in sharp contrast to man's weaknesses. Take Madeline B.'s mother who persuaded her husband not to file for bankruptcy after his grocery store failed. He was ready to give up but she "moved all of the supplies into the house and it was she who sold them out of the house. She said that as long as we have our health, two feet and two hands, we will not go bankrupt and lose our family name. And when they bought a farm, my mother would do all the harvesting."[23]

Bahia K., a four-and-a-half-foot dynamo, began sewing in a kimono factory at the age of fifteen, four days after her arrival in Boston in 1912; she didn't stop working until 1972. The man she married in Detroit failed in business several times because "people could take advantage of him." She altered clothes at home, took in laundry, baked sweets to sell, worked in a garment factory, raised a family, and when her family was to be dispossessed for faulting on mortgage payments, it was she who "cried and lied" to turn the sheriff away; and it was she who obtained a loan that saved their home, because her husband, she said, was "too shy."[24]

Many homekeepers displayed a surprising capacity for economic aggressiveness, pushing, prodding, driving their husbands and sons forward. Neither the threat of poverty nor the incapacity of their men, nor any other adversity compelled them to work. Cases of women—ambitious to accelerate the family's upward mobility or to fill the expectation-achievement gap in its goals—who exhibited energy, imagination, and determination equal to their men's are surprisingly common. Joe C.'s mother bore nine children. Meanwhile, she peddled during the first year of her marriage while her husband worked for the railroad company. The next year, 1908, she rented a store. By 1916, each parent operated a store, and in 1924 they bought a third. As soon as they were able, the children joined the enterprises.[25] Mitchell M.'s mother peddled in a horse and buggy before World War I, while his father worked as a laborer for an iron company. "She did very well," recalled Mitchell. In the evenings, both parents sewed articles which the mother sold the next day. After the war, the father opened a grocery store and, by the mid-twenties, the mother stopped peddling to repair rugs in her husband's rug-cleaning business and continued to work when they sold the store to expand the rug-cleaning business.[26]

Inevitably, immersion in the working world and a taste of assertiveness slowly eroded the conventions that restricted women. Although women in homes that gained in economic and social standing gained also in personal standing and respect, it was the working women who set a trend for nonworking women to follow. "Once a woman goes to work and associates with Americans," said Bahia K., "she learns quickly from them about her rights. . . . Here, in the United States, men and women are equal. She has to break [her husband's] old-country habits and train him."

The gains of the first generation remained, however, slight. Women moved cautiously so as not to overstep the bounds of Syrian convention lest society and their men reprove them. "Too much freedom is not good," cautioned Negebe S. "If one goes too far, that is not good; she must know her limitations." Those limitations, according to Claire A., came from the Syrians' "lack of sophistication; they were held back because people talked."[27]

If the gains were gradual, however, their impact was not benign. Their effects would become clear only with the passage of time. The competition for brides, dependence on women's economic assistance, and the American environment had begun to smooth the roughest edges of male dominance. Segregation of the sexes—in social gatherings and churches for Christians and almost everywhere for Muslims—remained the rule throughout the interwar period, but now and again, at Christian informal gatherings, the rules were breached without serious reaction. Protection of a daughter's virtue was unyielding to change, but the practice of early and arranged marriages began to bear the taint of backwardness and foreignness as some, admittedly relatively few, daughters began to insist on romantic love and personal choices, oblivious to family obligations. Letters written to the editor of the *Syrian World* in the second half of the twenties, by American-born and American-raised daughters, ventilated their resentment and revealed the breadth of the cultural chasm opening between daughters and their parents. In the freedom from traditional restraint and the equality they sought, they were supported by antitraditionalists such as A. Hakim who denounced, in his article on "The Marriage Problem among the Syrians," the "pathetic" old customs of arranged marriages and the stringent moral rules that restricted the liberty of women, and he praised the "modern method of personal choice with the sanction and approval of the parents." Marriage, he concluded, "which is the foundation of happy family life, which in turn is the basis of the property and progress of the nation, should be our principal concern in our present stage of transition. For upon the outcome of our efforts along this direction will depend either the improvement of the status of the race or its deterioration."[28]

Al-Sayeh, the Arabic newspaper most devoted to the works of the literary community in New York, frequently criticized parents for their fidelity to outdated customs inapplicable to life in America. Those customs belonged, it wrote, to a country about which their children knew absolutely nothing and had never seen.[29]

If unmarried females were deprived of sex education at home and were prohibited from unchaperoned social contact with the opposite sex, they nonetheless followed the wider vogues in fashion. Shorter skirts and loose waists replaced the cumbersome long skirts and tight bodices in their closets and in those of many of their mothers. Younger women, married and unmarried, adopted the prevailing styles, rouged their faces, and marcelled their hair; but only the youngest and most daring cut their hair.

Covering the head, a custom common to Christians, Muslims, and Druze, was relinquished by Christians and Druze, except by the elderly and most traditionally minded. Even Muslim women, if they had ever worn it, had abandoned the veil in America and began to uncover their heads to the dismay of men like Shaykh Kalil B. "Few women covered their heads in America," he complained. "For a woman to . . . uncover her head is to go contrary to her religion. A Muslim woman should not be uncovered except her face, hands, and feet; no one other than her immediate family should see her otherwise." Old World customs seemed to linger longer in American Muslim households than in Christian ones, not only because they were characteristically more cherished in Muslim households, but because a generation or more separated Muslim from Christian migrations.

Their diverse responsibilities in America impelled working wives and mothers to adjust in other ways. They began to have fewer children, to cook fewer time-consuming Arabic meals (many taking hours of preparation), and gradually to adopt the custom of prearranged social visits. Even the time-honored preference for male children began to lose much of its force between the wars.

Indicative of the shift in the position of women was their pivotal role in community building and group cohesion. In order to preserve and perpetuate the native culture and values, and to arrest the growing drift of the youth, women became increasingly involved in many facets of the community's social needs, building on a trend that began before World War I. They took charge of, if they did not always initiate, charitable societies to help the needy and clubs to build and support churches. "In the early days," wrote Courtemanche of the Syrians in Worcester, "the women would go from house to house, collecting 25-cent pledges for the church. They scrimped and saved on household budgets to bake pastries and buy coffee that was sold at church functions. The proceeds went to the church." Frank George of Paxton told her that "If it weren't for them, we wouldn't have a church. . . . The woman of the house was really the boss— and it was the same in the community."[30] When the Muslim community of Cedar Rapids decided to build a mosque in the late 1920s, the women formed a club to raise money and "had to coax the men to form one," said Negebe S. In addition, they sponsored and supervised church socials to bring youths together.

When men sought the company of men for "men's talk and things," they could find them in a coffeehouse, if one existed, or they formed men's social clubs where they played cards. Women had to depend on visits to neighbors or relatives, until they discovered that they too could socialize, as well as perform good works, in their own clubs. For many women, clubs and societies represented an escape from domestic drudgery, and for others, a search for status. And, for a few others, they were a forum for innovative and creative ideas. Spring Valley had Mrs. Salimi Aboud. She was, perhaps, the creator of the Syrian women's society in the twenties that worked to build a church. The Orthodox of the town prayed in a converted house at the time, and the women met in a "room off the one used for the church." Mrs. Aboud wrote and directed plays, recitals, and other programs for special religious and social occasions that were presented in the church basement or the Moose Hall on Main Street. Her Easter programs, when children and adults alike stayed up to welcome the dawn, were favorites. In addition, recalled Amelia A. M. and Budelia M., "the women would have evenings in which they'd recite panegyric poems to God and they'd wear a blue-ribboned button as the 'Ladies of Saint George's Church' . . . and Mrs. Aboud made up the poems." The creative work of such women provided opportunities for the women they influenced to develop self-expression and confidence. Women whose creativity found no opportunities for public expression, like Mrs. Essa M. of Manchester, New Hampshire, Tafaha al-T. of Montreal, and Yamna N. of Detroit, filled notebooks with Arabic poetry and prose for their own gratification.

Children who passed their formative years in a household of recently immigrated parents, integrated Syrian values with little resistance. Relatively unadulterated, the values were communicated in Arabic, the children's only language, until they entered American schools, some in their adolescent years. It was in these children that continuity of tradition appeared scarcely disturbed. It was also they who usually experienced the severest problems of disorientation when, beginning about their teens, they found themselves living by two sets of values: Syrian in their parents' world; American in what was essentially their own world where they strove to gain acceptance. Their dilemma was further complicated by their inability or unwillingness to shed, free of guilt, the cherished Syrian values—family honor and obedience to, and respect for, parental authority. Restraints, because they were generally wrapped in family love and protection, encouraged burdensome feelings of guilt, even when the children reached adulthood. "The conflict started," said Laurence S., the youngest of eight sons, "when the children grew up and wanted to do what their parents didn't want them to. Even after I got married, my mother wanted me to take her out. Even then, I felt my responsibility was still to her and to the family name."[31]

The parents' dilemma was as profound as the children's. Their insistence on continuity of family values repeatedly caused tensions. If they worried about what their children absorbed away from home, they were unable to comprehend the pressures their children suffered at school and on neighborhood streets to be and act as Americans. They were, therefore, torn between denying the validity of their beliefs and enduring family conflict as well as the possible alienation of their children. In Syrian family life, there was little or no tolerance for either.

Enforcing Old World values on New World children opened a generational gulf that seemed to widen with each successive child and in proportion to the stage at which parents had evolved from traditional folkways. On a broad scale, the extent of a child's rejection of his parents' values and customs varied with the place of the child in the roster of siblings as well as its sex. Older children, when they rejected the values, tended to be more passive—sometimes painfully passive—then aggressive; daughters were likely to keep their objections unarticulated. The youngest, growing up in a household which, by the time they were born, had advanced further toward assimilation and, defended by their middle siblings, met with far less parental displeasure for deviations. From among the middle children usually arose the staunchest rebels, and it was this group that suffered most psychologically. Over the long period, change was invariably the victor as parents cautiously edged toward their children's views.

Other dynamics were gradually softening the rigidity of the old forms. The Syrian's ambivalence toward, and careless relations with, American culture undoubtedly had an effect. Contacts with Americans by working mothers and fathers and the acquisition of a better home and other middle-class material symbols were important indexes. More important, perhaps, was the infiltration, into the home, of the English language, new ideas, tastes, and manners by growing children who engaged in the kind of vital contacts with American values provided by public schools. Parents could either accept them or tolerate them, but they could not ignore nor shut them out. Less significant but nonetheless contributive was that many of the erstwhile child brides, who had grown up or were growing up with their children, developed more sympathetic and understanding attitudes toward tradition than their older less compromising husbands did.

Military service was very significant in stimulating change. Numerous Syrian youths, naturalized and unnaturalized, prodded by the Arabic press and patriotic clubs, served in World War I—over three hundred from Massachusetts alone[32]—and while in service, they experienced more directly than their civilian compatriots two effective Americanizing forces—living and socializing with Americans and patriotic consciousness-raising. Many gave their lives in defense, they believed, of American ideals they had come to cherish as fervently as their American buddies. Civilian Syrians, on the other hand, avidly bought many thousands of dollars of Liberty bonds.

The beneficiaries of this softening were the younger children. Never completely free from the restrictions experienced by their older siblings, their assimilation was eased by parental liberalism, however gradual and slight, while they, in turn, added to the Americanization of their parents. Each successive child—boys and girls—experienced almost as wide a sibling gap with their older brothers and sisters as the gap that separated them from their parents. Furthermore, to each successive child, the exercise of strict parental authority appeared less and less tolerable. They were more selective in the values they adopted from their parents' culture and tended to internalize the feeling of being American. Thus, from schools, newspapers, radio, and motion pictures, they brought home a disdain for things foreign. Their foreign names, the parents' strange food, music, and alien language and customs, all became so many badges of shame. If they

visited the homes of American friends or ate there, they
sparingly invited their friends home. They yearned for aspects of American middle-class life, to which they were being
exposed, without the liability of any foreignness.

Children fully participated in the domestic life of the family. Generally, Syrian parents lavished their children with
affection and as openly as they were reprimanded for
transgressions, they were freely coddled and kissed in public
and private. Not infrequently, reprimands were accented
with corporal punishment. Children also shared in the family's social activities, being permitted to mingle among visiting
relatives and friends who usually warmly acknowledged their
presence; and, much as in Syria, they accompanied their parents, dressed in their finest, on family visits, many demanded
by traditional religious and social etiquette. They participated in group outings and religious celebrations and were
taken to weddings and funerals. Even when the pleasure of
doing so had evaporated with growing up, they were expected to attend. Furthermore, just as they shared in the
joys, they shared in the griefs and anxieties of family crises.
Because of the intimate contacts within their group, their
closest friends, even as adults, might, more often than not,
be cousins and Syrian neighbors. At about the age of puberty, the behavior of daughters was reined in, while sons
were guided toward their adult roles of independence and
authority. In what they wanted for their children and what
they expected from them, parents were strong-willed and
resolute.

From the community point of view, the consequences of
such socialization of Syrian children were positive. Aside
from family unity and group cohesion, children learned to
respect their elders and provide for their parents until the
parents' last days. Significantly, moreover, the number of
Syrians who turned to crime, delinquency, or government
relief, by all accounts—informants' testimonies and community studies—was among the lowest of any ethnic group.

In attempts by the immigrant generation to maintain and
transmit its cultural heritage to its progeny, it ran afoul of its
eagerness to succeed; cultural heritage was, accordingly, rel-

egated to second place. Much of what the immigrants transmitted was folk knowledge—glorified nostalgic reminiscences of village life—which constituted the villagers'
perception of their heritage. Village songs and lullabies and
occasionally the Syrian national anthem were sung; moral
anecdotes, fables, and stories were told. Stories about heroic
and noble escapades of ancient Arab heroes frequently were
conveyed as family and village history.[33] About the great
Arab-Islamic contributions to world civilization, they knew
little and what they did know was selective and biased in favor of the immigrants' religious affiliations. Their village view
of Syrian culture left their children poorly informed about
their ethnic heritage. Consequently, of the significant Syrian
national and political events that had produced national heroes (heros with which all Syrians identified) and which, in
other nations, kindled national pride and historical continuity, the descendants knew little. Historic events, such as the
Christian massacre of 1860 in Mount Lebanon, were specific
to one or two groups, and, rather than unite, they tended to
divide.

Thus, the Americanized children of the pioneers showed
scant interest or knowledge in their ethnic origins. Their
identification with the parents' homeland bore little relation
to the American reality. Later attempts by parents, churches,
and organizations to arouse an interest were, on the whole,
unsuccessful. However, because they could not completely
divorce themselves from their ethnic background, the Americanized generations held on to what they came to accept as
Syrian culture—food, dance, and music. They were, at this
point, more American than Syrian, but more Syrian than
Arab.

The cultural void was filled from the well of American
myth and history. Lacking ancestral legends and heroes that
had an organic relevance to their lives, they adopted American heroes as role models and American legends as their
own—presidents, cowboys, athletes, and men like Charles
Lindbergh whose historic trans-Atlantic flight was celebrated
in a song. The first verse, roughly translated from Arabic,
was sung by Agia B. and began:

Lindy, Lindy, Oh Aviator
You are the hero of heroes
You braved the sea day and night
You, you, Oh Aviator.[34]

TRANSPLANTING THE FAITH

Institutions presuppose permanence, and both were well advanced in the New York colony by the 1890s where newspapers, voluntary associations, and places of worship first appeared and symbolized its transformation from temporary colony to permanent community. Often these three most common types of Syrian institutions were interconnected. Sometimes the need for a place to worship preceded the church or mosque; sometimes it was the other way around and newspapers were identified with a particular faith.

Churches and mosques, although the most revered, were neither the first nor the most numerous of the Syrian institutions. For one thing, they required a settled congregation holding the same beliefs and financially able to build and maintain them. To form a congregation, in many cases, might require uniting co-sectarians dispersed over several towns and counties, which often was neither practicable nor possible. Perhaps for this reason, no mosque was known to have been erected before the late 1920s. It was, therefore, simpler to form a club than to build a place of worship.

Christian Syrians, even in a Christian country, could not take their faith for granted. Just as the faith and its rituals were central to group cohesion, so its moral imperatives dictated behavior. The longer a group remained without its own church, the more difficult it was to maintain group cohesion and impose moral standards of its own. While the Syrians attended "American" churches, they also yearned for the spiritual gratification of familiar liturgies in languages they could understand.

Yet, churches did not keep pace with Syrian immigration and distribution. Before 1920, 60 Eastern-rite churches were scattered among half of the states of the Union. By 1920, there were 82, and by 1930, 112. But more than half re-

mained concentrated in the East, leaving vast regions un-
served by one. Some communities built churches after more
than a generation; some awaited the sporadic visits of itinerant priests for important ceremonies; many simply joined
the "American" churches they had been attending. A very
large segment of the Syrian population maintained little or
no contact with churches of their native rite. While many Maronites and Melkites attended Roman Catholic churches,
many Syrian Orthodox found the Episcopalian compatible
with their sense of ritual and beliefs; others attended Orthodox churches of Greeks, Slavs, or Russians all under the jurisdiction of the Russian Orthodox Archdiocese in America.
By the estimates of those in the three Eastern-rite archdioceses who have tried to retrace the history of their faiths
in America, the erosion of numbers of adherents was considerable. The greatest gains were made by the Latin church
because of the centuries-old affiliation of the two Uniate
churches with Rome.

Although possessed of their own theology, liturgy, language, music, and rituals, and despite attempts to resist ab-
sorption as one of Rome's ethnic churches, neither the Maronites nor the Melkites sufficiently asserted their own ethnic
and religious distinctiveness from the Latin churches in
America. Of the Melkites, it was written that "often they
adopted the theology and practices of the numerically and
intellectually superior Western Church. Western laws and
customs, forms of devotion, feast days, and liturgical practices current in the West were accepted by the Easterners. . . .
When Eastern Catholics arrived in this country, they were at
a disadvantage, both numerically and psychologically. . . .
Faced with misunderstanding on the part of the Latins and
often indifference on the part of their own parishioners, they
often attempted to 'Americanize' (i.e. Latinize) their
churches."[35]

Notwithstanding the thirty-six Maronite and twenty-three
Melkite parishes and missions which existed by 1930, neither
rite, because of official Roman Catholic opposition, organized a diocese nor were they permitted to appoint their own
bishops. By 1966, when finally permitted to establish exar-

chates in America, the battle to win back the "Latinized" descendants of the immigrant generation had been virtually lost.[36]

Syrian Orthodoxy developed with far less jurisdictional restraint in America. The Russian Orthodox Archdioceses, under whose jurisdiction it fell, ordained the first Syrian bishop, Archimandrite Raphael Hawaweeny, in 1904. The young priest had been requested to come to America by Dr. Ibrahim Arbeely, president of the Orthodox Benevolent Society of New York, "to provide for the spiritual, educational, cultural and economic needs of the new Arab immigrants." On his arrival in 1896, he was appointed by the Russian bishopric to head the Syro-Arabian Mission in North America. When he was ordained bishop eight years later, it was in the Brooklyn church which he had founded.[37]

In order to "bring back those of his flock who had strayed," Bishop Hawaweeny sent a "Pastoral Letter" in late 1912 "to his clergy and people forbidding them to accept the ministrations of Episcopalian clergy who at that time were deceiving people into believing that Orthodoxy and Anglicanism were synonymous."[38] A comparison between the development of the Orthodox church in America and the churches of the Eastern Catholic rites is unavoidable. It is doubtful that one of the Eastern Catholic bishops could have been as forceful against the ministrations of the Roman Catholic church to his "Catholic" communicants.

During his nineteen-year tenure, Bishop Hawaweeny consecrated between thirty-five and forty Syrian Orthodox churches throughout the United States. His death in 1915 ushered in a sixty year period of factionalism within the Syrian church. Only twenty-four churches would be founded in the next two and a half decades.

The first twenty-year schism, hotly debated in print and pulpits, was over the issue of jurisdiction. Some, in the Orthodox community, opted to remain under Russian jurisdiction; others preferred to be administered by the Antiochian Patriarchate of Damascus.[39] The consequence of having competing jurisdictions, each with its Syrian bishop, was that many Syrian Orthodox were served by two, often bitterly, opposed churches. The community, finally unified under the Antiochian Patriarchate of Damascus in 1934, almost immediately faced a second administrative controversy which kept it divided until 1975.[40] In spite of the internal conflicts, the independent church increased its churches and wooed back much of its flock.

Circumstances in America altered the way in which immigrant churches of the three Eastern rites were established and administered. For one thing, congregations usually initiated and financed church buildings and their maintenance. For the Orthodox, this meant a large measure of control over their church through an administrative body. It began when Orthodox adherents in a community, as a rule, formed a society, elected officers, and authorized them to raise parishioner funds and search for a permanent priest. Secondly, there was a chronic shortage of ordained priests. When a congregation was able to obtain one—either from their respective American archdiocese, from the homeland, or by persuading an itinerant priest to become its spiritual leader—it considered itself fortunate. The shortage prompted the bishop to ordain men from the immigrant community—men who had some education and could be quickly trained. Catholic sects often had to wait as much as a year or two before the assignment and approval of a priest by a Latin bishop.

The intermingling of religious and nationalist identities, however, was unchanged and was strengthened in America by overzealous and, at times, poorly educated clergy who migrated to serve their people. The Maronite church has historically viewed itself as a national Lebanese institution; it employs Syriac as its liturgical language. Melkites and Orthodox, on the other hand, use Arabic as their primary liturgical language and historically have identified with Greater Syria. Identity with Syria narrowed the difference between Melkites and Orthodox whose liturgies were almost identical, while it made the Melkites less tolerant of "Latinization" in America than it did the Maronites who formed a closer affinity to the Latin church.

The effects of the Latinization or the anglicanization of

Eastern-rite liturgies on Syrian ethnic identity to 1940 are difficult to measure, given the large attendance, in some cases for extended periods of time, at non-Syrian-rite churches. Yet, individual experiences show that not in all cases were the factors of Syrian identity—religion, sect, family, and place of origin—eroded. Edward A., for example, was born in 1899 to a family from Zahle on a homestead near Grand Forks, North Dakota. Syrians were few and scattered throughout the state. Since the nearest Syrian-rite churches were several hundred miles away in Minneapolis and St. Paul, he attended a Latin-rite church. Knowing nothing of being Melkite or Maronite, he dismissed as irrelevant his Maronite wife's remark that his family was Melkite. He was not, however, indifferent to his family's Zahle origins nor the Arabic language which he barely remembered—the two remaining links to his ethnic identity of which he was proud.[41]

Christine L., unlike Edward, has lived in a community of her people all of her life. Peoria is presently reported to have about 330 Maronite families, all immigrants or descendants of immigrants from the Maronite village of Itoo in Mount Lebanon. In fact, the word "Itoo" in Peoria is synonymous with being Maronite. Itoos constitute the largest majority of the Syrian community and are a tightly knit group. For almost ninety years its members attended a Roman Catholic church. When in 1978, a Maronite church was established, only eighty-two families returned to their native church. Christine, a widow and a retired businesswoman, was not among them. She was five when she immigrated with her mother in 1900 and, she said, "I went to the Irish Catholic church and school all my life and I still go there. Now, there is a Maronite church, but I won't go. My parents never told me I am a Maronite. They were Catholic. I wasn't aware I was a Maronite then and I am not one now." Yet, she added, "I speak Arabic and I am proud of it." Ethnically, she is an Itoo first and a Lebanese second. "I used to call myself Syrian, but was told not to say that anymore. I don't know why."[42]

Fort Wayne, like Peoria, had no Eastern-rite church until

1980 when a small Orthodox community established a church. It is attended by many of the "anglicanized" and "Latinized" descendants of the pioneer peddlers who, nevertheless, retained their ethnic identity which had been, by and large, Syrian, until the independence of Lebanon.

If any trend emerges from these and other testimonies, it is that religion, as the paramount identity factor in Syria, had, by World War II, lost much of its paramountcy in the United States.

Churches of the three Syrian-rite faiths usually depended for their financial existence on a lay board of trustees or council selected from among the most prominent and wealthy of the parish. It was administered by a priest, and since the board hired him, he was dependent on and accountable to it. Thus the relationship between clergy and laity was conditioned in advance, frequently strained by factional disputes within the parish and continual congregational pressure for additional operating funds, not only to administer the church, but to enhance and expand it. To parish, priest, and board members, the aggrandizement of the church symbolized not only dedication to the faith but pride and prestige to which they contributed time, effort, and money. However, its mounting annual budgets relied most heavily on the generosity of its affluent parishioners, many of whom found in this symbiosis a way to acquire status.

The rapid assimilation of Syrians began to affect attendance at all Eastern-rite churches. In order to arrest the defection of parishioners who could not understand the language of the liturgy and to attract new members, the leaders acknowledged the inevitable; even before the end of World War I, aspects of their respective masses were gradually Americanized. Americanization of the Eastern Catholic chruches had begun when they came under the administration of the Roman Catholic authorities in the United States,[43] while the Orthodox church, virtually independent, Americanized itself. As early as 1917, Archpriest Basil M. Kherbawi recognized that "a need is always felt for a book in the English language of the most necessary prayers of the Holy Orthodox Catholic Church for practical use by the young people especially. I have therefore ventured to publish this Breviary in both English and Arabic languages for the benefit of those who know them both or know either one."[44]

Then in 1920, Antiochian Metropolitan Germanos published parts of the Orthodox mass in English accompanied by music for choir and organ, arranged and adapted to Western music by the Metropolitan himself, including a prayer he had composed for the president of the United States.[45] By 1929, the native churches were "finding it necessary to bend the general trend and partially conduct their services in English."[46] The church would further anglicize the liturgy, Westernize the Byzantine chants, phase out cantors in favor of choirs, and shorten the liturgy.

More than one irony flowed from the Americanization of the Eastern-rite churches. By fostering assimilation and diluting the distinction between themselves and the "American" churches, they weakened the effect of religion on Syrian ethnic identity. On the other hand, the rites not only survived on American soil but were strengthened. With the help of educated and trained clergy, they were able to produce social and educational programs aimed at the descendants of the immigrant generation and invited their participation in the church, with the clergy participating more actively in the life of their communities.

Only in four Muslim concentrations were mosques known to have been built before World War II, three of which survived into the postwar period. Yet, Muslims fulfilled their spiritual obligations without fear of perdition. Highland Park, Michigan, appears to have been the site of the first. An imam whose brother was a successful construction contractor lived in Highland Park and, as his son, Imam Mohammad K. reflected, "everything came together." The mosque was consecrated in 1923. However, it became embroiled in a factional controversy and after faltering for four years, it was closed. The Muslim population, in any case, had been gradually migrating to Dearborn to work in the Ford Motor Company's expanding River Rouge plant.

In 1929, the Muslims of North Dakota built their mosque and set aside land for a cemetery. "That only a temporary roof was built, indicates that the Moslems had desires to see the Arab-American community strengthened, but such was not to happen," recorded the State Historical Society of North Dakota. With only a few families remaining and isolated by the Great Depression, the mosque was barely operational until the mid-fifties when it was abandoned.[47]

On 18 February 1925, the Muslim community of Michigan City, Indiana, acquired a cemetery for $825 and a few years later, perhaps in the late twenties or early thirties, it purchased a building and divided it into two parts—"one for prayer as a mosque, and one for social events, with a room for instruction of the Arabic languages [sic]." The building is still in use.[48] In 1929, a fourth mosque was being planned in Cedar Rapids, Iowa. Delayed by the depression, it was not completed until 1934.

It had long been apparent to Muslims in the United States that the American time schedule and calendar were not adjusted to the Islamic way of life. For peddlers, shop owners and factory workers, bowing in prayer, ritually cleansed, to the East five prescribed times daily and fasting during the daylight hours of the holy month of Ramadan were impracticable. Nor could they attend a mosque on the Friday Sabbath, even had these institutions existed. Pious elders, agonizing less over the obstacles in the path of Koranically and canonically correct behavior than over the temptations that threatened to lead their youth away from cultural values, began to relax their fundamentalism and allowed the liberal aspects of their religion to govern the conduct of believers.

As uncompromising as official Islam is on such taboos as eating pork and drinking alcohol, it makes allowances for unusual circumstances and environments. A Muslim, for example, may find it more expedient to make up missed prayers or perform charitable deeds—feeding the poor, donating for religious education, or endowing a school or mosque—as substitutes for unfulfilled obligations. Imam K. elaborated, articulating perhaps an overly liberal view of Islamic canon:

Missing a prayer was not serious because Islam has *qada*, meaning to satisfy a claim or duty. That is, you can make prayers and offer qada prayers to God and the claim is satisfied. If a Muslim backslides too far and gets caught up in the American environment, God will give you the opportunity to make up even five thousand prayers in addition to the regular prayers. A believer can make up five or ten or twenty prayers a day before he dies. Or, there is *kaffara*—"penance" or "atonement." One may feed the poor of any faith, help widows or orphans or they may choose to give up sex, saying to his wife: "From this day forward, you are to me as my mother." This is called *zihar*. If a man wants to break zihar, an imam could advise him to feed, say, ten poor people, turning a weakness into a benefit.

For Muslims, any uncontaminated place at home or work could be a place to pray. And, for both Muslims and Druze, immigrants compensated for the lack of consecrated religious institutions by coming together to pray, read, discuss religion, or celebrate religious festivals. Most would, if they could, have sent their children back to the home village for Islamic education and upbringing. Many, but by no means a majority, did.

For the devout, unlettered Muslim villagers, observance of their faith in this way was less than spiritually satisfying and did not always alleviate the fear of canonical error in the absence of an imam. Yet, it permitted them to live and work in a Christian culture and to maintain their heritage and identity. The apprehension before immigration was harsher than the reality after it, as Shaykh B. discovered:

> Before, the [Highland Park] Muslims prayed in their homes. Each believer read his own Koran. He didn't need a leader. . . . This is a free country; no one asked you about your religion or faith. Personally, I prayed and fasted as I had done in the village. No one asked or bothered me. Nothing changed. I worked on Friday. It was not necessary to stop working to pray. This is a matter of choice; I worked and prayed on Friday. I prayed after work. . . . I fasted all day while working during Ramadan. Difficult? Don't ask how difficult! But I did, even when I felt very weak. It is required.
>
> As a Muslim, it never came to my mind to be concerned that

my way of life would be changed or that it would be difficult
for me if I came to the United States. I was not afraid. There
was no reason to be afraid.

The Druze emphasis on interpretation of the inner meanings of sacraments which they inherited from Islam allowed
the sect's adherents greater flexibility in adapting to American life. The Druze faith had long since made fasting during
Ramadan and corporate prayer voluntary and had dropped
the requirement to bow toward Mecca in prayer. Rather, a
Druze could pray anywhere at relative, rather than precise,
times and needed only to declare his intent to perform the
ritual ablutions. "Since a Druze is striving for the highest degree of piety individualistically," explained Samah H., an
American-born Druze, "he is less concerned about obligatory
acts missed or achieved than he is about the condition of his
spirit in its progress toward *Tauhid*, or 'unity,' with God's
spirit. . . . The Druze do not believe that 'acts' earn Paradise.
Only the degree of spiritual perfection has merit in God's
view." Liberalism, however, was more apparent in the faith
than it was in the rigid social system governing the way Druze
lived and identified in the homeland.

If the first mosque was not built in the United States until
1923, the first Druze majlis has yet to be considered, since
none can be established without the fundamental requirement of a resident member of the religious elite to officiate—
and these men are forbidden to emigrate. Mr. H., a member
of the American Druze Society which, among its other objectives, questions the relevance of religious secrecy in modern
times in general, and in America in particular, pointed out:
"Can one have a church without a minister?"

When asked to define their faith, informants, unable to
articulate their religious beliefs clearly, invariably emphasized their fealty to Druze-Arab values over that of faith.
Haifa R. was once asked about her religion by a priest in her
town and she candidly replied that she "didn't know much
about it. All I know is that I believe in God and I believe in
everything that the Ten Commandments tell you to, and
that's very important. If you believe in those things, that's all
you need to know." Interjected her sister-in-law, "We know

more about the Bible than we do about our own Druze religion."

Samia S.'s view was more typical. To be a Druze, she said, meant the way she was brought up, her ancestry, and the fact that she was born in Lebanon and was an Arab. She was brought up in a strict Druze tradition by her father who was a shaykh, and she owns a copy of the *Book of Wisdom*, parts of which she had memorized as a child. But, her "Druzeness" is not specifically related to her religious beliefs, she said, because all monotheistic religions have similar beliefs and accept each other's tenets.[49] The Druze heritage which defined the identity for most Druze immigrants, was frequently transmitted to them and their children in heroic stories. Jack H. stressed the Druze courage, tolerance, and "keeping the family as a solid unit" in the tales he told his children.

When an enclave of men became a community of families, the services of self-made religious leaders became especially essential. Marriage contracts, circumcision rituals, and burial rites had to be officiated over by one who understood the processes; pious men rose from within the communities of the Muslim and Druze faiths to meet the needs. Since Islamic clergy are trained and not ordained, the most learned or self-trained men filled the role of imam or shaykh—men such as Shaykh Kalil B., the senior Imam K., and Sam Juma in North Dakota.[50]

Kalil was an illiterate nineteen-year-old Shi'a immigrant in 1913 when he took a job with the Ford Motor Company in Highland Park. He taught himself to read Arabic by studying the Koran and he learned to perform burial and marriage services "because the Shi'a people had no one else to do this for them." For his piety during his selfless services for almost seven decades, his people honored him with the title of shaykh, usually conferred on prayer leaders and religious teachers by the Shi'a of Syria and Lebanon. Najem B.'s cousin and a Druze from Cleveland acted as itinerant Druze shaykhs, officiating at burials and weddings. The senior Imam K. ministered to Muslims in such distant places as Kansas, Massachusetts, West Virginia, Iowa, and North Dakota.[51] He also officiated at some Druze funerals.[52]

Islam changed in spite of, or perhaps because of, the vigilance of such devout guardians of the faith in America. When after World War II, educated and trained imams arrived to take up posts in mosques, they considered Arab-American Muslims undisciplined and ignorant of Islam and Arabic and complained about their Americanized practices. Such developments were perceived in the twenties and had begun to alarm Muslim leaders. Shaykh B. published an article in *Al-Bayan* in 1925 urging Muslim parents to teach their children Arabic as well as religious traditions and customs. He especially stressed the imperative of teaching religion to the American-born children who, he feared, were beginning to lose their heritage and becoming "foreigners and atheists."[53]

In the interview, as in the article, he blamed parents who neglected the religious training of their children: "All young [Muslim] people in the United States are unconcerned with religion, not for lack of places to worship, but from lack of training at home. . . . Because of climate and water and the [nature of] the country, children who are born and raised here are not concerned with religion."

His concern was reiterated by delegates at an "important" meeting of the Moslem Young Men's Society of New York City who resolved, among other matters, to take "the necessary steps for regulating religious observances by Moslems in America."[54]

The esoteric nature of the Druze faith and its beliefs and practices placed no pressure on the Druze in America to establish religious structures, even if they could have done so. "Worship was not the main reason for Druze coming together; it was because they were Druze," commented Samah H. Moreover, because the majlis, unlike the mosque and Christian church, did not play the central role in the religious and social lives of Druze, and because of the principle of dissembling and the rule of intent, many Druze in America freely attended Christian churches, mainly Protestant and sometimes non-Catholic Syrian churches. They participated in the social activities in these churches, unthreatened by the fear of conversion or loss of identity and unhampered by conflicting loyalties. "In America," asserted Henry Flehan, "the foreign-born Druze who could not attend a majlis . . . , basically lacked no spiritual belief, but totally believed in God's spoken word as practiced by all religions. [A Druze] tried to teach the same to his children. [That is] the reason why so many attended Christian churches in this country in the absence of his [own] place of worship." "If there had been a Druze majlis," said Samia S., "I probably would not have joined the Methodist church." Mrs. Helen D. was baptized a Christian. "My parents were broad-minded," she said. "They never taught us how to be [religiously] Druze; they probably didn't know much about their religion." In the small Pennsylvania town where he settled, her father took his family to a Protestant church, "but it didn't change my feelings about being a Druze."[55] All of the Druze informants had either attended a Christian church, been married in one, or had sent their children to one.

The Druze system, based on tribal values and an esoteric religion known only to an elite minority, had been strengthened over the centuries by persecution and was ultimately forged by the Druze in Greater Syria into a "nation"—a people with an identity distinctive from their neighbors in the Ottoman provinces where they resided. In the United States, that feeling, rather than the faith, bound, and continues to bind, the Druze community.

CLUBS, SOCIETIES, AND UNIFICATION

It was in the United States that the erstwhile Syrian villagers, perhaps even city dwellers, learned to organize around a common purpose or cause, and they practiced it with a vengeance. Syrians developed such a propensity for organizing that at any given time the number of organizations was out of all proportion to the number of Syrians in America, albeit most of them short-lived.

During the early pioneer period, the Old World practices of village leaders consulting with the heads of prominent families living close to each other, was adapted to American settlement conditions. Men convened around a supplier, in-

formally and irregularly to discuss issues relevant to the
needs of the group—helping the needy and burying the
dead. Broader colony issues might bring other leaders into
the discussion. Sometimes, these informal meetings evolved
into formal societies, employing democratic rules of proce-
dure, to implement the wishes of the group as when the Orthodox of Spring Valley, in 1914, organized a society to purchase their own cemetery. They met regularly, elected
officers, set dues, kept ledgers, and recorded the minutes of
their meetings.[56] The men and women of the Cedar Rapids
colony also formed a club to help the needy and to raise
money to build a church.[57] Membership of such groups
might have cut across family, village, and creed, but not typically. From such single-purpose organizations, clubs proliferated to serve a variety of aims.

It is reasonable to assume that the first clubs and societies
were formed in the New York colony. By the early 1890s
there were sectarian social and charitable societies, women's
societies, societies to teach English and good citizenship, and
others to assist and encourage naturalization and promote
patriotic ideals as well as to promote understanding between
Syrians and other Americans. As part of the trend toward
specialization, merchants and manufacturers formed their
own societies and a literary society was also founded.

Political organizations were precluded not only because
Syrians in America were disunited, but because the Syrians
were "too busy to pay attention to Turkey," according to a
member of the Young Syrian Society founded to foster the
welfare of Syrians at home; but it had disbanded by 1909.
Moreover, most of them, he told Louise Houghton, had become American citizens but would certainly not join in any
move against the Turkish government.[58] The Young Syrian
Society was succeeded by the United Syrian Society, whose
aim was to improve "the social and political status of Syria"
by enlightening public opinion in America. That there were
no religious restrictions for membership, impressed Mrs.
Houghton, given, as she said, the "bitter religious hostility"
that characterized the Syrian community.[59] The Society was
apparently short-lived, since nothing more is known about it.

A more influential organization was the Lebanon League of Progress founded in 1911 to support a French-backed Maronite-dominated Lebanon. With these known exceptions, homeland politics were not generally reflected in the aims of Syrian- or Lebanese-American organizations until after World War I.

Syrians organized for many civic and social purposes and performed beneficial services for their people in the United States and abroad, but, by and large, many were for the purpose of socializing. If they had a central theme, it was the underlying one of group solidarity and continuity, mainly through in-group marriage. They tended, therefore, to be exclusivist.

As was the Syrian's natural inclination, groups insulated their members, much as did the churches and mosques, by cultivating their own clubs and creating a social life centered on identity of the group. Membership was based on religion, sect, village, or family. In many, such as the Itoo Society of Peoria, even spouses with no blood ties to members of the group were excluded. Victoria S. had to resign from the Douma (Mount Lebanon) Society when she married a non-Douma man.[60]

Divisions were, of course, an ancient and timeless characteristic, activated by the concept of family honor as if it was an immutable law of nature. Gatherings for purposes that transcended narrow group identity could be expected to split along a constellation of ancient fissures. Najla S. of Detroit, described a typical case. Her Melkite church club was started by Melkites from various parts of Mount Lebanon and Syria. However, "they couldn't get together because each was from a different village or city. Everybody wanted to come forward in the name of the place he came from, or for his family's name or for himself—selfish—so they separated. Each group went its way. . . . And then each group began to infight on some pretext. The Damascenes ended up as a group of families. Then a few families dominated and wouldn't follow the rule of the majority. The club broke up and no one knows where the money from the treasury is. . . . One brother won't see anything his brother's way. Everyone wants

his own way." Factional and clannish tendencies, combined
with an ingrained individualism, inhibited the Syrian's ability
to sustain, enthusiastically, anonymous support for causes or
participation in organizations or institutions involving non-
primary groups.

The number of clubs and societies increased markedly in
the 1920s. The first generation, to arrest the growing drift
of the youth away from the group and its mores and to maintain group solidarity, formed, in addition to other types,
clubs based on family and village (or city) of origin. They
drew together dispersed members from various parts of the
country to annual meetings and festivities at which patri-
archs and matriarchs reigned; youths were matched, old and
young socialized, and through it all continuity and unity were
reinforced. The Rashid and Attiyeh family societies were
only two of several such in the United States.

Since 1927, various branches of the large Rashid family
have met at annual reunions "to keep up acquaintances," because the family was losing its "togetherness." Its members,
in 1979, numbered 1,200.[61] Every year since it was founded
in 1935 by some members of the Attiyeh families from Ayn
Arab in Cedar Rapids and Sioux City, Iowa, the Attiyeh Society has reaffirmed and renewed family ties annually. It was
founded, it was said, "to help the young members of the Society financially, in pursuit of a higher education."[62]

Societies based on place of origin are more numerous.
With the idioms and accents of the homeland still on their
minds, immigrants first came together in village and town
clubs to preserve old relationships. Hardly a village or town
in the homeland had not been thus linked to its émigrés. The
Itoo Society may have been representative. It grew out of an
incident in 1914 when a young Itoo laborer was killed on the
Illinois River and funds for his burial had to be collected
from his fellow villagers. About fifty Itoo families then
formed their society "so we don't have to take collections or
go on relief," explained Christine L. "We're a proud people."
They wanted "to keep the Itoo community together and prevent marriage outside the group," she added. Later, the
group began to send money to the needy in the home village,

four or five times a year. . . . and keep up Itoo ancestry" so that the children and grandchildren will "get to know each other and not lose their identity," said Oscar A.[63] "Through the Itoo Society," declared Joseph C., "I pass Itoo culture to my children."

At one time the society split temporarily; one faction "which did not get along with the others, especially concerning homeland politics and about who was going to be the 'mayor' of Itoo," formed its own club. Two years before the Itoo Society was established, the Syrian men of Peoria had joined together in a nonsectarian Society of Love and Brotherhood, better known as the Barrel Club for the barrel of beer they consumed on meeting nights. When the Maronite Itoos formed their society, the Barrel Club disbanded and the non-Itoos, a tiny group of Melkites from Zahle, formed the Zahle Club. Nostalgia for the Syrian town prompted its members to re-create in some craggy hills near Peoria, the famous symbols of their town—a wooded glen and picnic area at the head of a mountain stream.[64]

Many civic improvements as well as new churches, orphanages, hospitals, and schools were funded by the contributions of societies to their villages, motivated by the traditional desire of emigrants of all nationalities, who had prospered elsewhere, to benefit their people and to be recognized at home for achievements. In marked contrast, however, Syrians did not establish comparable ethnic charitable or educational institutions in the United States, although individuals did contribute generously to American philanthropic causes.

The 1920s also marked the acceleration of associational activity among Muslims. Druze had already formed their Bakurat al-Dirziyya in 1911, but in the twenties, with the arrival of women and families, that society began to form chapters to "help each other out and . . . to keep ourselves informed in what is going on between our people here and our people back home and also to keep ourselves well informed on our culture," explained Nafe K. Muslims, like Christians, bonded together in social and charitable clubs. Some Muslims of Michigan City, for example, founded several before World War I, based on fellowship, on their common religion, and even on their common villages, but they were short-lived. Hussien Hussien Ayad, a prominent member of the community, told John P. Brennan of the Public Library of Michigan City that Muslims decided to form societies because "unity and sincerity insure [sic] success of fruition." In the twenties, however, the arrival of families changed the character of the group and by 1924, these families—two hundred, it was reported—formed the Society of the New Era. With the help of their women, the society purchased a cemetery to which Muslims had access, free of charge, and two buildings, one "as a haven for the incapacitated free of charge" and the second was turned into a club hall for meetings. Later, the society purchased the building that became a mosque.[65]

In its "important" meeting of April 1929, the Moslem Young Men's Society of New York City attempted to organize on a broad scale. Its delegates from other cities resolved to "join hands with other Moslem organizations throughout the world for the defense of Islam."[66]

If politics was omitted as an organizing principle, Syrian organizations were not immune from its effects as news of events reached the Syrians from the homeland, particularly from Mount Lebanon. Maronite ideologies, justifying Maronite preeminence in the Mountain after World War I and aimed at separating the Maronites from a developing Syrian nationalist movement, adopted a secularist identity with the Phoenicians of the region's distant past. In America, the movement spawned a number of "Phoenician" clubs and at the same time ignited a widespread controversy, fueled by the creation of Greater Lebanon under the French Mandate. Many non-Maronites from both Mount Lebanon and the incorporated Syrian lands, as well as their descendants who, as a consequence, had to change their national identity, rejected the new Lebanese identity. For more than two decades, the issue was hotly debated in homes and churches, but nowhere more heatedly than in clubs and societies. Many split over whether they should be called Syrian-American, Lebanese-American, or both. Only when Lebanon and Syria achieved full independence after World War II did the controversy subside.

Some Syrians gravitated to "American" clubs in addition to Syrian organizations. Among the favorites were the Odd Fellows, the Moose, and the Eagles. Louis L., when he lived in Chicago, made many friends in the Knights of Columbus and even attended an opera and played golf with them. Syrians of all creeds were attracted to Masonic clubs for the fellowship but also in some cases, for the precepts and rites. Frank A. found that the Masons taught humanity and the Odd Fellows taught brotherly love.

The persistence of traditional restraints in the associational life of Syrians, after more than a generation in the United States, began to disturb increasing numbers of the Americanized second generation. They complained of the factional tendencies of the Old World views and practices, not the least of which was sexually segregated clubs.[67] New clubs, more American in outlook, which seemed to appear everywhere in the country toward the end of the twenties, found a medium for their grievances in the English-language *Syrian World*. The new clubs announced themselves and communicated their views to its readership. The names and purposes of the new clubs revealed a new outlook and a developing trend. The immigrant offspring were attempting to reconcile the disparate halves of their identity—preserving elements of their parents' culture within their own American culture.

The Syrian-American Confraternity of Grand Rapids, for example, was organized in 1927 "to inculcate and impress the doctrines of Americanism upon, and to make better citizens of, the Syrian people; to create the spirit of brotherhood and unity regardless of religion or creed, in the Syrian colony of Grand Rapids and its environs." It chose to express its purpose by presenting an Arabic play which, curiously, was "favorably commented upon by many American papers in the city."[68] From Los Angeles, in October of that year, came a notice from the Syrian Young Men's Society which hoped to facilitate "friendship among the young Syrian generation," maintain "traditional customs of their forefathers," and create a "social atmosphere . . . in order to invite and strengthen family ties."[69] Calling itself "Flower of the East," in January 1928, the New Syrian Society of Wilkes Barre, Pennsylvania, worked for "unity and understanding, uplifting the Syrian name, encouraging higher education, and prompting the Syrian youth to the desire of emulating the achievements of their forefathers."[70] The New Syrian American Society of South Carolina stood for the "promotion of Americanization without losing sight of the rich cultural heritage of our race;"[71] and the Syrian American Club of Tucson stressed nonsectarianism—"the new trend of thought among the younger generation."[72]

As organizations learned about each other, there were appeals in letters published in the *Syrian World* to break the cultural isolation some sensed—appeals which eventually led to calls for federation. The idea, advanced by the Good Fellows Club of Tyler, Texas, in May 1927, initially aroused no interest, but it was revived in the fall of 1928. One of the advocates, Fred S. Rizk of Jacksonville, Florida, expressed concern about the loss of the Syrian heritage and the Arabic language and suggested that the erosion was salvageable only with unification. The Syrians, scattered throughout the forty-eight states are "absorbed in the irresistible American tide," he said. These "true Syrian-Americans," nearer to the vanguard of modern American life, know very little of their history, heritage, and language.

> Far more serious . . . , they lacked the interest to inquire and learn. . . . The result is a dying class or race consciousness. . . . In almost every city of any size there are young Syrian societies. But their local character is their principle weakness. They are completely out of touch with other societies sharing with them a common heritage. Usually after a little flourish they die, only to be supplanted by another equally weak and equally purposeless association. Can we not get these different Syrian clubs into one embracing society, having the purpose not only of bringing into intimate and wholesome contact the great number of our Syrian young men and so impress each one of the existence of the others, but also of promoting periodical discussion of contemporary Syrian events? Can we

not have representatives from the various communities meet
yearly to exchange ideas and propose constructive policies?[73]

The *Syrian World* may, in fact, have been an important ca-
talyst in the spread of the new type of clubs. It was conceived,
wrote Salloum Mokarzel, its editor-publisher, "in the spirit of
service to the Syrian-American generation" based on the assumption that lack of sufficient knowledge of its "racial traits
and historical background renders them somewhat unsym-
pathetic with their parents' attitude." True to the stated aims
of the publication, he invited the use of its pages as a "forum
for the discussion of existing problems among Syrians in
America in an effort to arrive at their best solution."

The conflict between the views of the Syrian-Americans
and those of their parents was sharpening, and Mokarzel
hoped his publication could mediate. He promised to "give
them a broader vision of their racial heritage; and all this to
the end that our Syrian-American generation will come to
better understand the country of their parents and appreciate more fully their racial endowments which constitute a
valuable contribution to the country of their birth."[74] Thus
his readers read articles about Syrian social, political, and
economic affairs, perhaps for the first time. They learned
about the achievements of fellow Syrian-Americans in business, which Mokarzel was wont to emphasize, as well as in the
arts, sciences, and literature. One of the publication's regular
features was a variety of interesting and romantic, if not always illuminating, glimpses into Syria's historic and literary
past.

A zealous champion of Americanization and a critic of tra-
ditionalism, Mokarzel generally subscribed to the goals of
Americans of Syrian descent. But, dedicated to his cultural
heritage, he also pledged to help them discover themselves
and "to breed in them a consciousness of appreciation for
their racial qualities and inheritances so that they may com-
port themselves with a befitting sense of honor as citizens of
this great American nation."[75]

In the proliferation of new societies, he also discerned the
seeds of future unification of the Syrians in America. "It is a

sign of a healthy social condition for the Syrian young folks
to establish societies of their own," he wrote in an editorial.

It is also a sign of intelligent understanding on the part of the
parents not to thrust themselves in the affairs of their youth
and insist on managing things their own, old way. . . .

The young folks should not be ridiculed or discouraged in
any of their legitimate efforts. Coming together in a social
club, a fraternal or benevolent society is a most laudable un-
dertaking. . . . The parents, if they value their traditions and
wish to see what is best in them perpetuated, should encourage all forms of social activities leading to cooperation among
their youth. This is the best method for holding together the
scattered fragments of the Syrian race. . . .

. . . [The formation of scores of new organizations] may
prove to be the nucleus of a nation-wide movement for the
unification of the race in what is bound to become a great
force for good.[76]

The call and the hope for a federation did not materialize;
yet, the formation of new organizations with a greater interest in their ethnic cultural heritage continued and, judging
only by what appeared in the *Syrian World* and in the absence
of any other known source, it reached at least the proportions of a small movement.

Mokarzel wrote inspiring editorials and articles on the
merits and necessity for unification. In "Can We Retain Our
Heritage? A Call to Form a Federation of Syrian Societies,"
which appeared in the November 1928 issue, he argued that
the "healthy awakening of racial consciousness among the
younger generation of Syrians in the United States" is a constructive form of Americanism and an antidote to hatred and
class prejudice. He called for cooperation and understanding among Syrians so that they may claim their "rightful
place and to express our resentment at the imputation of
inferiority," since Syrians as well as other races are not classed
"among the so-called Nordics." Ignorance fosters fear and
mistrust. America, above any other country in the world,
needs the cementing influence of mutual understanding
among her heterogenous elements." Establishing societies

would be beneficial to Syrian Americans, he continued, in that they

> would help us first understand ourselves where this understanding has heretofore been woefully lacking. Our young generation had not in the past what it is now beginning to show of its appreciation of its splendid background. This was a negative situation which not only did not help to breed self-respect, but rather tended to destroy it. . . . substantial progress could be made toward taking the next logical step which would be to diffuse knowledge of our race, through the co-ordinated collective efforts of these societies, among the general body of the American nation. . . . Then it would be that we will not feel ourselves secluded and misunderstood and misjudged, nor would Americans remain in that state of ignorance about us as to cause their resultant lack of appreciation of us. . . .
>
> But now a broader duty suggests itself, . . . It consists of forming a national federation of Syrian-American societies in the country for the purpose of promoting policies of general interest to the race as a whole. Local organizations would retain their independent status, simply adhering to the general policy of the Federation in national affairs as affiliated members. . . . The numerous communications published so far in the *Syrian World* prove the existence of such a tendency. What seems to be lacking is a central agency to act as a clearing house of information and interchange of ideas on the general plan. In the absence of any organized body for such a purpose, the *Syrian World* willingly offers itself as this necessary medium.

He presented a four-point plan for implementing the "bid for national unity" and promised to publish the list of responding societies.[77]

In December, the Reverend W. A. Mansur, a regular contributor to the journal, published a detailed seven-point statement of "spirit, purpose and methods;"[78] and, during the next year, the journal published enthusiastic responses, pledges from associations, and progress reports. By April 1929, the pledges totaled only nineteen and never reached the expectations of the unification advocates. Mokarzel warned that final action could not be deferred indefinitely

and criticized those suspicious of unity. "No single organization need fear the loss of its individual identity and autonomous prerogatives as the fundamental purpose of the Federation is to bring the scattered units together in matters of
national policy only. . . . every constituent member will have
a voice."[79]

The movement foundered for another year. It was too
frail to survive the country's economic plunge in October
1929. "Perhaps it has been for the best to have held the con-
summation of the movement in abeyance after once having
aroused widespread interest in it," conceded Mokarzel in December 1930. "Its resumption in the future might prove of
immensely greater benefit owing to the large possibilities offered."[80]

Even had the depression not intervened, the likelihood
that the unification movement, advocated by a minority of
the Syrian-Americans, would fail, was certain. Ironically, the
very obstacles that the movement had hoped to eliminate,
immobilized it. Ambiguous references to "Syrian" heritage
were irrelevant to the majority of the Syrian-American generation. On the other hand, perceptions of what that heritage consisted of varied with each sectarian and religious
subgroup. Because the immigrants had been unsophisticated
in the broader and deeper meanings of their culture, "Syrian
heritage" translated into parochial and regional heritage.
Therefore, references to "Arab" culture or heritage were
meaningless and remote. Neither could the Syrian-American
generation long be held to its parents' and clergy's definition
that to be Syrian was to live by the traditional virtues and to
think of themselves as having their own traditions and customs that they must preserve. Moreover, a unification movement, to stimulate an interest in and preserve the Syrian heritage, required an impartial leadership or an institution that
could transcend the diverse Syrian identities. Also required
was a consensus definition of that heritage—one that would
transcend conflicting interpretations and emphases—Islamic
versus Christian, for example, or Arab versus "Phoenician."
The *Syrian World* itself could not conceal its own Lebanese
Maronite leanings, politically or culturally, despite Mokarzel's

lofty aims and attempts at impartiality. Ultimately, undefined and unexplained, the Syrian heritage found its own uncontroversial level in the common denominators of food, music, and dance.

The unification movement was hampered by two other factors. Many Syrian clubs and societies were ephemeral. Exacerbating the situation, the Syrian-versus-Lebanese identity controversy, kept alive by continuing political events in the homeland, was taking its toll. Secondly, the cultural stimulus of the Syrian-Americans between the wars was overwhelmingly that of America. Motion pictures, radio, jazz, bobbed hair, short skirts, new dances, and other modern attractions, far removed from the parents' old-fashioned culture, captured the youth's attention.

Wedad F.'s perception of Syrian culture was characteristic. In 1921, at the age of six, she immigrated to Spring Valley and subsequently lived in Fort Wayne, Detroit, Milwaukee, and Los Angeles. She was reflective for a few moments before she said:

> Syrian culture? It's hard to say. I've heard my parents say that Syria was the seat of all learning and culture. They always beat that drum but us kids didn't know what that meant. But because of that, they pushed my brothers to go to college. Beyond that, it was what we did and what we heard in our home: how sweet the air and water and how delicious and large was the fruit—peaches the size of grapefruit and grapes the length of your first finger—and we used to laugh. Not that they wanted to go back to live, but they talked about it and told us stories—village folktales. We loved them. Many had morals to them and there was a proverb for everything. We ate Syrian bread and we talked the Syrian language and we went to a Syrian church, that is, after we had attended a Methodist or Catholic one on Sunday. . . .
>
> My parents were from Syria and the people who lived on Congress Street [in Detroit] were Maronites from Mount Lebanon. I didn't know why, but I had the impression, when I was growing up, that I shouldn't like them. I later learned that Orthodox didn't get along with Maronites. I knew I was supposed to hate Druze; they killed my grandparents in 1925. I never met a Druze or Muslim until I was well grown up after

the war [World War II] and they were foreigners to me—they
might have been from another world. I liked those I met and
I wondered to myself what my mother would say if I told her
that. She was already dead. I never lived in a Syrian neighborhood like Congress Street, but our house was always full
of Syrians.

So, what is Syrian culture? Was it the same for Druze and
Muslims and Maronites who were supposed to be different
from Orthodox? I don't know. I couldn't tell you then and I
can't really tell you now. I suppose it was to be hospitable in
your home, serve tons of food, speak the [Arabic] language,
respect your elders—well, you know, marry someone of your
own religion. Oh yes, protect that family name! and so on.
Syrian literature and history? No. Maybe the old people
talked about it, but not us. To tell you the truth, I don't know
anyone of my generation who cared much. In my group, we
joined clubs to be social—to find husbands or wives. After
1939, when our club joined the Midwest Federation, it was for
the same reason. Maybe the officers had some such notion in
mind and wrote letters to the president of the United States
on behalf of Lebanon or Syria, or something, but it didn't get
through to the membership. We wanted to have fun and we
did. I met my husband at a federation convention in 1941. He
was born here and he's ten times more old-fashioned and
strict than I am. He can't even pronounce his name properly
in Arabic.[81]

Without its initiators recognizing why, the movement
failed. The failure of subsequent unification movements to
comprehend the failure of the first, jeopardized their
chances of success. In 1932, a regional federation of local
organizations "of any persuasion or purpose" was formed in
Boston. Although hampered by the depression, internal conflicts, and World War II during the next fifteen years, the
Eastern Federation was successful enough to inspire other
regional federations. All sponsored social activities, provided
scholarships, and worked to improve relations between
Syrian-Americans and others. Aside from interest in Arabic
food, music, and dance, little of the Syrian, Lebanese, or
Arab ethnic heritage was apparent in their purposes or activities before the end of World War II.

The Syrian-American descendants of the pioneer generation entered the post–World War II era lacking a unifying
institution and program of cultural education and preservation. Well assimilated, they nevertheless perpetuated the values and virtues that are rooted in an Arabness they understood in its irreducible elements: family unity and honor,
hospitality, and generosity. Lack of a unified identity in the
United States militated against the development of a single,
sustained national secular institution until the 1960s.

PRESS, POLITICS, AND THE ARTS

The impetus for the development of an Arabic-language
press was provided by a few intellectual immigrants. Graduates, for the most part, of religious and secular schools of
higher education in the cities of Syria, they had been influenced by the émigré Syrian literary revival in Cairo. It was
both coincidental and fortuitous that in New York, the publishers of the Arabic press, many of whom had little or no
prior journalistic training or experience, came together with
émigré Arab writers and poets in a symbiotic relationship to
form an immigrant intelligentsia.

Before World War I, Arabic publications appeared and
disappeared regularly. So keen was the Syrian penchant for
publishing that between 1892 and 1907 (the lifetime of the
first Arabic newspaper) twenty-one Arabic dailies, weeklies,
and monthlies were published, seventeen of them in New
York City and the others divided between Philadelphia, Lawrence, Massachusetts, and St. Louis. In 1907, when the Syrians numbered only about fifty thousand, eleven publications
struggled for existence.[82] By 1930, their numbers may have
exceeded fifty, with only a handful having appeared after the
war. The competition for a readership that was limited in
number and literacy was made sharper by the religious and
political biases of the individual newspapers. Thus, some
newspapers vanished almost overnight; others lasted between five and ten years, several lasted two or more decades.
Al Jamiʿa (*The League*, 1906–13) which, like its publisher,
Farah Antun, was unmatched for its intellectual standards

and diversity, lasted only seven years, primarily because it exceeded the literary capacity and interests of its immigrant readership.[83]

The most durable newspapers, publishing for over sixty consecutive years, were *Al-Hoda* (*The Guidance*), *Meraat al-Gharb* (*Mirror of the West*), and *Al-Bayan* (*The Explanation*). In 1928, despite the decline in the number of Arabic readers, there were six Arabic dailies in New York, a daily and a semiweekly in Detroit, a weekly in Lawrence, and three monthlies, one in Detroit and two in New York.[84] What is remarkable is that so many publications, at any given time, could be supported by so small a population, for most of whom newspaper reading was a habit acquired in America. It may be, as some old-timers suggested, that the seeds of the mission schools in Syria were bearing fruit in America.

The first newspaper to appear in America was *Kawkab Amrika* (*Star of America*) in 1892. Founded by Najib Arbeely, who had been the interpreter for Arab immigrants, and his brother Ibrahim, it was first published as a weekly and then a daily. It printed three pages in Arabic and one in English of local and homeland news. From 1901, it included a Syrian folklore supplement. The Arbeelys are credited with introducing the first Arabic characters used in typesetting in the United States, an accomplishment that required a release from the Ottoman sultan who had forbidden their export.[85] Typically, its publishers took a political position, remaining loyal to the sultan. They differed from subsequent publishers in that they did not espouse an overt religious orientation.

Al-Hoda began publishing in Philadelphia in 1898 as a weekly, then as a semiweekly. Its publisher, Naoum Mokarzel, a Lebanese-Maronite, was motivated by his opposition to the religion and the Ottoman allegiance of the Arbeely brothers. When his brother, Salloum, arrived to join him, Naoum moved the paper to New York in 1903 and it appeared daily. If *Kawkab Amrika* introduced Arabic characters to publishing in America, *Al-Hoda* was the first to use them in a linotype machine, replacing the traditional and slower method of setting type by hand.[86]

Najeeb Diab, a Syrian Orthodox, an anti-Ottoman Arab

nationalist, and former editor of *Kawkab Amrika*, launched his *Meraat al-Gharb* in 1899 to oppose the political and religious biases of *Al-Hoda*.[87]

The Druze *Al-Bayan*, which also spoke for the Muslims, appeared in 1911 reflecting a growing Druze and Muslim population opposed to the Christian biases in the interpretation of homeland politics. Until World War I brought about the dissolution of the Ottoman Empire, it was staunchly pro-Ottoman. Thereafter, it espoused Arab nationalism and supported an independent Syrian Arab nation.[88]

The editors reported events in the homeland, social news of Syrians in America, immigrant success stories, feature items, and literary works. *Kawkab Amrika*, for a time, published the names of immigrant arrivals. And, as has been noted, it guided their adjustment in editorials. Among their contributors were immigrants who asked questions, voiced opinions, and reflected on their aspirations. Usually, four to eight pages, the newspapers carried advertisements of products and services of Syrian businessmen.

From its inception, the Arabic press had presented many aspects of American social, economic, and political life to its eager readers. While it educated, it also idealized and oversimplified. On the other hand, it kept the homeland alive in their minds and stirred their emotions. Many Syrian immigrants, for the first time, became informed about the society, politics, history, literature, and culture of Arabs in general and Syrians in particular. In addition, Arabic books published in the United States, Beirut, Damascus, and Cairo were made available by newspaper publishers and lists were printed in papers.[89] Never before had these predominantly village-centered, unschooled readers learned so much about their heritage.

In the early years, before self-reform improved their quality, the papers printed paid self-serving articles and laudatory or insulting (sometimes anonymous) paragraphs. Many of the authors and recipients as well as the publishers became enmeshed in sectarian animosities as a result. The harmful practice of accepting such paragraphs for printing and the attempt to eradicate it were among the causes which sparked the 1905 riot in New York. In the opinion of the *New York Herald*, the Syrian press "tried to adapt methods of the society journal and the personal and political editorials of the country newspaper to Oriental conditions."[90]

Several other Arab entrants (hardly a complete list) into the crowded journalistic arena before World War II, deserve mention. *Al-Kalimat* (*The Word*) appeared as a bimonthly journal in 1905, the creation of Bishop Raphael Hawaweeny, a year after he was ordained the first Syrian Orthodox bishop in America. Its primary objective was to guide the spiritual and cultural behavior of his flock, but he also included news of marriage, births, baptisms, church building, and other church-related items.

Syrian publishers had, from the start, befriended the intellectuals and used the pages of their newspapers to launch, test, and advance the early literary output of such luminaries as Kahlil Gibran, Ameen Rihani, Naseeb Arida, Mikhail Naimi, Iliyya Abu Madi, and Abd al-Masih Haddad. In return the contributions of these men of letters added to the quality and prestige of the newspapers as well as their publishers.

Some of the literati had been influenced in the mid-nineteenth century by the Syrian literary revival in Cairo. There Syrian exiles had, among other innovations, adapted rigid, centuries-old Arabic poetic forms to the English tonalities of Protestant hymns worked out previously by leading Syrian poets and American missionaries at the American University in Beirut. In America, according to Shmuel Moreh, author of a study on the influence of free verse on modern Arabic literature, the movement, further influenced by Freemasonry and free verse, was revolutionary.[91] Only in 1912 did Ameen Rihani confess that a piece published in *Al-Hilal* in 1905 was in free verse modeled on Walt Whitman; Kahlil Gibran later achieved greater perfection in this genre.[92]

As the literary movement in America coalesced into an American school of modern Arabic literature, it inspired the formation of Al-Rabitat al-Qalamiyya (The Pen League), an influential literary society, led by Gibran. As it gained momentum, some of its accomplished participants turned to publishing, focusing on the output of the Pen League. In the pages of their publication, the writers exchanged ideas, challenged traditionalists, and invited imitation.

Al-Funun (The Arts), a literary journal founded by the poet Naseeb Arida in 1913 to publish the works of the Pen League, nurtured the art, the artists, and the literary movement until, lacking popular appeal to an undereducated and, in some cases, barely literate readership, it closed permanently in 1919. Its objectives were assumed by Arida's friend and fellow artist, Abd al-Masih Haddad whose *Al-Sayeh (The Traveler)* had, since 1912, been a biweekly, semiliterary paper. Until the dissolution of the Pen League in 1931, it devoted itself entirely to literature. Illiya Abu Madi, a giant of the literary movement, whose poems and articles had appeared in *Meraat al-Gharb*, published his influential fortnightly literary magazine, *Al-Sameer (The Entertainer)* from 1929 until his death in 1936.

Two publications that testify to the Americanization of the press are *Al Akhlaq (The Character)* and the *Syrian World*. In 1920, Yaqoub Rufail launched an innovation in Arab-American journalism and patterned it on some of the most respected American magazines of his day. Its articles, until it closed in 1932, contributed by many of the intelligentsia and other male and female writers and poets, were topical, literary, and educational. It seemed to encourage contributors from talented women. Among the most distinguished was Afifa Karam, the feminist who had contributed articles to *Al-Hoda*. Her *Al-Alam an-Nisa'i (Women's World)*, founded in 1912, was among those forays into publishing whose early demise was ordained by its untimeliness.[93]

The Syrian literati of America, notwithstanding the revolutionary effect they had had on literature in the Arab world, exerted minimal influence on Syrians in the United States. In truth, Syrian-Americans little appreciated Arabic literature whose content was so alien to their experience that hardly a single name except for Gibran (1883–1931) was known to them. Even his works were introduced to most Syrians by literary Americans who popularized them. Since the

Syrian literati were concerned primarily with their influence on Arab literature, this elite failed to preserve or transmit works of lasting ethnic social or cultural significance in the United States. Of the few recognized American authors and poets of Syrian descent, such as William Blatty (1928–), Vance Bourjaily (1922–), and Samuel Hazo (1928–), little or no influence either of their Arab predecessors or of their ethnic origins is discernible.

The appearance of the *Syrian World* in English in 1926 at a crucial period in the maturation of the Syrian experience, signified the publishers' recognition of the end of an era as well as a language crisis. The apathy toward, and ignorance of, cultural heritage was paralleled by apathy toward the Arabic language and consequently threatened the survival of the Arabic press as an ethnic institution. With new Arabic speakers and readers from Syria limited to one hundred annually under the Immigration Quota Act, hardly equal to the community's mortality rate, the use of Arabic inexorably dwindled. Even in immigrant homes, English was increasingly replacing the native language; in the homes of their married children, English prevailed. The colloquial Arabic spoken in many homes was shot through with the twisted, corrupted Arab-English patois invented by their parents. English, the key to becoming American, could not be avoided, not even by Muslims who were under the greatest pressure to maintain Arabic as fundamental to their religion. English, by the twenties, was becoming dominant, if not in most homes, then in most social functions as well as in business.

Attempts by concerned leaders and parents to teach Arabic at home, churches, mosques, private schools, and clubs were, more often than not, defeated. Once past the alphabet or primer, both teacher and student lost patience with the complexities and mysteries of classical Arabic, which possessed no similarity to the grammar or syntax of English nor with spoken Arabic—and had little relevance to the American life and schooling which had first claim on the interest and concentration of Syrian-American children.

Traditionalists, expressing a feeling, suddenly acute, that spread through the Syrian community, pressed for keeping

Arabic alive in the United States. They preached and published articles, but the hour was late. Shaykh B. wrote of its importance to preserving Islam in America.[94] Naoum Mokarzel, plagued with declining subscriptions to *Al-Hoda*, appealed for the maintenance of Arabic more pragmatically. He urged Syrians to be proud of their racial origin and not to turn away from their language. If they gave serious consideration to its study, he wrote, "they would make of the Arabic language a valuable capital yielding them sufficient compensation both in pleasure and profit. Anyone combining a knowledge of Arabic and another live language—be it English, French, Spanish or any other—has a better chance of inducing mercantile and manufacturing and educational interests to employ him in manifold capacities—a salesman, foreign representatives, correspondent, translator, instructor, etc."[95]

The consensus of the Syrian-American readers of the *Syrian World* where Naoum's article appeared, however, was clearly that knowledge of Arabic in America was useless. George Bowab of Atmore, Alabama, challenged Naoum's statement that charged parents with "criminal negligence" in neglecting to teach their children Arabic, and he reminded the publisher that even Syrians in Syria spoke more French than Arabic. "I personally think," he continued, "it will behoove every father and mother to concentrate their efforts on making their children better fitted with English, than to waste their efforts on a language whose only literature is myths, dream stories, and fables, and whose Classics are about the same type of stories as found in the popular American magazines as sold on the streets for a price within the reach of all (five cents). . . . only in the case where our parents neglect any and all forms of education then and only then are they guilty of criminal negligence."[96] Another reader believed that the language of the Arab conquerors of Syria was no longer important, since "the Europeans have given the modern world all the progress of civilization."[97]

The Arabic language crisis in the United States evoked a variety of suggestions, including the founding of a Syrian university for the second generation. That proposal met with criticism from Salloum Mokarzel. He asked his readers to accept "the inevitable fact that Arabic cannot be perpetuated in America except as an academic language." It would be preposterous, he continued, to expect Syrian-Americans to accept it as "a medium of general utility," without first developing pride in racial culture and tradition, not through an expensive university, but through centers within existing universities.[98]

But the language crisis was most severely felt in the publishing community. At its height in 1928, the *Syrian World* reported: "Although the oldest Arabic-language newspaper in the United States barely exceeds the age of thirty years, a serious discussion has now developed as to whether the Syrian press has not reached the end of its usefulness. There seems to be a concession in all quarters that the life of Arabic-language newspapers in America has become very limited, and as this consciousness takes greater hold on the minds of publishers and editors, serious consideration is being given to the discussion of the future."[99]

The *Syrian World* would become an early casualty. It was a singular publication with a limited and elitist readership. Subscribers were lost because it was, some of its readers complained, "too erudite" and "above their understanding."[100] Although Mokarzel asked for recommendations and instituted features to attract a wider audiences, it remained hightoned. The depression further reduced its subscribers. After announcing, in 1931, its policy to modify its standards, the journal ceased publication in 1932 as Mokarzel assumed management of *Al-Hoda* on the death of his brother Naoum. No successor of its stature or quality replaced it in the Syrian-American community. In its time, its influence was, arguably, out of proportion to the size of its readership.

By World War II, at least four New York dailies, and one weekly had survived the crisis, albeit considerably reduced in readership and quality. The restriction of immigrants and the diminished use of the Arabic language were not the only reasons. Homeland political and social news competed unsuccessfully with expanding interests in America. To compete for readers' attention, the Arabic press tried to adjust to the new circumstances. Although much of what appeared in it was to some degree pedestrian, its intellectual content began to yield to local news and social gossip. To compete with the American press, it adopted the latter's techniques and style and simplified Arabic for readers whose lack of facility with the language called for an easy, clear journalistic style—a style which has since influenced journalism in the Arab world.

To its detriment, the Arabic press as an ethnic institution, for all its rhetoric about unity, succeeded, in effect, in exacerbating parochial divisiveness. By establishing itself on a sectarian basis, its individual publications did not address themselves objectively to the overall Syrian community and were thereby unable to generate a broad readership. Nevertheless, the quality and national status achieved by the major newspapers before the Great Depression have not since been equaled. It played a decisive and responsible role in the adjustment and assimilation of Syrian immigrants and spurred Syrian villagers toward literacy and self-education. It linked the immigrant colonies with the homeland and with countrymen in the rest of the Western hemisphere. To their credit, the publishers and editors as well as their contributors, with their fingers on the pulse of the changing Syrian-American community, exhibited enough insight and vision in American life to recognize that the old ways and values no longer sufficed. Yet, even as they announced their bold faith in the new land, they retained almost worshipful praise for the ancestral qualities. If at times they presented an ambiguous impression about the importance of their cultural heritage, they, nevertheless, were determined to sort out confusions and mark a new route for the immigrants in the New World.

For decades before World War II, the Syrians felt no need to gain influence as a group in American life. Emphasis on individual achievements, whether in business or later in prestigious professions, required neither political parties nor unions, although factory workers benefited from membership in unions. When George Addes worked with Walter Reuther to organize the Detroit automotive industry in the mid-thirties and gained prominence in the movement, he did so not as a Syrian for the benefit of Syrian laborers, but for an American cause. Syrians, however, voted at least as faithfully as the rest of the population and joined Rotary and Kiwanis clubs, if only because these were the "American" things to do. If city machines thought them too few to court, small-town ward bosses did not. And yet, they were too individualistic and scattered to be relied on as a political bloc. As early as 1910, one or two Syrians aspired to public office.[101] After World War II, Syrians won elections as mayors, city councilmen, and state legislators, and were appointed to public office.

The majority of Syrians were conservative and generally Republican, in part because most began climbing up the economic ladder in the twenties when the Republican party was ascendant. Those who were Democrats generally adhered to the party's social and economic platform, conservative in the South and more liberal in the North.

Because economic achievement was valued over intellectual recognition, little stimulus remained for intellectual and artistic pursuits within the Syrian and Syrian-American community. With some exceptions, those who were inclined in that direction left the community. Richard H., an accomplished pianist and his sister who had studied theater, like their cousin, John K., a recognized member of the American art community, had to "veer away" from their own people. "We would go with people who were interested in the arts. . . . The Lebanese people, generally speaking, are not culturally inclined. . . . In my generation very few were in the arts. . . . As a child, I would feel left out; I am sure, I alienated myself from them, sure." John K. left home at eighteen to attend an art school in Chicago and has achieved recognition in his field. Although, he feels "very warm" in a world that is no longer his among his extended family, he cannot live with them, he said. When developing his talent at home, he remembered, "they'd think I wasn't working because I didn't go to work at eight to five every day." Even now, he doesn't think he is respected as a positive or successful person in the Syrian community outside his family. "They wouldn't take my work seriously, even if I earned $500 a day to their $400 a week."[102]

Most Syrians survived the miseries of the Great Depression by their own resourcefulness and group assistance. Relatively few were forced by economic circumstances to resort to public relief, and then only between odd jobs or unsuccessful petty entrepreneurial activities, peddling among them. The force of family pride and their faith in America seemed little diminished by the depression which proved to be a temporary set back in their economic progression. Few gave up and returned to Syria; and socialist ideologies, prevalent in the thirties passed them by.

The persistent identification with the homeland continued to wane; loyalty to America began to take precedence. The pioneer generation registered its rush to assimilate in the saying "We came to America to become Americans and we exceeded." They will say it about themselves, often critically and sarcastically, when they reflect on how readily they adopted Americans ways without fully integrating them.

The Syrian-Americans who went into the post–World War II period with many of their parents' values and traits usually dropped those which were not compatible with their own American perspectives. They raised their children according to local practices; they relished ethnic food but usually only on special occasions; if they did not attend church regularly, they at least observed religious holidays. They maintained family bonds but also developed relations with non-Syrian Americans of their own economic class. However, family honor, group identity, and success-orientation were stamped indelibly on their character by their pioneer parents who had not only found their own course and knew what they wanted for themselves and their descendants but transmitted that self-confidence on to their progeny.

The third and fourth generations are considerably more remote from the culture of the first. A recent awakening to their ethnicity has caused them to turn to their parents for cultural pegs on which to hang their identity; but parental knowledge is often superficial, based only on being Syrian of one religion or sect. Grandparents add little more than nostalgic reminiscences of an outdated past. If political and economic events had not reactivated Arab immigration and an interest in Arab culture, Syrian-Americans might have assimilated themselves out of existence.

NOTES
SELECT BIBLIOGRAPHY
INDEX

Notes

INTRODUCTION

1. The early Arab immigrants are included in Adele Younis's study entitled "The Coming of the Arabic-speaking People to the United States" Ph.D. diss., Boston University, 1961).

2. "Experience in Peace and War Justifies Detroit Plan of Americanization Work," *Detroiter*, 24 Nov. 1919, p. 4.

3. "A Motto Wrought into Education" (9 [Apr. 1916]: 409).

4. "Picturesque Colony," 2 Oct. 1892, p. 2.

5. "New Colony," *Cedar Rapids Evening Gazette.* 9 Mar. 1897, p. 8; "Arabian Colony," *Detroit Journal*, 21 July 1897, p. 3.

6. H. A. R. Gibb, *The Arabs* (New York: Oxford University Press, 1940), p. 3.

1. LAND, HISTORY, AND SOCIETY

1. Charles Issawi, ed., *The Economic History of the Middle East: 1800–1914* (Chicago: University of Chicago Press, 1966), p. 220.

2. Philip K. Hitti, *History of the Arabs* (New York: Macmillan, 1963), p.]43.

3. G. E. von Grunebaum, *Classical Islam: A History, 600 A.D.–1258 A.D.* (Chicago: Aldine, 1970), p. 147.

4. John L. Burckhardt, *Travels in Syria and the Holy Land* (London: J. Murray, 1822), p. 28.

5. A. H. Hourani, *Syria and Lebanon: A Political Essay* (London: Oxford University Press, 1954), p. 33.

6. *Lebanon in History* (New York: Macmillan, 1967), p. 447. See

also A. Ruppin, "Syrien als Wirtschaftsgebiet," in Issawi, *Economic History*, p. 272.

7. *Syria and Lebanon under the French Mandate* (London: Oxford University Press, 1958), p. 24.

8. Tax farmers are men, frequently notables, who were granted the "license" by the government, as a favor or as highest bidder, to collect the revenues from a given area. The tax farmers traditionally guaranteed the government its allocated sum. No limits were placed on the amounts they could collect as their profit nor on methods of collection. Corruption was endemic.

9. Records of the Governor of the Administrative District of Zahle (in Arabic) 1870s and 1880s.

10. Zeine N. Zeine, *Arab-Turkish Relations and the Emergence of Arab Nationalism* (Beirut: Khayat's, 1958), pp. 61–62.

11. Bernard Lewis, *The Emergence of Modern Turkey* (London: Oxford University Press, 1961), p. 183; also Albert H. Hourani, *Arabic Thought in the Liberal Age, 1798–1939* (London: Oxford University Press, 1962), p. 245.

12. Victor Ayoub, "Resolution of Conflict in a Lebanese Village," in Leonard Binder, ed., *Politics in Lebanon* (New York: John Wiley & Sons, 1966), p. 123.

13. A. L. Tibawi, *American Interests in Syria, 1800–1901* (Oxford, England: Clarendon Press, 1966), pp. 201, 277.

14. Many of these publications, including grammar books, were brought to the United States or were sent for by immigrants.

15. Hourani, *Syria*, p. 36.

16. Zeine, *Arab-Turkish Relations*, p. 45.

17. Hourani, *Syria*, p. 36.

18. William R. Polk, *The United States and the Arab World*, rev. ed. (Cambridge, Mass.: Harvard University Press, 1969), p. 88. Gabriel Charmes, comparing education in Egypt and Syria concluded that "in Syria, . . . education was widespread. Each city, each village, had excellent schools. It was above all in the area of teaching that the communities rivaled each other. Those who had been behind, in the last years, made enormous sacrifices to catch up with their predecessors" (*Voyage en Syrie* [Paris: Ernest Leroux, 1891], p. 183).

19. Issa Skandar al-Ma'lūf, *History of the Town of Zahle* (in Arabic) (Zahle, Lebanon: Matba'at Zahle al-Fatāt, 1911), p. 280; also Vital Cuinet, *Syrie, Liban, et Palestine* (Paris: Ernest Leroux, 1896), pp. 273, 414.

20. Personal interviews with Tafeeda B., Pasadena, Calif., August 1962, and Lateefi C., Windsor, Ont., July 1980.

21. A. L. Tibawi, *American Interests*, p. 311.

22. Records of the National Administrative Council of Mount Lebanon, 9/114/28 Safar 1291 A. H. (in Arabic) [16 Apr. 1874].

23. Issawi, *Economic History*, pp. 259–60.

24. Ibid., 272.

25. Ibid., 261.

26. I. M. Smilianskaya, "The Disintegration of Feudal Relations in Syria and Lebanon in the Middle of the Nineteenth Century," in ibid., 241–42. This tradition seems to continue into the present as indicated in John Gulick's study of a village in 1952: "it can be deduced that most of the men do not derive all or even most of their income from the land they own. However, as far as can be determined, each landowner, even though he may be a white-collar worker in the city, maintains his plots, . . . which are usually widely scattered over the village territory, with the assistance of a resident family or village worker" (*Social Structure and Cultural Change in a Lebanese Village* [New York: Wenner Gren Foundation for Anthropological Research, 1955], p. 64). See also Anne H. Fuller, *Buarij: Portrait of a Lebanese Muslim Village* (Cambridge, Mass.: Harvard University Monograph series, Harvard University Press, 1966), p. 75.

27. Issawi, *Economic History*, p. 274.

28. "Western Development and Eastern Crisis in the Mid-Nineteenth Century: Syria Confronted with the European Economy," in William R. Polk and Richard L. Chambers, eds., *Beginnings of Modernization in the Middle East: The Nineteenth Century* (Chicago: University of Chicago Press, 1968), p. 220.

29. Letter to the author from Henry Flehan, Mebane, N.C., 12 Mar. 1981.

30. *The Druze: Millennium Scrolls Revealed*, trans. Fred I. Massey (n.p., ca. 1965), p. 31.

31. Flehan letter.

32. Najjar, *The Druze*, p. 27.

33. Although the millet system ceased to exist in 1918, communal jurisdiction, headed by the respective religious leaders, in personal law continues into the present.

34. Zeine, *Arab-Turkish Relations*, pp. 40–41.

35. Alixa Naff, "The Social History of Zahle, the Principal Market Town in Nineteenth-Century Lebanon" (Ph.D. diss., UCLA, 1972).

36. This attitude was expressed in interviews with several Damascene immigrants in the United States.

37. Personal interview, Earlville, Ill., Aug. 1962.

38. Gabriel Baer, *Population and Society in the Arab East* (London: Routledge & Kegan Paul, 1964), p. 148.

39. "The Story of My Life from the Age of Twelve to the End of My Days" (memoir, 1952).

40. Personal interview, Los Angeles, Calif., May 1962.

41. *The Development of the Gazal in Arabic Literature* (Damascus, Syria: n.p., 1960), pp. 44–45.

42. Naff, "Social History of Zahle," Appendix I; also interviews. Morroe Berger wrote: "Though bedouin society plays a declining role in the modernizing Arab World, certain bedouin values persist through the changes. They persist as personality traits . . . and as ideals. . . . These qualities are both fact and legend in all types of Arab communities but the factual element is greatest in the nomadic" (*The Arab World Today* [Garden City, N.Y.: Anchor Books, Doubleday, 1964], p. 49).

43. Berger, ibid., chap. 5, "Personality and Values," pp. 133–65.

44. (In Arabic), *Al-Hoda*, 17 May 1898, p. 6. See also A. Hakim, "The Sage of Washington Street on the Display of Wealth," in which the author took his people to task for their "offensive air of superiority" and "false sense of pride" (*Syrian World* 3 [Sept. 1928]: 24–30).

45. *Syrians in America*, (New York: George Doran, 1924), p. 94.

46. Naff, "The Social History of Zahle" p. 129.

47. *The Muqaddimah and Introduction to History*; trans. Franz Rosenthal, vol. I (New York: Pantheon Books, 1958), p. 304.

48. Conversation with Dr. Afaf Tannous, Arlington, Va., Oct. 1982.

49. Personal interview, Spring Valley, Ill., Aug. 1962.

50. Personal interview, Spring Valley, Ill., Aug. 1962.

2. MIGRATION

1. "The Coming of the Arabic-speaking People," pp. 182–83

2. Records of the Governor of the Administrative District of Zahle (in Arabic), 13 Rabiᶜ I, 1294 [Mar. 1877].

3. Lewis, *Emergence*, p. 178.

4. Younis, "The Coming of the Arabic-speaking People," pp. 184–88.

5. "Syrians in the United States," pt. 1: "Sources and Settlement," *Survey* 26 (1 July 1911): 483.

6. Ibid., 485; Hitti, *Syrians*, p. 48; al-Maᶜluf, *Zahle*, p. 266. The

fifty-fifth annual report of the Board of Foreign Missions of the Presbyterian Church of the United States noted the following observation in 1892: "There are men, boys, women and children from Zahleh in every large city of the New World, in Australia, and in the islands of the sea. The stories of their experiences will make a strange chapter in the history of modern Syria," quoted in Clark S. Knowlton, "Spatial and Social Mobility of the Syrians and Lebanese in the City of São Paulo, Brazil" (Ph.D. diss., Vanderbilt University, 1955), p. 45. With regard to the origins of the early Syrians from other urban centers, the *New York Daily Tribune* of 1892, cited previously, reported that "a majority of them [the Syrian colony of New York City] came to this country from Syria, principally from the cities of Beirut and Damascus."

7. Personal interview, Spring Valley, Ill., July 1980.

8. Personal interview, Montreal, Que., Aug. 1962.

9. Ministrie des Affaires Etrangères, 1888–94, vol. 9, doc. 6, p. 110 of the report.

10. Ibid., vol. 100, doc. 9016, p. 327.

11. Ibid., "Rapports commerceaux," no. 135, Turkie d'Asia, pp. 380–81.

12. Quoted in Zeine, *Arab-Turkish Relations*, pp. 41–42.

13. Record of Bonds, Court of the Administrative District of Zahle (in Arabic).

14. Personal interview, Cedar Rapids, Iowa, June 1980.

15. "United States Melkite History Changed," Sophia 2 (Jan. 1981), based on "research in city and archdiocesan archives conducted by Fr. Nicholas Samra.

16. "Syrians in the United States," pt. I, p. 486.

17. Lucius Hopkins Miller, *Our Syrian Population: A Study of the Syrian Communities of Greater New York* (n.p., ca. 1904), pp. 4–5.

18. *Reports of the Immigration Commission*, vol. 3, *Statistical Review of Immigration, 1820–1910* (Washington, 1911), table 27, "Destination of Immigrants Admitted to the United States, Fiscal Year 1899 to 1910, Inclusive, by Race of People," pp. 269–92.

19. "A Picturesque Colony," p. 2.

20. Charles Issawi, "Economic Development and Political Liberalism in Lebanon," in Leonard Binder, ed., *Politics in Lebanon* (New York: John Wiley & Sons, 1966), p. 73. A similar opinion was expressed by Henry H. Jessup, *Fifty-Three Years in Syria*, vol. 2 (New York: Fleming H. Revell, 1910), p. 588.

21. Aliya H.'s father escaped sentencing for smuggling (personal interview, Dearborn, Mich., May 1980). Joe D.'s sentence for dis-

turbing the peace was military service and he fled his village reluctantly (personal interview, Grand Rapids, Mich., June 1962).

22. Personal interview with Mike H., Los Angeles, Calif. Apr. 1962; memoir, Fairs N.; Milhem S. Abu al- H., a Druze from Mount Lebanon, was the first of a large family to settle in West Virginia in 1885, according to a private conversation with his descendant and family historian in Washington, D.C., July 1981. Abdo A. Elkholy quotes an elderly Muslim woman who said that in 1885, her father left the ship and his Christian fellow travelers when they told him America had no mosques (*The Arab Moslems in the United States: Religion and Assimilation* [New Haven, Conn.: College and University Press, 1966], p. 17).

23. Personal interview with Mohammad W., Dearborn, Mich., May 1980, a Shi'a Muslim.

24. Personal interview with Mohamad S., Washington, D.C., Apr. 1980, a Druze.

25. "Western Development and Eastern Crises," in Polk and Chambers, *Beginnings of Modernization*, p. 220.

26. Faris N., memoirs; Elias L.

27. *The Lebanese Book in Celebration of the Silver Jubilee of the League of Lebanese Progress, 1911–1936* (in Arabic) (New York: Al-Hoda Press, 1936), p. 36.

28. "Objectives of the League of Lebanese Progress" (in Arabic), *Al-Hoda*, 5 May 1914, page number missing.

29. Personal interview with Jamal and Haifa R., Oelwein, Iowa, June 1980.

30. Personal interviews with Nafe K., Saginaw, Mich., May 1980, and Theodore H., McLean, Va., 1978.

31. Some of the large Christian and Muslim trading houses of Syria had offices in Liverpool, Marseilles, and Lyon.

32. Henry Pratt Fairchild, *Immigration, a World Movement and Its American Significance* (New York: Macmillan, 1913). The author contends that the "pernicious" recruitment of emigrants by steamship agents was "the purpose of the claim in the immigration law limiting the nature of solicitation that may be done by transportation lines" (p. 151).

33. Quoted in Knowlton, "Spatial and Social Mobility," pp. 40–41.

34. Many Christian immigrants assumed, no doubt erroneously, that all Syrian brokers were Muslims, perhaps because Muslims were predominant in the port cities.

35. *Al-Hilal* (all in Arabic), "Syrian Events in America," 5 (Apr. 1897):596; "The Arabic Language in America," 16 (1 Apr. 1907):46–49; "The Syrians and Their Naturalization in America," 13 (1 Oct. 1904):14–20; "Emigration to America," 15 (1 Apr. 1908):319–20.

36. Personal interview, Fort Wayne, Ind., June 1962.

37. "News about Syria" (in Arabic), *Al-Hoda*, 3 May 1898, pp. 12–13.

38. "Syrian Probe Comes to a Head," *Cedar Rapids Evening Gazette*, 11 Mar. 1910, p. 9.

39. "Indictment Returned against Joseph George," Ibid., 6 Apr. 1910, p. 9; "Joseph George Pleads Guilty and Fined $500," ibid., 8 Apr. 1910, p. 5.

40. Conversation, Moorhead, Minn., July 1982.

41. W. S. Nelson, *Silver Chimes in Syria* (Philadelphia: Westminster Press, 1914), p. 97.

42. "Spatial and Social Mobility," pp. 49–50.

43. The *Book of Khalid* (New York: Dodd, Mead, 1911), pp. 28–30.

44. Personal interview with Mike H.

45. North Dakota WPA interviews with Joe A., Williston, N.D., 1937; personal interview with Yamna A., Montreal, Que., Aug. 1962.

46. Personal interview, Temple, Md., Apr. 1980.

47. Personal interview, East Detroit, Mich., May 1980.

48. Personal interviews; also, Ann Novotney, *Strangers at the Door* (Riverside, Conn.: Chatham Press, 1971), p. 52; Thomas M. Pitkin, *Keepers of the Gate: A History of Ellis Island, New York* (New York: New York University Press, 1975), p. 92.

49. Personal interview, Los Angeles, Calif., May 1962.

50. Personal interview, Los Angeles, Calif., Apr. 1962.

51. Personal interview with Dan S., Grand Rapids, Mich., June 1962.

52. Houghton, "Syrian in the United States," pt. 1, p. 483. The book, *The Alien's Primer for Learning the English Language* (in Arabic) (New York: Eastern Press and Kawkab Amrika, 1895).

53. Pitkin points to the seriousness of the problem and the inability of the police to control it (*Keepers*, p. 89).

54. See, e.g., *Al-Hoda*, Jan. 1909, p. 8.

55. P. 17.

56. "Local News" (in Arabic), 7 Feb. 1911, p. 3.

57. "Syrians in the United States," pt. 1, p. 488.

58. "The Syrians in America" (in Arabic), *Al-Hilal* 15 (1 Apr. 1908): 424–27.

59. "The Syrians in the United States," 3 May 1919, p. 43.

60. *Syrians*, pp. 62, 65.

61. Salloum Mokarzel, "Arabic Newspapers in America," *Syrian World* 2 (May 1928): 39.

62. Pitkin discusses the confusion of identifying separate nationalities, inadequate facilities, incompetence of immigration inspectors, faulty recordkeeping, misclassification of immigrants on steamship manifests by fraudulent shipowners, etc. (*Keepers*).

63. Dan S.; personal interview with Habib T., Dorchester, Mass., Aug. 1962.

64. Personal interview with Essa M., Manchester, N.H., Aug. 1962, Essa S., Faris N., Tom C. and Elias L., to name a few.

65. *Statistical Review*, p. 44.

66. Ibid., table 9, "Immigration to the United States by Country of Origin and by Sex for Years Ending June 30, 1869–1910," pp. 30–44, and table 10, "Immigration to the United States, by Race of People, during the Period 1899 to 1910," p. 45.

67. Ibid.

68. Figures compiled from *Statistical Review* and working sheets provided to the author by the Department of Immigration and Naturalization, Washington, D.C., undated and pencil noted "OPEC."

69. Figures compiled from OPEC working papers and *Annual Reports of the Commissioner General of Immigration* (Washington, D.C.) published annually. Abdul Jalil al-Tahir's study of "The Arab Community in the Chicago Area: A Comparative Study of the Christian-Syrians and the Muslim-Palestinians," the only study of any pre–World War I Palestinian community in the United States does not, in his extensive use of statistical data, differentiate between Syrians and Palestinians (Ph.D. diss. University of Chicago, 1952).

70. Houghton, in 1911, stated that "the Centennial Exposition is known to have attracted a few Syrians, chiefly traders from Jerusalem, who brought olive wood articles and other curios" ("The Syrians in the United States," pt. 1, p. 483). Hitti wrote that the Columbian Exposition of 1893, "is known to have attracted especially traders from Jerusalem and Ramallah who brought with them olive wood articles and other curios" (*Syrians*, p. 48).

71. "OPEC" documents of the United States Department of Immigration and Naturalization.

72. For example, Hitti, *Syrians*; Houghton "Syrians in the United States"; and Miller, *Syrian Population of Greater New York*.

73. Although land was also measured in surface units such as *dunum* and *feddan*, the most common evaluation was, in the nineteenth century, in monetary units of measurement. One of them, the *dirham* of silver, divided into 24 *qirat*, was adopted in 1864 as the basis of measuring rural properties in Mount Lebanon. See André Latron Latron, *La Vie Rurale en Syrie et au Liban, Étude d'Économie Sociale* (Beyrouth, 1936), p. 24. For a discussion on agricultural measurements used in Mount Lebanon in the nineteenth century, see Naff, "The Social History of Zahle," pp. 548–53. The 1877 cadastre of Qadat Zahle shows land registered in dirhams.

74. *Statistical Review*, table 35, p. 357. It is interesting to note that "the immigration law of 1893 provided that steamship lists or manifests should state whether each alien possessed $30, and if less, how much. The law of 1903 retained this provision but changed the amount to $50. . . . The law does not require that aliens shall have a specified amount of money as a requisite to admission into the United States, but the financial resources of an immigrant frequently have an important bearing on his admissibility" (ibid., p. 349).

75. Ibid., 84.

76. *Annual Reports*, 1896–1910.

77. Faris N., Karam N., Mike H., and Essa M. A large variety of religious, historical, and literary books published before 1910 were collected by the author from first generation immigrants or their descendants.

78. *Statistical Review* and *Annual Reports* for the consecutive years 1919–30. Tables entitled "Immigrant Aliens Admitted Fiscal Year Ending June 30 by Race of People, Sex, and Age."

79. Ibid.

80. Several informants reported the practice in personal interviews, among them Oscar A., Peoria, Ill., July 1980, Amelia U., Peoria, Ill., July 1980, and Wardi N.

81. Interviews with several returnees in Rashayya al-Wadi, Syria, May 1965, and Zahle, Lebanon, summer 1969.

3. "AMRIKA"

1. Personal interview, Detroit, Mich., May 1980.

2. Allan Nevins and Frank E. Hill, *Ford: Decline and Rebirth, 1933–1962* (New York: Charles Scribner's Sons, 1962), p. 644.

3. Personal interviews with Eva F., North Hollywood, Calif., Apr. 1962, and Matt I., Warren, Mich., July 1962.

4. "Reflections of a Housewife on Buying at the Door," *House Beautiful* 38 (July 1915):40.

5. Personal interview, Cedar Rapids, Iowa, June 1980.

6. Conversation with Faris N., Los Angeles, Calif. 1950.

4. PACK PEDDLING

1. "Syrian Americans," in *One America: The History, Contributions and Present Problems of Our Racial and National Minorities*, eds. Francis J. Brown and Joseph S. Roucek (Newark, N.J.: Prentice-Hall, 1952), pp. 283–84.

2. "Syrians in the United States," pt. 1, p. 486.

3. See also Faris N., memoirs.

4. Personal interview with Darwish R., Los Angeles, Calif., May 1962.

5. "A Picturesque Colony," 2 Oct. 1892, p. 2.

6. *Greater New York*, p. 18.

7. Memoirs.

8. *Khalid*, pp. 43–44.

9. *A Far Journey* (Boston and New York: Houghton Mifflin, 1914), pp. 198–99.

10. W. Benough, "The Foreign Element in New York, a Syrian Colony," *Harper's Weekly*, 3 Aug. 1895, p. 746.

11. "A Picturesque Colony," p. 2.

12. "Syrian Society's Work," *New York Evening Post*, 23 Feb. 1906, p. 14.

13. *Fort Wayne's History*, a pamphlet published by the Fort Wayne Chamber of Commerce (n.d.), p. 4.

14. "Cedar Rapids' Population," *Cedar Rapids Evening Gazette*, 4 Jan. 1976. p. 13A. Figures based on U.S. census data.

15. "The City of Peoria Is Celebrating a Century of Progress," *Spirit*, p. 60.

16. "Spring Valley: Geography, Population, Economic Base" (Paper by Mrs. Bernice Sweeney, historian of Spring Valley), statistics based on U.S. census data.

17. See also Stewart G. McHenry for similar statements on upstate New York: "The Syrians of Upstate New York (a Social Geography)" (Ph.D. diss., Syracuse University, 1973), p. 56.

18. Arthur C. Pritchard, "Two Hundred Pounds or More: The Lebanese Community in Mannington," *Goldenseal* 4 (Apr., Sept. 1978):20.

19. Personal interview, East Detroit, Mich., June 1980.

20. Faris N., memoirs: Budelia M.; and personal interview with Nazha H., Detroit, Mich., May 1962.

21. Mike H.

22. Personal interview, Cedar Rapids, Iowa, June 1980.

23. Personal interview, Vicksburg, Miss., 1979.

24. Eva F., Louis L., conversation with Milton F., North Hollywood, Calif. Mar. 1982.

25. Letter to author from Dr. Eugene P. Nassar, Utica, N.Y., 23 June 1983, with supporting data from John Moses, author of *From Mount Lebanon to the Mohawk Valley: A Story of Syro-Lebanese Americans of the Utica Area*, Utica, N.Y.: privately published, 1981. See also Stewart G. McHenry whose study reveals a similar pattern of subnetworks among Maronites of upstate New York ("Syrians in Upstate New York").

26. Elizabeth B. and also Tafeeda B.

27. Tafeeda B., Mike H., Eli B., Elias L., Matt I., and personal interview with Essa S., Manchester, N.H., July 1962; also Faris N., memoirs.

28. Memoirs.

29. The bishop's census of 26 Syrian Orthodox communities in the United States was requested by *Al-Hoda* ("Readers' Contributions" [in Arabic], 19 Apr. 1898, p. 16).

30. Elizabeth B. and Tafeeda B.

31. Memoirs.

32. Tafeeda B.

33. Elizabeth B., Nazha H., and Eli B.

34. Memoirs.

35. Elizabeth B. and Tafeeda B.

36. Tafeeda B.

37. Nazha H.

38. Memoirs.

39. "New Colony," p. 8.

40. Negebe S.

41. Personal interviews with William A. and Hasebe A., Cedar Rapids, Iowa, June 1980.

42. Ibid.; also personal interviews with Mohammed H., Pottsville, Iowa, June 1980, and Mike A., Cedar Rapids, Iowa, June 1980.

43. Personal interview, Cedar Rapids, Iowa, June 1980.

44. Personal interview with Sam M. H., Cedar Rapids, Iowa, June 1980.

45. Lillian K. H.

46. *Directories of the City of Cedar Rapids*. The first directory appeared in 1900; the first year in which Syrian names appear is 1909.

47. Lillian K. H.; *Directories*.

48. Lillian K. H.

49. Negebe S.

50. "Wed in Syria," *Cedar Rapids Evening Gazette*, 12 Aug. 1897, p. 5.

51. According to Lateefi C., the Rochester settlement had twenty families, including one Muslim and one Druze, in 1909.

52. Personal interview, Grand Rapids, Mich., June 1962.

53. Personal interview with Hasiby A., Spring Valley, Ill., Aug. 1980.

54. Personal interview with Mrs. Bernice Sweeney and unpublished papers from the Cyril Sweeney Collection provided by Mrs. Sweeney.

55. Marion Kinneman, "John Mitchell in Illinois," *Illinois State University Journal* 32 (Sept. 1969): 21.

56. Amelia A. M. and William D.

57. W. H. Hoffman, *City Directory of Spring Valley, Illinois*, 1913.

58. "Syrians in the United States," pt. 4, "The Syrian as an American Citizen" (7 Oct. 1911), pp. 965–66.

59. Conversation with William A.; also Hasebe A.

60. "Ross, N.D., Area Is Home for Some 50 Mohammedans," *Fargo Forum*, 8 Aug. 1937, p. 10; "Time, Americanization Take Harsh Toll of Once-Thriving Moslem Colonies in N.D." (*Fargo Forum*, 8 Dec. 1967, p. 9).

61. *The Arab Moslems in the United States*, pp. 27–28.

62. Lawrence Oschinsky, "Islam in Chicago: Being a Study of the Acculturation of a Muslim Palestinian Community in that City," (master's thesis, University of Chicago, June 1947). p. 24.

63. Conversations in Washington, D.C., with Raymond Hamden, 12 Aug. 1980, and with B. H. Husn, 3 July 1981; see also letter from Flehan; personal interview with Najem B., Richmond, Va., 21 Sept. 1980; and "Syrians in America," *Sandusky* (Ohio) *Masonic Bulletin* 15 (Mar. 1935):130.

64. A copy of the Bylaws and the Articles of Incorporation were provided by Henry Flehan. See also "Proposed Association" (in Arabic), *Al-Bayan*, 7 Feb. 1911, p. 47.

65. Nafe K.

66. Nafe K. and Najem B.

67. Jamal and Haifa R., Najem B.

68. Personal interview with Jack H., Flint, Mich., June 1980; also see E. D. Benyon, "The Near East in Flint, Michigan: Assyrians and Druzes and Their Antecedents," *Geographical Review* 34 (April 1944):272–73.

69. Druze informants; Flehan letter.

70. An item in *Al-Hoda*, dated 1 July 1908, suggests that Toledo was a peddling settlement before Syrians were attracted there by its industrial growth. The article states that the son of Shaykh Nakhla Habib Nasr Kayruz, a prominent merchant, soared three times over the river, perhaps reaching Cleveland in an air balloon which he built ("Readers' Contributions" [in Arabic], p. 3).

5. ON THE ROAD

1. "Alas, Poor Z'aytar" (in Arabic), by Shukry al-Khuri, is an incomplete novelette in which the trials of a simple Lebanese villager, on his way to peddle in the New World, are satirized (São Paulo, Brazil: Abu al-Hul Press, 1911). See also a poem (title missing) published in *Al-Hoda*, 21 June 1898, which portrays peddling humorously. The anonymous poet writes in colloquial Arabic and incorporates numerous English words from the peddlers' jargon. More serious articles on the importance of "merchandising" or "trading" to Syrians' success in America are found on the pages of the early Arabic press. Mikha'il As'ad Rustum traveled to several Syrian colonies in the United States and recorded his impressions in poetry and prose. Among them is a light poem describing peddlers' wares and peddling lexicon. ("In the Notions Case and the Suitcase of Silks and Their Variety of Merchandise" [in Arabic], in *The Book of a Stranger in a Strange Land* [New York: Eastern Press, 1895], p. 19).

2. Personal interview with Anisee Z., Detroit, Mich., July 1962. Adapted from one of her husband's experiences.

3. Aliya H.

4. Personal interview, Detroit, Mich., July 1962.

5. Personal interview, Vicksburg, Miss., Aug. 1979.

6. Memoirs.

7. Personal interview, Spring Valley, Ill., Aug. 1962.

8. Matt I.

9. Nemer K.

10. Budelia M.; also Frank A., Aliya H., and Nemer K.

11. Nazha H.

12. *The History of Syrian Trade in the American Colonies* (in Arabic), pt. I, "1920–1921" (New York: Syrian American Press, 1929), p. 20.

13. Habib I. Katibah, *Arabic-speaking Americans* (New York: Institute of Arab American Affairs, 1946), p. 6.

14. Personal interview, Aug. 1980.

15. Arthur C. Pritchard, "Two Hundred Pounds or More," p. 21.

16. Personal interview with Mayme F., Vicksburg, Miss., Aug. 1979.

17. Louis L.

18. Budelia M.

19. Personal interview, Peoria, Ill., July 1980.

20. Houghton, "Syrians in the United States," pt. 2, "Business Activities," *Survey*, 5 Aug. 1911):665; also Salloum Mokarzel, "History of the Syrians in New York City," *New York American Newspaper*, 3 Oct. 1927, p. 13.

21. In 1831, Georgia passed an act requiring foot peddlers to pay a fee of $1,000 in each county. It was doubled for those traveling by horse and carriage. Not all fees, however, were so exorbitant, but they were prohibitive enough to curtail peddlers' activities and led them to devise means of circumventing the requirements. In both northern and southern states, the laws and fees imposed varied with time, place, and manner of travel at first, then they were extended to cover the peddling of wares manufactured outside of the state of sale and even those manufactured within the state. In Alabama, the tax was $50 per county; North Carolina taxed $20 per county and several other southern states, opposed to the Yankee peddlers of clocks, required them to pay a fee of $100 per county (Fred Mitchell Jones, "Middlemen in the Domestic Trade of the United States, 1800–1860," *Illinois Studies in the Social Sciences* 21 [1937]:63).

22. Matt I., Amelia U.'s father, was jailed for lack of a license in New Orleans. In Manchester, N.H., the license fee was $50 a year. Also Essa S.

23. Mary M. Another variation used by women was:

Qadmi, qadmi, ya Mrs., qadmi,
[Approach, approach, Mrs., approach],
Buy sumthin', father dead fil blād [in the old country],
Buy for shoes, lil awlād [for the children].

24. "She's 'Mama' to a Family of 100," *Look Magazine*, 28 Aug. 1962, 91, 94.

25. Tafeeda B.

26. Personal interview, Peoria, Ill., Aug. 1980.

27. "Syrians in the United States," pt. 2, p. 650.

28. Louis L.

29. *History of Syrian Trade*, p. 148.

30. "The Syrian Woman in the United States" (in Arabic), 5 Mar. 1899, pp. 14–15.

31. "She's 'Mama,'" p. 93.

32. Houghton, pt. 2, p. 650.

33. Mayme F. and Louis L.

34. Pt. 2, pp. 662–63.

35. "The Peddler," *American Magazine* 74 (Aug. 1912):411.

36. (New York: Young Scott Books, 1968), pp. 13–16. In another children's book by Maud Hart Lovelace, who grew up in Mankato, Minn., before World War I, the main characters stumble on a nearby Syrian colony and befriend the daughter of a peddler who is the granddaughter of an amir (*Betsy and Tacy Go over the Big Hill* [New York: Thomas Y. Crowell, 1942]).

37. Naff, memoirs.

38. Amelia A. M.

39. Eva F.

40. Pritchard, "Two Hundred Pounds," p. 23.

41. Elias L.

42. Memoirs.

43. Personal interview, Windsor Ont., June 1962.

44. "Two Hundred Pounds," pp. 23–24.

45. Personal interviews with Mary S., Grosse Pointe, Mich., May 1980; George F., Erie, Ill., July 1980; Johnny N.

46. Personal interview, Montreal, Que., July 1962.

47. Personal interview with Wedad F., North Hollywood, Calif. May 1962.

48. Conversation, 1950.

49. Aliya H.

50. For further discussion and examples, see H. L. Mencken, *The American Language, an Inquiry into the Development of English in the United States* (New York: Knopf, 1937), pp. 683–85.

51. Similar testimony was given by several other informants.

52. Memoirs.

53. Matt I.

54. Memoirs.

55. Hitti, *Syrians*, p. 76.

56. Pt. 2, 663.

57. Personal interview with Assad S., Boston, Mass., July 1962.

58. Mary M., Louis L., personal interview with Charles T., Dorchester, Mass., July 1962.

59. "Acculturation of an Arab-Syrian Community in the Deep South," *American Sociological Review* 8 (June 1943):270.

60. *A Doctor for the People*, 2d ed. (New York: Vanguard Press, 1939), pp. 36–38.

61. "Ghetto Sights," *Cedar Rapids Evening Gazette*, 3 July 1901, p. 4.

62. Pt. 2, p. 663.

63. *Syrians*, p. 8. Afif I. Tannous, in his article, "Emigration, a Force of Social Change in an Arab Village," states that as a result of the flow of cash into the villages, "emigration was the last step [after the silk industry, foreign missions, and contact with the city] with which the village plunged into the Western economic system and became 'money conscious'" (*Rural Sociology* 7 [Mar. 1942]:71).

64. *Fifty-Fourth Annual Report of the Board of Foreign Missions of the Presbyterian Church in the United States* (New York: Mission House, 1891), p. 225, quoted in Knowlton, "Spatial and Social Mobility," p. 45.

65. Personal interview, Mark, Ill., July 1980.

66. Personal interview with Selma D. N. and Maggie M., Spring Valley, Ill., July 1962; and Wedad F.

67. *U.S. Bureau of the Census Historical Statistics of the United States, Colonial Times to 1970*, Bicentennial ed., pt. 1 (Washington, 1975), Series F 1–5, "Gross National Product, Total and Per Capita, in Current and 1958 Prices: 1869–1970," p. 224; and Series A 119–34, "Population, by Age, Sex, Race, and Nativity, 1790–1970, by Census Years," p. 15.

68. Ibid., Series D739–64, "Average Annual Earnings per Full-Time Employee, by Industry, 1900 to 1970 (in Current Dollars)," pp. 166–67.

69. Houghton, pt. 2, 663.

70. Salloum Mokarzel, "Syrians in New York City, p. 13.

6. Off the Road

1. A list of Eastern Orthodox churches was published in *The Word*, the official monthly publication of the Antiochian Orthodox Christian Archdioces of North America, 25 (Dec. 1981):21–23. A brief history of Melkite churches is found in *Melkites in America: A Directory and Information Handbook* (West Newton, Mass.: Melkite Exarchate, 1971). An account of the Maronite churches was provided by the Maronite Chancery, Brooklyn, N.Y., in 1981.

2. Dolores Courtemanche, "Worcester's Lebanese-Syrian Community: An Ethnic Success Story" (Worcester, Mass.), *Sunday Telegram*, 14 Sept. 1980, p. 8.

3. Personal interview with Nellie B., Peoria, Ill., July 1980.

4. Personal interviews with Anthony L. and George J. B., Warren, Mich.; also Edna M., St. Claire Shores, Mich., June 1980.

5. Conversation with Faris N., 1950; also Alexander M.

6. Personal interview, Thelma W., Cedar Rapids, Iowa, June 1980.

7. "Don't Like Arabs," 16 July 1901, p. 8.

8. Louis L.

9. Amelia A. M. and Haseby A.

10. Personal interviews with Tom A., Spring Valley, Ill., Aug. 1962; also Mary M., Budelia M., Amelia A. M., and Assad S.

11. Nemer K.

12. Tafeeda B.

13. Haseby A., Nazha H., and Wedad F.

14. Personal interview with Peter F., Manchester, N.H., Aug. 1962.

15. Personal interview, Grand Rapids, Mich., July 1962.

16. Eli B.; also personal interview with Edward E., Grand Rapids, Mich., July 1962.

17. Personal interview, Vicksburg, Miss., Aug. 1979.

18. Personal interview with Edna S. A., LaSalle, Ill., Aug. 1980; Amelia A. M., Budelia M., and Wedad F.

19. Nemer K.; Elizabeth B.

20. Mayme F.

21. Conversation with Nazha H., Dec. 1982.

22. Tafeeda B.

23. Memoirs; also Essa S.

24. Tafeeda B.

25. Ibrahim Othman, in his study of Springfield, Mass., entitled *Arabs in the United States: A Study of an Arab American Community*

(Beirut: Dar al-Qalam Press Co., 1974), p. 52. See also Knowlton, "Spatial and Social Mobility," pp. 217–18.

26. Letter from Eugene P. Nassar.

27. *Reports of the Industrial Commission on Immigration and on Education* (Washington, 1901) 15:83, 88. See also Maldwyn A. Jones, *American Immigration* (Chicago: University of Chicago Press, 1900), pp. 191–92.

28. Ibid., "Syrians," p. 443.

29. Tafeeda B.; Elizabeth B.

30. Personal interview, May 1962.

31. "Armenian Justice," *Cedar Rapids Evening Gazette*, 9 Nov. 1897, p. 6. Frank A. praised Joseph George as a leader in the community.

32. P. 5.

33. "Factional War Is Waged," p. 4.

34. "Syrian Riot," p. 5.

35. *New York Times*, p. 5.

36. *New York Herald*, p. 4.

37. *Syrians*, p. 94.

38. *History of the United States and History of the Syrian Immigration* (in Arabic) (New York: Al-Dalil Press, 1913), p. 795.

39. "Foreign News: The Syrians in America" (in Arabic), *Al-Hilal*, 1 Apr. 1897, p. 596.

40. Amin Al-Gharib, "Some Causes for the Backwardness of the Syrians in the United States" (in Arabic), *Al-Hoda*, 17 May 1898, pp. 6–7.

41. "The Maronites and Orthodox in Butler, Pennsylvania, Fight in Name of Religion" (in Arabic), *Al-Hoda*, 5 May 1914, p. 3.

42. Pt. 3, "Intellectual and Social Status," *Survey* 26 (2 Sept. 1911):796.

43. *Immigrant Races in Massachusetts* (n.p., 9 Jan. 1922), a pamphlet written for the Massachusetts Department of Education, Division of Education of Aliens, p. 9.

44. Personal interview, Los Angeles, Calif., May 1962.

45. Personal interview, Detroit, Mich., May 1980.

46. "New Colony," p. 8.

47. Personal interview, Los Angeles, May 1962.

48. "Wed in Syria," p. 5.

49. "New Colony," p. 8.

50. "A Subject Affecting Immigrants" (in Arabic), *Al-Kalimat*, 15 Sept. 1909, pp. 349–50.

51. Pp. 14–15.

52. Pp. 15–17.

53. Page numbers missing.

54. P. 1.

55. Pt. 3, p. 802.

56. Statistical records for Spring Valley, Ill., for example, were checked in the Bureau County Office of Records, Princeton, Ill. The first laws requiring the recording of births and deaths were passed in 1916. Although earlier statistical records, including marriages, exist, they were quite incomplete. Another major problem was recognizing Arabic names in their anglicized or misspelled form.

57. U.S. Bureau of the Census, *Fourteenth Census of the United States, 1920*, vol. 2, *Population, General Report and Analytical Tables*, chap. 10, table 1: "Mother Tongue of Foreign White Stock by Nativity and Parentage for U.S.: 1920 and 1910," p. 973; table 2: "Increase in the Foreign White Stock by Mother Tongue for Nativity and Parentage Classes for U.S.: 1920 and 1910," p. 974 (Washington, 1922). Two individuals referred by other Syrians as pioneer Syrian informants were, in fact, Assyrian nationalists. The interview was conducted in Arabic.

58. "Speeches and Debates of the Meeting of the Maronite Young Men's Society." These were probably published originally as a pamphlet by Al-Hoda Publishing House in 1903. They were found in a collection of plays, essays, stories, and speeches published in New York, Beirut, Damascus, and Cairo, which seem to have been collected and privately bound by an unknown immigrant. The debate is on pp. 24–33 of the speeches and debates.

59. U.S. Bureau of the Census, *Fifteenth Census of the United States*, vol. 2, *Population, General Report of Statistics by Subjects*, table 4, "Country of Origin of the Foreign White Stock by Nativity and Parentage for the United States: 1930" (Washington, 1933), p. 268.

60. A. Hakim, "The Marriage Problem among the Syrians," *Syrian World* 3 (Nov. 1928):31.

61. Oschinsky, "Islam in Chicago," p. 28.

62. John W. Shuman, "A Mission in Syria," *The Builder, Official Journal of the National Masonic Research Society* 14 (Apr. 1929):108.

63. Nafe K., Mohamed S.

64. Personal interview with Imam Mohammad K., Detroit, Mich., June 1980.

65. Telephone conversation, Samah HeLal, Vienna, Va., July 1981.

66. WPA interviews, North Dakota, 1939; "Once Numerous

Moslem Community Now Reduced to Half Dozen," *Minot Daily News*, 7 Dec. 1968, p. 12.

67. Salloum Mokarzel, "Christian-Moslem Marriages, *Syrian World*, 2 (Apr. 1928): p. 14.

68. "Emigration: The Druze Opinion" (in Arabic), pp. 4–6.

69. "He Who Is Married in the Homeland" (in Arabic), page numbers missing.

70. "Once Numerous Moslem Community," p. 12.

71. Personal interview, Dearborn, Mich., June 1980.

72. Personal interview, Cedar Rapids, Iowa, June 1980.

73. "Once Numerous Moslem Community," p. 12.

74. For a concise and informative account, see George M. Fredrickson and Dale T. Knobel's "History of Prejudice and Discrimination," *Harvard Encyclopedia of American Ethnic Groups*, Stephan Thermstrom, ed. (Cambridge, Mass.: Belknap Press of Harvard University Press, 1980), pp. 829–47.

75. Mike H., William A., personal interviews with Hussein I., Cedar Rapids, Iowa, June 1980; and Rose C., Peoria, Ill., July 1980.

76. Personal interview with Nellie J., Spring Valley, Ill., July 1980; William D.

77. H. A. El-Kourie, "Dr. El-Kourie Defends Syrian Immigrants," letter to the editor of the *Birmingham Ledger*, 20 Sept. 1907; also, "El-Kouri Takes Burnett to Task," letter to the editor of the (Birmingham, Ala.) *Age-Herald*, 20 Oct. 1907. Taken from "In Defense of the Semitic and the Syrian Especially," reprints of the letters.

78. Wadi N., Abe A.

79. Conversations and correspondence with Sandra H. Bennett, St. Louis, Mo.

80. Unpublished documents and ledgers related to the founding of Saint George's Syrian Orthodox Church, the Syrian Men's Society, and the purchase of the Syrian Orthodox cemetery in Spring Valley, Ill., 1914–24.

81. Personal interview with Wadi al-S., Mount Clemens, Mich., May 1980.

82. Personal interviews with Kamel O., Taylor, Mich., May 1980; Alex E., Dearborn, Mich.; May 1980; and George B., Warren, Mich., May 1980; and others.

83. Courtemanche, "Worcester's Lebanese-Syrian Community," p. 8.

84. "Time, Americanization," p. 9.

85. The historical summary regarding naturalization legislation is drawn from Reed Ueda's "Naturalization and Citizenship," *Harvard Encyclopedia of American Ethnic Groups*, pp. 740–41.

86. Ibid., p. 741.

87. Ibid.

88. Darwish R., Essa M., Mike H.; Faris N., memoirs.

89. Joe D., Eli B., Mose N., and others.

90. *Fifteenth Census of the United States, 1930*, table 5: "Citizenship of the Foreign-born White Population, by Sex and Country of Birth for the United States: 1930 and 1920," vol. 2, *Population*, pp. 406–7. For table showing 40.4 percent Syrians and 48.7 percent Palestinians naturalized and having first papers based on 1920 census, see Niles Carpenter, *Immigrants and Their Children* (New York: Arno Press and the New York Times, 1969), p. 263.

91. Joseph W. Ferris, "Syrian Naturalization Question in the United State: Certain Legal Aspects of Our Naturalization Laws," Pts. 1 and 2, *Syrian World* 2 (Feb.–Mar. 1928). Discussion of the Syrian naturalization cases are based on this two-part article in which the author cites court records.

92. Ibid., Pt. 1; also "Syrians and American Citizenship" (in Arabic), *Al-Kalimat*, 1 Nov. 1909), p. 417, and 15, Nov. 1909), p. 437.

93. Ferris, pts. 1, 2.

94. Ibid., pt. 1, p. 7.

95. "The Syrian-American Problem" (in Arabic), *Al-Hoda*, 20, Apr. 1914, p. 5.

96. Ibid., 1 July 1914, p. 3.

97. "Open Letter" (in Arabic), ibid., 16, Sept. 1914, p. 3. Among other articles which appeared in *Al-Hoda*, in Arabic, are "Society for Syrian National Defense," 11, Mar. 1914, p. 3; "To the Struggle, Oh, Syrians," 4, Apr. 1914, p. 3; "The Syrian-American Case in the Higher Court," 21 Apr. 1914, p. 3; "The Syrian Problem in Washington," 17, Sept. 1914, p. 8; in *Meraat al-Gharb* (in Arabic), "About the Syrian Problem," 7, Apr. 1914, p. 4.

98. Elias Simʿan Theeb, "American Citizenship and the Syrians" (in Arabic), 8, Apr. 1914, p. 5.

99. Ferris, pt. 2, p. 19; see also *United States Reports of the Immigration Commission*, vol. 5, *Dictionary of Races or Peoples* (Washington, 1911), p. 139.

100. Ferris, pt. 2, pp. 21–22.

101. P. 16 (in Arabic).

102. "Factional War Is Waged," p. 4.

103. Jean Gibran and Kahlil Gibran, *Kahlil Gibran, His Life and World* (New York: Avenel Books, 1981), p. 333.

104. Vol. 1 (July 1927), p. 1.

105. "On the Display of Wealth," pp. 28–29.

7. FROM SYRIAN TO SYRIAN-AMERICAN: BETWEEN THE WARS

1. S. A. Mokarzel and H. F. Otash, *The Syrian Business Directory*, 1908–9 (New York: Al-Hoda Press, 1908), Introduction. The authors promised future issues which did not appear. Other publications on Syrian trade are: Salloum Mokarzel, *The History of Syrian Business among Immigrants in America* (in Arabic), 1920–21, with a historical essay on Syrian immigration by Dr. Philip K. Hitti (New York: Syrian American Press, n.d.). It traces the progress of Syrian business from the early immigration period and describes the establishment of distinguished business in New York and others elsewhere in the United States. Illustrated with photographs of the owners and their establishments. *The Syrian American Directory Almanac* (New York: Arida & Andria, 1929) lists businesses and residences of Syrians in Manhattan and Brooklyn; describes the social and educational organizations; provides questions and answers for applicants for citizenship; and includes numerous historical and informative articles on the homeland and America. *The Western Pacific Directory and Buyers Guide for 1954–1955*, ed. Samuel S. Mamey (Los Angeles: Saint Nicholas Orthodox Church, 1954) provides the names and addresses of Syrian business in the western states by city. Other regional and local directories were published as well.

2. Personal interviews with Louis A. and Najla S., Detroit, Mich., May 1980.

3. *The Directory*, pp. 61, 189–90.

4. Telephone conversation, George S., Detroit, Mich., July 1983.

5. Ibid.

6. Vol. 141, 1975 Oct. 11, p. 10.

7. Personal interview, Royal Oak, Mich., May 1980.

8. Personal interview, Dearborn, Mich., May 1980.

9. Personal interview, St. Claire Shores, Mich., June 1980.

10. Personal interview, Vicksburg, Miss., Aug. 1979.

11. Conversation, North Hollywood, Calif. 25 Feb. 1983.

12. Ibid.; also Nazha H.

13. Nemer K., Eli B., Eva F., and Matt I., among others.

14. *Al-Hoda*, 14 Jan. 1903, p. 2.

15. Ibid., 21 Aug. 1925, p. 5.

16. *The Directory.*

17. *The Almanac*, pp. 78–79, 120–21.

18. Personal interview, Dearborn, Mich., May 1980.

19. Personal interview with Alice G., Los Angeles, Calif., May 1962.

20. Mike H., Nagebe S.; personal interview with Ramza A., West Roxbury, Mass., Aug. 1962.

21. "Women's Talk" (in Arabic), *Al-Hoda*, 17, Dec. 1908, p. 4.

22. Ibid., 9 Jan. 1909, p. 4. Afifa Karam published in 1912, the short-lived magazine, *Woman's World*, in Arabic. Until her death in July 1924, she was a regular contributor to *Al-Hoda* and to the monthly Arabic magazine the *Character* (1920–32), which printed many articles of interest to women.

23. Personal interview, Detroit, Mich., May 1980.

24. Ibid. Among other women who experienced similar circumstances were Najla S., Zahia B., in a personal interview, Detroit, Mich., May 1980, George A.'s mother, and Haseby A.

25. Personal interview, Peoria, Ill., July 1980.

26. Personal interview, Peoria, Ill., July 1980.

27. Personal interview, Detroit, Mich., June 1980.

28. Pt. 1, pp. 27–32.

29. "Advice to Parents," *Al-Sayeh*, 22 Sept. 1928, reprinted in English translation in the *Syrian World*, 3 (Oct. 1928):51.

30. "Worcester Lebanese-Syrian Community," p. 9.

31. Personal interview, Oak Park, Mich., May 1980.

32. William I. Cole, *Immigrant Races in Massachusetts: The Syrians* (Massachusetts Dept. of Education, Division of Education of Aliens, 1922), p. 4.

33. Naff, "Social History of Zahle," app. 2, pp. 493–528.

34. Conversation, Washington, D.C. May 1978.

35. *Melkites in America: A Directory and Informative Handbook* (n.p.: Melkite Exarchate, 1971), p. 19.

36. Ibid., p. 15.

37. William Essey, "Lest We Forget: Raphael, Bishop of Brooklyn," *The Word* 20 (May 1976):12; also letter from Fr. Basil Essey to the author, 26 Sept. 1980.

38. Ibid., 14.

39. William Essey, "Lest We Forget: The 'Antacky-Russy' Dilemma," *The Word* 20 (Sept. 1976):7–9; also letter.

40. The very complex subject of disunity in the Syrian Orthodox

church in the United States, from 1915 to 1975, is detailed in Archimandrite Serafim's *The Quest for Orthodox Church Unity in America: A History of the Orthodox Church in North America in the Twentieth Century* (New York: Saints Boris and Gleb Press, 1973).

41. Telephone conversation, Grand Forks, N.D., 15 Jan. 1981.

42. Personal interview, July 1980.

43. Philip M. Kayal and Joseph M. Kayal have analyzed the Americanization of the Eastern Catholic-rite churches in their study *The Syrian-Lebanese in America: A Study in Religion and Assimilation* (Boston: Twayne Publishers, 1975).

44. *Abbreviated Arabic and English Breviary* (New York: Mir'at al-Gharb Press, 1917), Preface.

45. *The Paradise: Parts of Mass Services from the Byzintian Orthodox Church Music.* Arranged and compiled by His Grace Germanos, Metropolite of Solophkias and Baalbek, Syria, during his visit on the island of Triuna, Lake George, New York, in the month of September 1920 (n.p.).

46. A. Hakim, "On Perpetuating the Mother Tongue," *Syrian World* 3 (Feb. 1929):37.

47. "Arab Americans of the Stanley-Ross Region in North Dakota" (Typescript, State Historical Society of North Dakota, 5 May 1977).

48. "An Interview of Hussien Hussien Ayad: Early Immigrant to Michigan City, Indiana" (conducted by John P. Brennan, representing the Public Library of Michigan City, Ind., n.d., Typescript), pp. 8–10.

49. Personal interview with Samia S., Bethesda, Md., Aug. 1980.

50. "Time, Americanization Take Harsh Toll," p. 9.

51. Imam Mohammad K.; also ibid.

52. Conversation with Samah H., Vienna, Va., April 1983.

53. "Teach your Children" (in Arabic), 28 Mar. 1925, p. 6.

54. "Moslems in America," *Syrian World*, 3 (May 1929):55.

55. Personal interview, Fenton, Mich., June 1980.

56. Unpublished documents, Syrian Orthodox church, Spring Valley, Ill.

57. Thelma W.

58. "Syrians in the United States," pt. 4, "The Syrian as an American Citizen," 7 Oct. 1911, p. 960.

59. Ibid.

60. Personal interview, Los Angeles, Calif., May 1962.

61. Boris Weintraub, "The Bonds of Generations," *Washington Post*, 9 July 1979, pp. D1, D7.

62. "The Aims of the Attiyeh Society" (n.d., Typescript). The 500-member Jamail family, based in Houston, Texas, welcomed their relative, Amin Gemayel, president of the Republic of Lebanon, on 24 July 1983 (Barbara Canetti, "The Lebanon Connection," *Washington Post*, 25 July 1983, p. C1).

63. Personal interview with Oscar A., Peoria, Ill., July 1980.

64. "Neighbor of the Glen in the United States" (in Arabic), *Al-Bilad* [Zahle, Lebanon], 17 July 1968, p. 16.

65. Brennan, "An Interview of Hussien Hussien Ayad."

66. "Moslems in America."

67. "The Idea of Mixed Clubs," *Syrian World* 2 (Nov. 1927):51.

68. "Americanization Movement among the Syrians," ibid., 2 (Aug. 1927):59.

69. Ibid., 2 (Oct. 1927):60.

70. Ibid., 2 (Jan. 1928):59.

71. Ibid., 5 (Dec. 1930):57.

72. Ibid.

73. Ibid., 3 (Oct. 1928):51–53.

74. "Forward," ibid., 1 (July 1926):2.

75. Ibid.

76. "Our Bulwark," ibid., 2 (Oct. 1927):49–50.

77. Ibid., (Nov. 1928):36–40.

78. Rev. W. A. Mansur, "A Federation of Syrian Societies," ibid., 3 (Dec. 1928):3–9.

79. "Success of Federation Assured," ibid., 3 (Mar. 1929):35–36.

80. "Syrian Societies," Ibid., 5 (Dec. 1930):45.

81. Conversation, North Hollywood, Calif., Feb. 1983. Also with Nazha H., George N., Huntington Beach, Calif., Feb. 1983; and Nazha G., Adelphi, Md., Aug. 1983.

82. "The Arabic Language in America" (in Arabic), *Al-Hilal*, 1, Apr. 1907), pp. 46–47.

83. Henry Melki, "Arab American Journalism" (in Arabic) (Ph.D. diss., Georgetown University, Washington, D.C., 1972), pp. 9, 95–108. No reliable study of the Arabic press in the United States exists. Even this singular study is incomplete.

84. "Arabic Newspapers in America," ibid., 2 (May 1928):36.

85. Melki, "Arab American Journalism," p. 28.

86. *Al-Hoda, 1898–1968: The Story of Lebanon and Its Emigrants Taken from the Newspaper Al-Hoda* (New York: Al-Hoda Press, 1968), pp. 5–6.

87. Melki, "Arab American Journalism," p. 7.

88. Ibid., 112.

89. "The Library of Al-Hoda" (in Arabic), *Al-Hoda*, 1908 July 1, p. 7; "The Library of Meraat al-Gharb" (in Arabic), *Meraat al-Gharb* July 1925, p. 6.

90. "Factional War," 29 Oct. 1905, Also Melki, "Arab American Journalism," p. 4.

91. "The Iraqi Poet Nizih al-Mala'ika and Free Verse in Modern Arabic Poetry," English summary of main articles in Hebrew (*Ha Mizrah He Hadash* 16 [1966]:viii–ix); also *Al-Hilal*, "The Arabic Language in America," p. 48.

92. Moreh, "The Iraqi Poet."

93. Yaqoub Rufail, "How Afifa Karam Grew Up and Developed" (in Arabic), *Al-Akhlaq*, July 1924, pp. 5–7; also Melki, "Arab American Journalism," p. 10.

94. "Teach Your Children."

95. "Arabic as an Asset," *Syrian World* 2 (June 1928): 17–18.

96. "Teaching Arabic Deemed Unnecessary," ibid., 3 (Sept. 1928):56–57.

97. "Arabic Not Our Original Language," ibid., 56.

98. "A Syrian University in America," ibid., 3 (Nov. 1928):42–44.

99. "Arabic Newspapers in America," ibid., 2 (May 1928):36.

100. "Notes and Comments," ibid., 2 (Aug. 1927):51–52.

101. Houghton, pt. 4, 7 Oct. 1911, p. 962.

102. Personal interview with Richard H., in interview of Sam and Lillian H.; personal interview with John K., Cedar Rapids, May 1980.

Select Bibliography

UNPUBLISHED DOCUMENTS, MANUSCRIPTS, AND
INTERVIEWS

144 taped oral history interviews in 40 Syrian and Lebanese-American communities in the United States.

40 telephone interviews.

Aims of the Attiyeh Society. Typescript.

Brennan, John P. "An Interview of Hussien Hussien Ayad: Early Immigrant to Michigan City, Indiana." n.d., 20 pages.

Essey, Fr. Basil, Englewood, N.J. Letter to author, 26 Sept. 1980.

Flehan, Henry, Mebane, N.C. Letter to author, 12 Mar. 1981.

Knowlton, Clark S. "Spatial and Social Mobility of the Syrians and Lebanese in the City of São Paulo, Brazil." Ph.D. diss. Vanderbilt University, 1955.

McHenry, Stewart G. "The Syrians of Upstate New York (A Social Geography)." Ph.D. diss., Syracuse University, 1973.

Maronite Chancery, Brooklyn, N.Y. Brief history of individual Maronite churches in the United States. 1981.

Melki, Henry. "Arab American Journalism." Ph.D. diss. Georgetown University, 1972.

Ministrie des Affaires Etrangères, Paris, France. Rapport Commerceaux, 1888–94, 9, Doc. 6.

N., Faris. Handwritten memoirs. 1952.

Naff, Alixa. "The Social History of Zahle, the Principal Market

Town in Nineteenth-Century Lebanon." Ph.D. diss., UCLA, 1972.

Nassar, Eugene P. Letter to author from Utica, N.Y., 23 June 1983, with supporting data from John Moses.

Oschinsky, Lawrence. "Islam in Chicago: Being a Study of the Acculturation of Muslim Palestinian Community in That City." Master's thesis, University of Chicago, 1947.

Saint George's Syrian Orthodox Church, Spring Valley, Ill. Unpublished documents and ledgers related to the founding of the church, the Syrian Men's Society, and the purchase of a cemetery, 1914–24.

State Historical Society of North Dakota. "Arab Americans of the Stanley-Ross Region in North Dakota." Typescript. 5 May 1977.

Sweeney, Bernice. "Spring Valley: Geography, Population, Economic Base." Papers from the Cyril Sweeney Collection on the history of Spring Valley.

Al-Tahir, Jalil. "The Arab Community in the Chicago Area: A Comparative Study of the Christian-Syrians and the Muslim-Palestinains." Ph.D. diss., University of Chicago, 1952.

Works Project Administration. Interviews with Syrian immigrants in North Dakota, 1939.

Younis, Adele. "The Coming of the Arabic-speaking People to the United States." Ph.D. diss., Boston University, 1961.

Zahle, Lebanon. Records of the Court of the Administrative District of Zahle, Mount Lebanon. 1888.

———. Records of the Governor of the Administrative District of Zahle, Mount Lebanon, 1870s and 1880s.

———. Records of the National Administrative Council of Mount Lebanon. 1874.

PUBLISHED OFFICIAL DOCUMENTS

Bureau County Office of Records, Princeton, Ill. Records of births, deaths, and marriages.

Cedar Rapids, Iowa. *Directories of the City of Cedar Rapids.* 1900–1915.

Spring Valley, Ill. *City Directory of Spring Valley, Illinois,* 1913.

U.S. Bureau of the Census Historical Statistics of the United States, Colonial Times to 1970, Bicentennial ed. Pt. 1. Washington, 1975.

U.S. Congress. Senate. *Reports of the Immigration Commission: Statistical Review of Immigration 1820–1910 and Distribution of Immigrants 1850–1900.* Vol. 3 Washington, 1911.

U.S. Congress. Senate. *Reports of the Immigration Commission*. Vol. 5, *Dictionary of Races or Peoples*. Washington, 1911.

U.S. Department of Commerce and Labor. Bureau of the Census. *Thirteenth Census of the United States, 1910: Population*. Vol. 1. Washington, 1913.

———. Bureau of the Census. *Fourteenth Census of the United States, 1920: Population*. Vol. 2. Washington, 1922.

———. Bureau of the Census. *Fifteenth Census of the United States, 1930: Population*. Vol. 2. Washington, 1933.

———. Bureau of the Census. *Sixteenth Census of the United States, 1940: Population*. Vol. 2. Washington, 1943.

U.S. Department of Immigration and Naturalization. *Annual Reports of the Commissioner General of Immigration*. Washington, 1890–1930.

———. "OPEC." Unpublished working papers of immigrants from the Arab World.

———. *Reports of the Industrial Commission on Immigration: Commissions Reports*. Vol. 15. Washington, 1901.

U.S. Department of the Interior. *Eleventh Census of the United States, 1890: Population Statistics*, vol. 1. Washington, 1895.

———. *Twelfth Census of the United States, 1900: Population*. Vol. 1. Schedule no. 1. Washington, 1901.

BOOKS IN ARABIC, FRENCH, AND ENGLISH

Arbeely, Ibrahim. *The Stranger's Primer for Teaching English* (in Arabic). New York: Eastern Press and Kawkab Amrika, 1895.

Arida and Andria. *The Syrian American Directory Almanac*. New York: By the Authors, 1929.

Ayoub, Victor. "Resolution of Conflict in a Lebanese Village." In *Politics in Lebanon*, edited by Leonard Binder. New York: John Wiley & Sons, 1966.

Baer, Gabriel. *Population and Society in the Arab East*. London: Routledge & Kegan Paul, 1964.

Burckhardt, John L. *Travels in Syria and the Holy Land*. London: J. Murray, 1822.

Carpenter, Niles. *Immigrants and Their Children*. New York: Arno Press and New York Times, 1969.

Charmes, Gabriel. *Voyage en Syrie*. Paris: Ernest Lerous, 1891.

Chevallier, Dominque. "Western Development and Eastern Crisis in the Mid-Nineteenth Century: Syria Confronted with the European Economy." In *Beginnings of Modernization in the Middle*

East, edited by William R. Polk and Richard L. Chambers. Chicago: University of Chicago Press, 1968.

Christgau, Alice E. *The Laugh Peddler*. New York: Young Scott Books, 1968.

Cole, William I. *Immigrant Races in Massachusetts*. Written for the Massachusetts Department of Education, Division of Education of Aliens. N.p., 9 Jan. 1922.

Cuinet, Vital. *Syrie, Liban, et Palestine*. Paris: Ernest Leroux, 1896.

Elkholy, Abdo A. *The Arab Moslems in the United States: Religion and Assimilation*. New Haven, Conn.: College and University Press, 1966.

Fairchild, Henry Pratt. *Immigration, a World Movement and Its American Significance*. New York: Macmillan, 1913.

Fredrickson, George M., and Dale T. Knobel. "History of Prejudice and Discrimination." In *Harvard Encyclopedia of American Ethnic Groups*, edited by Stephan Thermstron. Cambridge, Mass.: Belknap Press of Harvard University Press, 1980.

Fuller, Anne H. *Buarij: Portrait of a Lebanese Muslim Village*. Harvard University Monograph Series. Cambridge, Mass.: Harvard University Press, 1966.

Germanos (Metropolitan). *The Paradise: Parts of Mass Service from the Byzintian Orthodox Church Music*. Lake George, N.Y.: by the author, 1920.

Gibb, H. A. R. *The Arabs*. New York: Oxford University Press, 1940.

Gibran, Jean, and Kahlil Gibran. *Kahlil Gibran, His Life and World*. New York: Avenel Books, 1981.

Gulick, John. *Social Structure and Cultural Change in a Lebanese Village*. New York: Wenner Gren Foundation for Anthropological Research, 1955.

Hitti, Philip K. *History of the Arabs*. New York: Macmillan, 1963.

———. *Lebanon in History*. New York: Macmillan, 1967.

———. *Syrians in America*. New York: George Doran, 1924.

Hourani, Albert H. *Arabic Thought in the Liberal Age, 1798–1939*. London: Oxford University Press, 1962.

———. *Syria and Lebanon: A Political Essay*. London: Oxford University Press, 1954.

Ibn Khaldun. *The Muqaddimah and Introduction to History*. Translated by Franz Rosenthal. Vol. 1. New York: Pantheon, 1958.

Issawi, Charles. "Economic Development and Political Liberalism in Lebanon." In *Politics in Lebanon*, edited by Leonard Binder. New York: John Wiley & Sons, 1966.

———. *The Economic History of the Middle East: 1800–1914*. Chicago: University of Chicago Press, 1966.

Jessup, Henry H. *Fifty-Three Years in Syria*. Vol. 2. New York: Fleming H. Revell, 1910.

Jones, Maldwyn A. *American Immigration*. Chicago: University of Chicago Press, 1900.

Katibah, Habib I. *Arabic-speaking Americans*. New York: Institute of Arab American Affairs, 1946.

———. "Syrian Americans." In *One America: The History and Contributions and Present Problems of our Racial and National Minorities*, edited by Francis J. Brown and Joseph S. Roucek. Newark, N.J.: Prentice-Hall, 1952.

Kayal, Philip M., and Joseph M. Kayal. *The Syrian-Lebanese in America: A Study in Religion and Assimilation*. Boston: Twayne, 1975.

Kherbawi, Rev. Basil M. *Abreviated Arabic and English Breviary*. New York: Mir²at al-Gharb Press, 1917.

———. *History of the United States and the History of the Syrian Immigration* (in Arabic). New York: Al-Dalil Press, 1913.

Al-Khuri, Shukry. *Alas, Poor Zᶜaytar*. São Paulo, Brazil: Abul Hul Press, 1911.

Kinany, A. Kh. *The Development of the Gazal in Arabic Literature*. Damascus, Syria: n.p., 1960.

Latron, André. *La Vie Rurale en Syrie et au Liban*. Beyrouth, Lebanon: Étude d'Économie Sociale, 1936.

The Lebanese Book in Celebration of the Silver Jubilee of the League of Lebanese Progress (in Arabic). New York: Al-Hoda Press, 1936.

Lewis, Bernard. *The Emergence of Modern Turkey*. London: Oxford University Press, 1961.

Longrigg, Stephan H. *Syria and Lebanon under the French Mandate*. London: Oxford University Press, 1958.

Lovelace, Maud Hart Lovelace. *Betsy and Tacy Go Over the Big Hill*. New York: Thomas Y. Crowell, 1942.

Maᶜlūf, Issa Skandar. *The History of the City of Zahle* (in Arabic). Zahle, Lebanon: Zahle al-Fatat Press, 1911.

Mamey, Samuel S., ed. *The Western Pacific and Buyers Guide for 1954–1955*. Los Angeles: Saint Nicholas Orthodox Church, 1954.

Melkites in America: A Directory and Informative Handbook. West Newton, Mass.: Melkite Exarchate, 1971.

Mencken, H. L. *The American Language, an Inquiry into the Development of English in the United States*. New York: Knopf. 1937.

Miller, Lucius Hopkins. *Our Syrian Population: A Study of the Syrian Communities of Greater New York*. N.p., ca. 1904.

Mokarzel, Salloum. *The History of Syrian Business among Immigrants in America, 1920–1921* (in Arabic). New York: Syrian American Press, n.d.

———. *The History of Syrian Trade in the American Colonies.* Pt. 1, 1920–1921 (in Arabic). New York: Syrian American Press, 1929.

Moses, John. *From Mount Lebanon to the Mohawk Valley: A Story of Syro-Lebanese Americans of the Utica Area.* Utica, N.Y.: By the author, 1981.

Najjar, Abdullah. *The Druze: Millennium Scrolls Revealed.* Translated by Fred I. Massey. N.p., ca. 1965.

Nelson, W. S. *Silver Chimes in Syria.* Philadelphia: Westminster Press, 1914.

Nevins, Allan, and Frank E. Hill. *Ford: Decline and Rebirth, 1933–1962.* New York: Charles Scribner's Sons, 1962.

Novotney, Ann. *Strangers at the Door.* Riverside, Conn.: Chatham Press, Ind., 1971.

Othman, Ibrahim. *Arabs in the United States: A Study of an Arab American Community.* Beirut: Dar al-Qalam Press Co., 1974.

Pitkin, Thomas M. *Keepers of the Gate: A History of Ellis Island, New York.* New York: New York University Press, 1975.

Polk, William R. *The United States and the Arab World.* Rev. ed. Cambridge, Mass.: Harvard University Press, 1969.

Rihani, Ameen. *The Book of Khalid.* New York: Dodd, Mead, 1911.

Rihbani, Abraham Mitry. *A Far Journey.* Boston and New York: Houghton Mifflin, 1914.

Rustum, Mikha'il As'ad. *The Book of a Stranger in a Strange Land* (in Arabic). New York: Eastern Press, 1895.

Serafim [Archimandrite]. *The Quest for Orthodox Church Unity in America: A History of the Orthodox Church in North America in the Twentieth Century.* New York: Saints Boris and Gleb Press, 1973.

Shadid, Michael. A *Doctor for the People.* 2d ed. New York: Vanguard Press, 1939.

Smilianskaya, I. M. "The Disintegration of Feudal Relations in Syria and Lebanon in the Middle of the Nineteenth Century." In *The Economic History of the Middle East: 1800–1914.* Chicago: University of Chicago Press, 1966.

Tibawi, A. L. *American Interests in Syria, 1800–1901.* Oxford, England: Clarendon Press, 1966.

Ueda, Reed. "Naturalization and Citizenship." *Harvard Encyclopedia of American Ethnic Groups.* Cambridge, Mass.: Belknap Press of Harvard University Press, 1980.

Von Grunebaum, G. E. *Classical Islam: A History, 600 A.D.–1258 A.D.* Chicago: Aldine, 1970.

Zeine, Zeine N. *Arab-Turkish Relations and the Emergence of Arab Nationalism.* Beirut: Khayat's, 1958.

ARAB NEWSPAPERS AND PERIODICALS

Al-Bayan, New York, N.Y.
Al-Bilad, Zahle, Lebanon.
Al-Hilal, Cairo, Egypt.
Al-Hoda, New York, N.Y.
Al-Kalimat, New York, N.Y.
Meraat al-Gharb, New York, N.Y.
Sophia, West Newton, Mass.
Syrian World, New York, N.Y.
The Word, Englewood, N.J.

AMERICAN NEWSPAPERS, JOURNALS AND MAGAZINES

"Dr. El-Kouri Defends Syrian Immigrant." (Birmingham, Ala.) *Age-Herald*, 20 Oct. 1907.

Van Slyke, Lucille Baldwin. "The Peddler." *American Magazine*, August 1912, pp. 405–14.

Tannous, Afif. "Acculturation of an Arab-Syrian Community in the Deep South." *American Sociological Review* 8 (June 1943):270.

El-Kouri, H. A. "In Defense of the Semetic and the Syrian Especially." *Birmingham Ledger*, 20 Sept. 1907.

"The New Syrian Society Has a School." *Brooklyn Daily Eagle*, 10 May 1892.

"Armenian Justice." *Cedar Rapids Evening Gazette*, 9 Nov. 1897.

"Cedar Rapids' Population." *Cedar Rapids Evening Gazette*, 4 Jan. 1976.

"Ghetto Sights." *Cedar Rapids Evening Gazette*, 3 July 1901.

"Indictment Returned against Joseph George." *Cedar Rapids Evening Gazette*, 6 Apr. 1910.

"Joseph George Pleads Guilty and Fined $500." *Cedar Rapids Evening Gazette*, 8 Apr. 1910.

"New Colony." *Cedar Rapids Evening Gazette*, 9 Mar. 1897.

"Syrian Probe Comes to a Head." *Cedar Rapids Evening Gazette*, 11, Mar. 1910.

"Wed in Syria." *Cedar Rapids Evening Gazette*, 12 Aug. 1897.

"Experience in Peace and War Justifies Detroit Plan of Americanization Work." *Detroiter*, 24 Nov. 1919.

"Arabian Colony." *Detroit Journal*, 21 July 1897.

"Ross, N.D. Area Is Home for Some 50 Mohammedans." *Fargo Forum*, 8 Aug. 1937.

"Time, Americanization Take Harsh Toll of Once-Thriving Moslem Colonies in N.D." *Fargo Forum*, 8 Dec. 1967.

"A Motto Wrought into Education." *Ford Times* 9 (April 1916):406–9.

Fort Wayne's History. The Fort Wayne Chamber of Commerce, n.d.

Benyon, E. D. "The Near East in Flint, Michigan: Assyrians and Druzes and their Antecedents." *Geographical Review* 34 (Apr. 1944):272–73.

Pritchard, Arthur C. "Two Hundred Pounds or More: The Lebanese Community in Mannington." *Goldenseal*, 4 (Apr., Sept., 1978):18–25.

Benough, W. "The Foreign Element in New York, a Syrian Colony." *Harper's Magazine*, 3 Aug. 1895, p. 746.

Tryon, Lillian Hart. "Reflections of a Housewife on Buying at the Door." *House Beautiful* 38 (July 1915):40–42.

Kinneman, Marion. "John Mitchell in Illinois." *Illinois State University Journal* 32 (Sept. 1969):21–35.

Jones, Fred Mitchell. "Middlemen in the Domestic Trade of the United States, 1800–1860." *Illinois Studies in the Social Sciences* 21 (1937):9–81.

"Syrians in the United States." *Literary Digest* 3 May 1919, p. 43.

"She's 'Mama' to a Family of 100." *Look Magazine*, 28 Aug. 1962, pp. 91–94.

Rankin, Lois, "Detroit Nationality Groups: Syrians." *Michigan History Magazine*, 23 (Spring 1939):195–200.

"Once Numerous Moslem Community Now Reduced to Half Dozen." *Minot* (N.D.) *Daily News*, 7 Dec. 1968.

Mokarzel, Salloum. "History of the Syrians in New York City." *New York American Newspaper*, 3 Oct. 1927.

"Picturesque Colony." *New York Daily Tribune*, 2 Oct. 1892.

"Syrian Society's Work: Teaching the Children of the Washington Street Colony." *New York Evening Post*, 23 Feb. 1906.

"Factional War Is Waged between Syrians of New York City." *New York Herald*, 29 Oct. 1905.

"Syrian Riot in Street, and Many Are Hurt." *New York Times*, 24 Oct. 1905.

Tannous, Afif I. "Emigration, a Force of Social Change in an Arab Village." *Rural Sociology* 7 (Mar. 1942):62–74.

"Syrians in America." *Sandusky* (Ohio) *Masonic Bulletin* 15 (Mar. 1935):130.

Azar, Raymond S. "The Grocery Days . . . Then." *Spectator* 141 (Oct. 1975):10.

"The City of Peoria Is Celebrating a Century of Progress." *Spirit*, n.d., pp. 3, 60–61.

Courtemanche, Dolores. "Worcester's Lebanese-Syrian Community: An Ethnic Success Story." (Worcester, Mass.) *Sunday Telegram*, 14 Sept. 1980.

Houghton, Louise Seymour. "Syrians in the United States." In 4 parts. Pts. 1–3. *Survey* 26 (July, Aug., Sept. 1911):481–95, 647–65, 787–803; pt. 4, *Survey* 27 (Oct. 1911):957–68.

Canetti, Barbara. "The Lebanon Connection." *Washington Post*, 25 July 1981, p. C1.

Weintraub, Boris. "The Bonds of Generations." *Washington Post*, 9 July 1979.

Index

Alixa Naff has taught at the university level, including the American University in Cairo. She has served as executive director of the Middle East Educational Trust and as program director of the Arab-American Project at the National Center for Urban Ethnic Affairs in Washington, D.C. Dr. Naff is author of *The Arab Americans*, an illustrated history for young adults. The Faris and Yamna Naff Arab American Collection of Arab immigrant artifacts and archival materials, which she donated to the Smithsonian Institution, is another result of her long commitment to the collection and preservation of the history of Arab Americans.